# ECONOMIC

Brian Atkinson

Peter Baker

and

Bob Milward

MACMILLAN

First published 1996 by
MACMILLAN PRESS LTD
Houndmills, Basingstoke, Hampshire RG21 6XS
and London
Companies and representatives
throughout the world

ISBN 0–333–65046–8 hardcover
ISBN 0–333–65047–6 paperback

A catalogue record for this book is available
from the British Library.

This book is printed on paper suitable for recycling and made from fully managed and sustained forest sources.

10   9   8   7   6   5   4   3   2   1
05  04  03  02  01  00  99  98  97  96

Copy-edited and typeset by Povey–Edmondson
Okehampton and Rochdale, England

Printed in Great Britain by
Antony Rowe Ltd
Chippenham, Wiltshire

# Contents

# List of Figures

# List of Tables

# Acknowledgements

The authors and publishers wish to thank the following for permission to use copyright material: Bank of England for Fig. 12.1 and Table 12.1 from MacFarlane and Mortimer-Lee, 'Inflation over 300 years', *Bank of England Quarterly Bulletin*, 34, 2 May 1994; Blackwell Publishers for Table 10.3 from Johnson and Webb, 'Explaining the growth in UK inequality: 1979–88', *Economic Journal*, 103, March 1993; Causeway Press Ltd for Fig. 9.2 from Whynes, 'Economic Aspects of Health Care in the UK', 1993, in Atkinson, *Developments in Economics*, Vol. 9, Causeway Press; Earthscan Publications Ltd for Table 8.2 from Hayes, Peter and Smith, *The Global Greenhouse Regime: Who Pays?*, 1993, and Fig. 8.4 from Markandya, 'Global Warming: The Economics of Tradeable Permits', 1991, in Pearce (ed.), *Blueprint 2: Greening the World Economy*, 1991; Edward Elgar Publishing Ltd for Fig. 8.1 from Kenneth J. Button, *Transport Economics*, 1994, p. 150; The Financial Times Ltd for Fig. 12.2 from *Financial Times*, 20 January 1994, Table 7.2 from *Financial Times*, 7 December 1994, and Fig. 6.5 from *Financial Times*, 5 September 1995; The Controller of Her Majesty's Stationery Office for Table 11.2 from *Employment Gazette*, August 1995, Table 13.1 from *Economic Trends*, May 1993, October 1995, 2.13, Fig. 7.1 from 'Assessing the Impact of Urban Policy', pp. 6, 7, and Figs 6.1, 6.2 and 6.4 from *Social Trends*, 1994; The Institute for Fiscal Studies for Table 10.5 from Giles and Johnson, 'Taxes Down, Taxes Up: The Effects of a Decade of Tax Changes', *Commentary*, 41; International Labour Office for Table 6.5 from *World Labour Report*, vol. 6, 1993, table 3.1, p. 34; Office for Official Publications of the European Communities for Table 14.1 from Neumann, 'Central bank independence as a prerequisite of price stability', *European Economy*, Special Edition, 1, 1991; Office for National Statistics for Table 11.2 from 'Monthly Regional Unemployment Figures', 1986, 1989, 1994, 1995, Crown copyright; Organisation for Economic Co-operation and Development for Table 4.1 from Madison, *The World Economy in the Twentieth Century*, 1989, Copyright © OECD, and Table 10.4 from *Revenue Statistics OECD Member Countries*, Copyright © OECD; Oxford University Press for data in Fig. 10.8 from Atkinson, *The Economics of Inequality*, Clarendon, p. 22, 1984, and Fig. 10.6 from Kay and King, *The British Tax System*, 1991, Oxford University Press,

Fig. 7, and Table 4.2 from Meen, 'International Comparisons of the UK's Long-Run Economic Performance', *Oxford Review of Economic Performance*, 4, 1, 1988, Table 4.3 from Feinstein, 'Economic Growth since 1987: Britain's Performance in International Perspective', *Oxford Review of Economic Policy*, 4, 1, 1988, and Table 9.1 from Drummond, 'Output measurement for resource allocation in health care', *Oxford Review of Economic Policy*, 5, 1989, pp. 59–74; Personnel Publications Ltd for Figs 10.1, 6.3 from Atkinson, 'Manpower strategies for flexible organisations', *Personnel Management*, Aug. 1984; The Joseph Rowntree Foundation for Fig. 1.1 from *Inquiry into Income and Wealth*, 1, 1995, p. 14; The University of Wisconsin Press for Table 9.3 for Psacharopoulos, 'Returns to Education: A Further International Update and Implications', *Journal of Human Resources*, 20, 4, Fall 1985, pp. 583–604; World Health Organization for Fig. 9.4 from *World Health Statistics Annual 1991*, WHO, Geneva, 1992. Every effort has been made to trace all the copyright-holders, but if any have been inadvertently overlooked the publishers will be pleased to make the necessary arrangement at the first opportunity.

# Introduction

Economics as an academic discipline has had a long period of gestation. Economic debates stretch back over the millenia, but it is common to date the beginning of the subject in a recognisably modern form to the eighteenth century. With a certain irony, the father of economics is often said to be another Adam. The author of the frequently quoted *Wealth of Nations* (1776), Adam Smith, is credited with the foundation of classical economics, from which the current economic orthodoxy has developed.

The influence of economic theories and ideas has been enormous in the last two centuries and even without consciously recognising the fact, many policy-makers have had their ideas shaped by economists. A famous quote from John Maynard Keynes makes this clear:

> The ideas of economists and political philosophers, both when they are right and when they are wrong, are more powerful than is commonly understood. Indeed the world is ruled by little else. Practical men, who believe themselves to be quite exempt from any intellectual influences, are usually the slaves of some defunct economist. Madmen in authority, who hear voices in the air, are distilling their frenzy from some academic scribbler of a few years back. (Keynes, 1936, p. 383)

This book takes as its central theme the outcomes of economic policy-making in recent times. Economic policy-making does not take place in a political vacuum, but is subject to a range of forces, not least of which is political ideology. Politicians select the ideas of those economists whose views most neatly conform with their ideologies and then promote them as being self-evidently correct. The UK has developed as a predominantly capitalist economy and the economists whose ideas have been most influential in policy-making reflect this. The economic orthodoxy which has been in the ascendant throughout the twentieth century has been based on neo-classical reasoning. This reasoning gives the market the central role in the allocation of resources and stresses cost minimisation as a production necessity. Whilst the period from the 1950s to the 1970s saw some modification in the role of the market as an allocative mechanism in policy-making, the bedrock of orthodox theory remained. Since the 1970s policy-making has become even more firmly based on orthodox economic reasoning and the role of the market has been asserted more strongly than at any time since the Second World War.

In writing this book we have attempted to set economic policy in the context of the underlying economic principles that support it. We aim to be critical, as the authors feel a common disquiet with much that has occurred in the policy-making arena in recent years. Wherever possible we suggest that there may be alternatives, and point the reader in the direction of alternative literature. Although one would not think so in reading most mainstream theory and policy texts, there is a wide range of alternative economic thinking, stretching from Marxian political economy, Post-Keynesian, Institutional, Evolutionary to Austrian Economics, to name but a few. Each of these approaches has different policy implications and outcomes. It is our intention to foster debate and enquiry and to encourage the student to seek the alternative that best suits her/him.

## Reference

Keynes, J. M. (1936) *The General Theory of Employment, Interest and Money* (Macmillan, London).

# CHAPTER 1

# Making Economic Policy

> Economic policy is a set of recommended economic actions, the purpose of which is to achieve some explicit or implicit objective or set of objectives.
>
> (Grant and Nath, 1984, p. 1)

Writing in *The Wealth of Nations* in 1776, Adam Smith explained how in a perfectly working economy, resources will be moved around to the areas where they are required, by means of an *invisible hand*. The forces of supply and demand, operating through the profit motive, will dictate the destination of resources, and the invisible hand therefore dispenses with the need for economic policies on the part of the government. In this schema, the economy should be left to market forces to determine outcomes. Should it be necessary to concede a less than perfect outcome from the operations of the invisible hand, then it is assumed that some impediment has been introduced. The role of government is simply to remove this impediment and guarantee the free flow of economic forces. However, any attempt to go beyond this and attempt to intervene directly in the workings of the economy is guaranteed to distort the operations of the market and lead to a worse outcome for society.

Notwithstanding this school of thought, governments have assumed a far greater role in the operations of economies in the twentieth century and have become major employers, accounting for a growing share of national incomes. Direct intervention in the operation of the UK economy has grown considerably. The First and Second World Wars have been of crucial importance in understanding this development. During wars the role of the government increases and the resources of the country are mobilised for military conflict. Consequently, the resources deployed by the government increase substantially and the amount of direction dictated by the government grows. After the war ends, the share of the gross domestic product (GDP) accounted for by the state shrinks, but never back to the level it was prior to the conflict. War therefore has had a ratchet effect on government involvement in the running of the economy in the twentieth century.

Governments implement economic policies with the intention of achieving specific aims or goals. However, some objectives may be in conflict, and

1

consequently policy-making is fraught with difficulty. For example, at least up until the middle of the 1970s, all postwar UK governments aimed to achieve a high and rising standard of living, balance of payments equilibrium, full employment, a more equitable distribution of income and wealth, and low inflation. Whilst striving to achieve some of these policy objectives, however, others tended to stray from target. A much discussed feature of the postwar economy was the tendency towards stop–go policy. This arose from government attempts to solve one or more economic problems, which in the process resulted in the worsening position of other target variables. For example, if economic growth was sluggish and unemployment was rising, the government would deliberately engineer a boom, primarily through fiscal policy: the 'go' phase. This would often lead to overheating of the economy, resulting in inflationary pressures and balance of payments difficulties, causing the government to apply the economic brakes: the 'stop' phase.

Governments are responsible for the direction of economic policy and argue that they are promoting social welfare through their policies. As such, then, they would claim to be operating in the public interest. This leads us into the area of value judgements, for it is evident that there is disagreement, for example, over what is a fair distribution of income and wealth, whether health provision should be achieved through compulsory insurance, or whether school-level education should be allocated by means of a voucher system. Economists tend to argue over such issues on the grounds of efficiency, but the term 'efficiency' itself is value laden and open to a variety of interpretations (Turk, 1983).

Governments have assumed a crucial role within modern economies, and their sphere of influence means that all citizens are significantly affected by decisions taken on economic policy. Over time, various institutions have developed which have assumed key responsibilities with respect to the implementation of policy. Not least of these is the Bank of England, founded in 1694 to raise revenue for the Crown. Since this time its operational scope and responsibilities have increased significantly and the Governor of the Bank of England has assumed a key, if sometimes uneasy, position in advising the Chancellor of the Exchequer as to the wisdom of his actions. The Governor of the Bank of England for part of the 1980s, Gordon (now Lord) Richardson, frequently disagreed with the then Prime Minister, Mrs Thatcher, over policy, and in 1995 differences over interest rate policy between the Chancellor of the Exchequer, Kenneth Clarke, and the Governor of the Bank of England, Eddie George, were widely reported in the press.

## Policy objectives and policy instruments

As noted, governments have economic objectives and these will tend to change or vary in emphasis at different points in time. In order to achieve these policy objectives governments employ policy instruments. For example, in order to achieve the objective of higher employment the government may boost the economy by means of fiscal policy instruments (taxes and government expenditure). Conversely, if the government is concerned by the level of inflation then it may dampen down the economy by reducing aggregate demand, but this will have an adverse effect on employment. The *trade-off* here is apparent: in aiming for its objective of lower inflation the government has through its actions adversely affected the level of employment. If one assumes that all governments generally aim towards the highest possible levels of employment/lowest levels of unemployment, then in trying to achieve one objective the government has simultaneously moved further away from the achievement of another.

Policy instruments are interdependent, and this must be taken into consideration in their use. For example, the use of fiscal policy impacts upon monetary policy. If the government reduces taxation (*ceteris paribus*) then it may have to increase public borrowing and this will have implications for the money supply and the rate of interest. If the rate of interest rises then this may cause the rate of exchange for sterling to appreciate, making British exports less competitive/imports more competitive and causing the balance of payments to deteriorate.

One approach to economic policy-making is through the allocation of *specific* policy instruments to the achievement of *specific* policy objectives. For example, the main effect of changes in the level of government expenditure or taxation (fiscal policy) will be felt on the level of aggregate demand, output and employment. However, the main impact of a change in the exchange rate will be felt on the balance of payments. In order to deal with this problem the *Tinbergen rule* was formulated. This states that a government should have at its disposal as many independent instruments of policy as it has independent objectives. For instance, running the economy with a level of aggregate demand which is designed to deliver full employment will not necessarily deliver an acceptable outcome for the balance of payments. In this case the government could look towards a level of aggregate demand designed to achieve full employment whilst having an exchange rate target designed to deliver a satisfactory balance of payments position. This approach can be employed across the spectrum of policy objectives assigning a specific policy instrument to each.

Recent economic experience is littered with examples of conflicts between objectives. During the postwar period up until the 1970s all governments had a firm commitment to the maintenance of full employment. However, by requiring a full capacity level of aggregate demand and through the promotion of high levels of employment confidence in labour markets, major pressures came to be felt on prices. Governments attempted to contain these inflationary pressures through the use of policies which limited rises in prices in both product and factor markets (prices and incomes policies). Such policies had limited success, generally restricted to the short to medium term, and in general had destabilising effects on the economy contributing to other problems, especially in the sphere of industrial relations. Equally, postwar governments have tended to boost levels of aggregate demand in order to combat rising levels of unemployment, or in line with the electoral cycle in order to give the electorate confidence at the time of a general. election. However, by boosting the economy the UK government has frequently felt itself subject to constraints imposed by a deteriorating balance of payments position. In the past, as the economy has been boosted, additional imports have been sucked into the UK whilst exports have been diverted to domestic consumption. In order to deal with the balance of payments problem governments have frequently had to curtail their attempts to boost the level of demand in the economy.

The balance of payments has been a major source of problems for UK governments, and policy instruments have frequently been employed to address these difficulties. The conflict which exists between high levels of domestic demand with full employment, and a satisfactory balance of payments position, has been outlined. If we refer to full employment and price stability as the *internal balance* and balance of payments equilibrium as the *external balance*, then the achievement of both simultaneously is fraught with difficulties. Whilst a country's internal balance will generally be given priority, its external balance places a constraint on domestic management which must be recognised. Ultimately, a persistent and large deficit will cause a country problems which will require immediate attention. The level of aggregate demand within an economy has an effect both on the internal and external balance. Aggregate demand is adjusted through the use of fiscal and monetary policy. A major problem for policy-makers is that they have two objectives, internal and external balance, but policies which affect the level of aggregate demand impinge on both.

TABLE 1.1   Assignment rule: policy implications

| State of the economy | Monetary policy | Fiscal policy |
|---|---|---|
| Unemployment and surplus | Expansionary | Expansionary |
| Unemployment and deficit | Contractionary | Expansionary |
| Inflation and surplus | Expansionary | Contractionary |
| Inflation and deficit | Contrationary | Contractionary |

*Source*:   P. Asheghian, *International Economics*, West Publishing, St Paul, Minn., 1995, p. 328.

In order to deal with this problem an economy must abandon one or other of its objectives, or increase its level of output by raising productivity. It is often difficult to achieve the latter, at least in the short run, and therefore a compromise must be sought. Monetary and fiscal policy can be shown to impact differentially on the internal and external balance. This means that in operating demand management policies governments can vary their emphasis on monetary and fiscal policy in accordance with economic circumstances. Accordingly, policy-makers can assign the specific policy instrument to the objective it will have most effect on: this is known as the *assignment rule*. It has been demonstrated that monetary policy is most effective in achieving external balance, whilst fiscal policy has most effect on the internal balance (Asheghian, 1995). The differential effects of policy can be seen in Table 1.1.

## Economic policy 1945–79

Governments had a limited role in the operations of the economy in the nineteenth century but pressures for legislative change in areas such as protection of children from exploitation at work led to a growing role for the government in regulating the worst excesses of employers. In the early twentieth century the foundations of the welfare state were laid, to be extensively built upon in the second half of the century. In the nineteenth century the general attitude to the operation of the economy was based on economic liberalism. That is to say, that the government should involve itself as little as possible in the running of the economy and restrict itself to limited areas, such as law and order and defence of the realm. Neo-classical economics was the economic orthodoxy which informed the policy-makers of the day. According to this line of reasoning, the economy is self regulating and left to its own devices any problems such as unemployment will be eliminated by the working through of market forces, as long as these are not interfered with by outside agencies, such as the government. At the heart of this line of reasoning is Say's Law of markets, which proposes that supply creates its own demand. In other words, in the process of producing any goods or services just sufficient income is generated to purchase them. Accordingly, there should be no deficiency in aggregate demand and the economy should work at its full potential with no involuntary unemployment. However, the paucity of such arguments was demonstrated in the interwar period as unemployment in the UK and elsewhere rose to alarming levels. The economic orthodoxy of the day was to force cuts in wages in an attempt to stimulate demand by lowering the prices of goods, but the result of this policy was a worsening of the economic situation. It became clear that nineteenth-century attitudes to the operation of the economy were unsatisfactory in the interwar period, and this stimulated a search for new approaches to economic management.

An economist who has had an enormous influence in the twentieth century is John Maynard Keynes, whose seminal work, the *General Theory of Employment, Interest and Money* was published in 1936. In the *General Theory*, Keynes showed the futility of cutting wages as a means of stimulating the economy, arguing that if everyone's wages are cut then at best there is no change in the real level of aggregate demand as wages and prices will fall together, and at worst there will be a reduction, as price falls are likely to lag behind wage decreases. Consequently, as Keynes observed, a situation of chronic demand deficiency was being further exacerbated through the application of an economic policy based on neo-classical orthodoxy. In an attempt to produce policy recommendations which could provide a way out of the economic impasse, Keynes turned existing orthodoxy on its head. His emphasis was placed on the level of aggregate demand. If there is a deficiency of demand, then, Keynes argued, attention should be addressed to making good this shortfall. The agency best placed to achieve this is government. Through the use of deficit spending in times of unemployment, new aggregate demand could be generated as a means of kick-starting a stalled economy. Once the economy had recovered, the deficit would be reduced, turning to surplus as full employment was established. Keynes' ideas were not implemented on any substantial scale in the interwar period but the intercession of the Second World War led to a changed political and social climate which ultimately paved the way for the introduction of Keynesian policies. However, it should be noted that Keynes died in 1946, some time before the establishment of policies which came to assume his name. It is important therefore to distinguish between Keynesian, or neo-Keynesian policies and the policies of Keynes; had he lived to witness their implementation, Keynes might well have dissociated himself with some so-called Keynesian policies. Above all, Keynes was not a socialist; as Dasgupta (1985, p. 139) notes:

> The sole purpose of his exercise is to fill in the lacuna in laissez-faire capitalism and to make capitalism acceptable to society. The task of the state here is to raise entrepreneurs' expectation of profit and to stimulate consumption, so as to keep up the level of effective demand.

At the end of the Second World War it was necessary to rebuild war-torn economies. A major error made at the close of the First World War was to force Germany to pay severe reparations, helping to further divide Europe and enable Hitler to establish a power base. Before the Second World War had ended, thought was given to the structure of the postwar world economy and international institutions such as the International Monetary Fund (IMF) and the Bretton Woods system of exchange rate stabilisation were established. Furthermore, the USA was heavily involved in reconstructing the economic base of Europe, through the provision of Marshall aid. Further moves to unite Europe and reduce the possibility of future conflict came in the early 1950s with the formation of the European Coal and Steel Community which formed the basis for the development of the European Economic Community and saw the establishment of partnership between the old adversaries, France and Germany.

Another important issue here was a changed attitude towards the role of government on the part of citizens. This was noticeable in Britain. In 1918 the victorious British forces were promised a return to a land fit for heroes. However, within a few years many of these heroes found themselves destitute with no employment and no prospect of employment. For many this continued right up to the Second World War. Those who had suffered the privations of the Second World War remembered this 'betrayal' and on the cessation of hostilities elected a Labour Government pledged to full employment and with a programme of measures designed to give it greater control over the economy. The Labour Governments from 1945 to 1951 embarked on a major programme of nationalisation in which the so-called 'commanding heights' of the British economy were taken into public ownership. This gave governments the means by which Keynesian policies of demand management could be expedited, for if demand was lagging, it was a simple matter to inject further demand into the economy through new investment in a public sector concern. The battle for the new orthodoxy of Keynesianism had been won by the time a Conservative Government was returned to office in 1951, and the similarities between Conservative and Labour policies were so marked that the term Butskellism (an amalgam of the respective Chancellors of the Exchequer's names), was coined by *The Economist* to describe the continity (Sked and Cook, 1984).

Keynesian-type policies ascribing greater power to governments were accepted in various forms in Western economies during the postwar period. Even the American Republican President, Richard Nixon, declared at the beginning of the 1970s 'I am now a Keynesian' (Stewart, 1977, p. 150). The degree to which the market was superseded by planning differed from country to country with nations such as France and Japan relying far more heavily on economic plans than the UK (Giddens, 1981). The UK's attempt to follow the French path of indicative planning with the publication of the National Plan in 1965 (HMSO, 1965) was ill fated and short lived. However, institutional mechanisms of various forms committed to general principles of managed economies and full employment were constructed. Moves to corporatism were undertaken in the UK with the establishment in 1961 of the National Economic Development Council (NEDC) a body which brought together the Trades Union Congress (TUC), the Confederation of British Industry (CBI) and Government (Johnson, 1991). The establishment of the NEDC was a clear indication that the management and direction of the economy was an issue that involved the participation not only of the government, but also of the representatives of workers, through the TUC, and of employers, through the CBI. In some countries, such as Germany and the Scandinavian countries, industrial democracy with rights of consultation and participation were established, though proposals made in 1979 by the Bullock

Commission in the UK to establish mandatory union representation on company boards came to nothing (Eldridge *et al.*, 1991).

Overall, then, the period from 1945 up to the 1970s saw the firm establishment of social democracy in the UK and elsewhere, with a raft of institutional mechanisms designed to deliver comprehensive economic management. It seemed that the problem of mass unemployment had been solved through the subjection of economies to 'scientific' principles of economic management. However, storm clouds were already gathering by the late 1960s and by the mid-1970s the whole postwar edifice of relative economic stability was beginning to crumble. By the late 1960s the pillar of international monetary stability, the system of fixed exchange rates known as the Bretton Woods system, was under severe pressure. This was largely the result of the American attitude of benign neglect. The USA had established a hegemonic position in the postwar period and in the absence of an international medium of exchange the US dollar had come to be accepted as the international currency. This was perfectly safe as long as the USA adopted a sound financial stance. Unfortunately, the USA took the opportunity to finance the Vietnam war largely through running a balance of payments deficit and thereby releasing large quantities of dollars onto international exchange markets. The Americans refused to devalue the dollar to accommodate this and enormous pressure was placed on the next major reserve currency, the German Deutschmark. The system ultimately collapsed through massive internal pressures, and by the early 1970s the world had returned to the prewar system of floating exchange rates. Further problems for the established Western economies came in 1973–4 with the Arab–Israeli war and the subsequent quadrupling of oil prices. Postwar expansion had been built upon the availability of cheap oil for fuel. In the absence of cheap oil, thought had to be given to new industrial processes and new products (such as smaller-engined cars) which would make more efficient use of fuel. The established Western economies experienced severe dislocation, and the result of this was economic recession. At the same time new threats to the established North American and European economies were evident from the growing economic strength of the Japanese economy and other South-East Asian 'tigers'.

The 1970s was a period of growing uncertainty and challenge for established economies. If the 1950s and 1960s had in general been a period of economic certainty, the 1970s can be seen as a period of transition and struggle. This is reflected in growing industrial militancy in the UK and elsewhere, as workers struggled to maintain or improve their living standards in straitened economic circumstances.

### The regulation approach

Academics have attempted to understand and explain the major shifts in economic policies and attitudes in recent years, and one of the most influential approaches is that of the regulation school. It is argued that economies go through periods of stability or harmony in which strong GDP growth is registered. During these periods a particular technological paradigm is paramount and gives a lead to the whole economy. After the Second World War it is claimed that the technological paradigm called Fordism was in the ascendant (Amin, 1994a). Fordism (named after Henry Ford) revolves around the mass production of relatively undifferentiated goods. Here, standardised products are produced using standardised processes. The consequence of this is deskilled workers using single-purpose machinery in large factories. Whilst workers tend to find the work tedious and monotonous, nonetheless their material rewards can grow as long as productivity is rising. Up until the second half of the 1960s, productivity growth in Western economies was maintained and both shareholders and workers could achieve real increases in rewards. However, in the later stages of the 1960s and into the 1970s productivity growth could no longer be sustained (Boyer, 1988). Workers and shareholders had become accustomed to increases in profits and wages, and neither party was willing to surrender its position. This growing struggle became increasingly evident in the 1970s with significant increases in industrial action. At the same time various economic pressures manifested themselves through ever-growing levels of inflation.

The regulation school argues that periods of stability as described under the heading of Fordism can be styled regimes of accumulation. In order for such a regime to exist there must be synchronisation between a mode of production and a mode of social regulation. Under Fordism the mode of production, as noted, was mass production. However, in order to sustain mass production there must also be mass consumption. This is where Keynesian policies are of utmost importance. Keynesian policies as they evolved in the postwar period were centrally concerned with the maintenance of high levels of aggregate demand. Mass production was underpinned by the guarantee of mass consumption. Full employment was a policy priority into the 1970s, and the development of a comprehensive welfare state and a progressive tax system provided a framework which stabilised and supported the system of mass production. There was, then, a regulatory system which underpinned the production system and was in harmony with it.

However, by the late 1960s the stability of this system was being challenged, and during the 1970s enormous pressures built up. Those of the regulation school would argue that we have now moved away from the relatively stable paradigm of Fordism, but that there is no clearly defined successor. The present economic situation in these terms, then, is described as being one of crisis. The collectivist, full-employment, welfare-driven approach has been dismantled, but no coherent successor has come to replace it. Some academics argue that a new regulatory system is being assembled and that the state is now performing a different role from that of the earlier period. Jessop argues that the structure of the Keynesian welfare state is in terminal decline. A contender for the role of successor is what he styles the *Schumpeterian Workfare State* (SWS). The key economic and social objectives of the SWS can be seen to be 'to promote product, process, organizational, and market innovation and enhance the structural competitiveness of open economies mainly through supply-side intervention; and to subordinate social policy to the demands of labor market flexibility and structural competitiveness' (Jessop, 1992, p. 2).

With this in mind it is now necessary to analyse the economic policies undertaken by UK governments in the 1980s and 1990s.

## Economic policy since 1979

Margaret Thatcher's Conservative Government was elected in 1979 and came to power with a programme to roll back the influence of the state and challenge trade union power. The Labour Government, under James Callaghan, had from 1976 onwards faced a number of difficult challenges. In 1976 Callaghan was the first postwar Prime Minister to publicly renounce a commitment to the maintenance of full employment. He delivered a speech in September which seemed to close the policy option of Keynesian reflation which had been applied by all postwar governments.

> We used to think that you could just spend your way out of a recession and increase employment by cutting taxes and boosting government spending. I tell you in all candour that that option no longer exists, and that insofar as it ever did exist, it worked by injecting inflation into the economy. And each time that happened the average level of unemployment has risen. Higher inflation, followed by higher unemployment. That is the history of the last twenty years. (Budd, 1994, p. 8)

Callaghan also elevated monetary policy to a more important position on the policy agenda, influenced in part by his journalist son in law, Peter Jay, and by the strictures of the International Monetary Fund. The period from 1976 to 1979 was described by John Fforde of the Bank of England as a period of 'monetarily constrained "Keynesianism"' (Riddell, 1983, p. 60). The Callaghan Government also had particular problems with the trade unions, culminating in the 'winter of discontent', 1978/9, during which large numbers of public sector workers went on strike (including, famously, gravediggers) over the Government's imposition of an incomes policy. Incomes policies, often introduced with prices policies, were attempts to contain pay rises either mandatorily, or through exhortation. Such policies were a central feature of the Keynesian approach.

The new Conservative Government immediately established its credentials on assuming office in 1979 by reducing the levels of direct taxation, whilst increasing those of indirect taxation. This was in line with its major tenet that there was insufficient incentive to work in the British economy due to high levels of taxation on earned income. The emphasis then, was to be shifted from *pay as you earn* to *pay as you spend*. At the same time, policy was shifted to full blown monetarism, with the setting of monetary targets, initially on the main target variable known as Sterling M3. By setting monetary targets, year on year, through the Medium Term Financial Strategy, it was intended that the money stock would be reduced and inflation eradicated (Gilmour, 1983). The dangers of inflation had become all too readily apparent again in the mid-1970s as the retail price index in Britain rose to well over 20 per cent. High levels of inflation are generally regarded by economists as a bad thing, but market economists in particular emphasise the manner in which inflation distorts market signals and consequently introduces inefficiencies into the system (Friedman and Friedman, 1980).

In a market economy, profit is the motivating force to produce and price is the signal of how much to produce. If prices of products are rising in general (*ceteris paribus*) then producers will have an incentive to produce more as greater profits can be made. However, in times of high and unstable inflation it is not possible to estimate how much of a price rise is due to real forces and how much is due to monetary forces. The consequence is that people in business may gauge their reactions incorrectly and produce too much, or too little. Mrs Thatcher, promoting the importance of the market, saw inflation as public enemy number one. In the 1970s Milton Friedman had shown there to be a strong correlation between the growth of the money supply and the reaction of prices, with a time lag of some 12–18 months. It was demonstrated, that over the period 1972–4, Sterling M3 had risen by over 20 per cent and, after a time-lag, inflation had mirrored this almost exactly. The solution therefore, seemed to be easy: set money supply increases in line with projected increases in output and the price level should not rise. This was the reasoning which informed the monetarist approach of the 1980s.

Keynesians had accepted the reasoning of the Phillips Curve which suggested that there was a stable relationship between unemployment and inflation (Hare and Simpson, 1993). If this was the case, then it was possible to use this relationship for policy purposes and choose a level of inflation which went with a given level of unemployment (see Chapters 11 and 12). If unemployment was politically too high then this could be remedied, albeit at the cost of a small rise in inflation. During the period that this achieved the status of orthodoxy the money supply was simply allowed to rise to accommodate the level of economic activity. Friedman rejected this, arguing that governments, by operating in this way, had injected inflationary pressures into the economy by keeping the level of unemployment below its market clearing rate and boosting the money supply (Trevithick, 1980). The argument of Friedman and others, who could be categorised as new classicists, was that in an attempt to stabilise their economy by applying Keynesian measures governments had in fact achieved the opposite. The policy conclusions are then obvious. 'All the new classical arguments tend towards the conclusion that the government should abstain from an active stabilization policy. The basic claim is that systematic changes in policy variables have no effect on real variables' (Klamer, 1984, p. 20).

Mrs Thatcher was particularly influenced in the formulation of her policies by Milton Friedman and Friedrich von Hayek. Friedman, as a staunch proponent of the free market, was influential in promoting the growth of monetarism in the 1980s. He feels that government has grown too large and needs to be severely reined back. Whilst government is important, he argues that it principally has four duties and should be restricted to these.:

> It [government] enforces law and order, provides a means for formulating the rules of conduct, adjudicates disputes, facilitates transportation and communication, and supervises the issuance of currency (Friedman and Friedman, 1980, p. 55).

Hayek was particularly concerned with individual freedom and saw the collectivist approach of socialism as a denial of individual freedom. He was opposed to most varieties of planning and championed market solutions. 'Economic liberalism is opposed, however, to competition being supplanted by inferior methods of co-ordinating individual efforts' (Hayek, 1976, p. 27).

Hayek was opposed to many of the policies introduced during the high period of Keynesianism and saw prices and incomes policies as a major impediment to individual effort.

The Conservative Governments of the 1980s were heavily influenced by thinkers such as these, and both Mrs Thatcher and the American President from 1980 to 1988, Ronald Reagan, advocated neo-liberal policies which resonated with policies from earlier epochs. In Britain, a new role for government was sought, with the emphasis being placed on government as an enabler, or facilitator, rather than as direct participant. This approach can be seen in a wide range of areas. Perhaps the most spectacular form of withdrawal from direct participation in the economy can be seen in the privatisation programme. The 1980s and 1990s saw a reversal of the nationalisation programme after the war with substantial sales of formerly publicly owned industries such as gas, coal, electricity, water and transport (Letwin, 1988; Ferguson and Ferguson, 1994). As well as providing billions of pounds of revenue for the exchequer, this policy also enabled the government to withdraw from conflict with former public employees over pay and conditions.

Increasing emphasis has been placed on supply-side policies. Rather than stressing the importance of demand management, the balance has shifted to facilitating supply. Wherever possible, attempts have been made to remove restrictions to the provision of goods and services and stimulate an adequate flow. This underlies the logic of cutting taxes on both private and corporate incomes. Another area which has received attention is the provision of training and education and labour market flexibility. Significant changes have been made in the provision of public sector training (see later) and university-level education has been greatly expanded. Furthermore, legislative change has weakened the power of trade unions, and individual workers have less redress against their employers in many situations (see later). In those sectors which have remained within the public arena such as health and education, new organisational structures and financial arrangements have been introduced. Wherever possible, quasi market arrangements have been introduced in an attempt to encourage 'efficiency' and accountability. In the case of health, hospitals have been encouraged to adopt trust status which places them in the position of independent cost centres run by a chief executive. Equally, family doctors have been encouraged to become budget-holders, giving them new financial responsibilities and placing the local family doctor on more of a business footing. In the case of education, schools have been encouraged to opt out of local authority control and become grant maintained. At the same time, further education colleges and ex-polytechnics have been granted independent status and removed from the aegis of local authority control. Central government has indeed reduced the sphere of influence and control of local government significantly. Cochrane (1993, p. 29) notes that there has been 'an increased involvement of the departments of central government . . . in the details of local government finance'.

### Constraints on economic policy-making

There are a number of constraints on economic policy-making. It was shown earlier that multiple objectives such as the maintenance of high levels of employment and balance of payments equilibrium cause governments to 'mix and match' policies in accordance with conflicting requirements. However, there are additional constraints which emerge explicitly from the processes of government.

Economic policy-making has to be viewed in its political context. In the UK, Parliaments are elected for a maximum five-year term. During this time the government, operating with the majority within Parliament, has power to implement its policies, economic and otherwise. However, all governments are aware that they face re-election and that if their policies are unpopular then they will suffer defeat at the next election. Unpopularity is less of a problem in the early term of a Parliament, but becomes a serious problem in the last two years. In between elections, the electorate has limited scope in influencing economic affairs, for as Miliband (1982, p. 1) notes, in a 'capitalist democracy' there is 'a permanent and fundamental contradiction or tension, . . . between the promise of popular power, enshrined in universal suffrage, and the curbing or denial of that promise in practice'.

However, general dissatisfaction with a government as manifested in opinion polls or through other demonstrations of discontent, may lead backbenchers belonging to the governing party to put pressure on the government to implement change in policies. Afraid of losing their seats at the next election, MPs may threaten a refusal to support the Government in Parliamentary Divisions. In the Parliament elected in 1992, the Major Government faced a number of threats from unruly backbenchers, notably over its policy towards Europe. However, as the Parliament approached the end of its life, increasing disquiet was felt amongst backbenchers as opinion polls constantly registered the fact that the Conservative Party's popularity was waning fast. This was generally attributed to a lack of a 'feel good' factor, particularly related to a weak housing market.

One of the Conservative's key themes in the 1980s was centred on the extension of the 'property owning democracy'. Many of the government's policies contributed to this ideal, notably the enforcement on local authorities of the sales of council houses. As the 1980s progressed, the percentage of the population owning their own houses increased, as did the real value of property. In fact, at many stages in the 1980s, people were gaining more from the appreciation in value of their property than from their salary. The property market gained a momentum of its own, with a seeming upward tilt under which property investment was a win-win option.

A final fillip to an already dangerously inflated property market was given in 1988, when the deadline for the ending of double tax relief on mortgages held by two persons (who were not married) was extended from March to August. Thousands of unmarried couples raced to take advantage of this tax break, increasing the demand for property (especially in parts of London) and with it, the price of houses. By 1989 the property boom was over and the 1990s has seen a property market continually in the doldrums.

Thousands of people continue to have negative equity (where the value of their mortgage exceeds the saleable value of their property) and this has a depressing effect on household expenditure. Indeed, the economic recession of the 1990s has been deepened by the problems in the housing market. People's expenditure patterns are influenced by what is known as the wealth effect. The amount an individual spends is determined in part by the value of his/her assets. In the heady days of the property boom of the mid to late 1980s, people's main asset, their house, was increasing rapidly in value. As a result consumers were more prepared to spend, often by incurring extra debt through such means as overdrafts and credit card expenditure. This was made easier in a climate of increasing financial deregulation. However, as property prices fell, the reverse procedure was set in motion. People felt less financially secure and reined back their spending, causing demand in the economy to fall. Additionally, in the 1990s, households faced a 'double whammy', as mortgage interest relief was considerably reduced.

Many supporters of the Conservative Government's policies in the 1980s felt betrayed and were quite vocal in displaying this. Worried Conservative backbenchers repeatedly called on the Chancellor of the Exchequer to introduce economic measures to relieve the gloom in the housing market. Such suggested measures included special tax relief for those with negative equity, or a general increase in mortgage tax relief for all. Furthermore, backbenchers repeatedly called for reductions in interest rates and continually counselled restraint on the Chancellor, even when economic circumstances may have suggested that interest rates should be raised to account for changed economic circumstances.

These political pressures are particularly important in the crucible of economic policy-making. Governments make economic policy, but they are dependent upon backbenchers to support them in the lobbies in the passage of legislation. The Government has, through the 1980s and 1990s, established a pattern within its overall economic policy whereby people should be allowed to spend more of their money in the way they see fit. Consequently, the emphasis has been on reducing the burden of direct taxation, whilst the burden has been transferred to indirect taxation. However, to maintain consistency within this strategy it is necessary to reduce tax concessions such as tax relief on company cars. In the days of the 1960s and 1970s, when direct taxes were relatively high, a number of generous tax concessions were in operation to partly compensate for this. As tax rates fall then it seems reasonable that generous tax concessions should be reduced or ended. By leaving tax relief fixed on the first £30,000 of a mortgage for a long period, its real value has been eroded over time by inflation. Furthermore, by reducing the rate of relief below the basic tax rate its value has been further reduced, especially for top-rate taxpayers. However, by arguing for additional help for homeowners, backbenchers pressurise their government to introduce inconsistencies into their economic policies. If the Chancellor was to give way on such a policy then he would have to rearrange his other expenditure and revenue policies to compensate. Furthermore, by subjecting interest rate policy to the dictates of the domestic housing market, the Chancellor could be seen to be acting against the longer-term interests of the UK economy.

Political and electoral pressures are of importance in shaping economic policies; however, relationships are often complex. Research has shown that voters hold Governments responsible for a large number of outcomes and not just management of the economy (Heath, Jowell and Curtice, 1991). To the extent that voters focus on economic issues they may need a number of months to absorb what is happening in the economy and then have a short memory span, giving greater importance to immediate perceptions rather than even fairly recent events. As Grant notes: 'In other words, voters are relatively myopic, but their myopia incorporates a short time lag. Economic improvement may need to be secured some months before the election' (Grant, 1993, p. 29).

Economic strategy and the electoral cycle have been closely intertwined in the postwar period. Governments of all political persuasions have boosted the economy by cutting taxes and/or increasing expenditure towards the end of their term of office in order to create a feeling of economic wellbeing amongst the electorate and, in effect, 'buy' votes.

The media is also an important contributor to the political process in a modern democracy. It was said that the Prime Minister, Margaret Thatcher, was a regular listener to the 'Today' news programme on BBC Radio Four. Whilst it is not suggested that this programme in any way shaped her thinking on economic policy, the fact that she was concerned to listen to it suggests that she felt that it had an important influence in the country as a whole. Popular news programmes such as ITN's 'News at Ten' and the BBC's 'Nine O'clock News' can be influential by focusing on key economic issues and presenting them, often with strong visual images. Newspapers and magazines are also important in conveying information on economic policy, as is perhaps evidenced by the number of newspaper owners and editors who have received titles at the behest of governments.

Pressure groups are also important in the framing of economic policy. As noted earlier, in the 1960s and 1970s the TUC and the CBI, both of which operate as pressure groups, were influential in shaping economic policy. With the demise of tripartite economic policy-making in the late 1970s, the influence of these groups waned, and whilst Margaret Thatcher was concerned to listen to the views of industry in the 1980s, her audiences seemed to be increasingly with the right-wing pressure group, the Institute of Directors.

It is argued that the world is becoming increasingly integrated in terms of industrial and commercial trade. The term 'the global economy' is often used to indicate this increasing integration and interdependency. With international financial deregulation, the collapse of the Soviet Empire, the gradual integration of China into the world economy and the growth and increasing sophistication of communications networks, the opportunities for international investment appear almost boundless. Capital has become increasingly mobile and as an economy such as the UK is primarily governed by capitalist dynamics, the growing internationalism of capital has reduced the level of control that any government can exercise on the British Economy. Transnational corporations have enormous influence and are feted by governments all over the world as they try to entice them to invest in their country and consequently create jobs.

The limits to the extent to which a nation-state can operate its own economic policies regardless of the policies of other nations was perhaps shown by the experience of the Mitterrand Government in France in the early 1980s. On his election to office in 1981, President Mitterrand introduced a Keynesian-style reflationary package intended to pull France out of recession. However, the result of this policy was a balance of payments crisis and severe pressure on the franc. By 1983 the French Government had introduced a new austerity package (Grant, 1993), demonstrating the fact that France was now so integrated into the international economy that its freedom to manoeuvre in isolation with regard to economic policy was now limited. Increasing sophistication in financial markets with the growth of new financial instruments has led to increasing financial interdependence at the global level. Increasing financial globalisation has occurred with growing volatility in financial markets, but the political apparatus to deal with and regulate this at the international level does not exist. As a consequence, domestic economic policies could be effectively derailed by an international financial crisis which individual nation-states are powerless to control. It could be argued that this globalisation of financial markets makes the co-ordination of national economic policies and the development of effective international regulatory institutions imperative.

In the face of a deregulated international capital market nation-states are powerless to deal with global movements and, in particular, currency speculation. Speculation in all financial markets has been greatly facilitated by increasingly complex and interdependent relationships. Whilst speculation is not a new phenomenon, 'the increased internationalization of finance has enhanced the scope for propagation of disturbances from one market to another within, as well as across borders' (Akyuz, 1995, p. 57).

Membership of the European Community is a further constraint on economic policy-making in the UK, as policies which are incompatible with the Community's founding treaties will be challenged (Grant, 1993). The signing of the Maastricht Treaty (albeit with the UK's refusal to agree to the social chapter) is a further step along the route to an integrated European state, and the establishment of full European monetary union (see later) would require greater co-ordination of economic policies. The UK has generally lagged behind other member states in promoting moves which lead to significantly greater integration and impinge on freedom to construct national economic policies. However, the UK is integrated into Europe in terms of its trading patterns and this is likely to become increasingly important as the Single European Market continues to establish itself.

## An evaluation of economic policy

In the 1950s and 1960s the UK economy grew at a rate which had not been matched for such a lengthy period in earlier times. Whilst the UK's rate of growth lagged behind our main European competitors, such as France, Germany and Italy, the Prime Minister, Harold Macmillan, was moved to state in 1957:

> Indeed, let's be frank about it; most of our people have never had it so good. Go around the country, go to the industrial towns, go to the farms, and you will see a state of prosperity such as we have never had in my lifetime – nor indeed in the history of this country (Childs, 1979, p. 106).

However, as has been demonstrated, by the 1970s enormous economic and social pressures had built up in the UK and the social democratic consensus of the earlier postwar period was no longer evident. In ushering in a new era of monetarism Margaret Thatcher was clearly announcing a break with the past in terms of economic policies and saw this as a necessary prelude to the working of an economic miracle. The verdict on the 'successes' of the economic policies of the 1980s and 1990s is somewhat qualified. Taking GDP growth since 1979 the figures are not suggestive of spectacular success, and are even less satisfactory when one considers that governments over this time have been the beneficiaries of substantial North Sea oil revenues, not available to earlier governments. Unemployment at well in excess of two million is considerably higher than was the case in 1979. Furthermore, as is shown later, work itself is far less secure and many more people are employed on a part-time or casual basis. Between 1979 and 1994 part-time employment increased in all the G7 countries, but the greatest increase was in Britain. In 1994, 23.8 per cent of British workers held part-time jobs, compared to 16.4 per cent in 1979 (*The Economist*, 29 July 1995). Public expenditure remains high at around the same percentage of GDP as in 1979, but a greater share of this is now accounted for by social security expenditure – perhaps a clear indication of economic failure rather than success. Indeed poverty levels in the UK have been growing rapidly in recent years, and the level of income inequality in the UK has grown faster than elsewhere, with the sole exception of New Zealand (see Figure 1.1).

It might be argued that the Government's overriding priority in keeping inflation levels down imposed substantial costs on the UK economy. Over the period 1979 to 1981 employment and capacity in manufacturing industry was reduced significantly, with subsequent balance of payments implications. Whilst inflation was to be checked through money supply control, the financial deregulation of the early 1980s made it difficult to operate monetary policy and to correctly interpret the chosen monetary targets. Sir Ian Gilmour, a member of the first Thatcher Government, comments on the methods used by governments to curb inflation.

> Governments have sought to bring down inflation by increasing unemployment. And they have done so because they have believed that only increased unemployment would prevent intolerable inflation. In consequence, they have produced intolerable unemployment (Gilmour, 1983, p. 10).

The early commitment to monetarism seemed to subside and by the end of the decade the UK had opted into the exchange rate mechanism (ERM) of the European Monetary System, thus surrendering its independence in monetary policy. Since leaving the ERM in 1992, the UK has not once again adopted the aggressive monetary stance of the early 1980s. Indeed in some respects economic policy in the 1990s has been more pragmatic than in the 1980s.

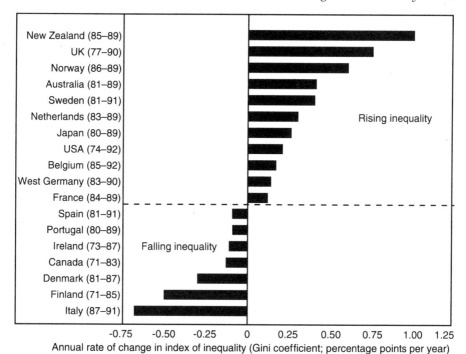

*Source*:    Joseph Rowntree Foundation; *Inquiry into Income and Wealth*, Joseph Rowntree Foundation, York, 1995, vol. 1, p. 14.

**FIGURE 1.1    International income inequality trends**

However, underlying the current approach there is still an obedience to the concept of rational economic man and a desire to further withdraw from direct intervention in the workings of the market.

### Conclusions

Current economic policies in the UK and elsewhere in the world seem to be failing to deliver prosperity for all, and indeed in the UK surveys have shown unease, amongst those in work, who feel that their jobs are insecure (Batchelor, 1995a). This lack of a feeling of security has been cited as a major reason why UK consumers have been reticent in their spending in the 1990s. In the 1950s and 1960s economists gained credibility because the economic policies they advised governments to adopt seemed to be leading to prosperity for the greatest number, in unprecedented fashion. In the 1990s the economics profession has come under increasing attack, not least because economists are implicated in the shortcomings of economic policy. A rash of books, including Paul Ormerod's *Death of Economics* (1994) have told of the powerlessness of economics to help in what many have styled a world economic crisis. Others have tried to defend economists, arguing that it is not the case that economics has failed entirely, just that the wrong economists have gained the ascendancy and have been major influences on policy in recent years. Lord Eatwell, for example, concedes that economics is failing, but argues that:

> It is failing not because some economists' ideas are not informing economic policy. They are, and they are not working. Rather, it is failing because economics today is built upon theoretical foundations which exclude the very substance of economic policy, namely, the economic institutions through which economic life is actually lived. (Eatwell, 1994, p. 36)

It is Eatwell's contention that the economic theory which informs policy-makers today is not rooted in the real world; in particular it 'either ignores institutions or treats them as imperfections' (Eatwell, 1994, p. 37).

The debate is set to run, but what is clear is that economic policies and policy-making are currently in a malaise. The early postwar consensus has evaporated and economic problems seem as intractable now as they appeared in the interwar years.

# CHAPTER 2

# Markets and Market Failure

In the previous chapter it was shown that market forces as a means of allocating resources have been, and remain, a powerful dynamic in Western economies. However, some economists feel that government has now grown too large and has encroached too far on the prerogative of markets. Consequently, they would like to see the powers and influence of government severely curtailed. Free market economists base their arguments on a sincerely held belief that, by reducing the influence of government, the welfare of society will be increased. Other economists see a strong and far-reaching role for government (in a variety of forms) and argue that this is the way in which society's welfare is best promoted. The branch of economics which deals with such ethical questions is commonly referred to as *welfare economics*.

Sen (1987) argues that economics has two different origins both of which are related to politics. One of these origins, which has a traditional association with ethics, can be traced back to Aristotle, if not further. This tradition sees economics contributing along with other sciences, to the living of a 'good life', and sees wealth creation as a subsidiary end. This standpoint transcends any notions of 'efficiency' and encompasses a broad view of what is for the good of mankind. The second origin sees human nature as being easily understood and reducible to simple describable moves and is traceable back to nineteenth-century economists such as Walras. This is often described as the 'engineering' approach. 'This approach is characterised by being concerned with primarily logistic issues rather than with ultimate ends and such questions as what may foster "the good of man" or "how one should live"' (Sen, 1987, p. 4). Whilst Sen does not dispute the fact that this engineering approach has helped to resolve a number of technical problems in economics he feels that it has shortcomings in a range of areas. In particular it is necessary that 'the deep questions raised by the ethics-related view of motivation and of social achievement must find an important place in modern economics' (Sen, 1987, p. 6).

The rather mechanistic, engineering, approach has been in the ascendant in economics in the twentieth century and, whilst various adaptations and modifications have occurred over time, this approach has established itself as the orthodoxy. Whilst early political economists such as Adam Smith were firmly convinced of the merits of the market, they were preoccupied with issues of welfare and clearly recognised the drawbacks of the market system. Smith was deeply concerned with moral issues and recognised the complexity of human behaviour. The economist/engineers of the late nineteenth and early twentieth century placed welfare issues in a technical and mathematised framework, but in so doing significantly reduced the 'human' dimension. However, this technical approach has had advantages to the economics profession as it yields precise and clear results, and as such has an appeal to policy-makers. This can be seen to be particularly the case in the situation of orthodox welfare economics. 'Welfare economics supplies the economist – and the politician – with standards, at least with some standards, by which to appraise and on the basis of which to formulate policy' (Scitovsky, 1951, p. 303).

This chapter outlines the established orthodox approach to welfare economics and the role of the market. However, it is argued that there are many shortcomings in the established orthodox approach and that the role of the market in particular requires careful consideration and evaluation. These are issues which will be dealt with in a variety of contexts in subsequent chapters.

## Key issues in orthodox welfare economics

In a pure market economy a large number of decision-makers contribute to an outcome which has no overall design or intervention. Such a system is not subject to planning or co-ordination exercised by agents such as the government. However, it is argued that each individual decision-maker pursuing his or her self-interest can contribute to an outcome which is in the best interests of society as a whole (Shand, 1990). This occurs because of the stimulus offered by the price mechanism and the limits to exploitation inherent within this mechanism. At the base of this theory is the concept of perfect competition. Here, producers of goods and services will be motivated by profit, but because of the conditions of perfect competition will be unable to charge excessive prices and earn excess profits in the long run due to the ease with which new firms can enter an industry where above normal profits are being earned.

At the core of neo-classical economics is the concept of equilibrium. Under the given circumstances of perfect competition, neo-classical orthodox reasoning shows that it is possible to achieve a state of equilibrium in goods and factor markets whereby no individual can be made better off without reducing the welfare of another individual. This is the well-known Pareto criterion named after the nineteenth-century economist Vilfredo Pareto. This criterion enables us to evaluate resource allocations and decide whether they are 'good' or 'bad' from the point of view of society.

In a simplified situation in which we have just two goods and an initial allocation of these goods between two individuals, if it is possible for a reallocation of these goods to take place whereby one individual gains in satisfaction whilst the other is no worse off, then this change in distribution is Pareto efficient. The welfare of society can be seen to have improved in these circumstances as total satisfaction must have risen. Those of a free market persuasion would argue that, left to itself, the market will move towards equilibrium in all markets (general equilibrium) and a Pareto optimal position will be established. The welfare of society is maximised, as no individual can be made better off without reducing the welfare of another.

This leads us to the *First Theorem of Welfare Economics* which states that

> if (a) there are markets for all commodities which enter into production and utility functions and (b) all markets are competitive, then the equilibrium of the economy is Pareto efficient. (Gravelle and Rees, 1992, p. 490)

However, the conditions of this theorem cannot be guaranteed in the real world, and whilst the ideal of perfect competition lies at the base of many economists' toolboxes, policy based on this reasoning can be misleading. There are a number of problems in accepting the theorem. For example, economic decision-makers, both firms and consumers, may not in effect be price takers because of the existence of monopolised or monopsonistic markets. As a consequence of this, prices will not accurately reflect the marginal value of activities to all parties to the transaction. Furthermore, the proviso that there should be markets for all goods or activities and that therefore markets should be complete, may not be fulfilled. For many goods, such as air, there are no markets. Finally, the requirement that markets be in equilibrium may not be met. Markets may be in disequilibrium, resulting in a lack of a unified set of prices to guide economic actors which leads to variations in marginal valuations and consequently inefficient allocations (Gravelle and Rees, 1992).

The Pareto criterion, though widely used, is controversial and by no means universally accepted. As Laidler and Estrin (1989, p. 408) note

> It [the Pareto criterion] identifies the welfare of society solely with the welfare of the individuals that make up the society. This is a defensible position but there are ethical systems which invest society itself, or groups within society (such as social classes) with a moral importance that is distinct from that attaching to individuals. In terms of such systems the Pareto criterion is at best inadequate and at worst meaningless.

Even if we accept the individualist ethical position of the Pareto criterion we are still left with unresolved problems. For example, the criterion does not equip us to select between say, two positions, both of which may be a Pareto improvement on the initial position, but result in welfare gains for different individuals.

A resource allocation that makes a poor person better off by a pound a year and lowers the welfare of no other member of the community represents a movement to a Pareto superior situation, but so does a reallocation that makes a rich person better off by the same amount if no one else's welfare is altered.The Pareto criterion gives us no way of choosing between the two reallocations (Laidler and Estrin, 1989, p. 409).

In the case described, either of the two positions may be seen to represent an improvement in the allocative efficiency of resource use, but the question of fairness or social justice remains unaddressed.

The ideal of a perfectly competitive economy delivering Pareto optimality in a condition of equilibrium can be used as a justification for a free-market, capitalist system. However, it is generally conceded, even by those of a free-market persuasion, that governments have a role in attempting to move an economy towards this ideal. As a basic minimum, governments may be deemed necessary to pass and enforce laws which deal with contracts and property rights. However, even this minimum role for the government involves the use of resources, as a judicial and law enforcement system has to be staffed and financed. The financing of such a system, it is generally accepted, must be achieved through some form of taxation system. When taxes are levied, either on income or on sales, then they act in such a way as to move the economy away from a Pareto optimal allocation of resources as a non-market element has been introduced into the pricing process (see Laidler and Estrin, 1989, p. 417).

Taxes can be seen to have a distorting effect on the allocative outcome in an economy compared to the ideal of Pareto optimality, but taxes can also be used to correct misallocations which the market seems unable to deal with. Such misallocations are said to be the outcome of *market failure.*

## Market failure

Externalities occur when there are relationships between economic actors which are not fully accounted for through market prices. An example of this occurs in the case of smoke pollution. In a situation where a firm pollutes the atmosphere with smoke and soot, a cost is imposed on all those who unwillingly are subjected to these effects. If someone is in the custom of hanging their washing outside to dry, then soot particles deposited on the clean clothing will be unwelcome and will necessitate the cost and inconvenience of rewashing the affected clothing. Quite obviously then, a financial cost is imposed on the householder. However, it must be less expensive for the firm to pollute the atmosphere in this way than to modify its processes and use different non-polluting fuels, or invest in pollution controls, or it would have done so. The firm, therefore, is producing its goods at less than the true cost. The fully accounted cost of the firm's actions would include the direct or *private costs* of production it incurs, plus the additional costs imposed on those individuals who suffer from its actions, the *social costs*. The output of goods produced by firms which are imposing a *negative externality* on society will be too high, as their cost schedules will not reflect the true costs of production. Consequently they will be able to sell their products at a lower price than would be the case if their cost schedules also incorporated social costs. In order to make good this failure of the market to allocate resources efficiently, a means must be devised by which both private and social costs are taken into consideration in deciding on the amount of a good or service which is to be produced.

In the same way as too much of a good may be produced which generates negative externalities, so also may too little of a good be provided which generates *positive externalities*. Here, the firm may provide a benefit to individuals which is not accounted for through the receipt of revenue. For example, a firm which landscapes its immediate environment will provide a pleasant sight for passers by and may even add to the value of nearby property. In this situation, individuals will benefit from another's actions without having made a financial contribution to the achievement of the outcome. The true benefits of the firm's actions exceed the benefits which accrue to itself. If some method could be found of rewarding firms for the benefits which they provide but which are not accounted for through market prices, then the level of this beneficial production should rise. Therefore, in addition to the private benefits accruing to a firm as represented by its demand curve (average revenue) it is necessary to add on the value of the social benefits which are also present.

It is therefore necessary to find methods through which resource allocation takes into account both private and social costs. In order to deal with a negative externality it may be possible to internalise it by making the producer bear the full costs of the damage done. For instance, the firm polluting the atmosphere could be charged the cost of rectifying the problems it causes and the victims of this pollution could thereby be compensated. Pigou (1932) advanced the notion of a tax on producers of negative externalities, that the consumers of the product would bear in the purchase price – an excise tax. This would have the effect of choking back demand, effectively moving the demand curve in towards the origin by the value of the tax. The production of the externality-creating good will be reduced and allocative efficiency will be achieved.

If one firm is imposing a negative externality on another, then a means of dealing with this would be to promote a merger between the firms. For example, assume that the smoke-emitting firm is exclusively negatively affecting a nearby orchard and the two enterprises merge. The resulting single enterprise would now have to decide on the best combination of smoke and soot and fruit. More smoke and soot means less fruit and vice versa.

Again allocative efficiency will be achieved as the firm will only continue to generate pollution up to the point where the revenue gained from extra production just equals revenue lost from depleted fruit sales. If pollution continues past this point, then extra sales from production will be less than the revenue lost due to reduced fruit crops, and the firm's overall revenue would fall.

Another means of dealing with negative externalities is through the allocation of property rights (Coase, 1960). Assume that two paper mills are situated along a river, using it as a common resource, both for water as an input for production and as a means of disposing of waste. If paper mill A is situated upstream and paper mill B downstream, then A's waste will be carried along by the river to B. If B then uses the water contaminated by A, the greater the level of contamination, the greater the cost of purifying this, preparatory to production. The way to deal with this would be to allocate the rights to the river to either of the two firms. One might assume that if B is given the rights to the river then it will simply prohibit the use of the river by A, but this is unlikely to be the case. As long as the revenue to A from production exceeds the costs to B of purifying its intake of water, then A can compensate B for the damage caused. A will be enabled to continue its production just up to the point where the revenue (in excess of other costs) gained from an extra unit of production is equal to the compensation necessary to account for the damage caused. A would not continue production beyond this point as its extra revenue would not be sufficient to account for the extra compensation it has to pay. The same result would also be achieved if the reverse were to occur and A was to be given rights to the river. In this situation B would pay A to cut back its output and therefore the amount of waste dumped in the river. B would be able to compensate A, for A's lost production, as long as its savings on purifying the water exceeded the lost revenue to A from its forgone production. Regardless of which firm was given the rights to the river, the outcome should be allocative efficiency.

Each of these attempts to deal with externalities has problems. For instance, in the case of taxes it is often difficult to identify clearly both the cause of an externality and all its victims. As a consequence, it is difficult to arrive at a figure for the tax and identify accurately those who should pay it. For example, many Swedish lakes are now devoid of fish life due to the effects of acid rain. This acid rain is due largely to the burning of fossil fuels in countries outside Sweden. The problem here is one of clearly identifying the culprits and apportioning blame – the difficulties are obvious.

In the case of a merger between two firms, similar problems arise. It is unlikely that a situation will occur in which there are only two parties to an externality. The more parties there are, the less likely it is that all can be included in a merged organisation.

The Coasian solution of assigning property rights appears plausible but again is fraught with difficulties. In order to achieve an efficient resource allocation it is necessary for firms to decide on the basis of accurate information where the balance of pollution and production should be. If each party knew accurately what the others' costs were, then the bargain struck should be an easy matter. However, in the absence of the free disclosure of information, expensive bargaining may be entered into as each party tries to strike a better deal at the expense of the other. In this case bargaining costs will offset gains from allocative efficiency.

## Public and merit goods

In some cases the market, if left to itself, will not provide some goods at all, or will provide them in insufficient quantities for the optimum benefit of society. The orthodox response is to devise methods by which an outside agency, government, can rectify these deficiencies and move the economy towards an optimal position. Government policy formed in the context of the failure of markets is often referred to as the theory of the second best. Lancaster notes: 'It is possible to conceive of policies (called *second best* policies) in which the government introduces distortions designed to counteract other distortions partly, which it does not choose to (or cannot) eliminate' (Lancaster, 1983, p. 313).

### Public goods

At the heart of the provision of public goods is the concept of the *free rider*. Some goods, whilst necessary for society and providing universal benefits, will not be provided through the market. For example, members of society may generally agree that the provision of national defence is a good thing and of public benefit. However, if asked to subscribe voluntarily for such provision, individuals are likely to decline, in the knowledge that provision will be made by others and that it is impossible for them to be excluded from the benefits. If everyone behaves in such a manner then no provision will be made. In such circumstances an external agency, the government, has to make a decision on the necessary level of provision and levy society accordingly through means of general taxation.

Public goods have two principal characteristics; *nonrivalry and nonexclusivity*. A good can be seen to be *nonrival* if at any level of production the provision of the good to an additional consumer incurs zero marginal cost. Most goods provided through the market have a positive marginal cost but some goods do not incur extra costs as extra consumers are added. Take the example of a lighthouse. Once constructed and operational, extra users of the services of the lighthouse do not add to costs.

A good is nonexclusive if it is not possible to exclude people from its consumption. An example of this is defence. Once a nation is equipped for defence then all citizens can benefit from this protection and it is not possible to exclude anyone from sharing in this.

Goods can be exclusive but nonrival. For example, a motorway at non peak time is nonrival as one car's progress would not be impeded by another and the additional cost of its use is zero. However, the motorway could be exclusive as it would be possible to exclude some traffic from using the motorway, or charge for its use. Equally, goods can be nonexclusive but rival. Air is nonexclusive but as we have already seen it is not nonrival because the use of the air by one firm or individual can impinge on the use of the air by others.

Defence is a public good as its characteristics include both nonrivalry and nonexclusivity. Just as no one can be excluded from the benefits of national defence neither does one individual's consumption of this defence in any way diminish another individual's consumption. However, the list of goods that are provided by the government includes far more items than can be subsumed under the strict definition of public goods. The majority of public goods are *non-pure public goods* or *quasi-public goods* as consumers can be excluded from their benefits. For example, roads and bridges can be converted to private use by means of levying tolls.

### Merit goods

Whilst it is possible that the market may fail to provide any quantity of a pure public good such as national defence, there are other goods that will be provided, but in insufficient quantities for full public benefit. In the case of a *merit good* such as health care or education, left to the market there will be underconsumption. The benefits to society of the consumption of such goods exceeds the benefits accruing to individuals. For example, left to themselves, some members of society, especially the poor, will under-invest in education, possibly denying children even the benefits of acquiring basic numeracy and literacy. By legislating that children have to follow a prescribed course of education for a minimum period of time, society attempts to ensure that all citizens acquire a certain level of educational attainment. This minimum level benefits society at large, for at the very least, in order to participate fully in a democracy and in the workplace, a citizen needs to be literate and numerate. Again, even at the most basic and self-interested level, society benefits from some general standard of health care. Take the spread of infectious diseases. It is in society's interest that citizens are protected from contagious diseases through innoculation or other forms of protection/treatment. The benefits of many forms of health care for the individual may be exceeded by the overall benefits to society. Having conceded the necessity to provide merit goods, society then has to decide at what level they should be provided and what is the best mechanism for their allocation. In the case of the UK, as was noted in the first chapter, the Conservative Governments in the 1980s and 1990s created surrogate markets for the provision of merit goods such as health care and education.

Orthodox economics incorporates a belief that state intervention is only justified when market failure can be clearly identified as the market is otherwise the guarantor of maximum efficiency. The state has a valuable part to play in raising the level of social welfare by intervening in cases of market failure. A technique widely used in assessing the welfare effects of public policy is cost-benefit analysis. If it can be shown that the (social) benefits resulting from undertaking a project outweigh the (social) costs then there is a gain in social welfare (Sawyer, 1989). However, this benign view of state action is not shared by all. Marxian economists argue that in a market economy the state operates in the interests of capital and against labour, thus reducing the welfare of society. Those of a free-market persuasion argue that the state is bureaucratic and inefficient. Members of the bureaucracy are seen to advance the role of government as this increases their own budgets and career development. However, the welfare of society is again reduced as resources are not put to their best use.

## Free markets and individual liberty

One of the main claims of those who hold a free-market position is that economic liberalism goes hand in hand with personal liberty (Hayek, 1944). The logical sequence here is that with the restriction of economic freedom comes the curtailment of individual freedom. Hayek, a leading member of the Austrian school, holds views which do not accord with the utilitarian wealth-maximising position of the orthodox neo-classical school. Whilst for Hayek the processes of the market are the only guarantor of individual liberty, he sees those market processes as being dynamic and not dependent on the attainment of general equilibrium (Gray, 1990).

> Distinguished liberal theorists, from Jeremy Bentham to Milton Friedman, have argued that capitalism is the only secure basis for democracy. In this view, the two systems are not only compatible: democracy positively needs capitalism in order to survive (Hodgson, 1984, pp. 110–11).

The New Right which focuses mainly on economics and stresses individualism, argues that the market must be allowed to operate more freely. Whilst some members of this group, such as Milton Friedman, trace their ideas on the role of government back to Adam Smith, others such as Hayek have a much broader view of the role of government (Bosanquet, 1983). The Friedmanite camp has had most influence in the UK, as was evidenced by the monetary policy experiments which played a key part in government economic policy in the 1980s.

The New Right argues that the period of Keynesian economics after the Second World War has led to an outcome which has moved us further away from the best allocation of resources. It is argued that government and other economic agents have increasingly impinged upon and distorted the workings of the market system. During the period from 1945 up until the end of the 1970s the trade union movement grew in terms of membership and influence. Over this time real wages grew, accounting for a greater share of GDP, and profits were squeezed. The New Right, echoed by the Conservative Prime Minister Margaret Thatcher in the 1980s, argued that this 'creeping socialism' and a growing administrative bureaucracy had led to a lack of consumer choice, with more and more decisions affecting welfare being made by bureaucrats. The prescription was to restore profit levels for firms, create an 'enterprise society' and provide mechanisms which allow more consumer choice.

However, there are problems here. Many advocates of the New Right rely on an orthodox model of the operations of the market based on general equilibrium and ultimately relying on perfect competition. In an attempt to restore greater freedom to labour markets, the representatives of labour, the trade unions, have been severely weakened by government actions (see later). However, it must be remembered why trade unions developed their strength in the nineteenth and twentieth centuries. A major reason for the growth of trade unions was the need for the individual worker to have support in dealing with the greater power of the employer. By joining together in the form of trade unions, workers could develop power blocs which enabled them to countervail the power bloc of the employer. Whilst the power blocs representing labour have been weakened, capital's position has not been challenged. Large companies are subject to competitive forces, but not to the same extent that small firms in the model of perfect competition are. If governments attempt to make labour markets operate along the ideals of the perfect market model, yet do little to curb the corporate power of mega corporations then an imbalance is obvious and both efficiency and equity are unattainable. In the same way that the new right argued that democracy was threatened by the power of trade unions, so too could it be argued that democracy is threatened by the power of major corporations, especially when they control large sections of the national and global media.

## Power

In the model of perfect competition firms are price takers. As a consequence, they have no strategy other than to accept the price determined in the market, and therefore their pricing and output policies are independent of other firms. In the real world, however, the mechanistic model of perfect competition does not hold and the deterministic outcome of this model is not realisable. Firms do not conform to the axioms of perfect competition, are not price takers, and do exercise market power. 'In contrast, more realistic models of the capitalist system, such as those of oligopolistic or imperfectly competitive markets, or of firms which do not necessarily act to maximize profits, often yield indeterminate solutions for output and prices' (Hodgson, 1984, p. 160).

In the case of the common real world situation of oligopoly, firms are interdependent, as the pricing and output strategy of one firm, has direct implications for another. The economic system therefore, is subject to an evolutionary process, constantly producing novelty, rather than a mechanistic process. In this uncertain climate, then, 'A better analogy than the machine is the game. Under capitalism, a game-like process is involved, played with a number of persons, some with much more power than others, and some with the exclusive ability to change the rules at will' (Hodgson, 1984, p. 160).

In the world of perfect competition power does not exist. Power is given up to the market and the free interplay of market forces. The market, which is seen to be entirely neutral, cannot but deliver outcomes which are fair and untainted by prejudice. Economics therefore:

> tells the young and susceptible and the old and the vulnerable that economic life has no content of power and politics because the firm is safely subordinate to the market and to the state, and for this reason it is safely at the command of the consumer and the citizen (Samuels, 1979, p. vii).

However, it could be argued that this picture is disingenuous in the extreme and that 'Such an economics is not neutral. It is the influential and invaluable ally of those whose exercise of power depends on an acquiescent public' (Samuels, 1979, p. vii).

Adam Smith wrote about the greater output forthcoming as a result of the division of labour. The only limit to the further subdivision of tasks in an effort to achieve technological efficiency was seen to be the extent of the market. However, as Marglin (1974) argues, extra output per day may be achieved because effort is intensified, more hours are worked, or less pleasant working conditions are experienced. In this case more output is achieved at the cost of greater input. Marglin (1974) argues that the development of the factory system was not primarily due to the possibility of greater technological superiority, but to the possibilities it opened to the capitalist to divide and rule – the exercise of power.

Economists have particular problems when dealing with issues of power and those of the orthodox school, as shown, simply dismiss power due to their faith in market forces. Non-orthodox economists, such as Galbraith, emphasise the importance of power and demonstrate its many variants. Galbraith (1985) divides power into three elements: *condign, compensatory* and *conditioned*. Condign power involves unpleasant consequences if a particular course of action is not followed. An individual or group has an alternative to their preferences imposed upon them owing to their wish to avoid the unpleasant consequences which would otherwise result. Galbraith (1985) gives the example of the galley slave whose preference would be to stop rowing, but who continues, due to his wish to avoid the consequences of the lash. By contrast, compensatory power brings submission to a particular course of action due to the promise of reward. This will usually mean monetary payment as a result of submitting to the preferences of others. Both of these forms of power are transparent, in that the individual, subject to either condign or compensatory power, is aware of her/his submission. The third element of power, conditioned power, is not transparent. This variant of power requires a form of conditioning or socialisation. In this situation one group in society operates through a variety of institutional mechanisms in order to achieve its own ends, whilst misleading others into thinking those ends serve them best also. The social order is organised in such a way as to benefit the few (those with power) at the expense of the many (Caporaso and Levine, 1992). Galbraith notes that in the context of conditioned power.

> The acceptance of authority, the submission of the will of others, becomes the higher preference of those submitting. This preference can be deliberately cultivated – by persuasion or education. This is explicit conditioning. Or it can be dictated by the culture itself; the submission is considered to be normal, proper, or traditionally correct. This is implicit conditioning (Galbraith, 1985, p. 39).

These forms of power can be manifest in all economic systems, from market economies to communist societies. In particular the non-coercive means of achieving and maintaining power of the conditioned variety requires far more research before a full understanding of how economies operate and how citizens' interests can be best served, can be achieved (Marginson, 1993).

## Firms and markets

In the basic model of perfect competition firms are price takers and the entrepreneur's role is a simple one of reacting to market forces over which he has no control. As we have seen, this is not a realistic position.Writing in 1937 Coase investigated the issue of why firms exist. The orthodox neo-classical theory has little to say on the subject of the firm, which remains an unexplored 'black box'. Coase noted that firms exist due to the expense of transacting in the market. So called 'transaction costs' are incurred in using the market (Dietrich, 1994). Participants in the production process have to discover information about relative prices and incur expense in negotiating and settling contracts for each market transaction. Market uncertainties also pose particular problems for planning for the future. Firms come into being as a means of internalising activities that otherwise would be undertaken in the market. According to Coase, the nature and scale of a firm's activities are determined by whether it is cheaper to undertake the activity in the firm or in the market.

In an attempt to show that the firm is not a means of circumventing the market, Alchian and Demsetz (1972) argued that the firm is in fact a form of surrogate market. In this schema employers are seen to be continuously bargaining with their employees and renegotiating contracts. They argue their case using a framework which Lazonick (1993) claims does not accord with the observed behaviour of business organisations. As he argues: 'That their arguments [Alchian and Demsetz] have received such widespread attention among modern economists, despite the absence of any attempt at empirical verification, can be explained only by economists' deep-seated ideological adherence to the myth of the market economy' (Lazonick, 1993, p. 188).

Alchian and Demsetz's account of the firm as a surrogate market is not convincing, but neither does the transactions cost approach adequately account for the nature and form of the firm in the real world. The account of transactions costs as formulated by Coase and later developed by O. E. Williamson (1975, 1985) continues to emphasise cost minimisation and efficiency as the explanatory mechanism behind the existence and form of the firm. This efficiency argument can be seen to have some consistency with the neo-classical approach (Hodgson, 1988). As noted, Marglin's approach (1974) emphasises power rather than cost-cutting efficiency as the motivational force for the firm. The firm cannot be viewed to the exclusion of the wider economic, social and political environment in which it exists. As Hodgson (1988, p. 216) notes, 'The current make-up of financial institutions, government policies, case law, etc., clearly favour the traditional firm.' However, if this environment was to change then a different form of organisation could well develop in the place of the firm. Organisational structures and markets themselves are to a very large degree dependent on institutional structures which determine form and interrelationships (Sawyer, 1989). The orthodox theory of the firm largely ignores institutions and therefore neglects a dimension of economic life which is of enormous significance. It is evident that current orthodox theories suffer from a neglect of institutional factors and, in their attempt to be universal, ignore important variables. Different localities (nations, regions, etc.) operate according to different economic rules, dependent upon their separate social, economic and historical antecedents and consequent institutional frameworks; orthodox theory neglects these crucial specificities.

## The pursuit of self-interest and sub-optimal outcomes

Adam Smith, in 1776, argued that each individual pursuing his or her own self-interest leads to the best outcome for society at large. Smith's reasoning was placed in a formal marginalist framework by the neo-classical writers of the second half of the nineteenth century, and this expression can be seen in the concept of Pareto optimality. However, Sen (1970) has demonstrated that making choices which lead to Pareto optimal outcomes and respect individual rights might be inconsistent. This is illustrated in the following paradox.

> Let the social choice be between three alternatives involving Mr. A reading a copy of *Lady Chatterley's Lover*, Mr. B reading it, or no one reading it. We name these alternatives a, b, and c, respectively. Mr A, the prude, prefers most that no one read it, next that he reads it, and last that 'impressionable' Mr. B be exposed to it, i.e., he prefers c to a, and a to b. Mr. B, the lascivious, prefers that either of them should read it rather than neither, but further prefers that Mr. A should read it rather than he himself, for he wants Mr. A to be exposed to Lawrence's prose. Hence he prefers a to b, and b to c. A liberal argument can be made for the case that given the choice between Mr. A reading it and no one reading it, his own preference should be reflected by social preference. So that society should prefer that no one reads it, rather than having Mr. A read what he plainly regards as a dreadful book. Hence c is socially preferred to a. Similarly, a liberal argument exists in favor of reflecting Mr. B's preference in the social choice between Mr. B reading it and no one reading it. Thus b is preferred to c. Hence society should prefer Mr. B reading it to no one reading it, and the latter to Mr. A reading it. However, Mr. B reading it is Pareto-worse than Mr. A reading it, even in terms of the weak Pareto criterion, and if social preference honors that ranking, then a is preferred to b. Hence every alternative can be seen to be worse than some other. And there is thus no best alternative in this set and there is no optimal choice (Sen, 1970, pp. 80–1).

The achievement of Pareto optimality and a liberal respect for individual rights can be seen from this example to be mutually exclusive.

Another example demonstrates how behaving rationally and in one's own self interest may result in an outcome which is not in the interest of society as a whole. This is the case of the prisoners' dilemma. Two individuals 1 and 2 have been arrested on suspicion of committing a crime and are being held by the police in separate cells. Whilst the police are confident that the two suspects are guilty of the crime, they have insufficient evidence to convict them. Each of the suspects is now offered a deal by the police. If neither suspect confesses then they will both be charged with the lesser offence of loitering, which carries a six-month sentence. If they both confess then they will each be gaoled for five years. If one confesses and implicates the other, who remains silent, then the implicated one goes to prison for ten years and the other is released without charge. This set of outcomes is shown in Figure 2.1.

If we think of the time spent in prison by both individuals as representing the total welfare of society then the lower the total sum of years spent in prison the better off is society. The best outcome is if neither confesses and each receives a six-month prison sentence resulting in a total period of imprisonment of one year. The best outcome for an individual is if he confesses and implicates the other whilst his partner remains silent. The worst outcome for an individual will occur if he remains silent yet his partner confesses. Taking the position of prisoner 1: if 2 decides to deny the offence

PRISONER 2

|  |  | CONFESS | DENY |  |
|---|---|---|---|---|
| PRISONER 1 | CONFESS | 5, 5 | 0, 10 | Years in |
|  | DENY | 10, 0 | $\frac{1}{2}, \frac{1}{2}$ | prison |

FIGURE 2.1   **The prisoners' dilemma**

then 1 is better off confessing as he will not serve a prison sentence. Equally, if 2 confesses, 1 is also better off confessing as the result will be a five-year prison sentence, rather than ten. Clearly, whatever prisoner 2 does prisoner 1 is better off as a result of confessing. The same logic also holds for prisoner 2: regardless of the actions of prisoner 1 he also benefits from confessing. The outcome is that, in the absence of an opportunity to collaborate, they will both confess and serve five years each in prison. However, had they been able to collaborate, the outcome would have been different. The position which maximises their joint best interest (and therefore the interest of society) is joint denial of the crime through silence. This policy would mean a total of one year in prison rather than the alternative of ten years. The implications of 'rational' independent actions are evident. 'Self-interested behaviour may be collectively self-defeating. This undermines the idea of a benevolent 'invisible hand' in the market system, in which the sum total of individual and selfish actions leads to a socially desirable outcome' (Hodgson, 1984, p. 45).

The prisoners' dilemma clearly demonstrates that the market system can lead to an outcome which is not in the interests of the majority of society.

### Economic 'efficiency' and crime

Given the choice of a range of products the study of consumer behaviour deriving from orthodox theory shows that consumers will choose combinations (bundles) of goods which maximise their satisfaction according to an income constraint. However, given this freedom of choice in the market, a possible outcome known as a *corner solution* may result, in which one or a number of goods is not consumed at all. As this is the outcome of consumer choice working within a framework of market forces this outcome may be seen to be of no concern. However, even if we accept that this is of no concern in the goods market, the situation has more consequences when applied to factor markets. Operating 'efficiently' in a Pareto optimal fashion, the market may determine that there is no demand for certain types of the factor labour. Unskilled labour, for example, may not be required at all, or the demand for such labour may be much smaller than supply, causing downward pressure on its price. As a result, some members of society may be unable to earn a wage at all, or may have to subsist on an income set below the poverty level. This outcome is not consequence-free, as individuals exist not only as economic units but also as social agents. Indeed, accepting the orthodox interpretation of human agents as rational utility-maximising individuals, the consequence for society of an outcome in labour markets which leads to poverty can be far reaching. Schotter (1990) argues that a worker assessing the wages (if any) on offer to him and the time available may reason in the following way. 'After weighing all of the probabilities, profitabilities, and costs, a worker who is facing a below-poverty wage may rationally decide to allocate some of his time to illegal activities, such as running numbers, prostitution, gambling, burglary, purse snatching, pocket picking, and mugging' (Schotter, 1990, p. 70).

In this scheme of things criminals may be viewed as 'utility-maximising entrepreneurs' (Schotter, 1990, p. 70) who, faced with an array of wages and prices, decide rationally how they will optimise time spent between criminal and non-criminal activities. In the UK, crime has shown a trend upwards since the end of full employment in the mid 1970s and property crime has risen and fallen in line with the general economic situation. John Wells (1995) argues that there is a clear link between crime and unemployment. If a 'market solution' leads to an optimal position in which there is high unemployment and/or very low levels of wages, then society may face increasing costs imposed by greater levels of crime, thus offsetting any gains accruing from 'efficient markets'. It has also been shown that with poverty and a decline in relative incomes comes a fall in self esteem, increased levels of sickness and lower life expectancy. Research has shown a rise in suicide rates amongst young men aged between 15 and 24 as unemployment rose and incomes from both benefits and paid employment declined relatively and in some cases absolutely (Hutton, 1995).

## Conclusions

Respect for market solutions and faith placed in the positive outcome of self-interested behaviour can be seen to be central to orthodox economics. However, as has been argued, the orthodox approach to welfare issues can be seen to have many failings.

Hahn (1993) argues that issues of welfare economics are usually approached in a utilitarian manner. By this he means that policies can be judged by the effect that they have on individual agents' utilities. He contrasts this with 'deontological views which appeal to some intrinsic "good"' (Hahn, 1993, p. 260). Perhaps the main reason why the utilitarian approach has stood the test of time is that it yields clear and precise results and provides a framework for policy. However, this is not sufficient defence in itself, and fierce debate continues about the efficacy of such a methodological approach (Hodgson, 1988). It can be argued (Eichner, 1983) that the concept of utility and the indifference curves which derive from this are purely metaphysical and therefore unprovable. Indifference curves are used extensively in welfare economics as a tool to gauge society's welfare, but as Koutsoyiannis (1979, p. 27) notes 'theory does not establish either the existence or the shape of indifference curves'. This begs the question as to whether such tools are a sufficient basis for important policy recommendations.

Sen (1987) feels that the methodological approach adopted in orthodox economics, with a narrow focus on ethics, has been unfortunate. This narrow view has led to 'the impoverishment of welfare economics as a result of the distance that has grown between ethics and economics, and particularly on the inadequacy of the evaluative criteria used in economics, especially modern welfare economics' (Sen, 1987, p. 51).

Viewed somewhat cynically, Sen is led to conclude that: 'It is arguable that the utilitarian criterion, and also that of Pareto efficiency, have appealed particularly because they have not especially taxed the ethical imagination of the conventional economist' (Sen, 1987, p. 50).

Hahn argues that it is difficult to 'make much of "innate" moral truths' (Hahn, 1993, p. 262) and that utilitarianism has served a useful purpose in exposing inconsistencies. However, he is well aware of the dangers of using such an approach in a mechanistic fashion and counsels for a more pragmatic approach. He feels that:

> many moral questions have no answer to which all rational agents must agree, and that the best we can do is to argue clearly with each other. In particular I believe that once a system like utilitarianism is treated like a machine which delivers answers we are blinded by bogus certainties and are bound, sooner or later, to do considerable harm to others (Hahn, 1993, p. 262).

It is evident that issues of competition and social welfare are extremely complex (Helm, 1990). Simplistic blanket policies can lead to unforeseen consequences which are to the detriment of society. It is necessary to further develop economic thinking in these crucial issues of welfare and to consider how human behaviour can better be analysed and understood, possibly through the greater use of experimental methods. The tools currently at the disposal of economists for the purposes of analysing questions of welfare are inadequate, and as such can lead to flawed policy. This should be borne in mind when reading the following chapters which outline government policy in action.

# CHAPTER 3

# Competition Policy

## The social costs of monopoly

Governments need a competition policy only if they believe that the existence of monopoly creates costs to society. If these costs are negligible, then there is little need for policies aimed at reducing monopoly abuses, particularly since devising and implementing such a policy has costs which may exceed any benefits. It is therefore necessary to begin by analysing the costs of monopoly. It will come as no surprise to learn that there is considerable disagreement among economists about the extent of monopoly costs, and also about the policies which are most appropriate to reduce these costs.

### Static efficiency costs

If we undertake a static analysis, and make the common assumption that monopolies try to maximise profits, it can be shown that monopoly does impose costs on society in the form of lower output and higher prices than would occur under competition. This is illustrated in Figure 3.1.

A profit maximising firm will produce where $MR = MC$ at B. The AR curve is the demand curve. To the right of point D consumers would be willing to pay more for extra units of output, and the amount that they would be willing to pay would exceed the marginal cost of producing the goods. If output was expanded along the AR curve, there would be a net gain of consumer surplus until output reached point C. This gain is measured by the triangle DBC, and since this potential gain is not achieved by a profit maximising monopoly it can be regarded as a measure of the losses arising from monopoly.

Although this kind of analysis does suggest that monopoly will lead to losses, it also suggests that these may not be very large. The reason is that the area of the triangle is 0.5 × change in price × change in quantity (assuming the demand curve is a straight line). If we assume for simplicity, that the monopoly can raise prices by 10 per cent and also reduces output by 10 per cent, the inefficiency arising for market power is $0.5 \times 0.1 \times 0.1 \times 100 = 0.5$

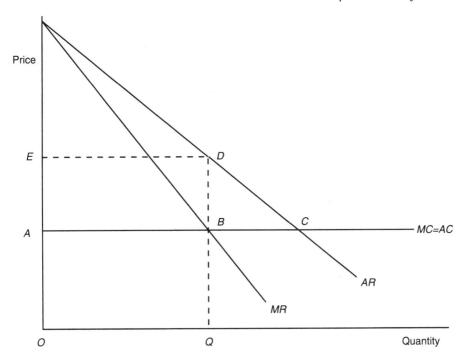

**FIGURE 3.1   The effects of monopoly**

per cent of the value of sales. Whilst for a large firm, this would be a substantial sum of money, it is not really large enough to justify an expensive competition policy. Even if the monopolist's market power is greater than that suggested in this simple example, the inefficiency arising from monopoly in this way seems relatively small, and indeed may be much smaller if the monopolist does not attempt to maximise profits, but instead is content with 'reasonable' profits .

*Distribution effects*

However, the static inefficiency effects are not the only consequences of monopoly. There is a distribution effect. In Figure 3.1 this is shown by the area *ABDE* and comprises the higher price paid by consumers, multiplied by the quantity bought. This is a loss to consumers, but a gain to producers. Note that this area is likely to be much greater than the triangle DBC measuring the efficiency loss: in other words, the distributional effects of monopoly are likely to be bigger than the short-term effects on efficiency as measured by the triangle.

*X-efficiency*

So far we have assumed that monopoly has had no effect on costs. However, in practice, the existence – or possibility of – monopoly profits may cause firms to devote resources to gaining or maintaining monopoly power. The rectangle *ABDE* is a measure of the potential gains from this course of action, and it would be rational for a monopolist or potential monopolist to spend up to this amount of money in order to gain this benefit. This could be done in several ways, for example by increasing spending on advertising. This would make it more difficult for new firms to enter the industry.

An alternative reason why monopoly may be less efficient than a firm in a competitive market is that, assuming that there are significant barriers to entry so that competition is unlikely, monopolists will have little incentive to look for ways to cut costs. 'The best monopoly profits are a quiet life', as Sir John Hicks said.

For either of these reasons, a monopolist may lack incentives to cut costs, and the result will be a higher cost curve than would be the case in a competitive market.

*Monopoly effect on the economy as a whole*

Monopoly does not exist in isolation: where there is one monopoly the economic and legal environment is such that there are likely to be many. If all the firms which are monopolists restrict output, they will employ fewer workers, so leading to a lower level of consumption than would be the case in a more competitive economy. This would lead to knock-on effects on aggregate demand and employment. Moreover, when output is restricted over a long period of time, the result will be an economy characterised by stagnation. For proponents of the school of monopoly capitalism, a high level of monopoly power in an economy is associated with a stagnating economy and high unemployment.

## The potential benefits of monopoly

*The Austrian approach*

So far we have been using a static approach, where firms are analysed at a particular point in time and the consequences analysed. A different approach is used by economists of the Austrian school, so called because the early leaders of this school such as Joseph Schumpeter came from Austria. The name is a little misleading because nowadays 'Austrians' come from any country. For these economists, monopoly power must be analysed in a dynamic context – the firm is never in equilibrium because the economy in which it operates is always changing.

For Schumpeter (1942, p. 84), 'in capitalist reality, as distinguished from its textbook picture, it is not the kind of competition that counts but the competition from the new commodity, the new technology'. In other words, in a capitalist economy, there will always be new innovation of both products and techniques. Schumpeter used the phrase 'creative destruction' to describe this process. Monopolists who rely on existing products and processes will find that their monopoly disappears as new products replace old ones and as monopolistic processes become obsolete. Hence, to keep their position, monopolists need to continually destroy existing technology and replace it with new. In terms of Figure 3.1, this means that the cost curve will be lower, so benefiting consumers.

The process of creative destruction is helped by the existence of super-normal monopoly profits. These can be fed back into the business to pay for research and development; firms in a competitive industry may not be able to afford such spending, and the banks may not be willing to lend to finance risky innovation which is a characteristic of competitive markets.

The research evidence on this point is mixed. Freeman (1982) summarises research suggesting that expenditure on research and development does increase with size, though large firms tended to have relatively fewer patents. However, firm size is not necessarily a good measure of monopoly; and the effect may depend on the industry. For example, Freeman suggests that in the chemical industry research and innovation is dominated by large firms; in engineering it is much easier for small firms to initiate new ideas.

*Stability*

One of the potential disadvantages of monopoly discussed above was that monopolists may opt for a quiet life; the mirror image of this is that they may provide stability – perhaps the opposite to Schumpeter's argument. Stability can be beneficial to consumers. They know the price they will have to pay and they know the characteristics of the product so that they do not make expensive mistakes by buying products which are not suitable. These benefits are not quantifiable, but they are undoubtedly advantageous to consumers.

**Empirical evidence on the effects of monopoly**

Given the wide variety of theoretical argument over the costs of monopoly, it is not surprising that empirical investigations into these costs also reflect considerable disagreement. Indeed, just posing the question 'How do you investigate the costs of monopoly?' suggests the difficulties involved in empirical investigations, for the obvious approach would be to compare monopoly and competition in the same industry – a comparison that the existence of monopoly makes impossible. This problem could be overcome to some extent by making cross-country comparisons, but the results obtained are unlikely to be conclusive since other variables such as labour and raw material costs will also vary.

The classic study of monopoly power is that of Harberger (1954). He assumed constant marginal costs, a price elasticity of demand for each industry equal to $-1$, and measured monopoly profits by calculating above average accounting profits. His conclusion: the American economy only lost the equivalent of 0.1 per cent of gross national product (GNP) per year as a result of monopoly. Other American economists have obtained much larger estimates, for example Kamerschen (1966) estimated that the cost of monopoly was 6 per cent of GNP.

In the UK, Cowling and Mueller (1978), using data gained at the firm level – the 103 largest firms – estimated that the welfare loss amounted to between 3.9 and 4.2 per cent of GDP. These calculations have been criticised by Littlechild (1981) on several grounds, for example that many of the rewards counted by Cowling and Mueller as monopoly profits are really profits arising from uncertainty and innovation. Moreover, Cowling and Mueller assume that advertising expenditure is 'merely an instrument for securing monopoly power' and add expenditure on advertising to actual profits when calculating the welfare loss triangle.

Littlechild develops an alternative model within which windfall gains result from unanticipated shifts in demand, while creativity and alertness generate entrepreneurial profits reflecting innovation and increased co-ordination rather than monopoly profits. This line of argument reflects that of Schumpeter discussed earlier.

Littlechild concludes that a systematic attempt to eliminate profit is more likely to destroy the competitive process than to stimulate it; what is needed is for policy-makers to pay less attention to the size of firms and the concentration of industries and more to the conditions of entry into those industries.

## What kind of competition policy?

There are two main approaches towards competition policy. One focuses on the *structure* of the industry – is it dominated by one or few firms? The other is to pay more attention to the *conduct* of the market: for example, how easy is it for new firms to enter the industry? – the approach suggested by Littlechild.

Traditionally, both UK and European Union (EU) policies have concentrated on business conduct, for example accepting that there is nothing wrong in one firm dominating an industry so long as it does not exploit its position. The emphasis was on the *abuse* of power, rather than its existence.

More recently, however, UK policy has given greater emphasis to the structure of the industry. In 1991 the then Secretary of State for Industry, Peter Lilley said 'I prefer to see clear structural remedies rather than behavioral remedies which involve long term monitoring by the Office of Fair Trading' (quoted in Yarrow, 1995). One example of this approach occurred in 1993 when the Monopolies and Mergers Commission (hereafter MMC) recommended that British Gas be required to divest itself of its gas sales business to stop it using its control of pipelines to hinder competition from rivals in gas sales. Rather earlier, in 1990, the electricity generating industry was restructured into four companies – the National Grid Company, National Power, PowerGen and Nuclear Electric.

Entry barriers are necessary if firms are to possess market power. If there are no barriers to entry, then the degree of concentration is unimportant because new firms could always enter the industry. Barriers to entry can take many forms. Legal barriers such as patents or restrictions on the right to practice medicine are the most difficult to surmount. Other barriers include scale – where there are significant economies of scale, new firms may find it difficult to compete. Firms' behaviour, such as signing long-term contracts with customers, also forms a significant barrier to entry.

The crucial concept here is that of contestable markets. Formally, this is one where entry and exit are costless and where all firms have identical cost functions, though its usage is sometimes widened to mean a market where it is relatively easy for new firms to enter. If a market is contestable, then established firms are effectively in competition with a very large number of potential rivals. Contestable markets are often presented as desirable; but, as Yarrow (1996) points out, one of the reasons why a firm may innovate is to cut its costs so that they are less than those of rivals. Not only would this mean that the market was no longer strictly contestable, but it suggests that contestability may not be compatible with dynamic efficiency.

Whilst the exact conditions for contestable markets may rarely be found in practice, the general implication of this argument is that strong competition may lead to greater concentration. This means that structuralist policies aimed at increasing competition may lead to undesirable results. Similarly structural policies aimed at reducing entry barriers may also sometimes be undesirable: for example, the removal of patent protection – often a large barrier to entry – may reduce the incentive to innovate. To give just one example, it is unlikely that Pilkington Glass would have spent large sums on researching float glass if their work could not have been protected by patents.

According to Yarrow it is possible to characterise four policy options. Option one is *laissez-faire* – where governments decline to intervene at all. Though this is unlikely, a modified form is found when competition policy is framed in ways which exclude large parts of economic activity from competition policy rules.

Option two can be called *rule of reason* where a government agency investigates and makes appropriate recommendations. UK monopolies policy is of this type: the MMC investigates where it seems that monopoly power may be exploiting consumers.

The third option can be called *prohibition with exceptions*. This prohibits certain practices such as price fixing, but exceptions can be given if the firm or firms involved can give good reasons for the practice to continue. This is the approach often adopted by EU competition policy.

The fourth option is for governments to declare that certain types of behaviour or industry structure are unacceptable whatever the arguments that firms could give to defend their dominance or activities. American monopoly legislation tends to take this option. It is at the opposite end of the spectrum from the laissez faire approach.

### Policies towards dominant firms

The MMC can be asked to investigate dominant firm situations in the supply of goods or services, general practices of an uncompetitive character and also mergers. In economic theory 'monopoly' is defined as one supplier, and this is the assumption underlying the analysis in Figure 3.1. In law, the position is different. The Fair Trading Act of 1973 is the British legislation that deals with monopoly and mergers, and here a dominant firm or monopoly is defined as one where the largest firm has 25 per cent of the market. Using this definition, the MMC has investigated a wide range of markets including gas, fertilisers, colour film, cinema films, infant milk foods, salt, metal containers, condoms and asbestos.

In the EU, authority for competition policy regarding single-firm dominance drives from Article 86 of the Treaty of Rome. This says: 'Any abuse by one or more undertakings of a dominant position within the common market or in a substantial part of it shall be prohibited as incompatible with the common market in so far as it may affect trade between member states.'

The contrast is clear: UK legislation focuses on structure – 25 per cent of the market – whilst EU legislation concentrates on abuse. In practice, however, the difference may be less than appears at first sight, since in the UK MMC investigations have not necessarily condemned dominant firms; their recommendations depend on what the dominant firm does with its power.

There are two problems in both approaches: what do we mean by a market? And, what constitutes abuse of a dominant position? There is no 'correct' way to define a market, and in practice there may be considerable disagreement between a firm and an investigator seeking evidence of a monopoly position. Firms being investigated favour a wide definition of 'market'. That is because the more narrowly a market is defined, the more likely it is that a firm will have a dominant position in that market. For example, no firm will have a dominant position (say 25 per cent of the market) for food, but it is quite possible for a firm to have such a position in the market for crisps or kiwi fruit. The issue has been extensively discussed, without much of a conclusion being reached. The European Court deliberated on this issue when it investigated the United Bananas case (quoted in Yarrow, 1996), and said that this depended on whether the banana could be 'singled out by such special features distinguishing it from other fruits that it is only to a limited extent interchangeable with them and is only exposed to their competition in a way that is barely perceptible'.

In practice, however, this does not take us much further, since it is still possible to argue about the extent to which products are interchangeable. Are matches interchangeable with lighters? Apples with oranges?

There is an additional complication when considering European legislation. That is because the EU is concerned with international rather than national markets; hence there is a geographical factor to be considered. The Commission has defined the geographical market to be:

> the area where the undertakings concerned are involved in the supply and demand of products and services in which the conditions of competition are sufficiently homogeneous and which can be distinguished from neighbouring areas because conditions of competition are appreciably different in those areas (Sapir *et al.*, 1993).

Sapir argues that in practice the Commission defines the geographical extent of the market differently in manufacturing from that in services. In manufacturing, the 'market' is often the *world* market. For example, when investigating a possible merger between Aerospatiale, Alenia and de Havilland, the market was for regional turbo-prop aircraft of 40–60 seats. Since there was mutual penetration between all large markets, the relevant geographical market was the world.

In services it is different, This has sometimes been defined nationally and sometimes locally, as in the case of foodstuff distribution. The fact that services are influenced more by language and cultural factors than manufactured goods creates difficulties for application of EU competition policy since they may affect only a particular country rather than the EU as a whole.

There are also difficulties in deciding what constitutes 'abuse', though it is relatively easy to find examples. Price discrimination is one form of abuse. This can take several forms. In some cases, prices are varied in different markets, not because costs differ but because competitive pressures differ so that lower prices are charged when there are competing firms. Sometimes price discrimination arises in the form of loyalty bonuses or discounts. These may benefit buyers in the short run, but make it difficult for competitors to enter the market and so may be disadvantageous in the longer term.

An example can illustrate the nature of price discrimination. In its examination of the Napier Brown/British Sugar case, the EU decided that British

Sugar was abusing its power. That was because British Sugar not only sold sugar in the retail market, it produced it in bulk and sold this wholesale to other firms such as Napier Brown. However, in order to reduce competition, British Sugar charged a high price for this bulk sugar, making it difficult for Napier Brown to make any profit. As a result of its findings, British Sugar was fined 3 million ecu in 1988. 'Commodity bundling' is another form of abuse. This occurs when a firm sells a range of goods, and offers a bundle of goods at a lower price than the buyer would pay if purchasing each item separately. Again, this may bring short-term benefit, but it also makes life difficult for other firms which may sell only one product. They will be effectively shut out of the market.

Vertical restraints can also be used to abuse a dominant position. These include exclusive distribution or purchasing agreements, exclusive franchises, refusal to supply and full-line forcing. This occurs when a firm sells two or more products, one of which is short supply and over which it has power. The firm will then only sell this product if the purchaser also agrees to buy other products which are available more cheaply elsewhere. Vertical integration can also be used to restrict competition. The most celebrated example of this was in the British brewing industry where the brewers also owned public houses, and used their ownership to make it difficult for small brewers who did not own pubs to sell their product.

The actual possession of a dominant position does not mean that this will necessarily be exploited. In 1991 the MMC investigated the market for instant coffee, where Nestlé had over 50 per cent of the market and a rate of return on capital of 114 per cent in 1989. The MMC concluded that Nestlé's profitability arose because of its success in meeting consumers' preferences in a competitive market, and not from exploiting its market power.

*Public interest*

If size does not automatically mean that there is abuse, then some criteria have to be used to decide if action is necessary in order to protect the public. The crucial notion here seems to be the 'public interest'. However, the meaning of this seems to have changed over the years.

Devine *et al.* (1985) analysed the MMC's approach over the years and concluded that there were three characteristics. First, the MMC had consistently condemned deliberately uncompetitive behaviour, especially artificial restraints on competition such as exclusive dealing, discount and bonus schemes designed to disadvantage potential competitors. For example, the MMC condemned Metal Box which had a dominant position in the market for metal containers because it offered long-term buying agreements that were not related to costs and which discouraged buyers from seeking alternative sources of supply.

A second characteristic of MMC investigations was that high levels of profit were condemned: for example Unilever and Procter and Gamble were making a rate of profit that was respectively twice and three times the average for manufacturing industry as a whole.

Devine's third finding was that the MMC rarely recommended structural change. Instead, it suggested changes in behaviour.

Since Devine's analysis, there seems to have been changes in the MMC's approach. The Nestlé example quoted above shows that high profits are not always condemned. And the MMC has recently urged structural change: for example, in making proposals to change the structure of the gas market so that it is open to competition.

*Appraisal of dominant firm policy*

UK and EU policies differ in their approaches to dominant firms. At first sight, the EU approach seems tougher. The EU Commission has power both to investigate and to decide particular cases, and it can impose fines of up to 10 per cent of the worldwide sales of the product of the dominant firm. And there have been some very large fines, though these have usually been imposed where two or more firms have acted together to abuse the market. For example, in 1991 TetraPak was fined 75 million ecu. This firm is the largest manufacturer of cartons for liquid foodstuffs in the EU and it took over Liquipak, a producer of milk packing machines which had an exclusive licence for a new sterilising technology. TetraPak used its new acquisition to prevent its rival Elopak from using this new technology.

So the EU can impose large fines, but the weakness of the EU approach is that it has been applied in so few cases, as Table 3. 1 shows. This limits the effectiveness of the policy.

TABLE 3.1   Individual Commission decisions relating to the application of Article 86

| Dates | Manufacturing | Services |
|-------|---------------|----------|
| 1964–69 | 0 | 0 |
| 1970–79 | 6 | 0 |
| 1980–90 | 10 | 5 |

*Source*:   Based on data from European Commission *Official Journal*.

One weakness of the UK approach is that the recommendations of the MMC have no power unless they are adopted by the Secretary of State.

This means that recommendations by the MMC may be rejected for political reasons rather then as a result of economic analysis. Moreover, the process can be very slow. The investigation into the brewing industry lasted three years and then it took a further three years for the legal orders to be implemented.

## Mergers

Just as single dominant firms can have advantages as well as disadvantages, so can mergers. According to Jacquemin (1990), there are two main types of benefit that may be attributed to mergers: a reduction in production and transaction costs, and an improvement in the efficiency of management. The reduction in production costs arises because of economies of scale, the fall in transaction costs because there need be no negotiations about prices between firms – these become an internal decision. Management may become more efficient if the merger results in old, inefficient managers being replaced by ones who are more efficient.

But mergers also have disadvantages. They may reduce competition, whilst take-overs absorb much management time and may cause managers to devote more attention to financial transactions affecting the share price than to running the business. Empirical investigations suggest that mergers had little or no effect on the profitability of merging firms, and that there were often few economies of scale to be found since the size of acquiring firms was usually greater than the minimum optimum scale for the industry (Mueller, 1980).

Because mergers may or may not confer benefits, there is a need for some policy to try to ensure that the benefits to the public of a merger exceed its costs. The UK approach to mergers was set out in the Office of Fair Trading's guide to the Fair Trading Act: 'There is no presumption that mergers . . . are bad in themselves. Many mergers can be to the country's benefit and in others no significantly adverse effects on the public interest can be foreseen'. Each case falling within the scope of the act is looked at on its own particular merits and not in accordance with any fixed rules or assumptions: the aim in each case being to assess and balance the advantages and disadvantages of the public interest (Office of Fair Trading, 1973).

In the UK, mergers are examined only if the two firms involved would have a share of the market of over 25 per cent, or if the value of the cases taken over exceeds £30 million. The Secretary of State need not refer a particular merger to the MMC for investigation. The 1990 Companies Act modified merger policy. It allowed companies proposing to merge to complete a questionnaire. If no reference to the MMC is made within twenty days, the merger can go ahead. This prevents the delay which would occur if an investigation was to be made. Moreover, the Act allows companies to sell off some assets in order to reduce the market share they would gain if the merger went ahead. For example, at the time of its bid for Distillers, Guinness agreed to sell off some of its whisky brands.

Merger policy in the UK affects only a relatively few companies, In 1989, for example, the Director General of the Office of Fair Trading (OFT) scrutinised 427 proposed mergers and recommended that only 14 should be referred to the MMC. Of these, two were abandoned after the reference and only two were rejected (Griffiths and Wall, 1993, p. 97).

Whether or not a merger is allowed to proceed depends on whether or not the MMC thinks it is likely to operate against the public interest. In this case, the public interest is usually evaluated against the effect the merger would have on competition.

However, 'competition' can be interpreted in several ways. Weir (1993) analysed 73 Commission reports covering the years 1974–90. He concluded that the Commission did not automatically take a potential high market share as a barrier to a merger. Probable price effects did have a significant effect: if firms could convince the Commission that prices were likely to fall as a result of the merger, then it was likely to get the go-ahead. On the other hand, the Commission were sceptical to claims that mergers would lead to an increase in efficiency.

There was no article in the Treaty of Rome which dealt specifically with mergers, and it was not until 1990 that a regulation came into force which dealt effectively with mergers. This was caused by a considerable increase in mergers resulting from the completion of the Single Market. This regulation applies to 'all concentrations with a Community dimension'. This is defined as worldwide turnover of all concerned undertakings of 5 billion ecu, an aggregate EU-wide turnover of the companies exceeds 250 million ecu, and each of the undertakings achieves less than two-thirds of its aggregate EU-wide turnover within a single state. Thus the regulation is an attempt to focus EU policy on mergers of large companies affecting more than one EU country; national mergers remain a matter for national policy.

According to Morgan (1995), in the first three years of operation, 178 transactions were notified to the Commission. Of these, only 14 went to full proceedings and the only ban on a merger was the Aerospaciale/Alenia/de Havilland case mentioned earlier (Sapir, 1993). More recently, in 1992, the Commission ordered Gillette to dispose of its 22 per cent interest in Eemland, the parent company of its main competitor Wilkinson Sword.

## Restrictive practices

Policy on restrictive practices – formal agreements between firms – is operated through the Restrictive Trade Practices Act of 1976. Agreements between two or more firms that involve restrictions of trade have to be registered with the

Director General of Fair Trading. The presumption underlying the law is that such restrictions are deemed to be against the public interest unless the firms involved can show that the agreement can pass through a 'gateway'. The gateways include showing that the agreement will protect the public from injury, that its removal will harm employment or exports, that it is necessary as a defence against measures taken by others to limit competition. Passing through a gateway is not enough; in addition, the firms have to show 'the restriction is not unreasonable having regard to the balance between these circumstances and any detriment to the public': in other words, that the restriction is in the public interest.

There is thus an important distinction between the approach to restrictive practices and that applying to dominant firms; restrictive practices policy is non-discretionary and legalistic with issues resolved in the courts rather than by ministerial judgement.

The most notable success in passing through the gateway was the Net Book Agreement. This enabled publishers to stop booksellers cutting the price of books. The argument was that, without this restriction, supermarkets would sell the most popular books at a discount, so cutting the profits of specialist booksellers who would go out of business, so making less popular books unavailable. The Net Book Agreement finally collapsed in 1995 when several major publishers abandoned it, so that shops were free to cut prices. Apart from pharmaceuticals, almost all other price maintenance agreements have disappeared, leaving the way open to supermarket competition on prices. Another successful approach was the Permanent Magnets case where the firms successfully argued that the absence of price competition had encouraged technical co-operation which benefited customers.

Unacceptable restrictive practices include fixing prices or giving discounts which do not reflect the real economic price of the commodity, collusive tendering, and sharing or allocating markets. The strongest form of restrictive practice is the cartel, but less formal methods can have similar effects, for example, dominant price leadership where smaller firms follow the example of the price leader. In 1990, companies who bought fleet cars accused car manufacturers of following the lead of Ford. This kind of accusation is difficult to prove, since firms can claim that their prices move together because they are all affected by changes in costs. For example, the Office of Fair Trading investigated pricing in the petrol industry in 1990. They found no evidence of collusion because the firms adjusted their prices according to changes in the world price of oil as reflected in the Rotterdam spot market. Prices charged by firms can change together even when there is no dominant firm; this can sometimes take the form of collusive price leadership where firms work together to decide prices.

One weakness of the UK system is that the Court of Appeal decided that a firm was not responsible for the actions of its employees. That occurred when a manager of Smith's Concrete Ltd entered into a price-fixing and market-sharing agreement in the Bicester area. The court's view was that Smith's was not a party to the agreement (Borrie, 1993, p. 6). However, in 1995 the Restrictive Practices Court fined nine concrete suppliers including RMC, Tarmac, Redland and Hanson £8.4 million for breaking a 1978 agreement that they would not fix prices and share out markets. In addition, five directors of the companies were fined £87,500 for aiding and abetting contempt of court by their companies. In this case the judge rejected claims that the companies had forbidden employees to undertake such practices, since the companies had not maintained a proper monitoring system.

The Government reviewed the operation of restrictive practices policy in a Green Paper (DTI 1988) and a White Paper (DTI, 1989). These argued that UK policy on restrictive practices was unsatisfactory because it caught too many small agreements, failed to catch some anti-competitive agreements, did not make it easy to detect violations and was costly to operate. For example, in 1991, details of 1327 agreements were notified to the Office of Fair Trading. Less than 50 per cent of these were actually notifiable, and very few of these required a reference to the Court. Processing such agreements involves a considerable expenditure of resources. Although the Government has not acted on the arguments put forward in its White Paper, a number of commentators have suggested that the UK should move to a EU-style approach.

Restrictive practices policy in the EU differs from that in the UK because it is concerned with the *effects* of a restriction rather than the form of it as in the UK. The basis of the policy is derived from Article 85 of the Treaty of Rome. This prohibits 'as incompatible with the common market all agreements . . . which may affect trade between member states and which have as their objective or effect the prevention, restriction or distortion of competition within the common market'. The Article goes on to forbid specific agreements, for example those which fix prices, limit or control markets, technical development or investment, share markets or sources of supply.

Agreements which fall within the jurisdiction of Article 85 are investigated by the Commission. They usually arise because of a complaint from a firm or individual who feels adversely affected. Other referrals come from firms wanting exemption. Table 3.2 shows that Article 85 has been used more frequently in recent years, particularly for manufacturing.

Because of the size of the EU, there is a danger of the system becoming clogged up with many cases. There has therefore developed a system of block exemptions, for example agreements relating to research and development are exempted because it can be argued that they usually lead to benefits to consumers.

Although the number of cases is small relative to the size of the EU, the policy can be very tough and companies can be fined up to 10 per cent of their annual turnover. In 1994 the Commission imposed fines of 140 million ecu on 19 companies for running a sophisticated price-fixing cartel in cardboard.

TABLE 3.2    **Individual Commission decisions relating to Article 85**

|  | *Manufacturing* | *Services* |
|---|---|---|
| 1964–69 | 25 | 2 |
| 1970–79 | 108 | 1 |
| 1980–90 | 120 | 28 |

*Source*:    Based on European Commision, *Official Journal*.

Later the same year cement companies were fined 248 million ecu. According to the Commission, the companies – including Britain's Blue Circle industries, Castle Cement and Rugby – began working together in 1983 to divide up the European market along national lines. The firms agreed to avoid sales to customers in other countries, and this was encouraged by the exchange of price information so that there was little incentive to export.

It is sometimes claimed that the EU's policy weakens European firms when they have to compete against larger companies overseas. That is not always the case. For example, in 1990 the Commission allowed an agreement between the French company Alcatel Espace and the German ANT Nachrichten regarding research and development (R&D), production and marketing of electronic components largely to help them compete against larger non-European competitors (Morgan, 1995, p. 7).

The Commission's decisions are subject to European law. Thus in 1988 sixteen chemical companies were fined 37 million ecu for running a cartel in low density polyethylene. In 1995 – illustrating how slow the procedures can be – the European Court of Justice threw out these fines because of the Commission's failure to follow proper procedures when it imposed the fines.

**Privatised utilities**

The privatised industries present a special problem for competition policy, because of the prevalence of natural monopoly. These industries are subject to the same laws as the rest of the economy, but there are also special features.

Each industry has a regulatory body such as OFGAS which is responsible for the gas industry. These bodies are constituted as non-ministerial government departments and are meant to ensure that the public interest is maintained in industries which would otherwise be in a position to exploit their monopoly power.

In order to do this they are given special powers, sometimes making use of existing institutions. For example, the Director General of OFTEL can refer

British Telecom (BT) to the MMC under the Telecommunications Act of 1984 to recommend a modification of the Telecom's licence. Similarly, under the Gas Act of 1986, the Director General of OFGAS can make referrals to the MMC in order to obtain licence modifications. This was done in 1988 and involved an examination of the supply of gas to non-tariff customers.

However, the regulators mainly interact directly with the industry and have considerable powers, most notably on prices. When BT was privatised, there was considerable concern that it would use its monopoly powers to exploit the consumer. Hence the regulator was given power to fix prices. This was done using a formula RPI − X, where X was decided by the regulator. From 1984 to 1989 X was 3 per cent, meaning that BT could only raise its prices by 3 per cent less than the rate of inflation. The regime was subsequently toughened so that in 1993 it became RPI −7.5 per cent, the reason being that this was an area of the economy where technological innovation cut costs. A similar formula was used for other industries, though in some cases X was positive; for example, the water companies are allowed to raise their prices faster than the rate of inflation to reflect capital investment needs. In all the industries privatised after BT, the formula has been adjusted to allow some costs to be excluded; this is called 'cost pass through'. The justification for this is that some costs cannot be influenced by the industry and should therefore be excluded, An example of this is the gas bought by British Gas from the oil companies. However, the exclusion of these costs is known to all the parties involved; and since they know that the costs can be passed on, there is no incentive to cut them.

There is a considerable debate as to the best method to regulate utilities. Two main approaches can be distinguished. The approach used in the USA has focused on the rate of return on investment earned by the firm. The disadvantages of this are that it encourages the over-use of capital. In addition, the regulator is involved in defining the costs of the industry in order to define 'profit'. Rate of return regulation can prevent monopoly abuse and it can achieve allocative efficiency if the allowed rate of return is close to the cost of borrowing. Where this approach fails is that it does not achieve allocative efficiency because of the over-use of capital and because the costs of regulation are high, both to the firm and the regulator (Price, 1994). American experience suggests that this approach leads to huge legal costs as firms challenge regulator decisions in the courts, though this might reflect the American legal system rather than the rate of return approach *per se*.

The British approach – controlling price – avoids these problems. The firm can only increase profits if it cuts costs, so this method creates incentives for efficiency; moreover, it is cheap to operate. However, these benefits only continue so long as the firm believes that the regulator ignores the firm's performance. If the firm believes that the regulator will choose the cap according to the firm's performance, it will adapt its behaviour. There is therefore a danger that if the regulator thinks that the firm is making too high a profit – i.e. is getting too high a rate of return on its investment – then the regulator will toughen the price cap. This means that the incentive to cut costs will disappear, and a price-capping approach will be little different from a rate-of-return approach.

There are potentially other problems with adopting an approach where the activities of the firm are strongly influenced by a regulator. There is a danger of what the Americans call 'regulatory capture'. In other words, working closely with an industry makes the regulator sympathetic to the problems of the industry so that eventually the regulation becomes little more than a symbol. One approach to this problem by the right-wing Adam Smith Institute (1994) is to suggest that the regulators should be answerable to a parliamentary committee and subject to annual policy reviews by the National Audit Office.

Another approach, also advocated by the Adam Smith Institute, is to suggest that the long-term policy should be to encourage competition. There is some evidence to suggest that competition from other firms has resulted in improved efficiency. Parker (1995, p. 44) reviews the evidence and concludes:

> it is increased competition that leads to allocative efficiency. . ... Regulation of dominant firms may be a poor second best . . . continued state regulation dulls efficiency incentives. So far, however, there is no clear evidence that regulated privatised enterprises in the UK are performing noticeably worse in productive efficiency terms than the non-regulated ones.

Price (1994) suggest four objectives for regulators: economic efficiency, managerial efficiency, equity and cost of regulation. She concludes that the evidence is mixed. For example, there have been improvements in efficiency in regulated industries, but there have also been similar improvements in other industries, and it may be that the improvements have occurred because of competition or from technological innovation which would have occurred irrespective of the form of ownership and control. She concludes: 'The effect of regulation on the industries' behaviour is difficult to measure given the number of changes they have experienced' (p. 97).

Underlying the government's approach to the privatised utilities has been the view that the best way to prevent consumers being exploited is to promote the entry of new firms. Thus Mercury was allowed to compete with BT. Similarly, British Gas now faces competition from other producers who are allowed to make use of its gas pipes. It is hoped that such competition will be an incentive to increased efficiency and lower prices.

But such a policy has limitations. BT and British Gas continue to dominate their respective markets and so still maintain the advantages which accrue to the dominant firm in an industry. Moreover, many of the benefits accrue to only a few consumers. British Gas's competitors are only interested in selling to large consumers; British Gas will be forced to compete in this market leaving small users to face higher prices.

### Evaluating competition policy

There is no such thing as an ideal competition policy. That is because there is disagreement about the role of such a policy – for example, should competition policy be subservient to industry policy? This could occur, for example, if a monopoly in one country was competing overseas against larger foreign firms. Competition policy might suggest that sanctions be imposed to help domestic consumers, industrial policy that the firm be encouraged to grow.

Even if the role and purpose of competition policy is agreed, the effects of policies are not always clear, not least because of the existence of trade-offs. For example, in some markets investment is 'lumpy' so that agreement between firms is necessary in order to prevent large amounts of investment coming on stream at the same time, giving rise to excess capacity.

Another difficulty concerns predatory pricing – almost universally deplored, but firms may claim that when they cut prices in markets where they face aggressive competition they are merely responding to competitive conditions and not attempting to see off competitors.

A third example of the complexities of competition policy is that advertising and product differentiation may give some benefits to consumers in the form of information and choice, but they also make it more difficult for new firms to enter the market. Hence in the long run they may lead to undesirable results. Finally, competition policy is difficult to evaluate since it may have an effect that is not discernible. This could occur if firms were deterred from anti-competitive behaviour by the fear of investigation.

Despite the difficulties, there is some agreement that UK policy towards competition has many weaknesses:

- Many mergers confer few if any advantages to the public, but are allowed because the burden of proof is that the MMC has to decide whether or not a merger is contrary to the public interest. A suggestion by some commentators (George, 1989) is that in referred mergers, the onus should be on firms to show that the merger will bring benefits to the public.
- The government's general approach to mergers is permissive. This is reflected in the statistics. In the decade following 1977, only 57 referrals were made out of approximately 2439 mergers covered by the legislation (Jacquemin, 1990).
- The permissive approach to monopolistic practices is reflected in the MMC's record. For example, the OFT urged an investigation into whether perfume manufacturers were operating a cartel to maintain high prices for their products. The MMC concluded that there was indeed a complex monopoly, but that the high prices which resulted were not against the public interest since factors such as exclusivity were more important to perfume buyers than price.
- The UK system allows considerable political intervention. In 1994 the Director General of the Office of Free Trading was ordered by the President of the

- Board of Trade to halt his investigation into bus services on the Isle of Arran. On another occasion he turned down an OFT recommendation to refer the proposed merger of Airtours and Owners Abroad to the MMC.
- Hay (1993) argues that the broad public interest criteria that are mentioned in the various acts are too wide ranging and have little to do with economic efficiency. For example, whether or not breaking up a monopoly affects regional unemployment ought not to be a matter for competition policy but for regional policy. He argues that these broad criteria and lack of clearly stated rules introduces great uncertainty for firms.
- 'The institutional arrangements in the UK are in a mess' (Hay, 1993). The Office of Fair Trading, the MMC and the Restrictive Practices Court all have different responsibilities not based on any real economic rationale. Consequently 'Anyone examining the UK's competition legislation . . . must be struck first of all by its complexity' (Borrie, 1993, p. 1).

Hence there is considerable pressure for reform of competition policy in the UK, and the consensus view which is emerging is that this should be based on the approach adapted in the EU.

The control of privatised utilities also seems unsatisfactory. Taking these industries back into public ownership seems impossible because of the cost – and also the lack of the political will – but there is little agreement on exactly how these industries can be prevented from being run in the interests of the shareholders rather than the public as a whole.

# CHAPTER 4

# *Industrial Policy*

## What is industrial policy?

In one sense all economic policy is an industrial policy since virtually all economic decisions by the government affect industry. A change in taxes, a large government order, a fall in the interest rate – all will have a greater or lesser impact on industry.

So in practice the term 'industrial policy' has a rather narrower meaning, and is concerned with policies that have as their primary aim 'restructuring or promoting the activities of particular firms or sectors' (Dietrich, 1992, p. 17). Industry policy is therefore one kind of supply-side policy, though it differs from most policies called 'supply side' since these are often advocated by those on the right of the political spectrum and focus on measures such as tax cutting. In this approach, the market decides what happens to industry, and the role of government is to facilitate the working of the market. On the other hand, 'industrial policy' is often advocated by those seeking government intervention in markets – the opposite to the policies advocated by most supply-siders.

Industrial policy can have both positive and negative aspects. A positive approach concentrates on encouraging new industries or new products or processes; a negative approach moves resources away from particular activities, for example those which it is believed are becoming obsolete. In practice, however, there are often strong pressures from those in declining industries for the state to give additional aid to help maintain employment.

The policies that can be adopted cover a very wide range of activities, including:

- Competition policy
- Government procurement policy – government purchases can help stimulate new innovations or help declining industries
- Education and training
- Fostering new technology, and R&D
- Finance for industry
- Regional and urban policy (discussed in Chapter 7).

## Does the UK need an industrial policy?

The argument for an industrial policy rests on the argument that the UK economy has performed relatively badly, and that better policies would do something to remedy this. So how has the UK economy performed?

This is a simple question; but the answer is not so simple, not least because there are no universally agreed criteria to judge performance. As Coates (1995) points out, 'Do we take employment levels, living standards, return on factors of production, overall rates of economic growth?'

Even if agreement can be reached on this, it is still a matter for argument what reference point should be used – for example should we judge the UK's performance against the best of the rest of the world, or against the historical record, or against the performance of similar countries? Finally, comparisons involve more than statistics; we need to develop reasons to explain the figures, and, as we shall see, there are numerous possible reasons which can be used to explain the performance of an economy.

The criteria used here will concentrate on economic growth, but it should be realised that this is a far from universally agreed measure. For example, it is quite rational – perhaps even desirable – to argue that a country should adopt a goal of reducing hours worked in order to increase leisure. That might lead to lower output but higher welfare. Similarly, those with 'green' values would argue that GDP is a very flawed measure of welfare, and that we ought not to aim at increasing industrial output but should seek to improve our environment. This would mean using some criterion such as 'sustainable growth' as a goal – i.e. maximising economic growth only to the extent that this would leave the earth's resources intact for the use of future generations.

### The UK record

A century ago, 'Britain was one of the highest income countries in the world, responsible for 40 per cent of world manufactured exports' (Saul, 1965, quoted in Crafts, 1988). However, the seeds of relative decline were already apparent. Much of the growth had occurred because people transferred from agriculture to industry, so increasing industrial output whilst agricultural output was hardly affected. Productivity in industry was not very high and politicians were aware of the threat from Germany and other countries. This was one reason for the 1890 Education Act which gave local education authorities responsibility for education, in order to ensure a supply of skilled labour for industry. Another indication of relative decline was that UK investment in industry in the UK was 7.3 per cent of national expenditure, compared to 18.6 per cent as the European norm, while school enrolment was 38.5 per cent of the population aged 5–19, compared to 58.2 per cent as the European norm

(Crafts, 1988). Moreover, the period from 1890 to 1913 showed very low growth in both productivity and GDP (M. Thomas, 1988).

Between the wars the story was mixed. The period was characterised by very high levels of unemployment and great poverty in many areas where traditional industries such as cotton, coal and shipbuilding were contracting. At the same time new industries such as cars and chemicals were invigorating many areas, and even today rows of houses dating from the 1930s still bear witness to high levels of activity in the construction industry.

But the underlying weaknesses remained. Gross investment averaged around 9 per cent of GDP, and productivity was much less than in competing countries: in the USA output per worker was 2.25 times that of British workers in 1935, and even in Germany, where poor economic conditions were a main factor in Hitler's rise to power, output per worker was 11 per cent higher than in the UK (Crafts, 1988).

The relatively poor performance of the UK economy is illustrated in Table 4.1 which shows that the UK performed worse than almost all the other countries in the table. The exceptions are those, such as Germany, which in 1950 were still suffering the effects of war devastation.

However, despite the relatively weak performance, its early start in industrialisation meant that the UK was still relatively rich at the end of the Second World War, and could look forward to a period of prosperity.

**TABLE 4.1    Annual average growth rates in GDP (% per year) 1913–50**

| | |
|---|---|
| Australia | 2.1 |
| Austria | 0.2 |
| Belgium | 1.0 |
| Canada | 2.9 |
| Denmark | 2.5 |
| Finland | 2.4 |
| France | 1.0 |
| Germany | 1.3 |
| Italy | 1.4 |
| Japan | 1.8 |
| Netherlands | 2.4 |
| Norway | 2.9 |
| UK | 1.3 |
| USA | 2.8 |

*Source*:   A. Madison, *The World Economy in the Twentieth Century*, OECD, Paris (1989) quoted in N.F.R. Crafts and N. Woodward, *The British Economy since 1945*, Oxford University Press, Oxford, 1991, p. 8.

*The economy in the postwar world*

In 1945 the UK economy faced several problems. Pre-war, the country had depended on earnings from overseas assets, but during the war the capital account had depreciated by £20 billion (Cairncross, 1990, p. 30). This weakened the balance of payments and limited the government's freedom of action in economic policy. Moreover, about three-quarters of the country's exports went to countries outside Europe; many of them to poorer less-developed countries, and this discouraged attempts to develop high technology products.

Since the Second World War, the UK economy has performed quite well if the criteria for judging performance is historical; growth rates have been high compared to those in Victorian times, and standards of living are far higher. However, if the appropriate measure of comparison is with competing countries, the picture is less rosy. Thus Madison looked at income levels adjusted for differences in the cost of living. He concluded that in 1950 the UK was fifth of the countries listed in Table 4.1; by 1973 it had fallen to tenth and by 1987 to thirteenth. This conclusion is supported by an analysis of percentage changes in GDP over a substantial part of the postwar era as shown in Table 4.2

A similar conclusion was reached by Feinstein who analysed GDP per head of population as shown in Table 4.3.

To obtain these figures, Feinstein converted GDP figures using purchasing power parities. Two things stand out. Unsurprisingly, the UK does rather badly, whether the comparison uses GDP per head or output per hour worked. More surprising is the relatively poor performance of Japan when the criterion is GDP per hour worked. Several explanations are possible for this. First, some parts of the Japanese economy such as the distribution system are very inefficient. Second, Japanese output per worker is high, but they work longer hours than workers in most other advanced countries and when this is taken into consideration, output per hour worked is relatively low.

TABLE 4.2    **Per capita GDP ($US 1980 prices), annual average per cent changes, 1960–87**

| | |
|---|---|
| USA | 1.9 |
| Japan | 5.5 |
| Germany | 2.7 |
| France | 3.0 |
| UK | 2.1 |
| Italy | 3.1 |

*Source*: G. Meen, 'International comparisons of the UK's long-run economic performance', *Oxford Review of Economic Performance*, vol. 4 (1988) no. 1.

TABLE 4.3   GDP per head of population and per hour worked, 1984

|  | *GDP per head of population ($US000)* | *GDP per hour worked ($US)* |
|---|---|---|
| USA | 15.83 | 21.31 |
| Sweden | 15.37 | 20.58 |
| Germany | 13.26 | 19.28 |
| France | 12.64 | 20.78 |
| Japan | 12.24 | 11.85 |
| Belgium | 12.15 | 19.84 |
| Netherlands | 11.71 | 20.72 |
| UK | 11.07 | 17.17 |
| Italy | 10.04 | 17.32 |

*Source*:   C. Feinstein, 'Economic growth since 1870: Britain's performance in international perspective', *Oxford Review of Economic Policy*, vol. 4 (1988) no. 1.

*More recent data*

A clear indication of the UK's industrial decline occurred in 1983 when trade in manufacturing went into deficit for the first time since the industrial revolution. In 1990 the UK was the only European state with a deficit in merchandise. And even the Government in its White Paper admitted, 'average productivity levels in manufacturing have not yet risen to those of our major competitors' (HMSO, 1994b, p. 13).

The decline of manufacturing industry – deindustrialisation – can have serious effects on an economy. First, it will lead to unemployment if the rise in other sectors is insufficient to absorb the labour shed by manufacturing. Second, manufacturing has unique growth-inducing characteristics. The faster the growth in manufacturing, the faster the growth in labour productivity in manufacturing and in GDP growth, largely because of the existence of economies of scale in manufacturing. If these arguments are correct, then the relative decline of UK manufacturing has serious consequences for the economy as a whole.

- in the 1980s, manufacturing productivity grew faster in the UK than in the USA, France and Germany (though cynics would point out that if very many factories close down, average productivity will show a rise even if those remaining are no more productive than they were at the beginning of the decade);
- UK share of the volume of world trade stabilised
- employment rose;
- overall growth rate of the UK was similar to that in France, Germany and Italy;
- the UK succeeded in attracting the lion's share of US and Japanese investment in the EU.

Despite these claims, there is no doubt that the relative position of the UK remains unsatisfactory, and that much needs to be done to remedy the position.

### Explanations of the UK's relatively poor performance

One explanation of the UK's relatively poor performance derives from the 'convergence theory'. Thus Feinstein (1988, p. 6) argues

> To a significant extent the superior performance of countries like Japan, Germany and Italy can thus be understood in the context of the lower level from which they started their postwar advance . . . there is broad agreement about the underlying forces responsible for the convergence phenomenon. It is generally considered to depend primarily on a process of technical diffusion from the leading nation(s) to other countries which have developed a certain threshold level of economic and social capability. Once a country has attained that crucial capability, the technology of more advanced countries can be obtained in various ways, and adapted to the borrowing country's specific circumstances and factor endowments. Latecomers can thus grow more rapidly than the lead countries where the pace of technical progress is effectively restricted to the advances which can be generated internally by R&D expenditure and other sources of domestic innovations.

Put another way, there can be benefits in 'backwardness' so long as a country has the preconditions for growth such as 'a minimum level of economic activity, of education and culture, of social cohesion, and of political and administrative stability' (Feinstein, 1990, p. 288). One advantage for less-developed countries is that they know that they are underdeveloped and need to reform. Second, they can borrow from more advanced countries – borrow not only money and technology, but also legal systems and corporate practices. Finally, less-developed countries usually have a large proportion of the population working in low productivity agriculture. Average productivity will rise as these workers transfer to industry.

However, whilst this convergence hypothesis may explain some part of the UK's *relative* poor performance, it does not give a complete answer: for example, 'advanced' countries can have very different growth rates, and some less advanced countries which seem to have reached threshold levels continue to fall behind. South American countries which were relatively developed at the beginning of the century have never really taken off. So we need to look at other explanations.

### Trade unions

The workers, and particularly the trade unions, are often held to be responsible for the UK's relatively poor economic performance. The criticism here is that unions are monopoly sellers of labour that distort the allocation of resources, resulting in inefficiency. For example. Friedman (1980, p. 277) claims:

> all of us . . . have indirectly been harmed as consumers by the effect of high union wages on the prices of consumer goods. . . Workers have been prevented from using their skills to produce the most valued items; they have been forced to resort to activities where their productivity is less. The total basket of goods available to us all is smaller than it would have been.

Friedman is primarily writing about the USA, but his argument, if accepted, applies more strongly to the UK because the UK has had strong unions for over a century. Thus British unions have been accused of preventing the full utilisation of productive capacity and the introduction of new techniques, and it is claimed that the insistence on collective bargaining results in inefficient workers receiving the same rewards as those that are more productive.

This line of argument led Hayek (1980) to claim 'that unions are the prime cause of the decline of the British economy' and led the Conservative Government elected in 1979 to enact a whole series of laws intended to weaken the unions. For example, the Employment Act (1980) introduced new restrictions on picketing, outlawed secondary picketing and introduced restrictions on the closed shop. This was followed by another Employment Act in 1982, a Trade Union Act in 1984, a Wages Act in 1986, another Employment Act in 1988, another in 1990 and culminated in a Trade Union Reform and Employment Rights Act in 1993 (Blyton and Turnbull, 1994).

There is some research evidence to support these criticisms of unions. For example, Metcalf (1989) reviewed some of the literature and concluded that 'the weight of the evidence suggested that union presence is associated with lower labour productivity'.

This emphasis on union strength as the cause of economic decline has been the subject of substantial criticism. In the first place, some writers argue that it is not the strength but the *weakness* of unions that has harmed the economy:

> if unions had been strong they would have obtained high wages which, in turn, would have been accompanied by modernisation and high productivity. Employers would have been forced by high wages to invest in new machinery, plants and methods of production in order to compensate for wage rises with productivity rises (Fine and Harris, 1985, p. 31, quoted in Coates, 1991).

There is evidence to support this argument. As Table 4.4 shows, for many years Britain has been a relatively low cost country. This has encouraged investment in labour intensive work rather than high-investment, high-output methods of production.

TABLE 4.4   Labour costs in manufacturing

| | Total hourly compensation ($)<br>1992 | Hourly compensation relative to USA<br>1975 | 1992 |
|---|---|---|---|
| USA | 16.17 | 100.0 | 100.0 |
| Japan | 16.16 | 47.2 | 99.9 |
| France | 16.88 | 71.1 | 104.4 |
| Germany | 25.94 | 99.8 | 160.4 |
| Italy | 19.41 | 73.4 | 120.0 |
| UK | 14.69 | 53.0 | 90.8 |
| Netherlands | 20.72 | 103.5 | 128.1 |
| Sweden | 23.26 | 95.8 | 143.8 |

*Source*:   US Department of Labor, quoted in P. Turner and Van 't dack, *Measuring International Price and Cost Competitiveness*, Basle, Bank for International Settlements, (1993).

*Note*: 'hourly compensation' includes non-wage labour costs such as holiday pay, employer social security contributions and payroll taxes as well as actual wages.

Research evidence also casts doubt on criticisms of the union effect on productivity. The work of Wadhwani and Nickell leads to the conclusion that there is no simple relationship between unionism and productivity. Thus Nickell *et al.* (1989) conclude 'Contrary to what is alleged, unions do not consistently reduce productivity growth' whilst Wadhwani (1990) finds 'no evidence here for the view that unions reduce productivity growth'.

One reason why unions may increase productivity is that unions improve communications within the workplace and so encourage organisational change: a conclusion supported by Machin and Wadhwani (1991) who studied 721 private sector establishments and found 'a positive association between unionism and organisational change'.

*Capital*

The argument that trade unions are responsible for the UK's relative economic decline comes largely from the right of the political spectrum; the suggestion that capital is responsible is associated with the left.

The basic idea is that the relationship between capital and industry in the UK has some features which are both unique and undesirable. The UK was the first country to industrialise, and this left British manufacturing firms to finance development from profits, leaving banks to invest overseas. This 'establishes a distance between industrial and financial interests and an international focus which had no parallel elsewhere' (Coates, 1991, p. 13).

The growth of financial institutions in the City of London led to a growing dependence on invisible earnings. 'As her industries sagged, her finance triumphed' (Hobsbawm, 1968, p. 151). The political power of the financial institutions led to economic policies which favoured finance rather than industry. 'The result has been a constant bias in British economic policy for well over a century. That bias has always favoured the interests of asset holders as opposed to wealth creators' (Cowling and Sugden, 1990, p. 3). This bias takes a number of forms. One is that finance benefits from high interest rates, but this puts up the cost of borrowing for industry and reduces investment.

Financial interests also give rise to short-termism. In the UK banks are often unwilling to lend long term, making it difficult for industry to undertake long-term planning. One consequence of this is the low level of civilian research and development in the UK. This contrasts strongly with the position in countries such as Germany and Japan where there are close, long-term relationships between manufacturing firms and banks. Where there is a close relationship, perhaps in the form of the bank owning shares in a manufacturing firm, then banks will continue to help even when a company runs into difficulties. They will also be willing to take a long-term view about the returns required on an investment. The disadvantage of this system is that it gives too much power to the banks; the directors of a few large banks have influence, not only over their own company, but over very many firms throughout the economy.

Support for this critique of the financial structure of the UK economy is illustrated by the dependence of British firms on the stock exchange as a source of finance. Very few rich countries except the USA have stock markets anywhere near as large as that in the UK. In other developed countries there is much greater emphasis on retained profit as a source of finance for industry. In the UK retained profit is relatively low because financial institutions which own or control most of the shares demand high dividends.

This critique of the UK's investment performance is not universally accepted. The Government (HMSO, 1995, p. 14) accepts that 'the UK has consistently invested a smaller proportion of GDP than its major competitors, with the exception of the UK', but it claims that this reflects the relatively low share of housing investment in the UK so that business investment and investment in machinery and equipment have been similar as a proportion of GDP to those of other members of the G7 group of countries. They also claim that other factors such as the skills of the labour force and management quality are as important as investment in determining productivity.

The short-termism criticism also manifests itself when we consider human as opposed to financial capital. Many firms are unwilling to spend much on training; and when they do it tends to be on training specific to the firm, on its operating systems, for example, rather than on long-term transferable training. That is because they fear that such training is expensive and that trained personnel will leave and join competitors.

The weakness of UK investment in human capital is a long-term phenomenon. Sanderson (1988) begins a review of the relationship between education and economic decline by quoting Sir Bernard Samuelson in 1882: 'The Englishman has yet to learn that an extended and systematic education is now a necessary preliminary to the fullest development of industry'. He also quotes Sir Bryan Nicholson who made the same point in 1986 rather more pithily 'We are a bunch of thickies'.

Chapter 9 reviews the arguments about skilled manpower; the conclusion reached there is that there is no overall shortage, but that there is a deficiency in some areas, particularly in the quality of scientific and technological education at the technician level. Another deficiency is that UK managers tend to be trained in accountancy and finance rather than engineering, and that they undertake too little training after they are appointed so that they follow innovations introduced elsewhere only after a long time lag.

## Culture

'The battle for British industrial supremacy was lost on the playing fields of Eton.' This view encapsulates the argument that there is a deep-seated culture in the UK, led by the products of the public schools, which is deeply anti-industrial. One of the leading proponents of this view is Wiener (1981) who puts the blame for the decline on 'the values of the directing strata' (pp. 5–6). Other writers such as Warwick (1985) support the view that British culture

> was non-industrial in the sense that it tended to uphold the outlook and lifestyle of the leisured gentleman. . . .. Education or training was generally disparaged to the extent that it appeared to have any practical or vocational relevance, and science and technology . . . yielded to the student schooled in the classics (p. 103).

To the extent that the public schools reflect the dominant ideology, the argument is that British culture is anti- manufacturing, anti-industrial, and dominated by a rigid class system which disparages wealth creation. Evidence for this can be seen in the destinations of the brightest graduates: they tend not go into managing the mines or mills but into advertising or the media which have replaced the colonies as desirable careers. This argument is not universally accepted. Rubinstein (1988) argues that it fails to present a persuasive nexus to account for the transmission of cultural values into economic performance, and that it may be based on a fundamental misapprehension about the essential nature of Britain's economy since industrialisation. He argues that for a young man of the middle classes, the imperative was to find secure employment, and that this was available in the army, the colonies and in the law, but not in manufacturing. Career choices were thus not determined by the dictates of an anti manufacturing culture, but by the need to secure employment.

He goes on to argue that 'British culture has been markedly *less* strident in its condemnation of capitalism than virtually any other Western culture' and cites writers such as Adam Smith and Samuel Smiles who vigorously defended capitalism.

Despite this defence, there is considerable support for the idea that anti-industrialism is deep rooted in British culture; if this is the cause of industrial decline, then the consequences for policy are ominous. A nation's culture is deep rooted, and minor changes in policy will do little to change it.

## Theoretical approaches to industrial policy

Theory underpins policy. No policy exists in a theoretical vacuum; all policies derive from some theory, whether or not this is recognised by the proponents of the policy.

In the case of industrial policy, there are three broad theoretical approaches. The market failure approach argues that markets are the best way to allocate resources, and that the role of government is to concentrate on the correction of 'market failure'. Generally, this gives only a minor role to government, though government intervention may be substantial if it is thought that monopoly and externalities are extensive. In this approach, industrial policy concentrates on micro economic measures and little attention is given to fiscal policy, for example. Competition will ensure that firms adopt suitable methods of production, and more active government intervention is seen as counterproductive since markets are better at allocating resources than governments.

In the Austrian approach, competition is also important, but it is seen as a dynamic process where entrepreneurs take advantage of opportunities. Competitive equilibrium may never be reached; instead the economy is a dynamic process of constant innovation. In the Austrian approach, as in the neo-classical, government has a relatively minor role to play. The role of the state is 'restricted to that of "nightwatchman" enacting and enforcing laws to protect property rights and market exchange' (Sawyer, 1992, p. 8). Since entrepreneurs and competition are the driving force of innovation, industrial policy should focus on the reduction of barriers to entry and the exercise of competition. This should be complemented by taxation policies to provide incentives to entrepreneurs.

In both the market failure and Austrian approaches, excessive state intervention is positively detrimental. Thus Bacon and Eltis (1976) argue that state activity takes resources away from the wealth creating market sector. And Price (1981, p. 32) suggests that 'if government takes it upon itself to attempt to guide the economy in a particular direction, it may discourage and finally extinguish private attempts to look forward into the future'. Moreover, 'The market's ability to work spontaneously is eroded every time a government takes decisions on its behalf'.

## The industrial strategy approach

A very different approach is taken by the industrial strategy approach. The central argument here is that market forces may play an essential part in the efficient allocation of resources, but that they are inadequate. Instead there is no sharp dichotomy between allocation through markets and allocation through planning. That is because 'The purpose is not to substitute the plan for the market, but to shape and use markets' (Best, 1990, p. 20, quoted in Sawyer, 1992). Whilst there is a role for competition policy in this approach,

> there is also the need for a developmental role for the state, which involves the active promotion of industrial development under which the state adapts an entrepreneurial role, either in its own industrial operations and/or in its promotion of private business. The state is therefore able to create opportunities which would otherwise not exist (Sawyer, 1992, p. 10).

Many advocates of the industrial strategy approach also give it a more openly political approach in that they seek to enhance democracy by increasing participation by workers in decision-making which can lead to higher production: for example, because workers can make better use of their knowledge.

## Industrial policy in Germany and Japan

One possible approach to industrial policy is to look at the policies that have been developed in more successful countries, though economic policies are not like plant seeds that can be successfully transported across national boundaries. Policies need to be adapted to their economic, political and social context, and a policy that is successful in one country may be a disaster in another.

The Federal Republic of Germany has a long history of intervention in industrial development; for example, Bismark introduced tariff protection to help the young steel industry. More recently, in 1966 the Stability and Growth Act gave the Federal Government the responsibility to achieve price stability, economic growth and full employment, partly through macro-economic policies designed to reduce fluctuations in the business cycle, but also through concerted action on the part of federal, state and local authorities (Price, 1981, p. 50). The approach which has been adopted does not involve planning as such, but rather concentrates on concerted discussions designed to concert expectations among different interests. Thus discussions take place between interested parties which seek to anticipate future problems, so that appropriate action can take place to prevent or mitigate the problems. The emphasis is on concerted action between employers, trade unions and the state rather than on actual intervention.

In some cases, government aid has been given to help problem industries; for example, grants were given to help shipbuilding face competition from subsidised yards elsewhere, and coal mining has been helped to compete with cheap oil imports. Extensive use has been made of subsidies which in 1987 amounted to 6.5 per cent of GNP (Stille, 1990, p. 95). Much of this money was directed at areas other than industrial policy, for example housing, but 12 per cent of the subsidies went to the railways which were seen as essential to efficient communications as well as being environmentally desirable. Rather more went to agriculture and 4 per cent to coal and 5 per cent to subsidise iron production.

In general, however, the German approach has been opposed to giving state aid to ailing industries. Thus in 1974 Volkswagen was making a large loss, but was refused direct state help; instead, money was made available to encourage the creation of new industries in the regions affected by VW redundancies.

According to the German concept of *Ordnungspolitik*, industrial policy has to play a subordinate role in enhancing structural change and reducing the social cost of change (Tomann, 1992, p. 184). State intervention is justified in three areas:

1. provision of basic sectors of national interest;
2. restructuring of declining industries;
3. fostering innovative activity.

Much of the action takes place at state rather than at national level. For example, the state of Baden-Wurtemberg encouraged technology transfer, especially to small and medium-sized firms. Overall, however, the characteristic feature of the German system lies in discussion and consultation rather than direct financial help.

The Japanese system has attracted wide attention. If there are two roles for the state in a market economy – a regulatory one and a developmental one – the Japanese model is developmental. Indeed, it is often described as the 'developmental state' model. Its industrial policy is very wide ranging and includes protecting infant industries, preventing excessive competition, industrial organisation as well as regional policy. At the heart of the policy is the Ministry of International Trade and Industry (MITI). To achieve its targets, MITI has used various measures – discriminatory treatment of permission to import, restrictive laws, subsidies as well as guidelines (Matsumoto, 1992,

p. 148) At the heart of the policy is 'administrative guidance' (*gyosei shido*) where companies are encouraged to follow MITI's guidelines and where informal get-togethers between companies are encouraged in order to exchange information before decisions are made.

In the period of Japan's most rapid economic growth, MITI concentrated resources on specific industries. This was not done on the basis of comparative advantage, but instead concentrated on industries with a high income elasticity of demand and where technical progress could be encouraged. The motor vehicle industry is a good example. For a time such industries were given tariff protection against imports, but that has since largely disappeared except for a few products such as rice.

Belief in the economies of scale led MITI to encourage large-scale mergers, for example in the steel industry where several firms were encouraged to merge in order to strengthen competitive power in world markets.

Since the late 1960s the policy has changed from modernising the capital-intensive industrial structure to concentrating on knowledge-intensive industries, in particular the computer industry. Here MITI promoted co-operative research and development.

Since Japan became an industrial giant, MITI's role has become less dominant. Japanese firms are now mature decision makers, and Japan has had to abide by GATT guidelines and has been subject to considerable external pressure to open up its domestic market to international competition, making it doubtful if MITI will be able to lead Japanese economy in the future as it did in the past. If this is so , the Japanese model may be more suited for developing countries than for more advanced economies.

## General policies

The British Government's approach to industrial policy was set out in its White Paper *Competitiveness: Helping Business to Win* (HMSO, 1994b). This emphasised the macro-economic context of industrial policy, and stressed the importance of low inflation. The paper argued that since inflation distorts price signals and creates uncertainty it was 'the enemy of growth and investment' (p. 21). The second aspect of macro policy in the paper is 'sound public finances' since 'high levels of government borrowing increase the burden of public debt, raising interest rates and ultimately forcing higher taxes or cuts in public spending'.

Both these claims would, of course, be contested by many economists. The relationship between investment and inflation is complex; since firms often borrow to finance investment, and since inflation benefits borrowers, it may be that inflation may increase investment. Similarly, the notion that public debt imposes a burden is too simplistic; it depends largely on how the money is spent. If it is spent constructively, then it may stimulate the economy, lead to higher incomes and hence higher government receipts in the future.

The 1994 White Paper also stressed the importance of making public services more efficient, for example through privatisation, and also by using the power of the public purse – i.e. public procurement. In exercising its purchasing power, the Government has two aims: value for money and improving the competitiveness of suppliers through a constructive partnership which can benefit both buyer and seller. The paper made little mention of other ways in which public procurement can aid industry, for example by encouraging innovation. Brunskill (1992, p. 69) suggests that government can help industrial policy 'by acting like a demanding customer'; setting stringent environmental targets and quality targets it can provide a stimulus to companies to upgrade their activities.

The DTI neatly summed up the Government's general approach in a press notice (DTI, 1993, quoted in House of Commons, 1994, p. 92): 'The government has "policies for industry" rather than an industrial policy or strategy'. Other writers are more ambitious. The Labour Party (1994a, pp. 4–5) stressed much more government intervention, for example, arguing that:

> It is not the job of government to run industry. It is, though, the role of government to promote within our industry and society those qualities that are essential if our industry is to be competitive. And nobody is in a better position than the government to take an overview of the economy and whether the relationships between the different players within it are functioning effectively . . . Britain will always be handicapped in international competition while we alone (under Conservative leadership) are ruled by a government prevented by its ideology from ever admitting that there could be a conflict between the short-term operation of the market and the long-term interest of the nation.

Some writers argue that this is insufficient; what is needed is 'to change the nature of strategic decision making within the modern corporation and, in the longer term, seek to displace its dominance within the market system' (Cowling and Sugden, 1993, p. 97). They come to this conclusion by concentrating less on market failure and more on the 'socially incomplete decision making' within the modern corporation. Power, they believe is too concentrated, and a more democratic structure is required. 'We need to confront the global strategy making of powerful transnational firms with our own national strategies. ' In the short run, this would mean that the DTI should assess those sectors of the economy that need immediate attention, such as car components and bio-technology where small firms are faced by high risk and long gestation periods. They suggest that the government should organise a catalytic role for itself; this would imply a vision statement for the sector, and then acting with the industry to achieve the vision – rather as the Japanese do.

## Specific policies

*Technology*

Technology is important. The ability of firms to develop or acquire new technologies is crucial to their future in a competitive world. Britain spends less on R&D than most competitor countries, and a relatively large proportion of this goes on defence-related activities which have a poor pay-off in terms of industrial development. Moreover, the quality of R&D seems to be declining. The best measure of a country's effectiveness in this area is the proportion of the country's patents that are used by other countries. The UK's proportion has declined slowly but continuously since the 1960s, and is now smaller than the French proportion, less than half that of Germany and far behind that of Japan (House of Commons, 1994, p. 48). The electronics and information technology industry is central to modern industrial development. They had a worldwide turnover of 700 billion ecu in 1990 and a European Union turnover of 175 billion ecu; roughly 5 per cent of GDP and probably rising to 10 per cent by the year 2000 (European Communities, 1991, p. 25). Even this under-estimates their importance, because they constitute an infrastructure through the enabling nature of their technologies, providing the hardware and soft-ware essential for nearly all industries. Hence they have a major part to play in the competitiveness of industry.

The information technology (IT) industry in the EU is relatively weak; for example Japan has a 49.5 per cent share of world semiconductor production, compared to 36.5 per cent in the USA and only 10 per cent for Europe (ibid., p. 27).

The importance of IT is one reason to adopt a policy specifically for the industry, but the economic argument also rests on the basis that this is an area where markets fail. Stoneman (1990, p. 125) summarises the reasons which also apply to many other industries:

- A firm may be unable to appropriate a return equal to the social value of its innovative effects, and so will under-invest.
- If firm A benefits from the innovative activities of firm B, then each firm will tend to hold back its technological efforts
- There may be duplication, with several firms doing identical research.
- It may be necessary for governments to intervene to gain a strategic advantage for firms in this country, or to offset strategic advantages being gained elsewhere, perhaps because of government help in competing countries.

There are many forms such government intervention can take: public provision, subsidies, co-operative R&D, competition policy, public provision, and policies for defence and standards. One example of such a policy is that produced by the Labour Party (1989). This suggested a system of automatic grants to stimulate R&D and also two large infrastructure projects to provide major benefits to the community whilst encouraging the development of technology. The areas suggested are the environment and the installation of a national broad-band fibre-optic cable network. The Party also suggested the creation of a new institution – the British Technology Enterprise – to finance new innovative activity and encourage new high-tech centres.

Geroski (1990) assesses these ideas. On the supply side, he dislikes the idea of automatic grants and tax incentives because they often reward creative accounting practices that shift some item of expenditure from one category to another. Moreover, they are a poorly targeted means of support and are based on eligibility rather than need, and finally, they may stimulate new innovation but do little to disseminate new ideas. This is particularly important since a country like the UK can only produce a small number of innovations, so that it needs to concentrate on disseminating innovation from the rest of the world. He argues that what is needed is a package of financial and management support, particularly for small firms. The proposed British Technology Enterprise may provide this.

On the demand side, Geroski suggests that more use be made of public procurement. In the USA, government purchases for defence purposes played a large part in the development and location of the American semiconductor industry. Military demand for innovative products or methods can enable firms to progress down the learning curve so that the private sector market benefits. Similarly, the Japanese Government formed a rental company called the Japanese Electronic Computer Company. This acted as a buying agency for computers and then hired them out to firms at low fees. The result was that computer use spread rapidly; the policy also encouraged firms to upgrade their computers regularly, and so stimulated innovation in the computer industry.

The British Government's approach to technology rests largely on the assumption that firms are the best judge of their technological needs, so that little governmental action is needed. The emphasis has therefore changed from the development of technology towards encouraging its adoption and diffusion, with particular reference to smaller firms (House of Commons, 1994, p. 118). One way in which this will be done is through a system of 'Business Links' aimed at improving support services for small firms. The first of these opened in 1993, and it is proposed to establish 200 centres. They will provide a single point of access for firms seeking advice. Among their staff will be Innovation and Technology Counsellors, funded by the DTI.

*Financial aspects of industrial policy*

Financial markets play a crucial role in industrial policy. In countries such as Germany and Japan, a large proportion of company shares are not freely traded on the stock markets but are held by banks, suppliers or customers.

This helps maintain commercial relationships so that hostile take overs are almost unknown, and firms can plan long term. The UK system 'focuses companies on strategies to support earnings and dividends rather than on strategies focused on firm or customer specific investments which are not easily traded' (Brunskhill, 1992, p. 59). She concludes that, while wholesale introduction of the German system is impractical, there are clear advantages to be obtained from the development of closer-knit links between companies and their financiers. One way to do this would be to provide tax relief for banks which invested in equities of their client companies.

One example of the problem occurred when British Aerospace sold Rover to BMW. The reason was that as Rover began to build up production it required risk finance and longer lines of bank finance. British bankers would not release the credit, because they said for every pound of capital British Aerospace had, it should not borrow more than £1. By contrast Honda in Japan can borrow £4 for every pound of finance (Hutton, 1994).

Smaller companies face particular financial problems. They obtain almost all their external finance from banks, whilst larger firms can make use of the stock market or other sources such as merchant banks. The central problem of financing smaller firms is that it is riskier and administratively costlier to lend to small firms than to large ones. According to the Midland Bank (House of Commons, 1994, p. 62), typical margins charged above base rate were 1.5 per cent for companies with turnover exceeding £10 million, but rose to 3 per cent where turnover was less than £1 million. Small firms employing less than 30 people were charged 3 to 5 per cent above base rate, and this was immediately doubled if the firm exceeded its overdraft limit even briefly. In other countries charges or interest rates were lower; thus in France small businesses can obtain finance at 2 per cent *below* base rates. Moreover, in the UK only 11 per cent of smaller firms' external finance is long term; in Germany it was 31 per cent, in France 23 per cent and in Italy 15 per cent. Another disadvantage of the UK system is that most of the money is borrowed by overdraft, and this is repayable on demand by the bank, so restricting the ability to plan long term.

Various schemes have been suggested to overcome this problem. The House of Commons Trade and Industry Committee suggested several methods such as a lower tax on retained profits. Another suggestion was to expand informal investment by private individuals ('business angels') who might also be able to offer management expertise – often a problem for small firms. This might be arranged through the Business Links network. Another suggestion was to make the tax privileges of pension funds conditional on them investing a proportion of their assets in small firms.

The Committee also noted Germany's KfW scheme. This is a quasi government body which can borrow funds on the international money market at low rates since it is guaranteed by the government. It then lends to small firms at low rates for long periods, with repayment only beginning in the third year.

The Government has also noted the problem; its solution has been to introduce an Enterprise Investment Scheme (replacing the old Business Expansion Scheme). In this scheme, investors may become paid directors. In this way it is hoped to encourage 'business angels' who want to invest in companies as well as contribute their expertise.

An alternative suggestion has been put forward by the Labour Party (1994b, p. 19). It suggests a Business Development Bank for Small Business. This bank will provide long-term loans to small businesses so that they are less dependent on overdrafts.

## Education and training

Many of our witnesses regarded the level of skills in the workforce as the central problem affecting UK manufacturing. Given that it is becoming ever easier to transfer capital and technology around the world, the skills of the workforce will increasingly be the determining factor in the competitiveness of different countries.

The House of Commons Committee (1994, p. 81) put the problem succinctly; countries need skills if their economies are to develop.

But it is much easier to make the generalisation than it is to develop desirable policies. In the first place, many jobs need little training. Thousands of people work as cleaners or drivers where training can be done quickly. Second, there is a large opportunity cost in training people to a high level of skills, since these are usually the people who are already well educated and therefore whose time is expensive. Third, who should pay for the training?

Neo-classical economists would argue that individuals should pay for the training if it benefits them, companies if they benefit. In this view, the role of the state is minimal: markets know best how much training is needed and the government's role is merely to reduce market imperfections.

More interventionist economists would argue that the market fails hugely in this context; for example, because of externalities. A worker trained by one firm may go and work for a competitor, so firms will tend to concentrate on training specific to the firm when what is needed are skills which will benefit the economy as a whole even if it does not pay the individual firm to pay for or provide some kinds of training. Moreover, individuals will not pay for the training because they lack knowledge of the labour market, and because the financial market does not function well in this area. That is because banks are usually unwilling to lend for training because they have little collateral – they cannot reclaim the training as they would a machine or factory.

One proposal is to reduce the difference between academic and vocational education; in the UK the introduction of General and Vocational Educational Qualifications (GNVQs) is one example of this, but it is likely that the brightest young people will ignore these and concentrate on traditional academic qualifications, leaving GNVQs as a qualification for those thought to be less able academically.

Perhaps more important than training potential workers is training existing workers. About 90 per cent of the workforce in the year 2000 is already in employment, so that if workers are to become more productive by then, existing workers will have to be trained. As Table 4.5 shows, there is some evidence to suggest that manufacturers in the UK spend similar amounts on training to that spent in other countries.

TABLE 4.5    **Manufacturing companies expenditure on training as a percentage of salaries and wages**

| | |
|---|---|
| UK | 2.7 |
| France | 4.3 |
| Spain | 2.1 |
| Germany | 3.0 |

*Source:*   House of Commons Committee on Trade and Industry, *Competitiveness of UK Manufacturing Industry*, 2nd report, HMSO, London, 1994.

However, this simple comparison may be misleading, because, as the Committee point out, the UK's relative failure in education and training means that UK employers start their training from a lower level than many of their competitors.

In response to this problem, the British government endorsed a series of targets drawn up by the Confederation of British Industry (CBI) (1992). These are summarised in Table 4.6.

TABLE 4.6    **National education and training targets**

| Target | % in 1990 |
|---|---|
| By 1997, 80 per cent of young people to reach NVQ 2 or equivalent | 52 |
| By 2000, 50 per cent of all young people to reach NVQ 3 or equivalent | 30 |
| By 1996, 50 per cent of the workforce to be aiming for NVQs or units towards them | 10 |
| By 2000, 50 per cent of the workforce to be qualified to at least NVQ 3 or equivalent | 31 |

*Source:*   CBI Manufacturing Council (1992) *Making it in Britain*, London, Confederation of British Industry.

The UK Government has developed this approach and devised targets for the year 2000:

*Foundation learning*
1. By age 19, 85 per cent of young people to achieve five passes at grade C or above or an Intermediate GNVQ or an NVQ level 2;
2. 75 per cent of young people to achieve level 2 competence in communication, numeracy and IT by age 19, and 35 per cent to achieve level 3 competence in these core skills by age 21;
3. By age 21, 60 per cent of young people to achieve two GCE A levels, and Advanced GNVQ or NVQ level 3.

*Lifelong learning*
1. 60 per cent of the workforce to be qualified to NVQ level 3, Advanced GNVQ or two Advanced level standard;
2. 30 per cent of the workforce to have a vocational, professional management or academic qualification at NVQ level 4 or above;
3. 70 per cent of all organisations employing 200 or more employees, and 35 per cent of those employing 50 or more, to be recognised as Investors in People (HMSO, 1995, p. 80). (The Investors in People project is a national standard for employers.)

However, it is one thing to set targets, quite another to achieve them, and the White Paper is rather vague on the measures to be taken. It proposes, for example, to 'promote the new targets' and to 'encourage schools, colleges and universities to set their own targets underpinning the national ones' (p. 81). The specific measures mentioned include piloting a scheme in one region to allow borrowers who have completed training funded by a Career Development Loan to delay the start of their repayment by up to 18 months in certain circumstances.

Another idea is 'maintaining the number of unemployed people allowed to study part time while on benefit, providing that they remain available for work and continue to seek it actively' (p. 84). Such ideas may be virtuous, but they are very short of commitment as represented by increases in government spending.

The Labour Party (1994b, p. 17) proposes several policies to remedy the UK's skills deficiency. They propose a new system of education and training for 16–19-year-olds which will provide a unified framework for academic and vocational courses. This is an attempt to remedy the anti-vocational attitude in the UK. They will also encourage company training by imposing a levy on those companies which do not provide adequate training for their workers.

Despite these policy proposals, the basic problems remain. *No one really knows how much training is really needed.* The general assumption is that more is better, and this may indeed be the case. But even if this is accepted, the question remains: who is responsible for providing training?

A Department of Employment witness to the House of Commons Committee (1994, p. 99) put the Government's position bluntly: the Government 'Cannot take responsibility for achieving the targets because a lot of the action which is required falls very clearly to other people'.

*Sponsorship*

In its White Paper (HMSO, 1995), the Government developed 'sponsorship' as a strategy in industrial policy. This involves working with industry on a sectoral basis, for example, to improve competitiveness, and by providing support to help UK companies win in world markets, minimising regulatory burdens and ensuring that government decisions take proper account of their impact on business. One example of this approach is that middle and senior managers are seconded to work in government departments. The actual activities seem rather limited in practice. For example, in aerospace, the initiatives include:

- supporting moves to improve competitiveness within the Airbus consortium;
- consultation on implementation of the National Strategic Technology Acquisition plan for civil aeronautics. To ensure best use of available resources, DTI and industry fund Technology Co-ordinators . . .
- supporting benchmarking and spread of best practice . . .
- supporting major export campaigns . . . (p. 43).

Such activities are no doubt desirable, but they will hardly revolutionise UK industry.

*Employment*

Underlying the British Government's approach to industry policy is its belief in the efficacy of markets, particularly the labour market.

The aim is a flexible labour market; in this context, this implies wage flexibility and in particular the introduction of the Jobseeker's Allowance. This requires all unemployed people to sign an individually tailored agreement as a condition of receiving benefit.

Clearly, an efficient labour market is a necessary feature of a successful economy, but many of the most successful postwar economies have had labour market features which are the opposite of flexible. For example, the Japanese economy is most successful in those large companies where workers can expect to have a job for life; though such workers are expected to be flexible in their approach to working conditions and the type of job they are willing to undertake. Also, the successful large companies to some extent rest on the back of a network of small firms where employment is not guaranteed.

Other examples of successful economies which exhibit many characteristics which are not 'flexible' are countries such as Germany, where trade unions are strong and where wage agreements are negotiated nationally. The Scandinavian economies also have these characteristics. Labour market policy is discussed further in Chapter 6.

*The European Union approach*

Whilst industrial policy is primarily a matter for national governments, the EU has a growing interest. This develops out of the completion of the single market and the free movement of labour and capital.

The EU approach (European Communities, 1991, p. 10) 'lays the emphasis on the need to concentrate on the creation of the right business environment and on the priority to give to a positive, open and subsidiarity-orientated approach'. The policy should therefore be built around an adequate balance between the following key elements:

(i)     First, laying down stable and long term conditions for an efficiently functioning market economy: maintenance of a competitive economic environment, as well as a high level of educational attainment and of social cohesion;

(ii)    second, providing the main catalysts for structural adjustment. In this respect, the completion of the internal market has a strategic role to play.

(iii)   third, developing the instruments to accelerate structural adjustment and to enhance competitiveness.

Whilst this may set out the underlying concept, in practice the role of the EU in actual policy is relatively small. That is because much policy requires finance, and the EU budget is tiny relative to that of national governments. Moreover, half the EU's spending goes on agriculture, leaving little for industry. In practice, much of the Union's industrial policy is effected through regional policy and is discussed in Chapter 7.

In general, it is fair to conclude that the EU's policy proposals are rather vague and general such as 'maintaining a favourable business environment' (p. 10), or 'Flexible, innovative, knowledge intensive industry requires strong social cohesion' (p. 13). No doubt in the future, the EU will play a more significant role on this area, but at present its activities are peripheral.

## Conclusion

In the last few decades, the world economy has become more competitive. Capital and technology can move relatively easily across national boundaries, and there is some evidence to suggest that the UK – and other EU countries – are in danger of falling behind. There is a growing feeling that governments need to take action, but relatively little agreement on exactly what this action should be.

# CHAPTER 5

# Small Firms

Recent years have seen a considerable revival in interest in the small-firm sector, both by academics and politicians. There has been a considerable growth in importance of the small firm in the UK and elsewhere since the 1960s (Curran and Blackburn, 1994). However, the position of the small firm in the UK economy is also important for ideological reasons, as the small firm is seen by some as epitomising the *enterprise economy*. The promotion of an *enterprise culture* has been a central plank of government policy since the end of the 1970s. Whilst governments have shown an antipathy to intervention in the operations of markets in recent years (Sugden, 1993), the small firm sector has been subject to a variety of policies which have been intended to promote its growth and strength.

### The fall and rise of the small-firm sector

A major cause of concern for UK policy-makers in the 1950s and 1960s was a decline in numbers of the small-firm sector. As noted in Chapter 1, this was the time at which Fordism with its emphasis on mass production was in the ascendant, and large factories with thousands of employees appeared to be the way forward. This emphasis on big being beautiful was further advanced by government economic policy. In the 1960s the Labour Government under Harold Wilson had a benign attitude towards mergers and this encouraged firms to grow larger by acquisition. At this time conglomerate firms, covering a range of economic activities with no obvious relationship to one another, developed rapidly. It was felt that this growth in firm size was in the public interest, as size and economies of scale were seen to be necessary to compete on the international stage. Small firms, by contrast, were seen to be associated with a bygone industrial age and were judged by many to be industrial dinosaurs.

The perilous position of the small-firm sector promoted concern in some quarters as it was felt that a supply of small firms was necessary to provide the new large firms of the future. As very few small firms ever grow to any size, a ready supply of such firms would be necessary simply to provide the few future success stories. The outcome of this concern was the Bolton Committee which reported on the state of the small firm in 1971.

However, the world economy moved into a traumatic phase in the 1970s, and established Western economies found the economic stability of the previous two decades undermined. The quadrupling of oil prices over the period 1973–4 required firms to rethink their production strategies and make more efficient use of energy. The growth of South-East Asian economies such as Japan posed further threats to markets for Western goods, whilst new technology facilitated innovative industrial and commercial processes and effectively 'shrank' the world by improving communications. At the same time, studies of the results of the mergers and acquisitions which took place prior to the 1970s showed that these had brought few, if any, benefits to the UK economy.

Against this background the certainties of the two decades before the 1970s came to be questioned. No longer was there the confidence that large firms would continue to grow whilst small firms would wither away. Increasing attention came to be focused on the potential contribution of small firms to an economy after the publication of a report in the USA by David Birch (1979). In this report Birch demonstrated that over the period 1969–76 two-thirds of net new jobs in the USA were created by firms with less than twenty employees.

### Definitions of the small firm

There is no single, accepted definition of what constitutes a small firm. The Bolton Committee report of 1971 identified a number of features which should be present if an enterprise is to be recognised as a small firm.

A small firm is:

1. An enterprise which has a relatively small share of its market.
2. Managed by its owners or part owners in a personalised way and not through the medium of a formalised management structure.
3. Independent in the sense that it does not form part of a larger enterprise and that the owner managers should be free from outside control in taking their principal decisions.

However, these economic definitions of what constitutes a small firm present a number of practical difficulties which the Bolton Committee recognised. It noted that the vast majority of firms in the manufacturing sector with fewer than 200 employees conformed to the criterion, but so did many manufacturing firms with 500 or more employees. As a consequence, the Committee found itself using a statistical rather than an economic definition in order to classify the small firm. This statistical definition, which is applied to manufacturing industry, has been widely used by researchers and encompasses all firms with 200 employees or less. For sectors other than manufacturing the definitions have tended to be somewhat arbitrary and dependent on the sector under consideration. Storey and Johnson (1987) comment on the multiplicity of definitions of the small firm and note that researchers have found over 30 definitions in use at the same point in time.

Even where the index for measurement is identical, as with employment or turnover, differences arise. For example, a manufacturing firm may be regarded as small if it has fewer than 200 employees, whilst a construction firm would generally be regarded as small if it has fewer than 20 employees. A small firm in retailing has a turnover of about one quarter of that of a small firm in wholesaling.

Whilst it is recognised that there is no 'official' definition of the small firm the Department of Trade and Industry adopt the following criterion in their 1995 report on small firms (DTI, 1995):

- Micro    –   0–9 employees
- Small    –   10–99 employees
- Medium  –   100–499 employees
- Large    –   500+employees.

## The small firm as generator of new jobs

Since the 1970s the small firm has come to be regarded by many as a panacea for ailing economies. A good deal of political rhetoric has been deployed in cataloguing the virtues of the small firm and its role in the creation of an enterprise economy. During the period of economic growth in the second half of the 1980s small firms were proclaimed as being crucial to the success of the UK economy. This can be seen in the 1987 Conservative Party Manifesto, *The Next Moves Forward*. In this document it was argued that self-employment 'is the seedcorn of the new enterprises of tomorrow. Without sufficient people to start new businesses, the future of our whole economy is in jeopardy.'

Industrial pressure groups such as the Institute of Directors have also championed the cause of the small firm, extolling its virtues and sounding a clarion call for support.

> Innovation, new products and the possibility of challenge to existing market dominances are vital to the effective functioning of a dynamic market economy. Without them, stagnation and inflexibility would result. Small and young enterprises provide a substantial element of these advantages (IOD, 1992, p. 40).

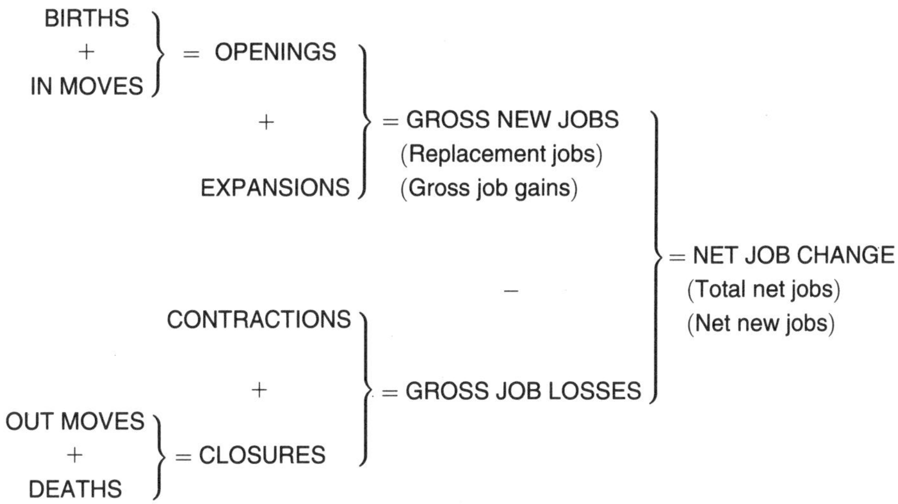

BIRTHS
+    } = OPENINGS
IN MOVES              } = GROSS NEW JOBS
        +              (Replacement jobs)
                       (Gross job gains)
EXPANSIONS }

                                        } = NET JOB CHANGE
                       −                  (Total net jobs)
CONTRACTIONS                              (Net new jobs)

        +           } = GROSS JOB LOSSES
OUT MOVES
    +     } = CLOSURES
DEATHS

*Source*: D. J. Storey, *Understanding the Small Business Sector*, London, Routledge, 1994, p. 162.

**FIGURE 5.1   The job generation process**

Politicians in particular have identified the characteristics of small firms which are seen to benefit an economy. These include a disposition to seek opportunity, take risks, operate flexibly and create jobs. By contrast, large firms are seen to be inflexible, bureaucratic, risk-averse and – owing to their more intensive use of capital – are more likely to reduce employment. However, there is much in these rather optimistic views of the potential of small firms that is questionable. Whilst the small-firm sector has an important part to play in an economy, both in terms of output and employment, the exaggerated claims made on its behalf are often due to a misreading of the evidence.

Birch's work on the American job market proved to be influential in the UK. However, this work is not without its critics (Loveman and Sengenberger, 1990; Keasey and Watson, 1993; Storey, 1994). Birch uses the definition of net job change to quantify employment change whilst a measure such as gross new jobs would give a smaller figure. This can be seen from Figure 5.1.

Over the period 1969–1976 there was significant loss of employment in large manufacturing firms, and net job change was negative. This has the effect of accentuating net new job gains in the small-firm sector. Storey also criticises the Dunn and Bradstreet data on which Birch's work was based as being subject to inaccuracies. For example, a number of firms remained in the database after they had ceased to trade. Storey agrees that small firms have made a disproportionately great contribution to net job generation in the USA but concludes that the magnitude of this contribution has been exaggerated.

Various estimates of the job generation contribution of small firms and self-employment have been made in the UK but again there are problems here in achieving an accurate picture. Whilst firms with a turnover of £46 000 a year have to register for the payment of value-added tax (VAT) and are therefore included in official government statistics, not all firms will reach this level of turnover. Many firms slip through the net for an official count, and the figures for new firms may well be inaccurate. For the 1984 and 1987 Census of Employment, estimates for the number of small firms with less than 25 employees were made, area by area. Information was based on a process of random sampling of small firms, and both the numbers of firms and the number of employees in those firms was open to statistical error. Notwith-standing these caveats, research has shown the significant contribution made to job generation in the UK by the small-firm sector. Daly *et al.* (1991) show that firms employing fewer than 10 people were responsible for the creation of over half a million jobs between 1987 and 1989. This was seen to represent about half of total net growth, even though these firms accounted for less than 20 per cent of total employment. Hakim (1989) showed the significant increase in self-employment that occurred in the 1980s. Over the period 1981 to 1988 Labour Force Survey estimates showed that the number of people who were self-employed in their main job increased from just in excess of 2 million to over 3 million. By June 1994 the figure for self-employment was slightly higher at 3 266 000 than in June 1988, but below the peak of 3 537 000 reached in June 1990 (DTI, 1995).

At the start of 1980 there were approximately 2.4 million businesses in the UK. This number grew, gaining pace in the second half of the 1980s, to reach a peak of 3.8 million at the close of 1989. The recession of the early 1990s saw this total decline to 3.5 million businesses by the close of 1992, rising slightly to 3.6 million by the end of 1993. Barclays Bank reported an increase in business start-ups in 1994, estimating a net increase of 24 000 businesses in the UK for the year (DTI, 1995).

The growth in importance of the small and medium-sized firms registered in the UK in the 1980s was mirrored in Europe. During the 1980s the total of small and medium-sized enterprises (SMEs) in the European Community grew by 25 per cent. At the end of the 1980s there were 3.6 million more European SMEs than at the start of the decade.

By far the greatest number of businesses are small. Micro businesses account for 94 per cent of all businesses. Around 10 million people in the UK work in micro and small businesses; this accounts for over 50 per cent of total non government employment, having risen from 40 per cent in 1979 (DTI, 1995).

TABLE 5.1   Employment in the UK by size of business and industry, 1993 (thousands)

| | | Size (number of employees) | | | |
| | | Micro | Small | Medium | Large |
| | *All* | *(0–9)* | *(10–99)* | *(100–499)* | *(500+)* |
|---|---|---|---|---|---|
| All industries[1] | 20 607 | 5 804 | 4 578 | 2 695 | 7 530 |
| A, B Agriculture and fishing | 441 | 367 | 52 | 11 | 12 |
| C Mining and quarrying | 137 | 11 | 13 | 21 | 92 |
| D Manufacturing | 4 827 | 675 | 1 181 | 1 095 | 1 876 |
| E Energy and water | 242 | 4 | 4 | 5 | 229 |
| F Constructuion | 1 553 | 953 | 303 | 134 | 164 |
| G Wholesale, retail and repairs | 4 246 | 1 262 | 980 | 420 | 1 584 |
| H Hotels and restaurants | 1 264 | 361 | 375 | 114 | 414 |
| I Transport and communication | 1 482 | 294 | 213 | 132 | 844 |
| J Financial intermediation | 1 001 | 95 | 83 | 93 | 730 |
| K Business services | 2 682 | 919 | 676 | 429 | 658 |
| M Education | 307 | 117 | 77 | 63 | 50 |
| N Health and social work | 1 558 | 302 | 436 | 93 | 726 |
| O Other services | 866 | 445 | 187 | 84 | 150 |

[1] Excluding public administration, private households and extra-territorial bodies (sections L, P and Q of SIC92).
*Source*:   DTI, *Small Firms in Britain: Report 1995*, London, HMSO, 1995, p. 56.

A major concern in recent years has been the so called de-industrialisation of the UK economy. This term is often used to denote the fall in absolute terms of employment in the manufacturing sector. Since 1966 the numbers employed in the UK manufacturing sector have fallen considerably. Within this overall decline in employment within the manufacturing sector there has been a redistribution of employment in favour of small firms. Over the period 1980–92 the numbers employed in the manufacturing sector continued to decline, whilst the numbers engaged in manufacturing in enterprises with fewer than 100 employees rose by 100 000. Firms with fewer than 100 employees accounted for 19 per cent of employment in 1980, but by 1992 this figure had risen to 29 per cent. Correspondingly, those manufacturing firms with more than 500 employees saw their share of employment fall from 68 per cent to 52 per cent from 1980 to 1992 (DTI, 1995).

Small and micro firms and self-employment are not evenly represented in all industries.

In manufacturing there are still economies of scale favouring larger firms in a number of sectors. For example, in industries such as food, drink and tobacco and chemicals a few giant firms are dominant. However, in some sectors, such as clothing and furniture manufacture, smaller firms are very strongly represented, and in publishing around half of all jobs are now in micro or small firms. The construction industry has traditionally been a sector where the micro enterprise is the norm. Self-employed craft workers are a common feature of this industry with micro firms accounting for the bulk of jobs in construction. The service sector has long been an important area for small and micro firm employment. The wholesale, retail and repairs sector accounts for in excess of half a million small and micro firms. Growth areas in the 1980s such as financial and business services have a strong small-firm representation, whilst the computer services industry has two-thirds of employment concentrated in firms with less than 100 employees.

Overall, the growth of the small-firm sector has been more rapid in the UK than elsewhere; though this has been achieved from a lower starting point. The European Commission noted in 1994 that the UK had more small firms per head of population than the EC average (DTI, 1995).

## Births and deaths of firms

At any point in time some firms are ending their business lives whilst others are beginning theirs. The total stock of firms at any point in time depends on the relationship between births and deaths. If deaths exceed births then the total stock of firms will be in decline, whilst if births exceed deaths the total stock will rise. The relationship between births and deaths of firms is complex. New firms may come into existence for a variety of positive reasons such as new market opportunities, but equally their existence may be attributable to negative factors such as redundancy. If a large firm in a given locality goes out of business then this has a number of implications. Ex-employees of the firm are now released on to the local labour market so the number of workers seeking employment will rise and the number of potential entrepreneurs will increase.

Whilst in secure employment and earning an acceptable wage, an employee may not consider going into business and exchanging the security of employment for the greater risk of self-employment. As the greater part of the population can be seen to be risk-averse then this is self-evident. However, if the conditions of employment were to deteriorate, then the number of potential entrepreneurs is likely to increase, reaching a maximum if the firm closes down.

Some people will probably never assume the role of entrepreneur, but many who would otherwise prefer not to may take the option of self-employment if the alternative is no employment, or significantly inferior terms and conditions of work to those to which they are accustomed. If a large employer, say in the engineering industry, was to close down, then this might lead to a growth of new small engineering firms in the locality as some of the displaced workers set up a business and recruit former workmates. The new business owner may be prepared to work long hours for little reward, as may his employees who fear that, having lost one job, they may also lose another. This in turn may put pressure on existing engineering firms who may now find their prices being undercut and who in turn may have to shed jobs or even go out of business. This situation will be exacerbated if the new firms have bought second-hand machinery at low prices (perhaps from their old employer whose plant is sold at liquidation) whilst existing firms are still paying for higher debt, incurred through higher machinery costs. Further threats to existing firms may also be experienced if stock from the dead firm is released on to the market at knock-down prices. Many smaller firms may find it difficult to survive a period of reduced demand for their products (even over a relatively short time period, reduced revenue may trigger a liquidity crisis which could tip an otherwise sound company into bankruptcy).

On a more positive note the death of a firm can lead to the opening of market niches formerly catered for by the larger firm which new small firms can successfully fill without displacing existing firms. Equally, new small firms may come into being to service other new small firms. Overall then, the death of a firm or firms can lead to births and/or deaths of other firms and complex patterns may emerge.

In a situation as described, what may well be observed in a local economy is a high degree of turbulence (births and deaths) (Beesley and Hamilton, 1984). Schumpeter (1942) argued that in a dynamic economy one could expect to witness such turbulence as it is evidence of creative destruction. Taking the analogy of a forest, it is to be expected that old dead wood is constantly being felled in order to make way for new dynamic growth. However, in some cases high degrees of turbulence may be evidence not of advance but of decline. This was the case in the Birmingham economy in the early 1980s. New firm growth increased at this time but this was more due to negative than positive factors. As existing firms, particularly in engineering, went out of business, so new ones sprang up. However, many of the problems here were structural and lay at the core of the industry. Ex-employees tended to set up businesses in those industrial sectors which were suffering major problems at a national level, thus leaving themselves with very little likelihood of success. As Storey and Johnson (1987) argue, Birmingham was at this time evidence not of the reborn mythological Phoenix but of the ashes that surrounded it.

## Reasons for the growth of the small-firm sector

There are a number of reasons why the small-firm sector has become increasingly important to the UK economy. As noted, the increasingly uncertain global economic climate has had an impact on large firms. This has caused such firms to take stock of their activities and in many cases to rationalise these. A number of firms had particular problems in the 1970s and early 1980s and this had the effect of conditioning their organisational strategies.

After a period of economic trauma in which a firm has had to reduce its employment levels, perhaps through compulsory redundancies, it will be less willing to commit itself to extra employment and new investment, even when economic circumstances improve. Large firms have sought new strategies to accommodate greater demand without committing themselves to significantly greater resource requirements (see later). One way of achieving this is through subcontracting work. Whilst this has long been an important feature of industries such as the motor industry, its significance here and elsewhere has increased. By subcontracting work to smaller firms a large company can reduce its risks should the economic climate worsen. This in turn has provided new opportunities for small firms.

In many cases large firms have hived off part of their activities through the medium of management buy-outs or buy-ins. In such cases the company may have taken stock of its activities and decided what it feels its main activities are. For example, in the 1980s the paper company Scott Ltd decided that its priority was to manufacture paper products, not to distribute them. As a consequence, it sold its transport fleet to the existing management team (a management buy-out) who proceeded to run this activity as a separate and financially independent entity – a small firm was born. Again, in the 1980s, Jaguar Cars evaluated its activities and decided that as primarily a motor car assembler it should reduce further the number of parts it manufactured in-house. The consequence of this was that it discontinued the manufacture of exhaust systems in-house and encouraged a former employee to set up his own business manufacturing exhaust systems locally and supplying these to the company.

Large Japanese manufacturers have traditionally made extensive use of small firms. In the case of the Japanese motor industry, large car assemblers will deal with large components firms which in turn subcontract to a large number of smaller manufacturers.

As the general level of income and wealth increases, consumer tastes become more sophisticated. In the decades immediately after the Second World War consumers were more prepared to accept undifferentiated products and services, as they had been accustomed to a relatively low material standard of life. As incomes rose, consumers increasingly demanded products which demonstrated some degree of individuality. Piore and Sabel (1984) argue that the increasing selectivity of consumers has been the key element in moving economies away from the technological paradigm of Fordism, based on mass production and consumption. They argue that a new paradigm based on flexibility of products and processes has now developed. This new paradigm of flexible specialisation has meant small batch production of differentiated products and has seen the development of new technology and organisational structures (Martin, 1988). This new paradigm is crucially based on economies of scope, just as mass· production was based on economies of scale. Small firms can operate at an economically viable level under these changed circumstances in a way that was not possible before.

The effects of recession and the rationalisation and death of firms has been an important contributory factor to new firm development. Recession push factors have been overwhelmingly important at certain times and in certain places. Storey (1982) showed that in the 1970s some 20 per cent of owner managers in Cleveland were 'pushed' into setting up their own businesses. Binks and Jennings (1986) argued that the figure for 'pushed' entrepreneurs in Nottingham in the early 1980s was as high as 50 per cent.

Another important factor has been technological advance. New technology has brought about entirely new markets. The development of home computers has meant a significant increase in the manufacture of computer hardware and related software, generating thousands of jobs both directly and indirectly. Small firms have been of crucial importance at the stage of innovation and development. It is notable that in high-tech areas small firms can make an enormous contribution to the development of new technologies such as virtual reality, and can open the frontiers of what can become billion dollar industries. Technological advance has also changed the configuration of industry. Computer aided design (CAD) and computer aided manufacture (CAM) have facilitated the entry of new small firms into areas which either previously did not exist or were dominated by larger firms.

The small firm has also featured as a cornerstone of the ideological advance of the enterprise economy. Governments in the 1980s and 1990s have promoted the virtues of the small-firm sector and have designed economic packages which have been intended to increase the size and strength of this sector. New enterprise has been championed through the provision of financial asistance, help and advice.

## Government and the small-firm sector

Governments since 1979 have stressed that their main contribution 'to improving the performance and productivity of business is the creation of a stable economic environment' (DTI, 1995, p. 12). At the heart of this policy is the government's intention to keep inflation at a low and stable level. In addition to this overall policy stance, government has also introduced a raft of measures which directly affect the small-firm sector. With regard to taxation, the rate of corporation tax for small firms has been reduced in recent years from 42 per cent to 25 per cent whilst the profit limit for this rate has been raised to £300 000. Simplified tax accounts and rules for small firms and the self-employed have also been introduced. The Government also argues that it has cut unnecessary red tape affecting small firms, through the introduction of legislation such as the Deregulation and Contracting Out Act of 1994. Financial assistance has been provided by means of such devices as the Small Firms Guarantee Scheme, with some 43 000 loans, worth £1.4 billion, being guaranteed since the scheme began in 1981 (DTI, 1995). The Enterprise Investment Scheme which replaced the earlier Business Expansion Scheme, exists to help small companies which are not quoted on the stock exchange to raise equity finance and to bring such firms together with potential investors – 'business angels'. Tax incentives are offered to outside investors to encourage them to invest in companies. Assistance based on geographical location is also available to small firms. Firms with fewer than 25 employees based in Development Areas (see Chapter 7) can apply for Regional Enterprise Grants.

Another feature of the government's programme is the provision of advice, information and training. A recent innovation which is currently being developed is the Business Links network. When completed it is intended that every business in England will have access to a Business Link (DTI, 1995). The Business Link is a service which provides a single focal point delivering an extensive range of support and assistance. Business Links are partnerships between Training and Enterprise Councils (TECs), Local Authorities, Enterprise Agencies, Chambers of Commerce and other agencies such as universities. A new initiative introduced by the TECs and Business Links entitled Skills for Small Businesses is intended to train key personnel in firms with less than 50 workers. This scheme is intended to cover some 24 000 workers at a cost of £63 million over three years.

### Evaluating government policies

In evaluating government or public policy towards small firms we first of all have to determine what its intentions are. Storey argues that 'public policy towards small firms has been mainly concerned with two issues: the creation of employment in smaller enterprises and the problems which smaller enterprises experience in obtaining access to finance' (Storey, 1994, p. 253).

As we have seen, governments in office since 1979 have delivered a political rhetoric which takes its economic principles from the New Right. The New Right is strongly identified with the promotion of a free market. According to such economic liberals the only condition *necessary* to justify intervention in the workings of the market is market failure. However, this is not a *sufficient* condition, for additionally it must be demonstrated that intervention leads to a welfare gain for society which exceeds any bureaucratic costs incurred. Storey (1994) argues that it may be seen to be a contradiction that the Government continues to promote small-firm policies yet at the same time it remains committed to the free market. Furthermore, he notes that the Government rarely justifies such policies on the grounds of market failure. Indeed, as Storey continues to argue:

> Subsidies by government to those wishing to establish their own firm results in the increased number of new firms and leads to increased employment in the small-firm sector. But subsidies to one group have to be raised by increased taxes or reduced reliefs to other groups, and it has never been shown that the *net* effect of subsidising small firms is to create more wealth in the community. In essence the argument must always return to the basic issue that, if there are economic factors which currently favour the small firm, these would be exploited by that sector *without* the assistance of government (Storey, 1982, in Storey, 1994, p. 255).

The costs and benefits of intervention in the economy by the government on behalf of the small-firm sector have never been carefully analysed. This is the case in the UK and in Europe more generally. A number of arguments for small-firm assistance have however, been advanced. Small firms are increasingly seen as major job creators. Consequently, attempts to increase new firm formation and the promotion of existing small firms can be viewed as contributing to job growth. However, if small-firm policies, by intervening in the market, can be seen to lead to job loss in larger firms, then this offsets partially, or wholly, any job gains in small firms. The welfare case here, then, becomes clouded. This is compounded if one considers research which argues that jobs in small firms may not be equivalent to jobs in large firms. Many people are 'pushed' into small-firm ownership, and the terms and conditions of workers in small firms may well be inferior to those in larger firms.

> For many individuals, it is unclear whether small-firm ownership and/or employment are more desirable alternatives to large firm employment: accident rates are considerably higher in small firms, employment is less secure and not as well paid, and there are usually less career advancement opportunities. Thus, the view taken of the move towards a greater emphasis on small-firm production might depend where the observer stands in the economic order (Keasey and Watson, 1993, p. 8).

In defence of small-firm assistance it is also argued that they face greater costs in dealing with government regulations – *compliance costs*. Complying with taxation and other legislative requirements imposes greater costs on small firms as a percentage of turnover than on large firms. This means that without compensating assistance small firms are at a disadvantage. As we saw in the orthodox model of competition, taxation moves an economy further from Pareto efficiency, and compensating action may be justified to offset this – the government intervenes on the *second best* principle. However, we then enter into very difficult territory once again. Should small firms be exempt from some regulations – a relaxation of red tape? Which regulations should they be exempt from and what are the wider social ramifications of this? Government policy has led to a relaxation of regulations for small firms but the specifics of this have not been determined after extensive cost-benefit assessments. In sum, there has never been, nor is there now, a cohesive and fully evaluated policy with respect to the small-firm sector.

> There has been no UK White Paper about the objectives and targets of public policy towards SMEs. Instead, policies have been introduced on a piecemeal basis, often in response to pressure from small-firm lobby organisations and to changes in the macroeconomy. It is therefore necessary to guess at the objectives of policy, rather than being able to view each initiative as clearly fitting into an overall conceptual framework (Storey, 1994, p. 257).

### Small-firm growth in the regions

A number of studies have analysed the performance of the small-firm sector in specific localities. Storey undertook follow-up research into the Cleveland economy in an attempt to compare experience in the 1980s with that in the 1970s (Storey and Strange, 1993). Estimates showed that there had been a significant increase in new firm formation in the later period. This can be interpreted as further development of an enterprise economy. However, a careful audit of the pluses and minuses leads to reservations in the proclamation of unqualified success. Amongst the positive factors it is noted that there has been greater take-up of public assistance for small firms and greater satisfaction with the providers of this assistance. Provision of premises was greatly improved. Furthermore, far more female entrepreneurs were represented. On the debit side, the new firms were largely concentrated in areas such as hairdressing and car breaking and repair activities. New small firms were smaller on average than in the 1980s. More new firm start-ups were due to the 'push' factor of unemployment.

One of the particularly concerning features of this study is the lack of export-base small firms in the Cleveland area. Export-base firms are those firms which sell their products or services outside the region (Fothergill and Gudgin, 1982). This is an important feature as income is then brought into the region through sales outside. If firms are trading locally, particularly in already saturated areas such as hairdressing and car-related activities, then the income and wealth of the area is less likely to grow. Indeed, in sectors such as hairdressing or window cleaning with a finite local demand, the birth of new firms is likely to lead to the death of existing firms and greater turbulence. As Storey and Strange conclude:

> Finally, the survey suggests that the new firms established in the 1980s, although more numerous, are less likely to achieve significant growth than the new firms established during the 1970s. Many of the 1980s' firms appear to have been established primarily for the lifestyle benefits which business ownership provides. For almost half of new-firm founders the prime lifestyle benefit is that of having a job at all (Storey and Strange, 1993, p. 68).

Mason (1988) compares two panels of firms: one group founded between 1976 and 1979, and another group founded between 1980 and 1985. In each case the locality is south Hampshire. Whilst growth in new-firm formation was registered for the second time period, a key feature of this study is the much greater incidence of negative factors contributing to new-firm formation in the later group. Furthermore, Mason 'found no evidence that government measures to promote small businesses had been significant in the rise in new firm formation' (C. Mason, 1988, p. 38). The most positive feature of government policy found in the promotion of firm start ups was the provision of small factory workshops through the Small Workshops Scheme. On balance Mason feels that it is 'plausible to suggest that the post-1979 cohort will exhibit modest growth and a high failure rate' (Mason, 1988, p. 38).

A study of a small industrial town in the East Midlands showed that there had been a significant increase in the number of small firms in the 1980s (Baker, 1993a). However, in common with the previous cases, push factors were a major contributory factor to new-firm formation. The reasons for small-firm formation differed according to the sector under consideration. Push factors were of greatest importance in the textiles and clothing sector, whilst business opportunities featured prominently in the engineering industry. Small firms in engineering were in particular gaining work from the motor industry and the defence and aerospace sectors. Whilst many firms seemed to be buoyant in 1989, at the time of the survey the power asymmetry between the small firms and large firms for which they were undertaking subcontract work was evident across all industrial sectors. Small firms felt the necessity to be extremely flexible in order to meet their customer's requirements and, in the case of one company working for a major car manufacturer, this meant the cancellation of all holiday leave over a recent Christmas period (Baker, 1993a). A major contributory factor to small-firm growth in this area was the increased provision of small-firm premises by local government. This again bears out the increased public sector provision and facilitation of premises registered in the other studies. Overall, it is felt that the growth in the small-firm sector was a reflection of large-firm restructuring, especially in engineering, whilst in the textiles and clothing sector the growth was strongly related to the failure of medium sized and large firms (Baker, 1993b). Prospects for the future in textiles and clothing firms seemed to be bleak, judging by the response of firm owners, whilst in engineering small-firm futures depended largely on the strategy and decisions for future sourcing of large firms.

## Small firms and local economic policy

Alfred Marshall, writing in the nineteenth century (1892), noted the dynamic qualities of agglomerations of small firms producing for the same industry. Taking examples from the Sheffield Steel Industry and the Lancashire Cotton

Industry he showed that such areas develop an 'industrial atmosphere' which is conducive to innovation and economic success. The term used to describe such areas is *industrial districts*. More recent writers have elaborated upon Marshall's work and have undertaken research into existing industrial districts. Claims for the existence of industrial districts have been made for many parts of the world and include areas of northern and central Italy, Baden Wurttemburg in Germany and Silicon Valley in the USA. It is generally argued that industrial districts are more than simply economic phenomena. In order for such areas to flourish, complex networking arrangements develop and social and economic relationships are intertwined (Malecki, 1991). Granovetter (1985) notes that industrial districts in areas such as Italy exhibit 'embeddedness', developing complex socio-economic patterns. Risk is often shared between firms and a variety of private and public sector organisations, and ideas spread rapidly and are diffused widely. In Italy the family is a very important feature of small firms in industrial districts, giving extra flexibility to the operations of such firms. It is possible to identify a number of features which are common to industrial districts; these include:

- a very high proportion of small or very small firms;
- clustering of firms in a geographical location;
- all firms are engaged at various stages of production of a specific product;
- dense networks of a social and economic nature;
- institutional support, embracing such areas as R&D, training, finance, information, etc.;
- intense specialisation of small firms;
- blend of competition and co-operation between firms;
- rapid diffusion of new ideas;
- adaptability and flexibility (Baker, 1995, p. 10).

In the development of industrial districts in Italy the state has performed an important role. For example, regional government in the Emilia-Romagna area of Italy has been of central importance in promoting small business enterprise. Centralised provision of business services and information has been provided and tailored to the needs of individual sectors. For example, a ceramics centre was established in the Sassuolo area, whilst one for footwear was set up in San Mauro Pascoli. Facilities for the metal/engineering industry have been provided in Bologna whilst the clothing industry is catered for in Carpi (Capecchi, 1990). The Italian state also assists small firms through advantageous tax arrangements (Magatti, 1993), low interest loans and grants for technologically advanced equipment (Lazerson, 1993). There are strong links and extensive co-operation between local authorities, trade unions and voluntary associations in an effort to maintain high standards and avoid destructive forms of competition, such as relentless price competition which undermines labour standards and encourages tax evasion. As Lazerson notes in the case of the clothing industry in Modena: 'The individual artisanal associations, especially the National Confederation of Artisans (CNA), voluntarily police the various labour and tax regulations because they believe that artisans should compete in terms of quality and efficient production, not through lower labour standards' (Lazerson, 1993, p. 214).

This is not to say that the industrial districts of Italy are examples of perfection. A number of authors have pointed to examples of labour exploitation which exist in such areas (F. Murray, 1987; Amin and Robins, 1990). However, there are a number of positive features in these areas such as relatively high incomes, investment in new machinery and high quality products, which stem from an attempt to combine co-operation with competition, whilst maintaining standards in labour markets. Nonetheless, recent developments are leading to problems. The progress of industrial districts after the Second World War in areas such as Emilia-Romagna owed much to the local state which was under the direction of the Communist and Socialist parties. These parties are now much more divided and may no longer have control of the regional government. Furthermore, new international pressures have introduced tensions into local policy. As international competition intensifies, some firms have switched production to low labour cost countries and concentration of industry has increased through mergers and acquisition (Amin, 1994b; Cooke and Morgan, 1994). The future of established industrial districts is clouded by uncertainty.

Many academics sought examples of industrial districts in the UK economy in the 1980s. Contendors such as Hertfordshire and Cambridge were advanced, but studies of these areas have been critical (Baker, 1995). In the case of Cambridge, Crang and Martin (1991) note the evidence of dualism in the local labour market, with a polarisation of incomes at the top and bottom ends of the labour market. Garnsey and Cannon-Brookes (1993) note the lack of local networking between Cambridge firms, whilst Henry (1992) finds evidence that Hertfordshire has industrial districts to be inconclusive.

The model of industrial districts as demonstrated in Italy in the 1970s and 1980s does offer some instructive lessons to policy-makers. The example of strong bonds of continuity, trust and co-operation evident in such districts can be seen to be positive features which transcend pure market relationships. However, market forces can undermine such positive features, as an unregulated labour market tumbles downwards in pursuit of the lowest common denominator. Wages may be cut, work intensified and hours increased. The necessity of establishing strong labour standards which cannot be undermined by the 'rogue' employer (Amin, 1994b) is evident if co-operation is to be maintained. 'such co-operation depends in turn on the establishment of rules limiting certain forms of competition such as sweated wages and conditions, as well as on collective institutions for the supply of non market inputs such as technological information or trained labour' (Hirst and Zeitlin, 1992, p. 76).

Whilst at the national level in the UK the emphasis has been on competition, at the local level attempts have been made to harness co-operation, collective provision and the promotion of 'labour friendly' practices and technology.

A number of local authorities in the UK have attempted to redress the increase in dualism in labour markets 'by using their own direct presence in the labour market, and their purchasing and property-holding power to establish wages and conditions that set standards within their local labour markets' [R. Murray, 1991, p. 52]. Furthermore, local authorities such as Sheffield City Council and the Greater London Council made attempts in the 1980s to develop production for social needs. The Greater London Enterprise Board, through its technology subsidiary, was active 'in developing human-centred technology – that is to say technology which builds on human skill rather than devaluing it' [Murray, 1991, p. 37] (Baker, 1995, p. 23).

It has been increasingly difficult for local government to carry out independent initiatives at the local level due to the accretion of power by central government. The emphasis now is on partnership and as such partnerships have to include the private sector and/or public bodies such as the TECs which are subject to the aegis of the private sector, there is much pressure to conform to the prevailing market ideology. Some schemes which have promoted a collective and co-operative approach within a market framework, include the Nottinghamshire Work and Technology Programme, implemented in May 1992 (Totterdill, 1992). This programme, launched by Nottinghamshire County Council and two local Training and Enterprise Councils (TECs), is intended to improve design skills, training and new production methods amongst small firms. However, it is no longer possible for local authorities to implement a comprehensive economic strategy of the form attempted in the 1980s by the now defunct Greater London Council. The problems encountered by the GLC in delivering an economic programme which ran counter to the economic orthodoxy of the Conservative Government were insurmountable. The GLC had major difficulties due to the scale of the problems it was dealing with, and these 'were then compounded by the attempts to swim against a powerful ideological tide of free market, non interventionism emanating from a determined central government with a large majority and, finally, the dissolution and emasculation of local authorities by the same government' (Curran and Blackburn, 1994, p. 23).

In the absence of strong legislative protection and enforcement of standards, workers in small firms are in a particularly vulnerable position. By subcontracting and outsourcing, large firms can transfer risks to small firms. This may result in small-firm owners exploiting both themselves and their workforce. Power continues to reside with large firms, and many small firms are left with the crumbs that fall from the table (Rainnie, 1993). Increasingly, small firms are likely to find themselves tied into dependency relationships which favour the large firm (Rainnie, 1991).

## Conclusions

There has been a clear increase in the importance of the small-firm sector and self-employment in the last two decades. However, government policy in this area seems to be unfocused. In general it would appear that the ideological commitment to the small firm overrides a true evaluation of policies which impact on firms of all sizes. If policies are not properly evaluated and their total impact accurately assessed then resources may be wasted and society's welfare may be damaged. In addition to its direct small-firm policies the government has been instrumental in promoting small-firm growth through its privatisation policies and its insistence that local authorities should tender out contracts for a variety of services such as cleaning and refuse disposal. Furthermore, deregulation of services such as public transport has also provided new opportunities for firms. Yet again the benefits provided by such policies are controversial and the contribution to overall welfare is disputable.

Overall, it is difficult to conclude that the growth in importance of the small-firm sector is evidence of a dynamic, thriving, enterprise economy. The issues underlying the development of the small-firm sector are complex and a great many negative as well as positive factors have played a part. There is no doubt that many people have prospered through small-firm growth but equally many have lost. It is necessary to carefully evaluate the role and contribution of the small firm before it can be stated that present trends have been to the benefit of society as a whole.

# CHAPTER 6

# Labour Markets

In the neo-classical world of perfect competition, labour is homogeneous and moves freely between jobs. In such circumstances the market for labour is indistinguishable from the market for any commodity. Wage levels are determined according to the forces of supply and demand and no involuntary unemployment exists as markets clear at prevailing wage rates. There is no need for government intervention as market forces establish equilibrium across all labour markets. However, once the assumption of perfect competition is relaxed, the situation becomes much more complex.

As Keynes pointed out in the *General Theory* (1936), economies can become 'stuck', resulting in high and persisting levels of unemployment. It was evident from the high levels of unemployment in the 1920s and 1930s that market forces were not clearing labour markets and the neo-classical policy prescription of reducing wages further in an attempt to price people into work was deepening the economic trough. During the Second World War considerable government intervention in the economy was deemed necessary to mobilise the country's resources for the war effort. During the Second World War the Ministry of Labour took direct responsibility for the labour market and this control over labour continued into the postwar period. Labour and Conservative governments introduced taxes and subsidies which were deliberately structured to shape the labour market and achieve a geographical dispersion of employment (see Chapter 7).

In the 1960s and 1970s the trend towards corporatism saw the continued subversion of market forces. It was felt that imperfections in capital and goods markets and high transactions costs (see Chapter 2) prevented the efficient operation of the labour market. Governments of both left and right felt that there were efficiency gains to be achieved from intervening directly in the labour market at all levels. This is exemplified in the founding of the National Economic Development Council in 1961 (consisting of the TUC, the CBI and the Government) which saw a further move in the direction of corporatism. The tripartite NEDC, bringing employers' and employees' representatives together with government in a planning forum, could be seen as an attempt to further insulate the economy from the full force of the market.

However, in recent years, in line with the general shift towards a greater reliance on market forces in the UK economy, labour markets have been subject to careful scrutiny and radical reform. According to Deakin and Wilkinson:

> Since 1979 government policy in Britain has been aimed at 'removing obstacles to the effective working of markets in general and of the labour market in particular' (Department of Employment, 1985). This policy of 'deregulation' has led to major changes in labour law and social security, in the name of removing rigidities and encouraging greater flexibility of wages and employment (Deakin and Wilkinson, 1991, p. 125).

The Government has promoted substantial change in many areas affecting labour markets since 1979, in the name of greater economic efficiency. Economies are constantly changing as dynamic forces (many of which are exogenous) impinge upon them. In what follows changes in labour markets generated by government policies and other factors are considered.

## The changing shape of the UK labour market

In the postwar period high levels of employment in the West became the accepted norm. The UK Government pledged itself in 1944 in the White Paper on Employment Policy to 'maintain a high and stable level of employment' on the cessation of hostilities. At the time it was envisaged that this would mean a figure of around 3 per cent unemployment, but in reality up until the 1970s the average national figure was well below this. Full employment came to be recognised as being a level of unemployment of around 2 per cent consistent with the fact that some unemployment (frictional unemployment) was inevitable as people changed jobs and that a small residual level of involuntary unemployment was unavoidable.

The population had become accustomed to full employment in the postwar years, and the electoral importance of maintaining this position can be seen by the policy of the Conservative Government at the beginning of the 1970s. In December of 1970 unemployment was below 600 000 or 2.6 per cent, but by the summer of 1971 it was approaching 800 000 or 3.5 per cent (Stewart, 1977). There was a clear danger that unemployment was about to reach its highest total since the war. This led the government to introduce a reflationary budget on 19 July 1971. Whilst unemployment did in fact fall after this, the underlying problems continued and unemployment remained significantly higher that in earlier periods, with the watershed figure of one million being reached by the mid-1970s.

In the 1980s the country became accustomed to levels of unemployment which were unimaginable in the 1960s. Double-digit figures for unemployment, something not experienced since the interwar years of depression, became commonplace in the 1980s. In March 1994 unemployment was

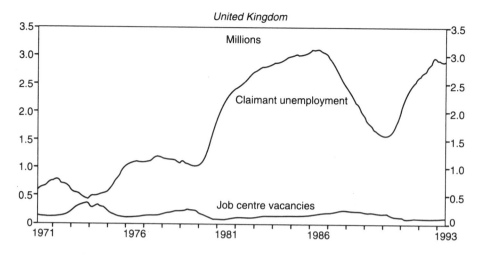

1  Seasonally adjusted unemployment (claimants aged 18 and over)
2  About one third of all vacancies are listed by job centres
3  Data before 1980 are not consistent with current coverage

*Source:*   HMSO, *Social Trends*, 24, 1994c.

**FIGURE 6.1   Claimant unemployment and job centre vacancies**


2 722 600, around 9.7 per cent of the workforce, and this was the lowest rate since June 1992. Unemployment continued to fall but was still 2 327 900 in April 1995.

Unemployment has affected some groups and areas more than others. In regions which were noted for their heavy concentration on traditional manufacturing employment the decline of these industries has left many workers (particularly male workers) without employment and with very few alternative prospects. Such workers have joined the ranks of the growing numbers of long-term unemployed (those out of work for more than one year). Inner-city areas have been particularly badly affected as traditional employment has evaporated, leaving little hope for the population that remains. Young people have also been particularly hard hit by unemployment, with this group constantly registering levels of unemployment well above the average (see Table 6.1).

The ethnic composition of unemployment is another significant factor. Pakistani/Bangladeshi and black workers experience particularly high levels of unemployment and, whilst the stereotype of the Asian self-employed worker is often portrayed, the high levels of self-employment in such communities are often due to lack of employment opportunities rather than choice (see Figure 6.2).

**TABLE 6.1   Unemployment rates[1] in the United Kingdom: by sex and age**

| Males | 16–19 | 20–29 | 30–39 | 40–49 | 50–64 | 65 and over | All males aged 16 and over |
|---|---|---|---|---|---|---|---|
| 1986 | 21.8 | 15.7 | 9.4 | 7.8 | 9.3 | 9.3 | 11.7 |
| 1991 | 16.5 | 12.3 | 7.8 | 5.8 | 8.4 | 5.9 | 9.2 |
| 1992 | 18.7 | 15.3 | 10.4 | 7.8 | 10.4 | 4.9 | 11.5 |
| 1993 | 22.0 | 16.4 | 10.3 | 8.8 | 11.9 | 4.6 | 12.4 |

| Females | 16–19 | 20–29 | 30–39 | 40–49 | 50–59 | 60 and over | All females aged 16 and over |
|---|---|---|---|---|---|---|---|
| 1986 | 19.8 | 14.4 | 10.1 | 6.7 | 6.1 | 5.1 | 10.7 |
| 1991 | 13.2 | 9.4 | 6.9 | 4.9 | 5.1 | 4.4 | 7.2 |
| 1992 | 13.8 | 9.4 | 7.2 | 5.0 | 5.0 | 3.1 | 7.2 |
| 1993 | 16.0 | 10.2 | 7.0 | 4.7 | 5.6 | 3.9 | 7.5 |

*Note:* [1] Unemployment based on the ILO definition as a percentage of all economically active. At Spring each year
*Source:*   Based on data from HMSO, *Social Trends*, 24, 1994c.

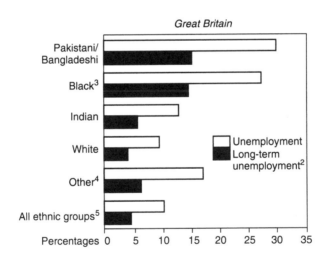

1   Unemployed based on the ILO definition as a percentage of all economically active.
2   Claimant unemployed for more than 52 weeks.
3   Includes Caribbean, African and other black people of non-mixed origin.
4   Includes Chinese, other ethnic minority groups of non-mixed origin, and people of mixed origin.
5   Includes ethnic group not stated.

*Source:*   HMSO, *Social Trends*, 24, 1994c.

**FIGURE 6.2   Unemployment rates[1]: by ethnic group, spring 1993**

**TABLE 6.2  Employees in employment in Great Britain**

| GREAT BRITAIN | All industries and services (0-9) | | Manufacturing industries (2-4) | | Production industries (1-4) | | Production and construction industries (1-5)* | | Service industries (6-9)* | |
|---|---|---|---|---|---|---|---|---|---|---|
| SIC 1980 Divisions of classes | All employees | Seasonally adjusted | All employees | Seasonally adjusted | All employees | Seasonally adjusted | All employees | Seasonally adjusted | All employees | Seasonally adjusted |
| 1974 June | 22 297 | 22 296 | 7 722 | 7 722 | 8 429 | 8 429 | 9 652 | 9 652 | 12 240 | 12 240 |
| 1975 June | 22 213 | 22 209 | 7 351 | 7 351 | 8 069 | 8 069 | 9 276 | 9 276 | 12 545 | 12 545 |
| 1976 June | 22 048 | 22 039 | 7 118 | 7 118 | 7 830 | 7 830 | 9 033 | 9 033 | 12 624 | 12 624 |
| 1977 June | 22 126 | 22 124 | 7 172 | 7 172 | 7 880 | 7 880 | 9 048 | 9 048 | 12 698 | 12 698 |
| 1978 June | 22 273 | 22 246 | 7 138 | 7 143 | 7 845 | 7 850 | 9 006 | 9 007 | 12 895 | 12 859 |
| 1979 June | 22 638 | 22 611 | 7 107 | 7 113 | 7 819 | 7 825 | 9 020 | 9 022 | 13 260 | 13 222 |
| 1980 June | 22 458 | 22 432 | 6 801 | 6 808 | 7 517 | 7 524 | 8 723 | 8 727 | 13 384 | 13 345 |
| 1981 June | 21 386 | 21 362 | 6 099 | 6 107 | 6 798 | 6 807 | 7 900 | 7 907 | 13 142 | 13 102 |
| 1982 June | 20 916 | 20 896 | 5 751 | 5 761 | 6 422 | 6 432 | 7 460 | 7 470 | 13 117 | 13 078 |
| 1983 June | 20 572 | 20 557 | 5 418 | 5 431 | 6 057 | 6 070 | 7 072 | 7 087 | 13 169 | 13 130 |
| 1984 June | 20 741 | 20 731 | 5 302 | 5 316 | 5 909 | 5 923 | 6 919 | 6 936 | 13 503 | 13 465 |
| 1985 June | 20 920 | 20 910 | 5 254 | 5 269 | 5 836 | 5 851 | 6 830 | 6 848 | 13 769 | 13 731 |
| 1986 June | 20 886 | 20 876 | 5 122 | 5 138 | 5 658 | 5 673 | 6 622 | 6 639 | 13 954 | 13 918 |
| 1987 June | 21 080 | 21 081 | 5 049 | 5 068 | 5 548 | 5 567 | 6 531 | 6 550 | 14 247 | 14 220 |
| 1988 June | 21 740 | 21 748 | 5 089 | 5 109 | 5 566 | 5 587 | 6 587 | 6 606 | 14 860 | 14 841 |
| 1989 June | 22 134 | 22 143 | 5 080 | 5 101 | 5 537 | 5 558 | 6 594 | 6 613 | 15 261 | 15 242 |
| 1990 June | 22 380 | 22 373 | 4 994 | 5 018 | 5 434 | 5 461 | 6 494 | 6 519 | 15 609 | 15 573 |
| 1991 June | 21 719 | 21 677 | 4 599 | 4 614 | 5 029 | 5 046 | 5 994 | 6 011 | 15 457 | 15 395 |

| Year | Month | | | | | | | | | | |
|---|---|---|---|---|---|---|---|---|---|---|---|
| 1992 | June | 21 395 | 21 359 | 4 412 | 4 419 | 4 806 | 4 815 | 5 723 | 5 737 | 15 412 | 15 361 |
| 1992 | Nov | 21 055 | 21 006 | 4 308 | 4 282 | 4 692 | 4 666 | 5 552 | 5 538 | 15 259 | 15 216 |
| 1993 | Dec | | | 4 274 | 4 267 | 4 653 | 4 645 | | | | |
| | Jan | | | 4 245 | 4 269 | 4 622 | 4 644 | | | | |
| | Feb | | | 4 238 | 4 265 | 4 611 | 4 636 | | | | |
| | Mar | 20 936 | 21 004 | 4 243 | 4 270 | 4 611 | 4 637 | 5 480 | 5 512 | 15 211 | 15 236 |
| | Apr | | | 4 235 | 4 265 | 4 596 | 4 627 | | | | |
| | May | | | 4 234 | 4 263 | 4 587 | 4 618 | | | | |
| | June | 21 082 | 21 058 | 4 269 | 4 277 | 4 615 | 4 624 | 5 476 | 5 492 | 15 349 | 15 308 |
| | July | | | 4 294 | 4 279 | 4 639 | 4 625 | | | | |
| | Aug | | | 4 302 | 4 274 | 4 644 | 4 615 | | | | |
| | Sep | 21 124 | 21 128 | 4 293 | 4 266 | 4 630 | 4 602 | 5 502 | 5 468 | 15 349 | 15 409 |
| | Oct | | | 4 300 | 4 278 | 4 636 | 4 613 | | | | |
| | Nov | | | 4 300 | 4 276 | 4 633 | 4 608 | | | | |
| | Dec | 21 130 | 21 084 | 4 256 | 4 252 | 4 583 | 4 578 | 5 453 | 5 443 | 15 408 | 15 393 |
| 1994 | Jan | | | 4 229 | 4 250 | 4 555 | 4 574 | | | | |
| | Feb | | | 4 231 | 4 249 | 4 554 | 4 571 | | | | |
| | Mar | 20 938 | 21 005 | 4 216 | 4 242 | 4 533 | 4 559 | 5 392 | 5 424 | 15 309 | 15 334 |
| | Apr | | | 4 215 | 4 241 | 4 530 | 4 555 | | | | |
| | May | | | 4 217 | 4 238 | 4 527 | 4 549 | | | | |
| | June | 21 011 | 20 993 | 4 227 | 4 233 | 4 534 | 4 542 | 5 398 | 5 413 | 15 366 | 15 332 |
| | July | | | 4 246 | 4 232 | 4 551 | 4 538 | | | | |
| | Aug | | | 4 267 | 4 239 | 4 572 | 4 543 | | | | |
| | Sep | 21 115R | 21 114R | 4 263 | 4 238 | 4 562 | 4 536 | 5 455 | 5 421 | 15 394R | 15 448R |
| | Oct | | | 4 255 | 4 235 | 4 552 | 4 530 | | | | |
| | Nov | | | 4 273 | 4 252 | 4 567 | 4 545 | | | | |
| | Dec R | 21 204 | 21 145 | 4 271 | 4 267 | 4 562 | 4 557 | 5 432 | 5 420 | 15 538R | 15 481R |
| 1995 | Jan | | | 4 253 | 4 274 | 4 542 | 4 562 | | | | |
| | Feb | | | 4 259 | 4 278 | 4 546 | 4 564 | | | | |
| | Mar | 21 045 | 21 134 | 4 256 | 4 282 | 4 540 | 4 566 | 5 383 | 5 416 | 15 429 | 15 474 |

*Source: Employment Gazette, May 1993, July 1995.*

In a report entitled *Black and Betrayed*, published in October 1995, the TUC argued that unemployment among ethnic minority workers was twice that amongst white workers. Unemployed black people were also seen to be more likely to be long-term unemployed than whites, and to have less success in gaining a job after taking part in a training scheme.

As economies develop, the balance of sectoral employment shifts. As the UK economy industrialised, the primary sector became a less important contributor to employment as the secondary sector grew. In turn, as the UK economy continued to develop, the secondary sector declined in importance relative to the tertiary sector. However, manufacturing employment was continuing to grow in the UK up until 1966. Over the period June 1979 to March 1995 employment in the manufacturing sector fell from 7 107 000 to 4 256 000, whilst over the same period employment in the service sector rose from 13 260 000 to 15 429 000 (see Table 6.2).

Women have come to constitute a quantitatively more important element of the labour force, with a growth in female participation rates since the end of the 1970s. In 1979 the total for male employment exceeded that for females by some 45 per cent – 13.1 million relative to 9.4 million. By 1993 the balance between these two groups was roughly equal, with both sexes registering employment totals of over 10 million. Much of this growth in female employment has been due to the expansion of part-time work. In 1993 some 45 per cent of all female employees worked part-time, compared to only 6.5 per cent of all male employees. The overall growth in importance of part-time work can be seen in Table 6.3.

TABLE 6.3    Full and part-time[1] employment in the United Kingdom[2]: by sex (in thousands)

|  | 1984 | 1985 | 1986 | 1987 | 1988 | 1989 | 1990 | 1991 | 1992 | 1993 |
|---|---|---|---|---|---|---|---|---|---|---|
| **Males** | | | | | | | | | | |
| Full-time | 13 240 | 13 336 | 13 430 | 13 472 | 13 881 | 14 071 | 14 109 | 13 686 | 13 141 | 12 769 |
| Part-time | 570 | 575 | 647 | 750 | 801 | 734 | 789 | 799 | 885 | 886 |
| **Females** | | | | | | | | | | |
| Full-time | 5 422 | 5 503 | 5 662 | 5 795 | 6 069 | 6 336 | 6 479 | 6 350 | 6 244 | 6 165 |
| Part-time | 4 343 | 4 457 | 4 566 | 4 696 | 4 808 | 4 907 | 4 928 | 4 933 | 5 081 | 5 045 |

*Note:*    [1] Full-time is based on respondents self-assessment. Excludes those who do not state whether they were full or part-time.
[2] At Spring each year. Includes employees, self-employed, those on government training schemes and unpaid family workers.
*Source:*    Based on data from HMSO, *Social Trends*, 24, 1994c.

However, despite the growth in importance of female employment, gender segregation in the workplace remains in evidence. Many jobs are still done predominantly by men whilst others are done by women. Women predominate in education, retailing and medical services, and the only manufacturing sector in which women are in the majority is clothing. Whilst women are concentrated in clerical and administrative work they are outnumbered by men in senior positions in professional, technical and managerial occupations. The Equal Opportunities Commission (1995) argues that this job segregation can result in discrimination, most notably in recruitment, promotion and pay levels. Furthermore, women are paid less when working with other women, whilst men are paid more if working with other men (EOC, 1995).

As employers have become increasingly cost-conscious in recent years and have sought ways of equating labour hours needed with those paid for in ever more precise fashion, then the attractions of part-time employment for employers have grown. Many part-time jobs are very poorly paid and are relatively insecure. Furthermore, part-time workers have not been given the benefits – such as sickness benefits and holiday pay – available to their full-time colleagues. Nonetheless, it is argued that most part-time workers choose this form of employment. However, a survey conducted by the Department of Employment showed that whilst in total in 1993 only 15 per cent of all part-time workers chose this option because they could not find full-time work, this figure rose to 29 per cent for male part-time workers (HMSO, *Social Trends*, 1994).

An Institute of Manpower Studies report showed that over the period June 1978 to June 1989 UK self-employment rose from 1.84 million to 3.18 million, or from 7.5 per cent to 12.2 per cent of the workforce. However, over this same period only two European countries, Belgium and Italy, registered a significant rise in self-employment, whilst in France and Germany growth was insignificant.

Various attempts to theorise developments in labour markets were made in the 1980s with the work of Atkinson from Sussex University holding much sway in management circles. It is argued that changing economic circumstances have dictated a need for new labour policies for firms. The deep recession of the late 1970s early 1980s and falling UK world competitiveness promoted a need for companies to reduce their unit labour costs. UK firms engaged in job cutting, which required expensive redundancy settlements to be made. The experience of recession in the 1970s and 1980s made firms more pessimistic and less certain about future market conditions. Furthermore, new customised production lines made possible by new technology, demands rapid response from firms. These factors, allied to a continued pressure for reduction of basic hours worked in firms, have led firms to pay close attention to their manpower needs.

Atkinson, researching for the Institute of Manpower Studies, proposed a model which attempts to describe and account for the new developments in manpower policy. This work, whilst having some similarities with earlier dual labour market theories (Doeringer and Piore, 1971), gives a clear outline of the possible labour market strategies open to firms. These strategies are shown in Figure 6.3.

In Atkinson's model, flexibility is broken down into three key types (J. Atkinson, 1984):

### A.  Functional flexibility

This describes the requirement for a smooth redeployment of workers from one set of tasks to another. In the past, some workers operated in strict demarcation zones and would only carry out tasks which were included in a narrowly defined job description. Now, workers are expected to have a much broader work remit and this is reflected in some cases by generic titles such as engineer, which replace a range of more specialist job descriptions, each carrying with it a commitment to a restricted range of activities. If the nature of their work changes, then workers have to be prepared to retrain to fulfil their new commitments, this can in some cases mean an entire change in career. In the very short run a lack of work for engineers could see them painting their own workplace.

Workers who meet the requirement of functional flexibility are often described as core workers. These workers are central to the company's operations and may be difficult and expensive to replace. Functional flexibility can be seen as being the necessary concession on the part of the worker in return for relative job security.

### B.  Numerical flexibility

Firms have increasingly attempted to match the number of hours of labour paid for at any point in time with the number of hours required. With increasing uncertainty in some product markets, considerable variations in work requirements can be experienced from one time period to the next. This has led to working contracts which can facilitate greater variation in hours worked. Such arrangements include casual labour, part-time labour, short contract labour and outsourcing. All of these forms of working facilitate a rapid readjustment of hours worked to changing needs. Workers outside the core group can be regarded as secondary workers and can be generalised under the heading peripheral. Those in the first peripheral group are full-time workers, but have less job security than the core and have fewer prospects for promotion. Those in the second peripheral group augment the numerical flexibility of the first group and are typically represented by part-time workers.

### C.  Financial flexibility

Collective bargaining between employers and trade unions led to standardised payment agreements for groups of workers and encompassed close attention to pay differentials between groups. On occasions, industrial disputes arose when accepted pay relativities between groups diverged. Firms have sought to introduce pay bargaining at the workplace level with a continuing move towards individual pay deals between the worker and employer. Increasingly, there is a move away from the

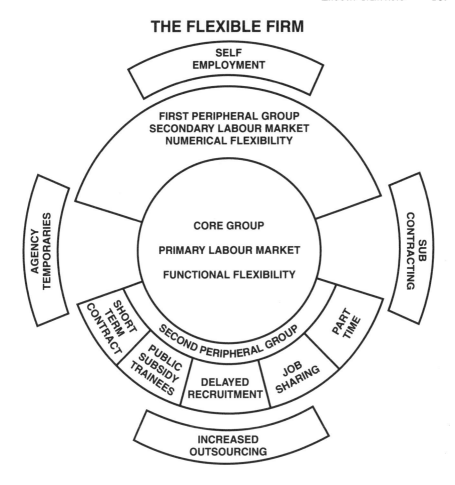

*Source*: J. Atkinson, 'Manpower strategies for flexible organisations', *Personnel Management*, Aug. 1984.

**FIGURE 6.3   The flexible firm**

rate for the job system to the rate for the worker approach. Rather than paying a standard rate for a particular task, regardless of the performance of the worker, attempts are made to appraise the worker's execution of her/his tasks and vary rewards according to the standard achieved. Consequently, workers who were previously paid the same wage in accordance with a collectively negotiated standard, may now receive markedly different rates of pay. Employers argue that this more flexible approach is efficient and equitable, as the individual worker can be rewarded, or penalised, according to his/her achievements.

The Atkinson model has been criticised on a number of counts, including that of undue simplicity and mere recognition of much that has been long evident (Pollert, 1988). Furthermore, data which suggests growth in the number of workers engaged on more flexible terms and conditions is not irrefutable evidence that firms are deliberately adopting a strategy of the flexible firm with a conscious development of a core and peripheral labour force. Work carried out for the Department of Employment covering some 877 employers with more than 25 employees argued that: 'Taking the responses as they stand they indicate that the flexible firm model built upon the core–periphery distinction is fairly unrepresentative' (McGregor and Sproull, 1992, p. 233).

The main reason given by employers for engaging part-time staff was for tasks that require a limited period of time for their completion. Such tasks include cleaning, usually done at the beginning and end of the day, and catering, occupying the middle hours of the working day. The main reason cited for engaging temporary staff was to provide short-term cover. Self-employed workers were engaged primarily to provide specialist skills.

The 1992 Employment Department study divided the reasons for employing non-standard workers into three categories.

1.  *Traditional*: need for short-term cover, tasks needing a limited time, equate staff levels to demand, specialist skills, etc.
2.  *Supply side*: workers preferred non-standard forms of employment, retain valued staff, easier to recruit.
3.  *New*: reduced wage costs, increase in flexibility of staff levels due to higher staff turnover, lower unionisation, fewer employment rights, etc.

The report concludes that traditional demands for non-standard staff continue to predominate, but interestingly an area where there is a much greater emphasis on the new rationale for employing staff is the public sector. Central/local government and health/education were areas which registered well above average response in citing the use of temporary workers. It would seem then that the Conservative Government through its actions has proved to be one of the greatest promoters of the use of non-standard labour and has helped to promote further the casualisation of the workforce.

Some firms have attracted media attention by making substantial shifts to restructuring their workforce away from full-time to part-time employees. In January 1993, as reported in the *Financial Times* (Buckley, 1993) the Burton Retail Group announced that it was cutting 2000 full-time jobs and replacing these with up to 3000 part-time jobs. In January 1994 Sock Shop also made the decision to shift to part-time working, shifting most of its staff from full-time to part-time contracts (Goodhart, 1994). Other firms which have pursued a similar policy include British Home Stores (BHS) and the Allied Maples Group. Nationally, around one third of all retail staff are employed on part-time contracts, though this is expected to rise. Whilst this often gives the spurious impression of job gain in the sector, the shopworkers' union USDAW has voiced disquiet at the trend, as it feels that part-time workers' career prospects are relatively poor.

While there is controversy over the reasons for the growth in numbers of non-standard workers, there is clear evidence to demonstrate the increased importance of such workers in the UK economy in recent years.

### Government policy

The first public acceptance by a government that full employment was no longer the overriding concern in the UK was made by the Labour Government in 1976. However, the major changes in economic policy and legislation which have impinged with far-reaching effect on the labour market have occurred since 1979, during the period of Conservative administration. On taking office in 1979, the Conservative Government under the leadership of Margaret Thatcher was pledged to rolling back the frontiers of the state and 'freeing' markets (Johnson, 1991). One of the markets that the government most wanted to free was the labour market.

At the core of the incoming Government's economic strategy was a need to provide incentives for people to work and for employers to reap profits and thereby employ more workers. It was felt that the main way to achieve this was by reducing the level of direct taxation, thus increasing disposable income and increasing the cost of leisure. At the same time it was the Government's opinion that labour markets were hindered from operating efficiently by restrictive labour laws and the actions of trade unions. A programme of legislation affecting the employer–employee relationship and reshaping the way trade unions could effectively represent their members was introduced, beginning with the Employment Act of 1980. Whilst these policy measures were implemented at the outset of the first administration (1979–83), a further policy which has had far-reaching effects on labour markets was not initially a key part of the Government's strategy. The policy of privatisation which was to assume such prominence in the mid and late 1980s was tentatively introduced in the later stages of the first administration and then gained momentum in the second administration (1983–87). Privatisation has had the effect of promoting part-time and temporary work and has generally helped to further develop the casualisation of the workforce. In those industries which have been privatised, such as Telecommunications, there have been substantial reductions in employment with an increase in importance for subcontracting out of work and short-term contracts. Local authorities are now obliged to tender out much of their work and this has led to an increase in subcontracting to private-sector employers.

The Government has had a marked effect on the labour market through its general policy of promotion of the individual against the collective. The 1980s witnessed a shift to a new set of values premised on an atomistic society in which self-interest was not to be derided, but applauded as the means of promoting overall benefits for society. This rediscovery of selective parts of Adam Smith's *Wealth of Nations* and the growing influence of monetarist economists such as Milton Friedman and Patrick Minford, witnessed the demise of the Keynesian treatise of regulated demand and market intervention. This neo-liberal ideology has seen a dismantling or reshaping of many of the institutions of the postwar welfare state.

In understanding the changes wrought in the workplace and elsewhere, it is important to note how society's norms and values can change over time, and the mechanisms through which this is achieved. During the postwar period up until the late 1970s, both Labour and Conservative governments operated according to principles of social democracy. Over this time, differentials in income and wealth were reduced and moves towards industrial democracy were made, though these lagged far behind the progress made in countries such as Germany. During this time, planning and regulation were seen to be necessary to overcome the vagaries of the market as demonstrated in the interwar period of high unemployment and poverty. However, as noted, the 1970s was a period of growing economic uncertainty and this provided an ideological vacuum into which new (or rather rediscovered 'old') policies and modes of thought could be inserted. The message of individualism, competition and market forces came together to form the new lexicon of the 1980s and policy was formulated in such a way as to become the embodiment of the message. The new ideology of the 1980s, then, revolved around competition in all spheres and the promotion of a philosophy which encouraged fragmentation rather than consolidation. Progressively over the 1980s, through a process of osmosis and amplification, the new ideology was absorbed, or at least accepted in acquiescence.

However, the role of conflict must not be underestimated in the progress of the new ideology which was promoted in the 1980s. The 1970s were characterised by high levels of strike activity, and it is argued that the Conservative Government of Edward Heath was brought down in February 1974 as a result of a protracted industrial dispute with the National Union of Mineworkers (NUM). The Conservative Government of 1979 was elected shortly after a bitter dispute between the Labour Government and public-sector workers, and both this dispute and earlier disputes gave the new Government ammunition for future propaganda offensives on organised labour and provided valuable lessons for future industrial relations strategies. This can be seen in the approach of the Government towards the National Union of Mineworkers in 1984. Prior to this time, in 1981, the Government found itself in direct confrontation with the NUM over possible pit closures, but this potentially explosive situation was not followed through by the Government and conflict was avoided. The NUM was still seen as being a powerful union in the early 1980s and its symbolic position, hedged around by its claimed defeat of Heath in 1974, was of importance to the Union movement. The Government could not afford to enter into any protracted dispute with the NUM which it was not confident of winning. Furthermore it was recognised that any dispute should involve a minimum of personal disruption to the population, as a failure to achieve this would demonstrate lack of control on the part of the Government and bring pressure from the electorate to end the dispute, possibly on terms favourable to the NUM. Bearing these considerations in mind, then, the start of the dispute with the NUM in March of 1984 acquires the patina of forward planning and deliberate execution. As Crick argues (1985, p. 98). 'Many in the NUM believe that the Coal Board deliberately tried to provoke a national strike, at its convenience. If so, then Yorkshire, one of the NUM's most militant areas, was the ideal place to do it.'

As the summer was approaching and coal stocks were at a high level, the possibilities of power cuts were a dim prospect in the distant future. Various intrigues developed during this dispute including a split in the NUM, with a splinter group of working Nottinghamshire miners, eventually assuming the title of the Union of Democratic Mineworkers, being formed. This splinter group of working miners helped to undermine the position of the NUM, as coal continued to be produced through the winter of 1984–5, further reducing the likelihood of power cuts. It is argued that the development of the working miners' group was not entirely spontaneous and indeed relied both on external finance and advice. Crick (1985) argues that at the outset, David Hart, a businessman and part-time adviser to the then Prime Minister Margaret Thatcher, played a leading role in the working miners' committee.

The dispute was allowed to drag on without resolution and in March 1985 the miners returned to work, having achieved none of their objectives. This was a damaging dispute for the trade union movement as it was demonstrated that possibly the most powerful union in the country could be subject to defeat in an industrial conflict, and this was bound to dent the confidence both of union members and leaders. The Government, whilst distancing itself publicly from the dispute and arguing that the resolution of the strike was a matter between British Coal and the NUM, had nonetheless conveyed a strong message to the Union Movement and had strengthened the hand of managements in their dealings with trade unions. Whilst other disputes, notably that between the print unions and Rupert Murdoch at Wapping in 1986, have occurred since this time, there is no doubt that the NUM dispute had the effect of reducing the likelihood of concerted collective industrial action on the part of labour.

## Government pay policy

From the 1950s until the end of the 1970s, UK governments attempted to deal with the problem of excess aggregate monetary demand through the operation of incomes policies, often aligned with restrictions on prices. Keynes himself recognised the serious dangers posed by inflation and the possibilities of this appeared to be greater in periods when demand was being maintained at high levels over sustained periods of time, in the postwar period. When the Conservative Government came into power in 1979 it pledged not to operate a statutory prices and incomes policy, and indeed it has not done so during its period of office. However, with respect to the public sector, the Government has operated cash limits which have had the effect of limiting the pay of public-sector workers. For example, in the 1994 pay round the Government allocated a sum of money for state teachers' pay which would enable teachers to have a pay rise of less than 2 per cent (below the rate of inflation). In the event, a negotiated pay settlement for the teachers was agreed which was in excess of 2 per cent. In order to avoid redundancies schools had to make 'efficiency' savings to meet the pay settlement. It is very difficult for schools to make further efficiency savings as their main outgoings are on teachers' salaries and they are not in a position to turn to the market and charge higher fees for the services provided. In June of 1994 Railtrack, the company in charge of track, equipment and signalling on the British Railways, seemed close to settlement with signalmen over a pay deal. However, it was then disclosed that the Secretary of State for Transport, John MacGregor, had reminded Railtrack of their need to stay within the Government's guideline for public-sector pay settlements of 1.5 per cent, and negotiations assumed a new character. Essentially, then, the Government has operated a form of incomes policy on the public sector alone. Exhortations to the private sector on pay increases have been made, but these have had very little effect, especially for private-sector company directors whose salaries have risen well in excess of average wage increases over the period since 1979.

### Trade unions

The trade union movement in the UK gained strength during the period following the Second World War and demonstrated a growing membership, reaching an all time peak of 13.289 million in 1979. With the growth of tripartism in the UK in the postwar period the trade union movement was increasingly consulted on economic issues. This development was embodied in the formal construction of the National Economic Development Council in 1961, which established a regular forum for the TUC as representative of the employees, the CBI as representative of the employers and the Government.

From its high level of membership in 1979 the UK trade union movement has suffered significant decline to 8.700 million members in 1993 (Table 6.4).

This decline in union membership has been a trend experienced across Europe and the USA and, in terms of an international comparison, the UK still had a relatively high level of union representation by the end of the 1980s (see Table 6.5).

**TABLE 6.4  Trade unions: numbers and membership 1979–1993**

| | 1979 | 1980 | 1981 | 1982 | 1983 | 1984 | 1985 | 1986 | 1987 | 1988 | 1989 | 1990 | 1991 | 1992 | 1993 |
|---|---|---|---|---|---|---|---|---|---|---|---|---|---|---|---|
| Number of unions at end of year | 453 | 438 | 414 | 408 | 394 | 375 | 370 | 335 | 330 | 315 | 309 | 287 | 275 | 268 | 254 |
| Total membership at end of year (thousands) | 13 289 | 12 947 | 12 106 | 11 593 | 11 236 | 10 994 | 10 821 | 10 539 | 10 475 | 10 376 | 10 158 | 9 947 | 9 585 | 9 048 | 8 700 |
| Percentage change in membership since previous year | 1.3 | − 2.6 | −6.5 | −4.2 | −3.1 | −3.2 | −1.6 | −2.6 | −0.6 | −0.9 | −2.1 | −2.1 | −3.6 | −5.6 | −3.9 |
| Cumulative fall in membership since 1979 (thousands) | | 342 | 1 183 | 1 696 | 2 053 | 2 295 | 2 468 | 2 750 | 2 814 | 2 913 | 3 131 | 3 342 | 3 704 | 4 241 | 4 589 |

*Source:*  Based on data from the Department of Employment, *Employment Gazette*, May 1995.

TABLE 6.5   Union membership (per cent) by sector, 1989

| Country | All | Private | Public | Manufacturing | Finance |
|---------|-----|---------|--------|---------------|---------|
| Sweden  | 81  | 81      | 81     | 99            | 72      |
| UK      | 39  | 28      | 55     | 41            | 25      |
| Italy   | 34  | 32      | 54     | 47            | 22      |
| Germany | 32  | 30      | 45     | 48            | 17      |
| Japan   | 26  | 23      | 56     | 32            | 50      |
| US      | 15  | 13      | 37     | 22            | 2       |
| France  | 10  | 8       | 26     | 5             | n/a     |

*Source*:   International Labour Organisation, *World Labour Report*, 1993.

A number of explanations have been advanced to account for the fall of trade union membership in the UK (B. Mason and Bain, 1993). It is argued that as inflation rises workers are more likely to join trade unions to defend their real earnings position. Over the period 1969–79 inflation was much higher than in previous decades, and this gave workers more incentive to join or remain members of trade unions to defend their real earnings. A further feature of the late 1970s was a fall in the earnings of white-collar workers relative to blue-collar workers, leading to an increase in the number of white-collar unionists, in an attempt to safeguard their relative position. Taking the period from the end of 1969 to the end of 1979 the growth rate of trade union membership was 28 per cent, some three times the rate registered in the 1960s.

Another factor which impacts on union membership is the level of unemployment. High and rising levels of unemployment have a depressing impact on union membership. This is said to have been the overriding factor in the early 1980s, for whilst prices rose rapidly at this time, a factor which should have promoted union membership, nonetheless total membership declined.

Accompanying, and strongly associated with, the new legislative framework which surrounds industrial relations is a changed attitude on the part of employers to the role of trade unions in the workplace (P. Smith and Morton, 1994). Until the 1980s the legislation regarding union recognition in the workplace was very supportive. Employers were consequently encouraged to accept unions in the workplace and to work with them. However, the legislative climate in the 1980s changed, weakening substantially the effectiveness of trade unions on many fronts. In a competitive environment which became increasingly fierce in the 1980s, some employers became increasingly hostile towards trade unions and found that both the law and the ideological position of the Government lent them support. This new, more aggressive form of management has often been referred to as 'macho management'. An outward manifestation of this hostility towards unions can be seen in a tendency towards derecognition of unions in previously unionised workplaces. Whilst this trend was not quantitatively important in the 1980s, ACAS (the Advisory Conciliation and Arbitration Service) (1992) has recently noted growing interest amongst employers in derecognising unions. This is especially so in the case of supervisory, technical and professional jobs. One company which moved in this direction in 1994 is Caterpillar (UK), the UK subsidiary of the world's largest manufacturer of construction and earthmoving machinery. In return for the surrender of rights to collective bargaining and derecognition of unions, white-collar workers at Caterpillar (UK) received a 2 per cent pay rise and a lump sum payment of £500. In the place of negotiated collective bargaining Caterpillar will introduce individual employment contracts, relating pay to individual performance. This move away from collective bargaining undermines one of the key reasons for union membership, and even in workplaces where unions continue to be recognised their usefulness to members is seen to be eroded in the presence of fragmented bargaining structures. Overall, then, the less supportive attitudes to unions from employers in recent years, coupled with a trend towards derecognition has helped to further reduce membership.

Other factors which have been advanced as explanations for falling trade union membership include the reduction in importance of the manufacturing sector which had historically high levels of trade union density and the shift in favour of service-sector jobs, often part-time and taken by females. As part-time employment, service-sector work and female employees all register lower levels of trade union density than their counterparts of full-time employment, manufacturing work and male employees, it is argued that employment shifts have been adverse for trade union membership. To this can also be added the reduction in average employment size of the workplace, as there is an inverse relationship between workplace size and level of trade union membership.

Taken together, these factors help to explain the reduction in trade union membership since 1979, but the question remains as to the future direction of trade union membership. David Metcalf (1990) argues that trade unions must adapt their behaviour in order to survive and grow. Metcalf argues that unions must strive both to avoid derecognition and to encourage recognition where this does not already exist. Trade unions must be seen as participants in the process of increasing productivity and profits in corporations. In order to do this they must emphasise the need for union voice in the workplace, coupled with co-operation. According to Metcalf the elements of voice 'might include training, flexibility on working time and jobs, monitoring the application of collective agreements and legislation and social planning associated with restructuring' (Metcalf, 1990, p. 33).

Over the years the trade union movement has accumulated a number of immunities from legal action for civil damages when performing duties relating to an industrial dispute. On occasions when these immunities have been under threat, or have been qualified by new legislation, the trade union movement has taken decisive action. One such occasion arose from the introduction of new legislation in the form of the Industrial Relations Act in 1971. Under this Act trade unions were required to register with the Registrar of Trade Unions and Employers' Associations, but in order to do so had to accept certain restrictions on their actions. These restrictions were traded in return for the continued right to the immunities which trade unions had previously enjoyed without conditions. The TUC recommended that this part of the Act should be boycotted by the trade union movement and members should refuse to register. This advice was widely acted upon and the Amalgamated Union of Engineering Workers went further by failing to recognise the authority of the Industrial Relations Court which had been formed to administer the new legislation. As a result of the refusal of the trade union movement to accept the new legislation and the new judicial apparatus introduced to administer it, the Conservative Government found its attempts at industrial relations reform were held up to ridicule. On its return to office in 1974 the Labour Government repealed the Industrial Relations Act, essentially returning the legal position to that which prevailed before 1971, whilst adding some extra provisions which extended the rights of those in employment.

A Conservative Government was elected in May 1979 immediately after the so called 'winter of discontent' which had arguably seriously damaged the Labour Party's likelihood of electoral success. This period of discontent had witnessed a series of public-sector strikes against the Labour Government's pay policy. The Conservative Government was able to capitalise upon this as it was felt that there had been a shift in sympathy away from the unions and, by association, the Labour Party. The climate then seemed right to introduce new legislation impinging on the trade union movement's freedoms. However, the Conservatives had learnt from the earlier débâcle under Edward Heath and did not intend to introduce a complex new judicial framework along the lines of the failed Industrial Relations Court. The policy adopted was one of relative caution introducing new legislation in stages and relying upon the ordinary courts of law to adjudicate. Over time, during the 1980s, the legislation built up into a comprehensive framework, changing significantly the position of the trade unions with respect both to employers and their members. In essence, it became increasingly difficult for trade unions to organise effective action against employers without punitive financial consequences, whilst it became easier for individual members of a union to seek damaging financial and/or judicial redress against their union. By exposing trade union funds to legal claims for damages which are enforceable by the ordinary courts of law, the Government felt that trade unions were more likely to abide by employment legislation and behave in a way acceptable to it.

*Some key elements of the legislation of the 1980s*

- The closed shop was initially restricted in its operations and ultimately had all statutory support withdrawn.
- Secondary picketing was outlawed. Secondary picketing occurs where an individual pickets at a workplace which is not his/her own. In order for picketing to remain lawful the worker or accompanying trade union official must picket at, or near, the place of work.
- The rights of workers to claim unfair dismissal if dismissed selectively were restricted.
- The requirement for secret ballots of union members prior to strike action was imposed.
- A ballot is required every ten years for those unions operating a political levy.
- A number of immunities for trade unionists were ended by narrowing the definition of a legitimate trade dispute, thereby exposing more cases of industrial action to the possibility of legal proceedings.
- The enforcement of contracts which stated that only unionised labour could be used was ended. Prior to 1982 some sectors, including the building industry, the printing industry and local authorities, frequently specified that contract work could only be tendered for by firms which had unionised workforces.
- The Commissioner for the rights of trade union members was introduced. This innovation provided both access to legal advice and funds for members who have a grievance against their union.
- The rights of a union member to take action against his/her union on a number of grounds were increased.

Further legislation has been passed in the 1990s which consolidates earlier pieces of legislation and introduces new elements. Under this legislation trade unions face a potential threat to subscriptions through the new check-off procedures for the collection of trade union dues. Many employers operate an arrangement with trade unions whereby the member's union subscription is deducted from his/her pay along with other deductions such as tax and then given to the trade union. From August 1994 employers can only deduct such subscriptions from the workers wage if written authorisation is given by the worker every three years. If workers have to make a conscious decision to 'opt in' in this way, then they may fail to do so, thus adversely affecting trade union membership and finances. Furthermore, some employers have refused to continue with the check-off system, whilst others have begun making a charge for the continuation of this service. In May 1994, shortly before the August deadline, the National Union of Civil and Public Services (NUCPS) civil service union had only secured 38 per cent of its members on check-off. The Union of Construction, Allied Trades and Technicians (UCATT), has 90 per cent of its members on check-off and by its best estimate felt that 10 per cent of these would be lost, costing the union an estimated £500 000 in income.

However, other trade unions are more optimistic, with the General Municipal and Boilermakers Union (GMB) claiming a slight increase in membership due to its check-off campaign.

Another important piece of legislation in the 1990s concerns the abolition of the remaining 26 wages councils which provided minimum basic and over-time rates of pay for workers in vulnerable occupations. Of these, the most important sectors affected are hotels, restaurants, hairdressers, shops and laundries. Wages Councils were established under the Trades Boards Act and came into operation in 1909. The intention was to provide a wage floor for those workers engaged in 'sweat shop' occupations. The then President of the Board of Trade, Winston Churchill, announced to the Commons 'It is a serious national evil that any class of His Majesty's subjects should receive less than a living wage in return for their utmost exertions' (Milton, 1992).

Unlike many European countries the UK has never had a minimum wage policy for all workers. The abolition of the Wages Councils removes the last vestiges of the piecemeal structure that remained. In sectors where Wages Councils did not operate, such as residential care homes and the private security sector, wage levels of £1.50 to £2.50 an hour are common. According to research undertaken by the Low Pay Unit in May 1995: 'Nearly half of all job vacancies in areas covered by the former wage councils, such as hair-dressing and shop work, are paying less than the rates would be now if they were adjusted for inflation' (Wood, 1995, p. 6).

The issue of the minimum wage attracts a great deal of controversy. Those against, including the Conservative Government, argue that minimum wages cost a country jobs by pricing workers out of jobs. According to this reasoning, if wages are allowed to gravitate to their 'market clearing' level then a position of full employment is more realisable. If employers are denied the flexibility of wage determination they will then employ fewer workers. In opposition to this, it is argued that countries with minimum wage levels, such as Sweden, succeeded in operating with lower levels of unemployment than the UK through the 1980s. Furthermore, it is argued that lower wage levels do not necessarily lead to more jobs, it simply means that those workers who would be employed anyway are paid less. It is argued that if workers are paid a reasonable minimum wage then they will work harder and will have higher morale. If the state does not enforce a minimum wage, but gives means-tested benefit to the working poor, then this can be seen to be a subsidy to employers who may well pay their workers as little as possible.

**Industrial harmony**

During the 1970s it was widely perceived that the UK had the worst record of industrial relations in Europe. The phrase the 'British Disease' was coined to describe the strikes, which are generally seen to be the first course of action taken by trade unions, rather than the final stage, after lengthy unsuccessful negotiations. The Conservative Government claims that it has cured the 'British Disease', and when one considers the much lower level of strike activity during the period of Conservative administration there seems to be evidence of a substantially changed industrial relations environment (see Figure 6.4).

However, when one looks behind the figures, the situation becomes far more complex. During the 1970s the number of days lost through industrial unrest in the UK economy was indeed substantially higher than in the 1980s and 1990s. However, in the 1970s the UK's record was by no means the worst in Europe, with countries such as Italy, with a higher rate of GDP growth, demonstrating a far worse record. Furthermore, whilst the UK record is now substantially better than it was, the UK is still not at the top of the table in terms of fewest days lost in Europe due to industrial activity. What has happened is that strike activity in Europe generally has reduced, due to growing economic uncertainty, changing sectoral balance and a host of other factors. However, what is noticeable about the UK economy is the growth in importance of other indicators such as absence from work and dissatisfaction with work. By 1985, the year in which the then Employment Minister Kenneth Clarke was able to claim 'Britain is enjoying its most strike-free year for nearly 50 years', Jane McLoughlin in the *Guardian* (16 Oct. 1985) stated that:

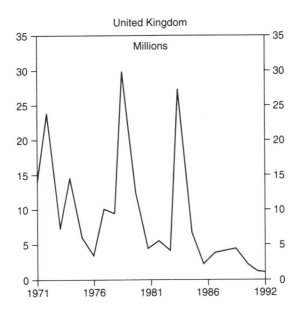

*Source*:   HMSO, *Social Trends*, 24, 1994c.

FIGURE 6.4   **Labour disputes: working days lost, 1971–92**

There are signs that the British Disease has not gone away – it has simply changed its symptoms . . . . Calling in sick for a day or two seems to be the new industrial weapon by which a worker can assert himself. British Industry loses 40 times more working days through this than it does through strikes.

In 1991 the UK had the second worst record in the European Union after the Netherlands for the percentage of the working week lost through illness (HMSO, *Social Trends*, 1994c).

A survey carried out in 1994 by the fifth largest union in Britain, the Manufacturing, Science and Finance Union (MSF), covering skilled and professional employees, showed high levels of staff dissatisfaction at work. A major problem identified in this survey was that of workers' perception of job insecurity, a factor causing anxiety and worry. This echoes the Employment in Britain Survey of 1993 which showed that since 1988 there had been an increasing level of insecurity amongst workers and growing dissatisfaction due to increased levels of work intensification. By the second quarter of 1995 concerns over job security had increased even further, according to a poll of 6000 people carried out by Gallup and Business Strategies (Batchelor, 1995).

The overall picture, then, is one which demonstrates a falling level of industrial strike activity since the 1970s, but in itself this cannot be interpreted as irrefutable evidence of increased industrial harmony. There is evidence to suggest that workers are experiencing increased levels of stress at work, but in the current legislative and managerial climate, coupled with high levels of unemployment, workers may well feel that the options available to them for displaying dissatisfaction in employment are limited.

### Education and training

Up until the First World War training was seen as something which should be left to industry. However, the needs of war brought a requirement for workers (especially women) who could be trained more rapidly than through the traditional apprenticeship system. In consequence, a new training apparatus was introduced by government. As the war drew to a close, requirements shifted from the rapid training of semi-skilled operatives to the skill training of disabled ex-servicemen. As the postwar depression deepened, emphasis shifted again, to training schemes for the unemployed. The Second World War once more saw the government extending its involvement in training. However, whilst the war brought a formalisation of training methods, 'The experience of the Second World War did little to change the emphasis of training in British industry . . . In the minds of employers, managers, trade unions and workers the place to receive training continued to be on the job' (Sheldrake and Vickerstaff, 1987, p. 25).

The emphasis remained firmly on the apprenticeship system. However, by the 1960s it was recognised that this voluntarist system was not providing sufficient numbers of well trained workers to meet the needs of a modern economy and 'Britain lagged behind its main European competitors in terms of the average skill levels and educational qualifications of its workforce' (Sheldrake and Vickerstaff, 1987, p. 31).

Since the 1960s a number of initiatives have been introduced by successive governments. However, the problems that have dogged industry remain. The UK continues to lag behind major competitors, including Germany and Japan, in the training of workers at technician level, and at the ages of 16–19 participation in education of Britons lags behind all our major competitors (Layard, 1995) (see Figure 6.5).

The *World Competitiveness Report* (World Economic Forum, 1995) argued that UK competitiveness as measured by workforce skills was in decline, with the UK slipping from 21st to 24th in the world league table over the year.

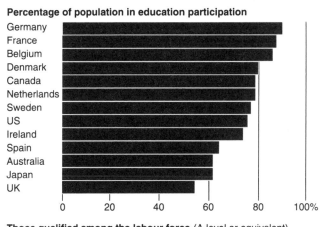

**Percentage of population in education participation**

**Those qualified among the labour force** (A level or equivalent)

*UK figures adjusted to include part-time further education.

*Source*: *Financial Times*, 5 September 1995, p. 18.

**FIGURE 6.5   Skills: Britain lags competitors**

It is argued that the UK approach to training has lacked focus and co-ordination. Sheldrake and Vickerstaff (1987, p. 54) argue that UK governments have responded 'merely as a matter of crisis management rather than calculated policy'.

Attempts to revitalise and refocus training through new initiatives such as the Training and Enterprise Councils (see Chapter 7) have met with much criticism, and training and education remains an area of considerable controversy and debate on the agenda of all political parties.

### The new industrial relations

It is argued that the system of industrial relations in the 1970s was an adversarial one in which unions and employers were fiercely opposed and had different objectives. Though this is an oversimplification, the evidence shows that the 1970s was a period of intense industrial conflict. Whilst the economies of western Europe and America suffered major dislocation in the 1970s and continued to struggle with high levels of unemployment and falling competitiveness, it became increasingly apparent that the Japanese economy was going from strength to strength. Industrialists in North America and western Europe came to pay increasing attention to the Japanese model of industrial relations and production in an attempt to emulate their evident success. Attempts have been made to distil the crucial elements of Japanese success and translate these to a Western setting. In the realm of industrial relations, Bassett (1986) argues that it is possible to identify a number of key features of the Japanese model of industrial relations.

According to Bassett there are six principal features of what can be recognised as a 'Japanese'-type deal. Not all of these features appear in every deal, and some do so in very tailored fashion, but nonetheless they are the key elements of a 'Japanese' package.

*Single unionism*: This practice developed at a growing pace in the 1980s and involved the recognition by management of a single union for purposes of negotiation. A result of this was the so called 'beauty contest' in which trade unions 'paraded' their wares in front of management in the hope of being selected as the union which would be chosen to represent the workforce. Single union deals were particularly associated with the setting-up of new greenfield site plants with no history of previous unionisation. The Electrical, Electronic, Telecommunication and Plumbing Union (EETPU) was a trade union which was particularly successful in securing single union deals with companies such as Sanyo and was seen by some as being a progressive union willing to work with the grain of management, whilst in other quarters it was vilified as having sold out the birthright of the union movement by becoming a token union which was the poodle of the employers. The EETPU was probably the most controversial of the unions of the 1980s, being expelled from the TUC for having transgressed the TUC's Bridlington Principles which seek to prevent unions from poaching members from established unions.

*Flexibility*: The Japanese are famed for their 'job for life' policy which guarantees a worker employment for life, dependent upon the worker's willingness to accept flexible working, including retraining if necessary. However, it is important to note that this security only extends to about 30 per cent of the Japanese workforce employed in the larger corporations, and much operational flexibility is achieved by the use of small subcontracting firms who cannot offer such security to their workers. A number of flexibility deals have been introduced in Britain, ending traditional demarcations between jobs. Rolls-Royce first introduced organisational changes in late 1990 at their plant in Crewe, Cheshire. These changes encompassed the introduction of a 'green book' which provided the basis for reorganisation of working practices. New practices involved the ending of traditional demarcation lines and the creation of teams of workers. The plant has been divided into 16 zones and each of these is operated under a manager and expected to assume responsibilities which include costs and quality. The traditional posts of foreman and chargeman have been dispensed with, flattening out the management hierarchy. Teams operate a policy of flexible working, with workers undertaking tasks regardless of their specific craft training. Management are very satisfied with the development so far and point to increases in productivity and reduction in the need for fault rectification.

*Single status*: It has been argued that the British workplace was highly stratified, with separate canteens for blue- and white-collar workers, managers' toilets, different holiday and pension arrangements according to status, and a whole host of other arrangements which denoted the individual's position in an hierarchical system of prestige and patronage. An increasing number of firms have rejected this approach in recent years and have moved towards a system of single status. This will typically involve clerical and manual workers having the same holiday entitlement, sickness benefit, pensions, and so on, and the use of common restaurant facilities. Workers at all levels from managing director to floorsweeper may also wear the same uniform and communicate at first name level.

*Participation*: One of the features of the 1960s and 1970s, it was claimed, was the low morale of workers engaged on production work. Workers, it was said, felt alienated from their work and had low levels of motivation. In an attempt to involve workers more closely in the work they are doing a number of developments have taken place. Workers are given more information about the company through newsletters, briefings and videos, and groups such as quality circles are often introduced.

In the 1970s there was a strong move in the trade union movement towards the achievement of greater industrial democracy in the workplace, with the German model of mandatory representation at company board level being a goal to aim for. In 1976 the Bullock Report proposed that those companies with over 2000 employees should have mandatory representation of employee directors on the board of the company. The structure of the company board would follow the $2x + y$ formula in which for each shareholder director there would be a worker director ($2x$) with an additional smaller number of co-opted directors ($y$). The Conservative Government of 1979 gave no support to such developments, and the current ideological climate is firmly against any such mandatory representation. However, Japanese companies do operate company boards consisting of worker and manager representatives and these boards discuss a variety of issues of concern to the employee. Members of these boards do not have to be trade unionists and their role is advisory. Critics of this approach argue that these boards have no real power and simply give an illusion of influence to the workers.

*Pendulum arbitration*: This is seen as being a feature of the strike-free agreement and was first used in Britain as part of such an agreement by Toshiba. Arbitration normally involves an independent third party considering the merits of a pay claim on the part of the employees and a pay offer on the part of the employers. It is argued that there is an incentive here for the employees to exaggerate their claim whilst the management may make a derisory offer. The arbitrator (who may well be appointed through ACAS) will, after due consideration, choose a position in between these extremes. Pendulum arbitration requires that the arbitrator should find for either one case or the other and not establish a settlement in between. The theory is that the danger of losing the case entirely will lead to more careful negotiations which will result in a moderate outcome and avoid any escalation of disagreement.

*No-strike arrangements*: These encompass an agreement between the union and the employer whereby strike action will not be resorted to whilst agreed negotiating procedures are under way. The final option in some cases where agreement cannot be reached voluntarily may be binding pendulum arbitration.

There is disagreement as to the major beneficiaries of the 'Japanese approach' detailed above. Those in favour would argue that a complete package benefits both employers and workers. Employers benefit through higher worker productivity, and employees benefit through increased involvement in their work, bringing greater satisfaction and increased material rewards. Trade unions such as the EETPU co-operated wholeheartedly with

Japanese and other companies which introduced such measures in the 1980s and stressed the need for a participatory rather than an adversarial relationship with management. Critics would argue that any extra involvement of the workers is one-sided and that such innovations as quality circles are merely an attempt to pass extra responsibilities to workers, without properly rewarding them for these responsibilities. Furthermore, it is argued that company boards are a method for excluding trade unions from representation and serve as a means of removing any effective representation of workers. Overall, then, critics would argue that the kind of package outlined above, as operated in most Japanese plants, serves to further exploit workers whilst attempting to persuade them that the employer has their best interests at heart.

**The UK in Europe**

The UK joined the European Economic Community in the 1970s, some two decades after its original foundation. During its period of membership the UK has frequently been out of step with the rest of Europe on a number of issues, and an issue of particular contention concerns European labour market policies.

A significant development of the European Union took place in the 1990s with the ratification of the Maastricht Treaty. The Maastricht Treaty carries the concept of the European Union forward a further stage by, amongst other things, creating citizenship of the Union, with consequent rights and duties for all individuals within member states. It is the intention within the European Union that close co-ordination of member states' economic policies will take place, and ultimately it is intended that a common currency should be established.

With the exception of Britain, all the other states of the European Union wish to advance along the course established by the Social Charter in 1989. The Charter represents a number of commitments covering employment protection, fair wages, holidays, working time, paid leave, safety and welfare and workers' participation. The right of trade unions to be recognised for collective bargaining is also established under the Charter. It is the intention of the European Union to promote through the Charter the achievement of decent standards of living and equality of treatment for all workers. It is recognised that national practices differ, particularly in the field of contractual arrangements, and the Union acknowledges this and the need to maintain competitiveness. The intention is that any changes should be implemented after thorough dialogue between management and workers. Over time, the European Council will implement directives which state minimum requirements, but particular sensitivity is to be applied in the case of small and medium-sized businesses where it is acknowledged that legal, financial and administrative restrictions could be unduly onerous.

Britain has throughout refused to be a signatory to the Social Charter. In signing the Maastricht Treaty the British Government opted out of the Social Chapter (the incorporation of the Charter) which binds the other European States. In defence of its action the Conservative Government argues that the Social Chapter places too many restrictions on employers, and that the UK economy would be damaged as a consequence of restricting the freedoms of employers. However, critics argue that by refusing to accept standards which are upheld in other Union states Britain may destabilise the Union and tempt employers to adopt 'sweated labour' practices which would be outlawed in other parts of Europe.

The behaviour of the UK Government in the field of labour issues has indeed attracted censure both from within Europe and beyond. The International Labour Organisation (ILO) chose to censure the UK Government in June 1994 for its continued withdrawal of union rights to workers at the Government Communications Headquarters (GCHQ) in Cheltenham. The ILO is also critical of the 'volume and complexity of legislative change since 1980' on industrial relations. In June 1994 Britain was found to be in breach of European Union laws on employment. British employers have been in contravention of European law by failing to consult with workers over redundancies, and British law has given insufficient protection to employees when they have been transferred to new employers or in cases where they have been made redundant. The ruling made on 8 June 1994 resulted from a case brought against the council by three Eastbourne refuse workers from a group of 18 who had been sacked in 1990 when the council transferred its work to a private company.

### European unemployment

Perhaps the most important problem facing the European Union by 1994 was the high level of unemployment faced by members states. In 1989 unemployment in the European Union states was 14.5 million, falling slightly to a cyclical low point of 8.3 per cent in 1990. By 1994 unemployment had risen to 19 million and represented 11 per cent of the workforce. The general governmental position with regard to labour markets in Europe differed markedly to that in the USA in the 1980s. Most European governments have afforded workers protection in terms of minimum pay levels and rights in the face of redundancy, whilst providing reasonable levels of unemployment benefit. Furthermore, public-sector employment is more important in Europe that the USA. Critics of this approach, including the OECD, have argued that the result has been high levels of unemployment, as wages have been protected from falling and employers have found themselves restricted by regulations. In the USA, which has a deregulated labour market, employment grew by an average of 2.1 per cent annually over the period 1982–90. Over the same period, European Union employment grew by 0.9 per cent annually (Balls, 1993). The superior employment performance in the USA occurred due to the expansion of very low paid service-sector jobs, so-called 'Mac' jobs (named after the fast food chain). The average wage in the USA hardly rose over the period, whilst the lowest paid 10 per cent of the workforce experienced a drop in wages of almost one third (Balls, 1993). The contrast between Europe and the USA is demonstrated by the fact that whilst in Europe unemployment rose, in the USA, the ranks of the working poor were swelled. The question to be addressed is how to deal with the problem of unemployment, and the Detroit Jobs Summit, convened by the American President Bill Clinton in 1994, was intended to tackle this. The UK Government has argued that Europe should go along the route the Americans took in the 1980s. However, others such as Jacques Delors, the President of the European Commission, have suggested other routes within a regulated framework of worker protection, including job sharing. The German Trade Union Federation has argued that jobs could be created by reducing working hours and accepting a fall in overall pay, whilst not reducing existing hourly pay rates. Robert Reich, the US Secretary of Labour, at a conference in London in June 1994, argued that there was a third way between the low skilled, low wage, job creation of the USA and the concentration on high skilled, but fewer, jobs in Europe. This, Reich argued, would involve training for new market conditions and the creation of national vocational standards. Furthermore, Reich argued in favour of the minimum wage as a means of protecting the poor and against the flexible hire and fire policies of the 1980s. A further issue which has entered debate is competition between the developed world and low labour cost countries. It has been argued that many countries intensely exploit their workforce by paying low wages for long hours and exposing them to unsatisfactory conditions at work. The USA has been at the forefront of debates to incorporate internationally recognised labour standards on the world trade agenda, and this is an issue that the successor to the General Agreement on Tariffs and Trade (GATT), the World Trade Organisation, will have to contend with.

## Conclusions

Major changes have taken place in labour markets since 1979, with an increasing emphasis being placed by government on the supply side. A notable change has been the significant decrease in power and influence of the trade union movement. The changes in labour markets have been due to a multiplicity of forces and one of the outcomes of these forces has been an increase in labour market flexibility. In summarising the reasons why this is so it is argued that: 'The main factors which are likely to have led to greater labour flexibility are: greater competition, both nationally and globally;

changes in production methods; changes in the structure of demand and supply; and government policies' (Beatson, 1995, p. 55).

The contribution of Government policies since 1979 to increased flexibility in labour markets is controversial. The TUC argue that labour is now in a weak position relative to the powerful position of the employer and this unequal power relationship is unhealthy in a modern economy. The Government would argue that its legislation in recent years has reduced the restrictive practices of trade unions and has restored management's rights to manage.

Whilst trade union influence has been substantially eroded, labour markets are increasingly flexible, and wage rates in the UK are very competitive compared to its close competitors, the UK's position in terms of work competitiveness is still not assured. The UK slipped from 14th to 18th place on the world competitiveness scoreboard between 1994 and 1995 (World Economic Forum, 1995). It is evident that in an increasingly competitive world in which capital is extremely mobile whilst labour is relatively immobile, any nation must invest heavily in its people's skills to gain competitive advantage. The trajectory for any successful developed economy must involve significant growth in human capital levels rather than an emphasis on low pay and long working hours.

# CHAPTER 7

# Regional and Urban Policy

Regional and urban policy is concerned with the economic inequalities which exist between geographical areas. Regions have tended to grow at different rates, with some being left well behind the leaders. One of the major and most persistent regional problems has been differential rates of unemployment, with some areas displaying a chronic tendency towards unemployment rates above the national average. During the interwar years some UK regions suffered particularly high levels of unemployment and even during the long postwar boom in the 1950s and 1960s areas in the north of England, Scotland, Wales and Northern Ireland had persistently higher rates of unemployment than the national average. According to the principles of market economics, if left to operate freely the market should eradicate unemployment differentials between areas. Ultimately, all those who seek work should be able to find employment and there should be no *involuntary* unemployment. However, this work may be extremely poorly paid and unpleasant. Given factor mobility those who are dissatisfied with the employment prospects in their region can seek work elsewhere. At the same time if wages are low in a region this should have the effect of attracting new investment and new employment to that region.

The orthodox mechanisms of economic growth and development can be seen to rest on the principles of comparative advantage first advanced by the nineteenth-century economist David Ricardo. According to the theory of comparative advantage regions and countries should specialise in those areas of production in which they have a natural advantage over other areas. For example, it is evident that due to climatic differences Spain has a comparative advantage over the UK in the production of oranges. In the case of the industrial revolution in the UK certain regions had climatic and resource endowments which gave them advantages. This explains the development of the cotton industry in Lancashire, the wool industry in Yorkshire and the steel industry in Sheffield. The comparative success of some regions is often explained by differential resource endowments. However, this explanatory approach can only take us so far, for, as Kaldor argues:

It is when we come to comparative advantages in relation to processing activities (as distinct from land-based activities) that this kind of approach is likely to yield question-begging results. (Kaldor, 1970, p. 339)

If we consider the differences in real income between countries and regions, it is not the difference in resource endowments that explains this but the 'unequal incidence of development in industrial activities. The 'advanced' high-income areas are invariably those which possess a highly developed modern industry' (Kaldor, 1970, p. 339).

Location theories which focus on transport costs do not help us very much either. Transport costs are only a significant explanation in those cases where bulky and/or heavy items are transformed into much smaller or lighter products, thus reducing the costs of transport to the market. In the case of steel, which uses both heavy ore and coal in manufacture, there is economic logic in locating the steel plant close to such deposits, but this is increasingly the exception in the modern world where such industrial employment is significantly less important.

The major flaw in the Ricardian theory of comparative advantage is that manufacturing capacity and services are not natural endowments. As Eatwell argues: 'What was a weakness in Ricardo's story has become a basic error in the neo-classical account. Manufacturing capacity is not a natural resource: it must be built up. And the process of building it up can yield the cumulative benefits of technical change' (Eatwell, 1982, p. 89).

At this stage it is necessary to introduce Myrdal's concept of circular and cumulative causation. In essence, this means that initial disparities in growth become exaggerated over time; success breeds further success and failure breeds further failure. In sectors such as manufacturing which offer opportunities for high productivity gains, well in excess of those for land-based activities, this is most marked. If an area establishes an advantage in a manufacturing activity, for example, then the gap between itself and rivals can widen and gains become cumulative. There is, therefore, a virtuous spiral of growth and a vicious spiral of decline. It is here that the role of public policy is of crucial importance. In the absence of intervention successful regions may continue to develop apace whilst other areas sink into a slough of despair with all the concomitant resource waste and human misery. Intervention is necessary to arrest this vicious spiral of decline and to promote success.

The league table of success in the post Second World War period shows Japan to be a premiership contender. However, had Japan followed the principles of comparative advantage at the close of the Second World War it is unlikely that this would have been so. Japan had very little capital at the beginning of the postwar period, and the only resource it possessed in abundance was people. Consequently, the natural path for Japan to have followed according to the tenets of comparative advantage, would have been in the production of labour-intensive products. However, these are not the products that would have enabled Japan to join the world's leading industrial nations. Wisely, Japan rejected Western advice to manufacture labour-intensive products such as fluffy toys, and through the agency of the Ministry of International Trade and Industry followed a modernisation policy strongly orchestrated by the state. Japan specialised in 'inappropriate' industries such as electronics and vehicles, with resounding success.

## UK policy

Actions taken to promote regional and urban economic outcomes can be described as spatial policy. Until the 1970s there was a fairly clear delineation between regional and urban policy. Regional policy was concerned with reducing economic variations between the main regions of the UK, with respect to such variables as per capita incomes and output, but most particularly with respect to unemployment. Urban policy was concerned primarily with the necessity for planning in order to deal with the structural problems evident in urban decay and deprivation.

During the 1970s the distinction between these two policy areas became increasingly blurred. Over the period 1974–76 the national rise in unemployment caused great anxiety to the Government, but what was noticeable about this rise in unemployment was the degree to which the previously prosperous non-assisted areas in the South-East and West Midlands were affected.

From 1966 onwards, a continual decline in employment in manufacturing has been registered. It has been shown that the rate of loss of manufacturing employment is directly related to an area's level of urban concentration (Townsend and Champion, 1992). The areas which suffered most from the loss of manufacturing employment were the major conurbations such as London, Birmingham, Manchester and Glasgow, followed by large cities such as Leicester and Hull. The Government was spurred into the publication of *A Policy for the Inner Cities* (HMSO, 1977) which was a statement of the reversal of previous policy and a declaration of intent to re-establish the manufacturing base of the urban core of the cities. Furthermore, spatial policy was increasingly likely to collide with industrial policy. Selective aid given through the National Enterprise Board to British Leyland and to the aerospace industry in the 1970s can be seen to be a shift away from the provision of aid on a geographical basis to the provision of aid on an industry basis. The 1980s and 1990s have seen an increasing focus on specific targeted initiatives and a shift away from the generalised pattern of regional aid evident in the earlier postwar period.

## A brief history of spatial policy

The initial impetus for the formation of regional policy derived from the high levels of regional unemployment evident in the 1920s and 1930s. It was apparent that markets were not clearing in the classic textbook sense, and this disequilibrium manifested itself in the form of high and persistent levels of unemployment. Consequently government intervention can be justified in an attempt to improve factor mobility. In particular, the areas suffering from unemployment lack the investment necessary to provide employment. This lack of capital extends to physical investment in plant and machinery, but also to human capital in terms of education and training. As the market was failing to redress this shortfall, then the agency of government was seen to be necessary to remedy this deficiency. A justification which has often been made for regional policy is the absence of a consideration of social costs from the operations of the market. In economic theory, firms are assumed to be profit maximisers and therefore cost minimisers. If we accept that firms locate according to the principle of cost minimisation then their actions are logical considered from the perspective of the individual firm. However, these individual considerations may diverge from the interests of the nation as a whole. For example, if firms locate or expand near to the mass market, established suppliers, and so on, then they will be adding to congestion and concentrating pollution. At the same time, the stock of human misery resulting from the social and economic costs of unemployment is concentrated in certain localities. A more even spread of economic activity should lead to a welfare gain for the economy when both private and social costs are included in the equation.

The attempt by government to affect the location of industry can be seen as an element in the increased role of government in the economy in the twentieth century. The Government has adopted a number of strategies in its attempt to intervene in the location of industry.

1. The attraction by means of financial incentives of new industries to areas suffering from the decline of their staple industries;
2. Restrictions on the ability of firms to locate or expand in booming areas;
3. Property initiatives such as the building of industrial estates and housing for workers;
4. The development of infrastructure, particularly road networks.

### Interwar policy

Policy oriented towards regional employment issues dates back to 1928. In that year the Industrial Transference Board was founded and began the task of relocating people from areas of high unemployment to areas with lower unemployment. Financial inducements were given to people to encourage them to move, and in coal-mining districts the unemployed were retrained in advance of relocation to other areas. This policy was not a resounding success as many people returned to their areas of origin. Furthermore, the policy was not tackling the root of the problem, as there was a country-wide labour surplus, even though this was more obvious in some areas. An additional problem posed by this strategy was the tendency for the younger and more enterprising groups to leave the depressed areas: just the people who would be needed to rebuild the economic fortunes of these areas. After the great depression of 1929–32 the Government introduced new legislation in 1934 aimed at alleviating the unemployment situation in the most depressed regions. Special Areas were designated and through a succession of Acts in the 1930s, financial provision was made for the development of trading estates and financial help to firms. The policy initiatives of the 1920s and 1930s did little to alleviate the problems of the depressed areas; it took the threat of war and rearmament to increase demand for products such as steel, ships and textiles, and temporarily ease the employment problems of these areas.

**Postwar policy to 1979**

The first piece of postwar legislation was the Distribution of Industry Act which came into being in 1945. This Act saw the designation of Development Areas in place of the previous Special Areas. The criteria for inclusion in this category were the existence of unemployment or a specific threat of unemployment. Problems in the cotton industry after the war saw the inclusion of north east Lancashire in 1948, along with Merseyside and Inverness. During the early postwar phase of regional policy in the 1940s the Government restricted new industrial development in London and the South-East and encouraged growth in the Development Areas. Old munitions factories were adapted for private-sector use in the Development Areas, and purpose-built factories were constructed on industrial estates. The most active phase of this development occurred between 1945 and 1947.

A further element of policy came onto the statute books in 1947 in the form of the Town and Country Planning Act. This Act saw the granting of prohibitive powers over industrial development to the Board of Trade. Under this Act it was necessary for an industrialist wishing to build or extend a factory on an area covering over 5000 square feet to obtain an Industrial Development Certificate (IDC). These certificates would only be granted in cases where development was in line with the 'proper' distribution of industry. This strategy enabled the Government to prevent further industrial expansion in economically successful areas, as it was hoped to push new development into areas of high unemployment. By the late 1940s balance of payments problems led to increased focus on exporting potential and reduced emphasis on the application of regional initiatives. However, as the economic plight of the traditional industries in the Development Areas worsened, renewed attention was paid to regional unemployment in the later stages of the 1950s.

A new approach to regional unemployment was ushered in at the start of the 1960s with the passing of the Local Employment Acts of 1960 and 1963. Under the 1960 Act the Development Areas were abolished and a more flexible regime introduced. This new strategy enabled the Government to deal with problems of unemployment as and where they arose. Particular emphasis was placed on the need to promote employment in given localities in England, Scotland and Wales, where chronic and high levels of unemployment were in existence or threatened; such areas were accorded the title Development Districts. The legislation of the early 1960s saw a shift away from a concern to distribute industry throughout the country in accordance with an 'ideal pattern' and towards a policy which elevated the need to reduce unemployment disparities across the UK. The 1960 Act was predicated on the assumption that the Government could intervene when and where necessary, to eradicate persistent unemployment. A raft of further legislation was introduced as the 1960s progressed, amongst which was a controversial scheme entitled the Regional Employment Premium (REP). This scheme, introduced in 1967, recognised the need to orient policy not simply towards the development of industrial capacity in the lagging regions, but more especially towards the creation of employment. The REP brought a payment to the firm for each adult male employee of £1.50 a week.

The Labour Government, in office from 1964–70, presided over a substantial increase in expenditure on assistance to industry in deprived areas. A comprehensive framework of assistance was built up over this period, encompassing financial assistance for investment in plant and machinery; industrial construction and training; and grants towards operating costs on new buildings, plant and machinery; the direct provision of industrial premises and subsidised rents; subsidies for labour costs; grants to clear and prepare derelict land and further restrictions on office and industrial development in economically buoyant areas.

The major piece of legislation in the 1970s was the Industry Act, 1972, which amongst other things incorporated the phasing-out of the REP from September 1974 (finally ended in 1977) and the raising of the exemption level for the IDC to 15 000 square feet in all areas other than the South-east, where it remained at 10 000 square feet. At the same time, Regional Industrial Development Boards were set up in England, Scotland and Wales with a brief to give advice on opportunities for industrial development and financial issues. In the late 1960s it was recognised that some areas suffered from particularly acute problems, and this led to the designation of a new category of area: the Special Development Area. Equally it was recognised that those areas adjacent to scheduled areas had problems but were ineligible for assistance, and this led to the development of a further category of area: the Intermediate Area. The Industry Act of 1972 extended the coverage of the Intermediate Areas, meaning that 65 per cent of the total land area of Great Britain was now eligible to claim regional assistance.

Nationalism became an increasingly important feature of spatial policy in the 1970s, and the Scottish and Welsh Development Agencies were founded in 1975 and 1976 respectively. It also became increasingly clear that whilst regional differences in unemployment had not been eradicated by previous policies, new pressures were now developing. Not only was it evident that there were still differences between regions, but it now became apparent that there were major differences *within* regions. This was manifested most obviously in the case of the deteriorating situation in the inner cities. By 1976 it was apparent that the inner cities had major problems, many of which stemmed from the decline of manufacturing industry. The Labour Government set a number of studies in action in order to evaluate the nature and scale of the problems and in the mean time accelerated the Urban Aid Programme, a programme designed in 1968 for much smaller scale purposes. The publication of *A Policy for the Inner Cities* in 1977 heralded a recognition of the need for a focus of attention on the decaying inner cities. The shift in attitude towards spatial policy which became apparent in the period from 1976, with a movement away from a concentration on the geographical distribution of industry, was to be built upon in the 1980s and 1990s.

### Regional policy since 1979

The British economy suffered major problems in the mid-1970s, notably high levels of inflation and balance of payments difficulties. Public expenditure curbs and a deflationary climate saw a reduction in investment levels in the country. Consequently there was less footloose capital available to be channelled to the assisted regions. Regional policy was less actively pursued in the late 1970s, and this is reflected in the falling expenditure levels in this area. When the Conservative Government assumed office in 1979, a trend to the downgrading of regional policy was therefore already under way. The new Government was elected on a pledge to substantially reduce public expenditure as a means of restoring the competitiveness of the UK in the world economy. The relevance of this general policy to the specific case of regional assistance was made clear in July 1979. A new package of regional instruments was announced, based on a much weakened version of the 1972 Industry Act. Over a three-year period the regional aid programme was to be substantially curtailed through a series of measures. Whilst Special Development Areas were still to receive grants for capital expenditure, the value of these was to be cut; furthermore Intermediate Areas were now no longer eligible for automatic assistance but had to rely on discretionary aid. The overall aim here was to shift emphasis further away from automatic to selective assistance. One of the major criticisms of regional policy in the 1970s was its blanket approach, distributing aid 'confetti-like' across a wide geographical area. This led to anomalies such as the eligibility for regional aid of prosperous towns such as

Aberdeen and Harrogate, as they were situated within more depressed regions.

Further downgrading of regional policy occurred in the first half of the 1980s. Special Development Areas were abolished, location controls were ended and a substantial reduction of the geographical area eligible for assistance took place. Spending on regional policy was set for continued long-term decline, with announcements made in 1984 of £300-million cuts in annual expenditure on regional assistance by 1987–9. During the 1980s regional policy spending in the UK fell by more than half in real terms. This downgrading of regional policy in expenditure terms has taken place in a number of northern European countries, notably in Denmark, where there has been a complete abandonment of regional incentives (Bachtler and Michie, 1993).

However, the UK Government has remained committed to regional policy, albeit with a much reduced budget. In 1988 a number of reforms were introduced, again with increasing focus on targeting aid, and with particular emphasis on increasing business capabilities through the development of managerial skills, strategy formulation, marketing, design and innovation. Since the publication of David Birch's study showing that in the US over the period 1969–76 two-thirds of net new jobs were attributable to firms with fewer than 20 employees (Birch, 1979), increased attention was given to the job creating potential of small firms. The 1988 reforms included the development of Regional Enterprise Grants available to firms with fewer than 25 employees.

As noted earlier, the 1970s saw the growing recognition of urban problems, and with this the development of new urban policy strategies. This increased focus on urban issues is reflected in the changed priorities for spending between regional and urban policy, with a diminution in overt regional policy expenditure and growth in urban policy expenditure.

### Urban policy since 1979

Urban policy began to assume a new urgency and importance from the middle of the 1970s. Cameron (1990) highlights the problems of the urban areas, noting that British urban areas lost in excess of two million manufacturing jobs over the period 1951 to 1981 with three-quarters of this loss being experienced by the conurbations. This problem was compounded by the fact that these manufacturing jobs were not compensated for by growth in the service sector. During the 1970s, over 900 000 jobs were lost in manufacturing, whilst less than 100 000 new jobs were created in the service sector (Cameron, 1990).

It is possible to divide urban policy in the UK into five policy phases (HMSO, 1994a). The first phase was the Urban Programme of 1968, concentrating on projects centred in the community and focusing on social deprivation. The second phase came in 1978 with an acceleration and broadening of the Urban Programme. This policy phase was to be accomplished through local–central government partnerships.

The early 1980s saw a change in emphasis and the opening of the third phase. Here, the main emphasis was increasingly placed on economic issues, and infrastructural needs were given priority. Partnerships were again stressed, but this time they involved the central government and the private sector. New agencies were formed, most notably urban development corporations, which were at the core of the new agenda. It was during this phase of policy development that new strategies and instruments for encouraging the flow of private-sector funds into the urban areas were developed. For example, it was during this period that the Enterprise Zones were introduced, along with City Grants and Urban Regeneration Grants and Urban Development Grants.

During the fourth phase, in the later 1980s, attempts were made to achieve greater cohesion in the package of measures in operation. City Action Teams and Task Forces were added to the existing agencies. The Action for Cities programme was inaugurated, bringing together a number of programmes operating from different government departments.

The fifth and most recent phase, in the early 1990s, has seen an emphasis on streamlining and focusing activities. At the heart of this new phase has been an emphasis on competition. Urban areas now have to compete with one another in an effort to attract government funding. This is evident in the City Challenge programme and the most recent Single Regeneration Bid Funding programme. Urban areas must submit bids under such strategies, outlining their needs for funds and detailed programmes for the use of these funds. A crucial element in the Single Regeneration Budget process is the requirement that bids are made by partnerships representing both the private and public sectors.

Lawless (1991) argues that there are three main categories of initiatives carried out under the Government's urban policies since 1979. These are 'programmes designed to enhance the coordination of urban governance, policies intended to liberalise the urban economies, and urban development initiatives' (Lawless, 1991, p. 16).

Initiatives intended to co-ordinate intervention in the inner city include the City Action Teams (CATS) and Task Forces. Policies directed at liberalisation include the Enterprise Zone scheme, which brought with it a relaxation of 'red tape', simplified planning controls, rate relief and a number of other bureaucratic and financial reliefs. The third element, that of property development, became increasingly important as the 1980s wore on. The major vehicle here was the Urban Development Corporations (UDCs), incorporated in the Local Government Planning and Land Act and first established by 1981 in the docklands areas of Liverpool and London.

## Policy objectives

In the HMSO report *Assessing the Impact of Urban Policy* (1994b) it is stated that policy has two principal objectives. These involve the creation of employment opportunities and the development of cities which are more attractive places for people to live in. In achieving these higher-level objectives there are ten contributory lower-level objectives. The relation between these higher and lower objectives is set out in Figure 7.1.

The ten lower-level objectives contribute to the achievement of one or both of the higher-level objectives. For example, the promotion of enterprise should strengthen existing firms and encourage new firms to start. The development of new sites and the improvement of existing sites is necessary for economic development and growth. Skills development and motivation are again essential ingredients in the employment nexus. The co-ordination of government departments and public, private and voluntary sector organisations, the removal of any barriers to recruitment and public services, and increased levels of security from crime and vandalism contribute to the achievement of objectives I and II. The improvement of both the private and public sector housing stock, the improvement of infrastructure and transport, and the building of community networks all contribute to a raising of the quality of life and increase residential attractiveness.

## An evaluation of UK regional and urban policy

Evaluating regional and urban policy is an extremely difficult and complex process. For example, measuring levels of unemployment in assisted areas against those in non-assisted areas might be used as a standard for comparison. However, this would not be an adequate comparitor even though the chief reason for spatial policy may be seen to create employment. Regional policy may be successful in creating employment whilst unemployment figures continue to rise. This becomes obvious when one considers that assisted areas are chosen in the first place due to their specific problems stemming from the decline in their industrial base. If old industries are dying and have no prospects of revival, then the loss of employment here may well outweigh the new jobs attributable to policy; the net effect is a rise in unemployment. Furthermore, a successful regional policy may well slow down migration from an area, keeping the labour supply at a higher level than would be the case in the absence of policy. Additionally, if regional policy creates some hope and prospect of employment then more people are likely to register for employment thus keeping unemployment levels at a higher rate than would have been the case had these people dropped out of the labour market. There is no question that over the years regional policy has both created and safeguarded jobs in the assisted areas: the main issue is at what cost to the Exchequer for each job? This is a difficult figure to arrive at,

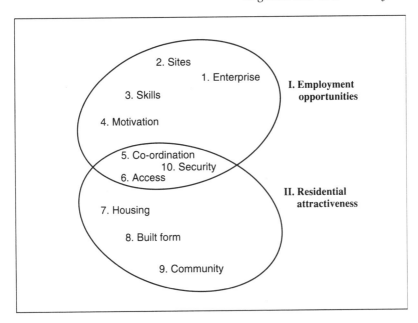

First is a *lower-level* set in which we can identify the following ten principal objectives:

1. *Enterprise development:* to improve the performance of existing enterprises and to encourage the formation of new enterprise;
2. *Sites for economic development:* to increase the rate of reclamation of sites and the improvement of existing buildings for private-sector development;
3. *Skills development:* to improve vocational and employment-related skills, adult numeracy and literacy; .
4. *Motivation to work:* to enhance personal development and enterprise in job search;
5. *Inter-agency co-ordination:* to improve interdepartmental and intergovernmental co-ordination and public/private/voluntary sector joint working;
6. *Access to employment and services:* to remove barriers to recruitment and to access to publicly-provided services;
7. *Housing development:* to improve the quality of the housing stock and the quality of management of public housing and to increase the quantity of private housing;
8. *Built environment:* to improve infrastructural services and the provision and running of transport networks;
9. *Social fabric:* to strengthen communities and increase local self-help and community care; and
10. *Safety and security:* to reduce the incidence of crime and vandalism and of accidents.

Second is a higher-level set which identifies two principal objectives:

I. the creation of employment opportunities; and
II. the creation of cities which are more attractive places in which to live.

*Source:* HMSO, *Inner Cities Research Programme: Assessing the Impact of Urban Policy,* HMSO, 1994b, pp. 6, 7.

FIGURE 7.1 **Higher-level and lower-level objectives**

and requires far more complex calculations than simply dividing through the estimated number of jobs by total spending on regional policy. A fuller appraisal of the merits of regional policy would require a comprehensive cost-benefit analysis. However, many of these costs and benefits would be difficult to measure accurately. For example, regional policy has meant that people have been able to remain in their homes and continue in employment. It would be possible to estimate the costs that moving to another area would have involved in financial terms, but there are other social costs which would have been incurred by what would have been involuntary relocation. By distributing industry more evenly, congestion and pollution costs can be avoided, but again these benefits are difficult to calculate accurately. Commenting on the effectiveness of regional policy since the war, the House of Commons Expenditure Committee noted in 1974 that governments had tackled regional problems in an uncoordinated manner. In a critical report it was suggested that large amounts of public funds had been spent on regional policy and much of this might well have been wasted. The report felt that greater monitoring of expenditure and accountability would have led to more effective use of resources.

However, whilst there is widespread criticism of individual regional policies carried out over the years, general concern at the many twists and turns policy has taken and a feeling that much policy has been rather hit and miss, this is not to say that regional policy should in the past, nor now, be abandoned. Professor Brown, writing in 1972, noted that 'There is no indication that the tendencies towards disparities of regional growth or the forces behind them have slackened or are likely to do so' (Brown, 1972, p. 337). However, he noted that regional policy was essential if regional disparities were not to widen and that there was a human and not simply an economic issue involved in assisting the least advantaged areas.

As outlined, the shift in policy in the 1980s has been away from regional policy and towards urban policy. Gudgin (1995) argues that in the 1960s a divergence in regional unemployment rates of 2–3 per cent was regarded as a serious social problem. In the period after 1979 there was a significant increase in regional disparities with the unemployment gap growing to 6–8 per cent. However, as Gudgin (1995, p. 20) notes 'but by this time belief in the efficacy of traditional regional policy had been greatly eroded'. After 1979 the emphasis has shifted to the problems of the urban core and notably the major conurbations. What follows is an evaluation of some of the major policy developments in the urban field since 1979.

## Urban Development Corporations

Urban Development Corporations (UDCs) have been in operation since 1980 and have been the cornerstone of urban policy since this time. Their main purpose was to take responsibility for the physical regeneration of their areas. This was to be achieved through the UDC, bringing agents and resources together. As Imrie and Thomas (1993, p. 4) note:

> The UDCs were forerunners in reorienting urban policy towards new economic imperatives in urban regeneration with the objective of pump-priming inner city land values through infrastructure projects, creating, and enabling, the new spaces of production and consumption, and utilising private-sector capital as a mechanism for revitalizing the cities.

In many senses the UDCs symbolised the Conservative Government's approach to urban problems, being market oriented and having their basis in property-led regeneration. The UDCs were seen as enablers, pump-priming development and unlocking the entrepreneurial potential to regenerate the urban areas. This was a departure from the previous managerialist state bureaucratic approach, with the new bodies being seen as facilitators and enablers, rather than as the major financial actors. As the 1980s developed, an element which has come to be more pronounced became clearer in the agenda of the UDCs: this was the growing role of business leaders in public policy areas. UDCs are non-elected bodies, assume the role of planning authority in place of the local authority and are directly accountable to central government.

In assessing the UDCs, Parkinson and Evans (1990) identify three key policy issues. These are efficiency, equity and accountability. Efficiency refers to the degree of success that UDCs have achieved in the physical regeneration of their areas and the degree to which private-sector investment has been levered in. Equity is concerned with the extent to which the wider community in the area concerned has benefited from regeneration and job creation. Accountability relates to the way in which the UDC interacts with other agencies in the area and its degree of responsiveness to the community and to the local authorities.

As Parkinson and Evans (1990) note, whilst the UDCs in general have helped to improve significantly their impoverished environments, the performance across all UDCs has been uneven. The London Docklands scheme has led to the regeneration and redevelopment of a significant area, levering in large amounts of private-sector investment. In contrast, the Liverpool Docklands project has had limited success in attracting private-sector funding. The extent to which an area will benefit from UDC status depends to a large degree on the state of the local economy and its future potential. Liverpool has deep-seated economic problems which make it a less appealing investment prospect than London, and this is reflected in the relative levels of investment. It is claimed that over the first six years of its operation the London Docklands development created 8000 jobs (Parkinson and Evans, 1990). However, over this period of time the number unemployed in the immediate area rose. Unemployment in 1992 was still higher than in 1981. The problem here is one of mis-match. Most of the unemployed people in the area had been displaced from manufacturing industry, whilst the new jobs were in service sector work, demanding different skills and aptitudes. Furthermore, by emphasising property development and attracting large scale investors, local property, land prices and rents were bid up, often to the detriment of existing industry and existing jobs.

The Liverpool scheme operates on a much smaller scale and its claims for job creation have been much smaller. A number of the jobs created have been semi-skilled and these therefore are more accessible to the local population. However, the level of public-sector expenditure has been high and the number of jobs created relatively small. Furthermore, the inhabitants of the most depressed areas of Liverpool such as Toxteth have seen little benefit from the Docklands development. With regard to housing in the London Docklands, the image created in the 1980s was that of a gentrified area catering for the young, rich and upwardly mobile. The displacement of many of the previous residents added to a general atmosphere of injustice.

The relationship between UDCs, the local community and local authorities has therefore often been strained. This has been accentuated by the tight time frames in which the UDCs have been expected to achieve their objectives. Due to their lack of local accountability they have been able to avoid local (and potentially lengthy) liaison and follow their own strategy. However, the early conflicts in the London Docklands between the UDCs and other agencies has served to lead to a mellowing of approach and a less conflictual model for later UDCs to follow.

The UDCs are now to be phased out over a number of years. There are a variety of reasons for this. To some extent it could be argued that the centralised model of the UDCs was a vehicle to overcome the possibility of hostility of unsympathetic local authorities to planning and development. The Local Government Act of 1989 has further stripped local authorities of their powers to operate in the area of economic regeneration, reducing the likelihood of conflict. The political atmosphere has also changed, with local authorities tending to come to agreements with the Government and developers, rather than enter into protracted appeals or public enquiries. As local government is no longer seen to be such an obstructive force, the UDC is no longer felt to be a necessary vehicle to counter this. A further factor in the demise of the UDCs is their growing and unanticipated costs. This is largely due to their property-led orientation which has become more expensive due to the recession and the collapse of land and property prices.

**Enterprise Zones**

The first eleven Enterprise Zones were introduced in 1981, since which time more have been added, leading to a total of over twenty creations since their inception. At the heart of the concept is a conviction that in the past, enterprise has been stifled by 'the dead hand of bureaucracy'. With this in mind, the first Enterprise Zones attracted a number of exemptions and allowances. Firms in the designated areas had exemption from: industrial training levies, local authority rates, Development Land tax and Industrial Development Certificates. In addition, firms could claim 100 per cent capital allowances for tax purposes against expenditure on commercial and industrial buildings, and were subject to simplified planning regimes and reduced government demands for information. The Enterprise Zone scheme has proved to be controversial and a number of academics have commented on its ideological basis which rests on faith (Vickerman, 1984). There are a number of problems with a scheme targeted on very localised assistance; not least of these is the sense of grievance of those firms which are located just outside the designated boundaries. A further problem is the extent to which existing firms have relocated to the zones without generating a net job increase for the country as a whole. Additionally, some of the firms which have located have been extensive users of space, as in the case of distribution depots, but relatively small providers of jobs. Talbot (1988) also notes that the 'cushioning' effect of financial and other exemptions may make firms in the zones complacent and less innovative.

By the late 1980s it was argued that Enterprise Zones had led to the creation of 35 000 jobs, but as many of these were attributable to firms which had relocated to the zones the net figure is placed at around 13 000 jobs which can be said to be due directly to the policy. The cost of each of these jobs is estimated at £23 000, rising to £30 000 if construction costs are included (Miller, 1990).

**City Challenge**

As noted earlier, the principle focus of urban policy in the 1980s was property-led regeneration. However, increasing social problems and the collapse of the property market witnessed a shift in policy direction. One manifestation of this changed orientation is the City Challenge initiative, introduced in 1991. Policy in the 1980s had largely excluded local authorities, but this new initiative gave local authorities a key role in local strategies. It is extremely difficult to evaluate the success of this initiative, not least because 'its objectives have shifted and evolved over time' (Davoudi and Healey, 1995, p. 79).

At the heart of much of the 1980s policy was the much vaunted 'trickle down' effect. This was supposed to work according to the principle that by concentrating on creating wealth, incomes generally would be raised, and, whilst those who were already well provided for would further their position, so too would the least well-off be raised to a higher standard of living: all boats are lifted on a rising tide. However, it was evident that this had not occurred and the new policy sought to benefit, directly, those in the most disadvantaged localities. This was to be done in part by preparing residents for jobs through training and education, thereby building up marketable skills profiles. Another element was that of furnishing communities with the institutional apparatus which would enable them to have an input into decisions which would affect them. A major intention was the construction of partnerships between the private sector, the public sector, local authorities, voluntary groups and the local community, as a means of developing and executing effective local plans. The City Challenge Boards were to decide for themselves what their problems were and were charged to put forward workable plans to deal with these. The Government was to provide variable funding over a five-year period, controlled initially through the bidding process under which 'winners' were chosen, and then by annual monitoring of projects.

Davoudi and Healey (1995) emphasise the objective of successful partnership between local authorities, the business sector and the local community. However, in their study of City Challenge initiatives in north Tyneside and Newcastle City, they observe little move 'towards participatory democracy' (Davoudi and Healey, 1995, p. 93). Robinson and Shaw (1994) note that a recent National Council for Voluntary Organisations Report, covering seven City Challenge initiatives, had expressed disappointment in the overall level of community involvement. Two rounds of City Challenge were undertaken, but a third was cancelled and the funds have been absorbed into the most recent initiative, the Single Regeneration Budget.

### Single Regeneration Budget

This is the most recent initiative and consists of the lumping together of 20 existing regeneration programmes operated by five government departments. The component parts of the Single Regeneration Budget (SRB) are shown in Table 7.1.

Under this new scheme, partnerships are formed at the local level and detailed proposals for the use of funds are submitted in a competitive bidding process similar to City Challenge. The Government has made it clear that bids must be made by partnerships which show representation from a range of relevant parties in the locality. Typical groupings will consist of representatives from local authorities, the business community, Training and Enterprise Councils (TECs), community groups and the voluntary sector.

The results of the first round of the SRB bidding process were announced in December 1994. Of the 469 bids made, less than half were successful, while others were awarded less than they had bid for. Overall, £125 million was made available for 1995–6, with the largest single recipient being London (Table 7.2).

TABLE 7.1   **Programmes in the Single Regeneration Budget 1994–5**

| Programme | Amount (£m) |
|---|---|
| Urban Development Corporations | 286 |
| Housing Action Trusts | 88 |
| English Partnerships | 181 |
| Estate Action | 373 |
| City Challenge | 213 |
| Urban Programme | 83 |
| Task Forces | 16 |
| City Action Teams | 1 |
| Safer Cities | 4 |
| Section II (part) | 60 |
| Ethnic Minority Grant/Business | 6 |
| Programme Development Fund | 3 |
| TEC Challenge | 4 |
| Local Initiative Fund | 29 |
| Business Start Up Scheme | 70 |
| Education Business Partnerships | 2 |
| Compacts | 6 |
| Teacher Placement Service | 3 |
| Grants for Education Support and Training | 5 |
| Regional Enterprise Grants Initiative | 9 |
| Total Single Regeneration Budget | 1442 |

*Source*:   Tony Baldry MP, Parliamentary Written Answer: *Hansard*, 31.3.94, Col 918.

TABLE 7.2   **How the regeneration cookie crumbled**

| Region | 1995–96 funds | Total funds |
|---|---|---|
| London | £36.584m | £316.710m |
| North-west | £18.267m | £143.293m |
| North-east | £18.286m | £80.667m |
| Merseyside | £10.382m | £78.004m |
| East Midlands | £7.378m | £55.876m |
| South-west | £4.050m | £34.090m |
| South-east | £5.263m | £31.798m |
| Eastern | £2.749m | £20.721m |

*Source*:   *Financial Times*, 7 Dec. 1994, p. 7.

The total committed over seven years through this first round is £757 million. There has been much criticism of the process of selection, not least of which is levelled at the selection panels which consist of civil servants. There is also criticism that the SRB scheme is simply intended to disguise the fact that overall cuts in budgets are being made. Sir Jeremy Beecham, Chairman of the Association of Metropolitan Authorities noted that the announcement of the SRB funds for the first round 'came days after the Government's revenue support settlement for local authorities had cut £900m from the amount local authorities could spend on capital projects next year' (Authers, 1994, p. 7).

Robinson and Shaw (1994) suggest that the SRB initiative represents at the least a retreat from urban policy, as any area can now compete for funds. Rather than targeting funds on the most severely deprived areas, allocations now depend on open competition, and an area with a proficient bidding partnership may be successful in its bid for funds, whilst an arguably more deserving case with a weaker partnership may fail.

### Training and Enterprise Councils (TECs)

Whilst not directly a part of regional or urban policy, the TECs are major contributors to local economies and, as noted, are an integral part of local strategy formulation under the SRB bidding process. The TEC scheme was first announced at the end of the 1980s through the publication of the White Paper, *Employment for the 1990s*. Since this time 82 TECs have been launched in England and Wales (now 81 due to the financial failure of South Thames TEC in 1995) and 21 LECs (Local Enterprise Companies) have been founded in Scotland. The main purpose in initiating the TEC scheme was to overhaul the training system in Britain. TECs have a two-thirds private-sector majority on their governing boards and are intended to be market-led, responding directly to the needs of the business community. As TECs take their lead from the private sector, it was felt that they would be more responsive to the real training needs of industry and, as a consequence, would ensure relevant and cost-effective training. However, many commentators have argued that the skills revolution anticipated by government has not taken place (Peck and Emmerich, 1993). One of the criticisms widely made of TECs is the limited extent to which groups in the local economy can influence decision-making (I. C. Thomas, 1994). Further criticisms concern the extent to which disadvantaged people can benefit in real terms from the TECs and the lack of a coherent national strategy for training within the TEC framework (Peck and Emmerich, 1993). The Organisation for Economic Co-operation and Development (OECD) has also criticised the TEC initiative in an unpublished note on the UK labour market produced in 1994. The *Financial Times* (6 July 1994) reported the OECD as being critical of the UK's educational and skills base. With respect to these the OECD notes: 'Improvements are required if the UK is to reduce the large discrepancy between its ratio of skilled to unskilled workers compared with those of Germany and Japan' (*Financial Times*, 1994, p. 10).

In 1995 the TECs were subjected to a new funding regime which was intended to provide greater value for money. However, some feel that the new funding regime, which places emphasis on workers finding employment at the end of training, will encourage TECs only to train those who it is felt have a very high likelihood of success of gaining employment. This will militate against training weaker groups, thus further worsening their position. In the financial year 1995–6, TEC budgets were slashed overall by 19 per cent, to £1.4 billion (Taylor, 1995).

## Regional policy in the European Union

When the European Community was initially founded in the 1950s regional problems did not present themselves as an issue for Community action. During the 1960s debate on the formation of an economic and monetary union led to the observation that chronic regional disparities could undermine this ideal. As a consequence, it was noted that the community should seek to promote a convergence of income levels across the member states. However, it was not until the community membership was widened in 1973 through the accession of the UK, Denmark and Ireland that steps were taken to establish the mechanism for regional assistance. In 1975 the European Regional Development Fund (ERDF) was formed. Initially the ERDF was intended to support and augment the member states' own regional policies. However, the further widening of the Community by the addition of Greece in 1981 and Spain and Portugal in 1986 has led to a more important profile for Community regional policy. The inclusion of Greece, Spain and Portugal meant that the Community had incorporated some of the poorer and relatively underdeveloped European nations into its membership, and disparities within the Community were now more marked. Another issue pushing regional development to the fore was the move towards a Single European Market (SEM). The SEM was seen to represent the possibility of significant economic gains for the Community, but it was noted that the weaker members might not be in a position to reap the full benefits. Furthermore, it was seen that the strongest countries would gain from a concentration of the benefits from economies of scale.

The Maastricht Treaty establishes the need to promote social and economic cohesion as a fundamental principle in achieving the further development and success of the community. Furthermore, there is a commitment to reducing disparities between regions and, in particular, helping the disadvantaged regions and rural areas. The scale of the problem here is substantial. Disparities between the richest and poorest regions are large, and over the last twenty years have shown little evidence of narrowing. As the *Economist* (1995b, p. 65) notes: 'Per capita income in the ten poorest regions is still less than a third of the ten richest, and the unemployment gap between the 25 lowest- and highest-ranking regions is more than five to one.'

However, the redoubled commitment to regional aid as a tool to ensure cohesion can be seen in the recent growth of the overall regional budget: for the next five years, 1994–9, this has been more than doubled from the 1989–93 base and stands at 156 billion ecu.

### Structural funds

The Union's regional policy is exercised primarily through the agency of the structural funds. These funds operate to promote development in those areas which are lagging, or to facilitate restructuring and convergence for those areas whose agricultural or industrial base is in decline. The five structural funds are:

1. The European Regional Development Fund (ERDF). The main purpose of this fund is to provide joint finance with member governments for the provision of infrastructure. This often takes the form of building roads and developing industrial estates. The fund will also support investments which either create new jobs or preserve existing ones. Other uses of finance include the promotion and encouragement of small and medium-sized enterprises (SMEs).
2. The European Agricultural Guidance and Guarantee Fund (EAGGF). The purpose of this is to provide price support for farms (over 90 per cent of funds), other forms of assistance for farms,and protection for the rural environment.
3. The European Social Fund. This is primarily concerned with training and education as a means of promoting the recruitment of marginalised members of the labour market, in particular the young.
4. A Financial Instrument for Fisheries Guidance. This measure was introduced as a means of smoothing out the restructuring of the fishing industry.
5. The Cohesion Fund. This fund was established under the Maastricht Treaty and focuses particularly on the development of infrastructure. However, it is targeted at individual states rather than regions and is available only to those poorer members whose GNP per head is less than 90 per cent of the EU average.

There are also a number of specific initiatives amongst which are schemes intended to assist regions which have problems caused by the retrenchment of key industries. These are RETEX for textiles, RECHAR for coal mining, RESIDER for steelmaking, RENAVAL for shipbuilding and KONVER, defence.

**Objectives of regional policy**

There are a number of objectives decided upon in 1988 which form the cornerstone of European policy. These are concerned with the development of the least advantaged areas, the employment of young people, restructuring in agriculture and forestry, development of rural areas, measures to deal with long-term unemployment, and restructuring of areas of major industrial decline.

These objectives translate into the use of the structural funds. In gaining access to funds regions must satisfy the requirements of certain categories for funding. These funds are categorised under the headings of objectives and relate to different conditions and uses.

*Objective 1:* Over two-thirds of structural funding is targeted at those regions which lag behind the rest. Initially, this covered those areas where GDP per capita was below 75 per cent of the EU average. This definition has now been relaxed to include regions close to this threshold such as Merseyside and the Scottish Highlands and Islands in the UK and parts of the Netherlands, Belgium and France along with the former East Germany. These areas join Greece, Portugal, the Republic of Ireland, Spain and Southern Italy. In the 1994–9 budget Objective 1 covers 26.6 per cent of the Union's population, compared to 21.7 per cent under the 1989–93 round. Spain continues to be the major recipient of funding.

*Objective 2:* This is for the use of areas which are suffering from economic decline and experiencing above average unemployment, but not eligible for Objective 1 funding. About 25 per cent of the Union's population will eventually be in areas receiving this funding, with the UK heading the list of recipients at present.

*Objective 3:* This is for the purpose of fighting long-term unemployment and integrating the marginalised elements of the labour force. The main mechanisms here are training schemes and aid for temporary employment. The UK, followed by France, is the largest claimant.

*Objective 4:* This is a recent addition and aims to help employees to adapt to changing industrial circumstances through reskilling. The UK does not participate in this objective.

*Objective 5a:* This is concerned with the restructuring of agriculture and fisheries.

*Objective 5b:* This is designed to assist those rural areas with high dependence on agriculture, low agricultural incomes, population loss and low economic development.

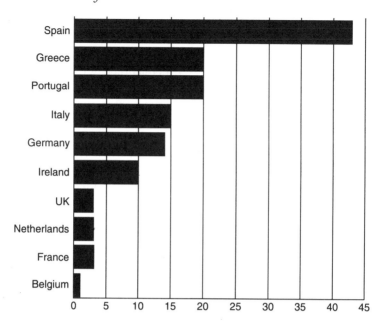

*Source*:    *The EIU European Yearbook* 1994–95, Economist Intelligence Unit Limited, 1995.

FIGURE 7.2    **The division of the spoils, 1994–8: allocation of structural cohesion funds, Ecu bn**

The allocation of regional funding is shown in Figure 7.2. As can be seen, the major beneficiaries are Spain, Greece and Portugal, all of whom joined the community in the 1980s. Until the 1980s the main exception to a fairly homogeneous economic grouping within the community was the Mezzogiorno (Southern Italy). The addition of the new members in the 1980s and more recently the new *Lander* in Eastern Germany, has meant a significant increase in disparities within the Union and a larger periphery. This increase in regional differences in labour market conditions and incomes has occurred at the same time as a policy shift towards greater economic integration. A number of frictions have developed in the application of Union regional policy, not least of which is the controversy over additionality. With the doubling of the structural funds after 1989 it was made conditional that European funding should be in addition to national expenditure not in place of.

A future problem for community regional policy will be posed if membership is widened to include some central and eastern European countries formerly in the Soviet bloc. Under current funding rules such countries would be recipients of substantial net transfers, and this would pose enormous financial and political strains on existing members (Begg, Gudgin and Morris,

1995). The future for Union regional policy, then, is fraught with difficulties and the closer economic integration necessary for economic and monetary union (EMU) seems to be a difficult task.

## Conclusions

Regional and urban policy has a long and controversial history. Those on the right of the political spectrum would tend to argue for less spending on such policy, as they would contest that much of this expenditure is wasted and the problems continue. Indeed the continuing divergence of regional fortunes is rather depressing. However, this may constitute an argument for spending more, not less. Leaving the market to solve the complex factors that contribute to regional disparities may be the route to social and economic disaster. Furthermore, it would necessitate the further postponement of such programmes as EMU as any convergence would be a lengthy process, even if ultimately possible. It seems clear that regional and urban policy is set to continue to be one of the most controversial policy issues at both the national and European levels for the indefinite future.

# CHAPTER 8

# Economic Policy and the Environment

## Introduction

The broad area of environmental economics represents a classic example of externalities whereby the actions of one individual (or group of individuals) have an effect on another individual (or group of individuals). The range of enquiry is diverse and extensive, covering, for example, noise pollution, urban congestion, air quality and global warming. As such, environmental economics can examine individual household behaviour, the behaviour of firms, intercontinental pollution and the global effects of collective actions. Therefore, policy prescriptions are equally diverse. Interventionist and non-interventionist debates spawn a vast literature. There are also the environmental 'fundamentalists' who advocate a return to the manorial economy to replenish the Earth's natural resources.

Although we may take an eclectic view of the problems that are involved in this area, it is necessary to narrow the debate somewhat and approach the subject, and thus the economic policy, in a much more systematic and subjective manner. Thus, after considering the alternative economic theory, we will concentrate on two areas where policy is required: urban congestion and global warming. Many of the debates in these areas have important implications and parallels in other areas of environmental concern.

## Philosophy and methodology

Associated with the Green Movement is the idea of 'zero-growth', whereby the objective of policy should be no economic growth, taking its premise from the Club of Rome report, *Limits to Growth* (1972). The report suggested that industrial activity on a global scale was increasing not in a steady, linear, fashion but at an accelerating rate, exponentially. As such, a 3 per cent per annum growth rate represents a doubling of production every 24 years, and the report foresaw scarcity, pollution and famine on a global scale within the next one hundred years, unless the current trend were to be arrested and even reversed. The major criticism of the report was that it does not necessarily follow that because the existing patterns of economic growth are damaging to the environment, the solution should be zero growth. It crucially depends upon what it is that is growing and to what extent an increase in GNP affects the environment. It is not necessarily the case that a rising GNP leads automatically to a worsening of the environment. Jacobs points to Japan, which had the highest growth rate in the industrialised world and the lowest energy intensity (Jacobs, 1991, p. 56).

The orthodox, or valuation approach, to environmental economics is to concentrate on the opportunity cost of environmental protection and where marginal cost equates with marginal benefit the amount of protection is said to be optimal. In practice, the costs may be known, but the benefits are difficult to measure. Even if the costs are known, we cannot evaluate the costs of any changes in terms of the economy or society as a whole. Therefore the approach depends upon the idea that the environment can be valued and an optimum value can be determined, but a large proportion of the value of the environment cannot be known as it holds an intrinsic value.

Jacobs (1991) sees environmental economic policy-making as a two-stage process whereby in the first stage targets are set for the major environmental indicators, and the second stage consists of influencing economic activity such that it does not exceed these targets. This involves a mix of instruments which could include taxes, regulations and expenditure by the state, designed to constrain individual firm and household behaviour. In addition he outlines two types of indicator for which targets should be set: first, the *primary indicators* which measure stocks of key environmental features such as soil, forests, land use, water resources, atmospheric composition and diversity of species. Then the *secondary indicators* which measure those economic activities that affect the primary indicators. For example, pollutant discharge rates which cause changes in land, air and water pollution. 'It is the primary indicator which means sustainability: but it is the secondary indicator upon which the economic instruments of the second stage of policy making can act' (Jacobs, 1991, p. 120).

## Neo-classical orthodoxy

The economic principles of the economics of environmental policy are located in the theory of externalities. Here pollution is viewed as a public 'bad', resulting from the output of 'waste' in the production process of private goods. Thus we can model the relationship in the following manner:

$C$ = goods consumed
$W$ = pollution level
$E$ = emission of waste which results in pollution from the production of $C$
$L$ = inputs of labour and capital

Thus:

$$U = U(C, W) \tag{1}$$
$$C = C(L, E, W) \tag{2}$$
$$W = W(E) \tag{3}$$

[it is assumed that the signs of the partial derivatives are:

$U_c > 0,\ U_w > 0,\ C_L > 0,\ C_E > 0,\ C_W < 0,\ \text{and}\ W_E < 0\,]$

Therefore, the utility of the so-called 'representative consumer' in (1) depends upon a vector of goods consumed and the level of pollution. Hence the level of consumer satisfaction depends upon the mix of 'goods' and 'bads' contained in the vector of goods consumed.

Equation (2) indicates that pollution emanates from the emission of waste in the production of goods consumed. It follows that the emission of waste is treated in this model as if it were another factor of production. Hence, the reduction in $E$ will result in a reduction in output in exactly the same way as if any other factor of production were to be reduced in the production process. In addition, the production function includes as an assumption the pollution level ($W$), because this may well have a detrimental effect on production in addition to the disutility to consumers that is produced. In the simplest case, $W$ will be equal to the sum of emissions of all producers. Extending the model, we can introduce the defensive activities of the victims of pollution and amend the utility function accordingly.

$$U = U[C, F(L, W)] \tag{4}$$

Now, individuals may employ a vector of inputs ($L$), to reduce their exposure to pollution. The actual level of exposure ($F$), would depend upon the extent of pollution ($W$) and the use of inputs in the defensive activities. Further, defensive activities of producers may also be introduced. With such a model it is therefore possible to evaluate the behaviour of individual households and firms within the system. By maximising the utility of the representative individual, we can produce a set of first order conditions for a Pareto-efficient outcome:

$$\frac{\partial C}{\partial e} = \left[ \sum \frac{\partial u}{\partial W} \cdot \frac{\partial W}{\partial E} \Big/ \frac{\partial U}{\partial C} + \sum \left( \frac{\partial C}{\partial W} \cdot \frac{\partial W}{\partial E} \right) \right] \tag{5}$$

This suggests that polluting firms should continue to extend their emissions of waste up to the point at which the marginal product of waste equals the sum of the marginal damage imposed on consumers and on producers. In other words, measures to control pollution should be followed by each polluting agent up to the point at which the marginal benefits from reduced pollution equal the marginal alleviation cost.

The first order condition relating to the 'efficient' level of defensive activities is shown by,

$$\frac{\partial U}{\partial F} \cdot \frac{\partial F}{\partial L} = \frac{\partial U}{\partial C} \cdot \frac{\partial C}{\partial L} \tag{6}$$

Here, the marginal value of each input should be equated in its use in production and defensive activities. We may then derive the first order conditions that characterise a competitive market equilibrium. The outcome is that competitive firms, with free access to environmental resources, will continue to engage in polluting activities until the marginal return is zero, where $\frac{\partial C}{\partial E} = 0$.

The conclusion drawn is that, in a competitive economy, firms will disregard the external costs imposed on others and will engage in socially excessive levels of polluting activities.

## Policy implications

Polluting agents should be confronted with a 'price' equal to the marginal external cost of their polluting activities in order to induce them to internalise at the margin the full social cost of their activities. As such, a Pigouvian tax could be introduced as a levy on the polluting agent, equal to the expression in equation (5). Hence decisions by producers and consumers could then be made in the light of full-cost prices. This tax would be negative, in the form of a subsidy, where there was an external benefit or positive externality. However, it has not been possible for governments to implement such a policy and there are no examples of a system of Pigouvian taxes being used (see Figure 8.1).

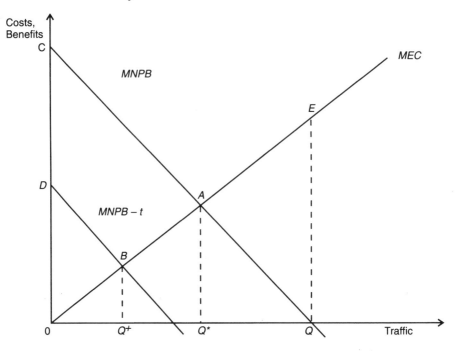

Costs,
Benefits

**FIGURE 8.1   A Pigouvian tax**

*Notes*
1.  Traffic level Q maximises net private travel.
2.  Marginal net private benefit falls as traffic increases until additional use adds no extra utility.
3.  Socially optimal traffic level Q* where *MNPB* = marginal environmental costs (*MEC*).
4.  To reduce traffic to socially optimal level, a tax is imposed of *t* per unit of traffic.
5.  Making road users aware of social costs, changing their decision-making perameter to
    *MNPB* – *t* (example of such a tax: differential tax on leaded petrol).
6.  Authorities gain revenue of *CDAQ**.

*Source*:   K. J. Button, *Transport Economics*, 2nd edn, Edward Elgar, Aldershot, 1994,
p. 150.

The Pigouvian solution to the problems of externalities has been repeatedly
attacked. Coase (1960) has argued that, in the absence of transactions costs and
strategic behaviour, the distortions associated with externalities will be
resolved through voluntary bargains struck among the interested parties.
Hence the inducements provided by the Pigouvian tax are not required to
achieve an efficient outcome. Turvey (1963) showed how a Pigouvian tax
would itself be a source of distortion in a Coasian setting and that 'any
general prescription of a tax to deal with external diseconomies is useless'.

Thus he argued that every case should be evaluated on its own merits, and no reason exists to believe that a tax would be preferable to alternative methods. In addition Turvey suggested that it is not certain that any methods would be particularly desirable unless information is costless as in the Coasian theory (Turvey, 1963). It is highly unlikely that voluntary agreements could be reached other than in the case of a small number of polluting agents.

### Urban congestion

The decision to build a road from point A to point B will have an effect on the uses to which the land at, around and between A and B can be put. In addition, this effect will last for as long as the road remains in existence. Also, the increased use made by people of this land, whether for residential, industrial or commercial purposes, will change the demand for transport in other parts of the region. It is also true to suggest that similar arguments will apply to rail supplies.

For economic analysis we can assume that the consumer is continuing to attempt to maximise utility/satisfaction. Thus the consumer will try to make the best of any situation with which he/she is confronted, given the very imperfect level of knowledge that will exist. However, it will be no longer possible to say that this represents the 'best' of all economic worlds: if the road had been constructed from A to C, or a railway instead of a road, would the consumer have been better off? The important point here is that of land usage and transport, and different modes of transport are interdependent. Thus a decision about one variable, taken without reference to the others, will put the consumer in the best possible position only by a highly unlikely and very lucky accident. Hence the decision to change anything (land usage or transport) must be made by reference to all the independent factors.

Apart from the problem of interdependence, there are several other reasons as to why the market is unable to supply transport services which would be regarded as 'efficient' in terms of relative quantities and qualities. For instance, road space is not sold in the usual manner, nor is it supplied whenever and wherever it makes a profit. Public transport systems follow price and supply policies which are a far cry from what would result in the absence of severe regulations of any alternative suppliers. Intervention takes place by various institutions to control, regulate, encourage and often to discourage, various transport activities. This non-market-generated information has to be taken into consideration, and a cost-benefit methodology can be used to evaluate alternatives.

Because road space is not sold in the usual way, high-demand road space has a 'price' that is similar to low-demand road space. Therefore high-demand road space is not rationed by price, but by congestion and overcrowding of transport services. In the absence of increased supply of road space where

TABLE 8.1   Car ownership in Great Britain

| Year | Cars and vans ('000s) | Cars and vans per capita |
|------|------------------------|--------------------------|
| 1930 | 1 056 | 0.023 |
| 1935 | 1 477 | 0.032 |
| 1940 | 1 423 | 0.030 |
| 1945 | 1 487 | 0.031 |
| 1950 | 2 258 | 0.045 |
| 1955 | 3 526 | 0.071 |
| 1960 | 5 526 | 0.108 |
| 1965 | 8 917 | 0.169 |
| 1970 | 11 515 | 0.213 |
| 1975 | 13 747 | 0.252 |
| 1980* | 14 772 | 0.277 |
| 1985* | 16 454 | 0.320 |
| 1990* | 19 742 | 0.374 |

*Not strictly comparable because of changes in the data collection method.
*Source*:   Transport statistics in Great Britain (various years) in K. J. Button, *Transport Economics*, 2nd edn, Edward Elgar, Aldershot, 1994, p. 58.

demand is high, the failure to ration by price, or by other means, has caused increases in the use of private motor vehicles and reduced public transport patronage during off-peak periods.

A substantial part of the increase in peak-hour traffic has therefore been met by overcrowding and infrequent services. It is possible to envisage the provision of better quality urban transport facilities both in terms of the technical constraints and from an economic point of view. However, the overriding question that needs to be addressed is what form of urban transport is likely to be the most efficient?

How do we define efficiency? To the consumer it may be a reflection of likes and dislikes; to the economist it may depend upon the relationship that exists between the value of the inputs (costs) and the value of the outputs (benefits) that are associated with alternative proposals. That is, in a fully employed economy, the economic (or opportunity) cost of producing more of a particular output (for example, road space) is the value of output foregone in some other service or good. Hence an 'efficient' allocation of resources is achieved when it is not possible to produce a combination of outputs which is more highly valued by the community. The technical constraints are quite clear-cut. In the absence of a transporter of the type found on the 'USS *Enterprise*', to costlessly dematerialise a person at point A, and costlessly rematerialise him/her at point B, then this is a very real (and less exciting) constraint on our ability to move people between two points. The economic constraints are less clear-cut: if prices are given, then different income levels and preferences of consumers will produce different demands for the same price. For example, standing on an overcrowded bus when the same journey could be made in a Rolls-Royce can be explained by either differences in preference or differences in income. However, it can be shown that a given sum of money transferred from the driver of the Rolls-Royce to the person standing on the bus will produce greater economic welfare for the bus user than would an equivalent amount of expenditure given to improving the quality of public transport, or on subsidising the price. This is because the bus user is able to decide as to how the sum of money is to be spent, and using it for better transport facilities is only one of many possibilities. But if public transport is subsidised, the bus user is forced to spend the extra income on public transport.

Price policy may be used as an inducement to guide people on to particular modes of transport at particular times of the day. For example, high parking charges at certain times and places may be an alternative to a complete ban on parking. However, there are basic problems involved in terms of the pricing of transport. The first of these involves the evaluation of investment. This can occur at many levels. For example, decisions as to the proper share of total national investment that should be allocated to transport will be made by central government, whilst investigations into small-scale road improvement schemes may be taken by local authorities. The decisions are therefore shared by central government and a variety of government bodies, local authorities, firms and individuals. There is then a problem of co-ordination and accountability. The second problem is one of resource allocation. 'Orthodox' economic theory suggests that the price mechanism is the best mechanism to allocate resources. However, there are many reasons why the price mechanism may not be wholly adequate in the area of transport. There is a widespread existence of joint costs, there is a problem of choosing between short-run costs, marginal costs and average costs as a suitable basis for charging. In addition, transport prices may be distorted by government taxes and subsidies, and by the difficulties involved in charging for the infrastructure of the economy.

Two major issues are implied: firstly, the place of government in an industry which in Britain is partly in the public sector and partly in the private sector. The government is both a direct provider of services and a source of taxes and subsidies as well as providing many regulations that directly affect the industry. Secondly, there is the requirement to be able to measure the value of time, because the main product of any transport investment is usually a reduction in journey time. It is essential, therefore, to have information on the money value of time when evaluating transport investment.

The decisions that are taken on road investment are made by central government and local authorities, but with the main responsibility firmly in the hands of the central government. The Department of the Environment pays the whole cost of investment in motorway and trunk roads and 75 per cent of the cost of principal roads. No government has yet been prepared to trust wholly either central planning or the market. The market solution would involve selling road space and linking road investment to the amount people are prepared to pay to use that road space. The main difficulty of allowing the market mechanism to determine transport investment has been the problem of charging for roads and bridges. In addition, it is a problem of social costs and benefits that are not reflected in the price mechanism. The aims of investment policy could be to maximise either consumer surplus, producers' surplus, or net total of consumer and producer surplus. Maximising consumer surplus would involve authorising the investment that would enlarge a transport system up to the point at which total demand could be met when the price equals zero. The major disadvantage of this is that it would mean the overexpansion of transport services in comparison with other goods and services and would lead to distortions through the necessity of raising subsidies to cover the losses of undertakings with zero revenue.

*The theory of pricing*

It can be shown that the satisfying of the first and second order conditions for a Paretian optimum position (that the marginal rate of substitution and the marginal rate of transformation for any two goods are equalised) can be achieved by setting price equal to marginal cost. It is possible to make allowance for any distributional effects of investment decisions by adding weights to the benefits (or costs) that will accrue to different individuals or groups. If utility is measured by the 'willingness to pay' criteria and the decision-maker makes allowance for the unequal distribution of income, then each £1 of gain or loss for lower income groups can be weighted more heavily than a £1 change in benefits for higher income groups. Therefore, if the costs and benefits of constructing a new road bridge over a river are to be calculated, the 'willingness to pay' data may be weighted to allow for the income level of the particular region involved. The weights would be determined by value judgement.

There exist four other major difficulties in the application of marginal cost pricing to transport: Firstly, there is the possible creation of distortions if marginal cost pricing is used in some cases but not in others. This would tend to divert demand from other sectors where the price is based on average cost. Secondly, there are major difficulties in using marginal cost pricing where there are discontinuities in the production process and output can be expanded only by indivisible 'lumps'. Thirdly, there is the problem of undertakings with falling long-run costs, making a loss and needing to be subsidised from some source. Fourthly, there are the technical difficulties that exist in identifying and measuring marginal costs and in devising an appropriate pricing system. Marginal costs differ in different situations. For example, they differ at different times of the day.

In practice, there are several objections to the introduction of tolls on road space: the costs of collection tend to be high and the likelihood of diverting traffic to other non-priced roads is high, with the consequences of a reduction in the benefits obtained from the toll road.

*Congestion tax*

This is another possible method of using the price mechanism to ration scarce road space. The theoretical arguments were again developed by Professor Pigou in his discussions of a firm's purchases under conditions of rising costs caused by decreases in the productivity of the factors of production. Figure 8.2 shows the case where the 'price' paid for the road space (vehicle running costs plus time costs) is $OC_2$, with the unconstrained traffic flow $OF_3$. However, beyond $OF_2$ (where marginal cost and average cost intersect) every additional road user imposes more costs on other road users than the benefits obtained from travelling on the road. The costs of extending 'output' from $OF_2$ to $OF_3$ are, $F_2EGF_3$, while the benefits are only $F_2EHF_3$. Hence, it is argued, a tax ($ET$) should be imposed to reduce traffic flows to $OF_2$ – a congestion tax.

Critics of a congestion tax have argued that the benefits to road users are measured by the size of the payments (in time and money) that consumers of road space are prepared to make. This measurement may be a misleading guide to the maximisation of utility or of economic welfare unless we are prepared to make the value judgement that income is optimally distributed.

In Figure 8.3 we have two alternative routes, one direct and one circuitous, from a suburban area ($S$) to the city centre ($C$) and there is a one-way traffic flow from $S$ to $C$. Assume that before the imposition of a congestion tax, 10 000 vehicles used the direct route during the rush hour, taking an average of 60 minutes to complete the journey. Thus total travelling time is 600 000 minutes. After the tax is imposed, 5000 vehicles continue to use the direct route, congestion is reduced and they complete the journey in an average of 40 minutes. The other 5000 divert to the longer route, taking 100 minutes. The overall average travelling time, after the imposition of the tax, would be 70 minutes (total travelling time of 700 000 minutes). Therefore, if the community accepted the value judgement that, for the journey to work, the time of all travellers should be given equal weight, then the tax would not be efficient and, as such, would not be imposed.

The tax would result in a net gain only if the time of the travellers continuing to use the direct route was valued at a greater level per minute of travelling time than that of the displaced travellers. However, there are other situations where the tax could have beneficial effects. For example, some road users without a strong reason to travel in peak hours would delay their journey to a different time. Car occupancy rates may be raised and more people may use public transport.

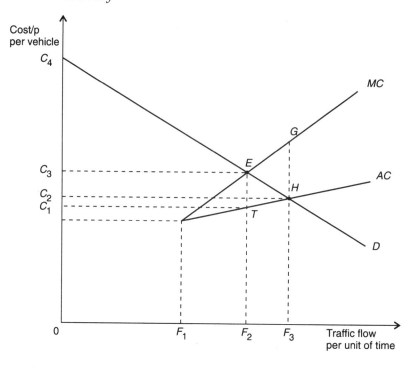

Notes
$C_4, D$ is the demand curve for space on the congested road
$AC$ = average cost
$MC$ = marginal cost
These include the time costs of the journey which increase with the traffic flow beyond $OF_1$ when
the road begins to get congested and each additional vehicle slows down all other vehicles.

**FIGURE 8.2    Congestion tax**

Governments throughout the world have appeared to prefer to live with
worsening traffic congestion rather than risk the political repercussions of
introducing any firm commitment to any form of road pricing. However, as
the effects of traffic congestion in the urban environment continue to grow
ever more damaging, the need for a solution becomes ever more urgent.

As the demand for road space increases, the response of an increase in the
supply of road space creates a further increase in demand due to the initial
reduction in journey times, and the increase in supply enhances the attractiveness of private travel. However, to take the policy decision not to increase
the supply of road space would lead to extended journey times, not only for
private travel, but also for public road transport. Hence, initiatives are

(1) Pre-tax

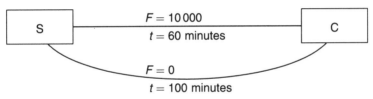

(2) Post-tax

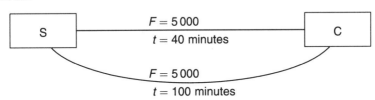

**FIGURE 8.3   Effects of congestion tax on traffic flow**

required to switch travel from road to rail, and therefore the supply of rail transport has to be increased. The implementation of this policy should result in freight moving from road to rail, reducing journey times for the non-freight traveller, making it more attractive and, possibly, increasing demand for road space. The outcome here could therefore be one where freight is moved by rail, but the roads remain congested.

There must therefore be a tax and/or subsidy policy, or a regulatory policy. That is, a combination of 'carrot' and 'stick', an element of public choice and an element of state force. This may be in terms of individuals choosing public transport in terms of relative cost, but also being forced to use public transport through the lack of any alternative: thus reducing demand without increasing the supply of road space.

## Global warming

The 'Greenhouse' effect is the increase in the atmospheric concentrations of gases that cause global warming, causing the possibility of climate change. There appears to be a general agreement amongst the scientific community that the concentrations of 'greenhouse' gases are increasing. However, there is less of a consensus about the possible outcomes of this increasing concentration. Disagreement is also apparent between the goals of the environmentalists and the needs of developing countries. This conflict of interests came to the forefront during the Uruguay Round of GATT. Poor countries tend to criticise those Western environmentalists who appear to place greater value on the preservation of ecosystems than they do on the requirements of people for increasing incomes and higher levels of energy use.

Pearce and Turner argue that transboundary pollution, which arises when one country's pollution can cause environmental damage in another, is an externality between the emitter and the recipient. Whereas, 'mutual externality is where the polluters damage both themselves and others', polluting what Pearce and Turner refer to as the 'global commons', the resources that are shared as common property by all nations such as the atmosphere, the stratosphere and the world's oceans (Pearce and Turner, 1991, p. 191).

The principle greenhouse gas, carbon dioxide, has increased by more than 12 per cent in the past three decades (World Bank, 1992, p. 61). Human activity is the main cause of the change in concentrations and the emissions of carbon dioxide have more than doubled over the period as a result of such activities (ibid., p. 61). The Intergovernmental Panel on Climate Change stated that 'sometime in the next century, heat trapping from increases in greenhouse gases is likely to reach a level equivalent to a doubling of carbon dioxide concentrations over the pre-industrial level' (ibid., p. 62). Many unknowns are involved in terms of scientific knowledge as to the implications for the planet of such increases in the concentrations of greenhouse gases: How will the climate change? How quickly will this change occur? What will be the distribution of the change on a regional basis? However, it is known that a threat exists and that something must be done to respond to this threat.

The response has to be global in scope because the effects are global. The emissions of greenhouse gases have many origins but affect the climate collectively. Therefore negotiations and agreements have to be international. However, national interests differ as between the richer industrial economies and the poorer developing economies, as well as those nations heavily dependent on the export of fossil fuels. The richer countries have been emitting larger amounts of greenhouse gases over a longer period, and as such have contributed a disproportionate amount of the accumulated gases in the atmosphere, approximately 60 per cent from fossil fuels (World Bank, 1992, p. 158). In addition, the emissions from the developing economies are growing more rapidly, although from a much lower base. Table 8.2 on pp. 166–7 shows the relative contributions from 62 economies. The climate change will affect different countries differently and will distort the costs and benefits of policies that may be adopted.

The 1992 Earth Summit in Brazil (the Rio Conference), offered the UN Framework Convention on Climate Change for signature. This had been signed by 158 nations by mid-October 1992 (Hayes and Smith, 1993). The major problem concerns the lack of any provision in the Convention for the funding of the proposals. These proposals may be expressed in four areas:

1.  An agreement to stabilise the concentration of greenhouse gases in the atmosphere at a level which would not cause change to the climate system. This would involve cutting emissions to 1990 levels by the year 2000;
2.  To achieve this at a rate sufficient to enable ecosystems to adapt naturally to any climate change that may occur;
3.  To enable sustainable development to occur;
4.  To ensure a lack of threat to food production.

The United Nations Conference on Climate Change in Berlin in March/April 1995 involved more than 40 developing countries and proposed sharp cuts in emissions of greenhouse gases. The proposal was put forward by 46 members of the G77 group of developing nations, and calls upon states to recognise the inadequacy of existing attempts to reduce the level of emissions. The group proposed that emissions should be reduced by 20 per cent by 2005, pointing out that only a handful of states are on target to meet their commitments under the agreement of Rio. It has been suggested that the 1995 proposal will meet heavy opposition from the US because of its hostility to the imposition of a timetable or of targets for reductions, and also from OPEC who fear reductions in demand for fossil fuels (*Financial Times*, 4 April 1995). However, the newly industrialising countries such as China, India, Argentina and Brazil gave backing to the Berlin proposals.

The World Bank Development Report 1992 suggested that there are three possible policy alternatives:

1.  *Do nothing* – Incur no additional costs, other than continuing research, until greater knowledge of the implications of global warming is available.
2.  Take out an *insurance policy* – by means of precautionary measures that minimise cost now, but reduce the costs of future action.
3.  Take *immediate action* to reduce, or at least stabilise, the emission of greenhouse gases (World Bank, 1992, p. 159)

According to the report, the choice of policy depends upon the relative costs and benefits of halting global warming. It is suggested that a form of hybrid policy is sought whereby economic performance is improved simultaneously with a reduction in the output of greenhouse gases. The conclusion of the report is that the case for doing nothing, based on the relative benefits and costs, is not supportable. However, neither is there a case for immediate action as the costs are too high in relation to the prospective benefits. Hence it is proposed that the 'wisest' course of action would be to make modest, but immediate, cuts in the output of greenhouse gases, and to make investments that are designed to reduce the cost of achieving greater reductions in the future (World Bank, 1992, p. 161). Yet this could be viewed as far too conservative and as a 'too little, too late' policy.

TABLE 8.2   Proportion of world carbon emissions by country

| | *1986*<br>*Per capita emissions*<br>*(% of mean)* | *1950–86*<br>*Carbon emissions*<br>*(% of world)* |
|---|---|---|
| USA | 503 | 30.1 |
| Czechoslovakia | 424 | 1.4 |
| Canada | 412 | 2.3 |
| Australia | 388 | 1.1 |
| Bulgaria | 362 | 0.5 |
| USSR | 361 | 17.8 |
| Germany, United | 352 | 7.4 |
| Poland | 334 | 2.4 |
| UK | 296 | 4.8 |
| South Africa | 280 | 1.2 |
| Belgium | 269 | 0.9 |
| Saudi Arabia | 260 | 0.2 |
| Netherlands | 242 | 0.8 |
| Romania | 242 | 0.9 |
| Japan | 212 | 5.6 |
| Hungary | 199 | 0.5 |
| Korea, Dem | 194 | 0.5 |
| France | 180 | 2.9 |
| Italy | 166 | 1.9 |
| Greece | 163 | 0.2 |
| Yugoslavia | 150 | 0.5 |
| Venzuela | 149 | 0.4 |
| Spain | 129 | 0.9 |
| Korea, Rep | 109 | 0.5 |
| Mexico | 91 | 0.1 |
| Argentina | 85 | 0.6 |
| Portugal | 80 | 0.1 |
| Syria | 78 | 0.1 |
| Algeria | 69 | 0.1 |
| Turkey | 69 | 0.4 |
| Iran | 68 | 0.4 |
| Malaysia | 58 | 0.1 |
| Iraq | 56 | 0.1 |
| China | 53 | 6.8 |
| Chile | 49 | 0.1 |
| Colombia | 44 | 0.2 |
| Egypt | 42 | 0.2 |
| Brazil | 38 | 0.8 |
| Thailand | 26 | 0.1 |
| Morocco | 23 | 0.1 |
| India | 19 | 1.8 |

|  | 1986<br>*Per capita emissions*<br>*(% of mean)* | 1950–86<br>*Carbon emissions*<br>*(% of world)* |
|---|---|---|
| Cameroon | 17 | 0.01 |
| Indonesia | 17 | 0.3 |
| Philippines | 16 | 0.2 |
| Ivory Coast | 13 | 0.02 |
| Nigeria | 13 | 0.11 |
| Pakistan | 13 | 0.15 |
| Vietnam | 8 | 0.1 |
| Sri Lanka | 6 | 0.02 |
| Burma | 5 | 0.03 |
| Ghana | 5 | 0.02 |
| Kenya | 5 | 0.03 |
| Sudan | 4 | 0.02 |
| Zaire | 3 | 0.02 |
| Bangladesh | 3 | 0.04 |
| Madagascar | 2 | 0.01 |
| Nepal | 2 | 0.002 |
| Tanzania | 2 | 0.01 |
| Mozambique | 2 | 0.02 |
| Ethiopia | 1 | 0.01 |
| Uganda | 1 | 0.01 |

*Source*:   P. Hayes and K. Smith, *The Global Greenhouse Regime: Who Pays?*, Earthscan, London, 1993.

There are three possibilities in terms of the problem of finance involved in the reduction of emissions. This is particularly the case where the developing countries' incremental costs are beyond their means to meet obligations to pay:

## 1.   Carbon taxes

Such taxes may be used to reduce demand to a level that equates with emission quotas or an overall emission target. The argument in favour of such a tax is similar to that of the congestion tax discussed earlier. In the absence of government intervention, those who make use of fossil fuels will not be the bearers of the full costs of their actions. Others will bear these costs, in different times and places. Government could intervene to ensure that it is the polluter who pays, by calculating the damage associated with the use of fossil fuels and making the users pay for such damage. One outcome could be that users reduce emissions as they attempt to avoid payment for damage, minimising the sum of damages and the costs of abatement. However, a major deficiency of a carbon tax is that the policy-makers are unlikely to know the level of tax that will be required to achieve a given target level of emissions.

In terms of equity, a tax on fossil fuels would be a regressive tax, as those on lower incomes spend a higher proportion of their total income on energy than higher income groups. This is exemplified by the imposition of value added tax on domestic fuel in Britain. However, Barrett has suggested that as the tax would generate revenue, a portion of this could be distributed to poorer households in what is termed a 'tax-benefit' policy (Barrett, 1991, p. 36). But this redistribution may well be used to pay for more energy use, and will depend upon the price/income elasticity of demand for the taxed fuels. Another obstacle to the introduction of a carbon tax is the effect that it will have on international competitiveness which would make it highly unlikely that a decision to impose such a tax would be taken by a state unilaterally. Thus international agreement would be required to overcome the problem of free-riders, and the problems of monitoring and enforcement need to be addressed.

## 2.   *Tradeable permits*

Such a system has been advocated as an alternative to, or a supplement to, carbon taxes (see Markandya, 1991). It is envisaged that targets for emissions reduction could be set by regulators, but rather than state intervention being the instrument of policy, as with the carbon tax, the market would be allowed to set the price of the permits to pollute which could be traded, and this price, in essence, would be a tax. Figure 8.4 shows the marginal costs of reducing emissions in two countries, one rich and one poor, where the level of emissions are higher in the rich country but it has a lower marginal cost of reducing emissions. Introducing a tax of $T^*$ reduces emissions from $OB$ to $OE$, and with this tax the emissions of the poor country would be cut from $OF$ to $OG$ and those of the rich country from $OC$ to $OD$. The tax $(T^*)$ is equated to the marginal cost of reduction. It follows, therefore, that the sum of $FG + CD = BE$. The revenue collected from the rich country would be $OD \times T^*$, that from the poor country would be $OG \times T^*$ and from both together would be $OE \times T^*$.

The total number of permits issued by the regulatory authority would be equal to $OE$ and each country's demand for permits will be given by the marginal cost of abatement. Thus, given a price of $T^*$ for the permits, the demand for permits would be $OG$ for the poor country and $OD$ for the rich country. The total demand for permits equates exactly to the supply, clearing the market at the price of $T^*$.

It has been suggested that an international market in carbon dioxide permits could be implemented within three years (*Financial Times*, 1 April 1995). Such a project may include the US and several European countries and

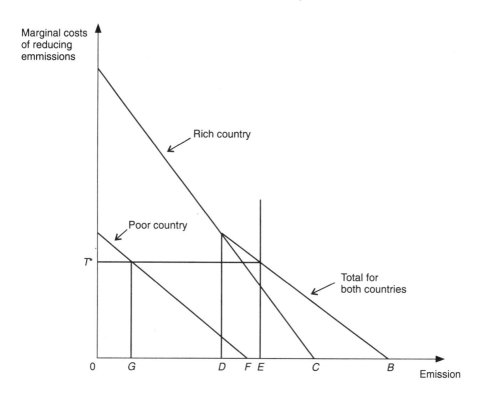

*Source*:   A. Markandya, 'Global warming: the economics of tradeable permits', in D. Pearce (ed.) *Blueprint 2: Greening the World Economy*, Earthscan, London, 1991, p. 54.

**FIGURE 8.4   Marginal costs of reducing emissions**

is recommended by the United Nations Conference on Trade and development (UNCTAD). The scheme has been based upon a US programme already in existence aiming to reduce acid rain by cutting sulphur dioxide emission by a third over a period of 20 years. The programme has been running since 1991 and consists of the allocation of certificates to emit sulphur dioxide to electric power plants that burn coal. If a power company reduces its emissions by introducing technology or switching to cleaner fuel, it may sell its surplus allowance to another company wishing to increase its emissions above its allocation. However, in practice, the companies have tended to be less than willing to trade their allowances.

A new United Nations Global Environment Protection Agency is proposed, which would organise and regulate the market as well as allocating carbon dioxide emission permits to participating national governments. Each government could then reallocate their permits to coal-powered power plants which are responsible for 70–80 per cent of carbon dioxide emissions (*Financial Times*, 1 April 1995).

However, the costs of monitoring will be very large indeed and it is not clear as to how it could be enforced on an intercontinental scale.

### 3.  *Emission abatement services*

This would involve the selling of low-cost abatement services by the developing countries to the advanced industrial countries. It makes the assumption that the developing countries have a large stock of inefficient energy-use equipment that is in excess of their own responsibility to reduce emissions. This excess potential for abatement gives the developing countries cheap abatement options available, relative to those available to the advanced industrial economies. In this view, the developing countries have a competitive edge in abatement services, if an international market for such services could be created. This may overcome the problems of monitoring and enforcement as these services could be provided by the private sector and would not require national governments to sign interstate agreements as in the case for tradeable permits. According to Hayes, abatement services would require:

(a)  that abatement targets be adopted by States and that these States devolve responsibility to meet the abatement commitments onto public and private entities within these countries.

(b)  that parties to the convention adopt rules recognising that abatement paid for by such an emission-reducing entity, but achieved at a saving relative to its own abatement costs in another country, can be debited from the emissions of the investors' country.

(Hayes and Smith, 1993, p. 163)

Hayes suggests that the price of the abatement services would settle at half of the difference between the advanced industrial countries and the developing countries marginal abatement cost.

One possible way of analysing the effects of individual rationality being in conflict with collective rationality is in the general form of game theory and, in particular, the prisoners' dilemma.

In Figure 8.5 the two countries, X and Y, are assumed to hold identical positions in terms of power, emissions, energy use, GNP, and so on. The pay-offs are a measure of the net gain after the costs of abatement have been deducted from the gross benefit due to the reduction in pollution. The first number in each pay-off pair of numbers relates to the pay-off to Country X and the second number relates to the pay-off to Country Y. Therefore, Country X will choose the non-agreement strategy aiming for the pay-off of 4 (rather

COUNTRY Y

| | | | |
|---|---|---|---|
| | Agreement | 3, 3 | 1, 4 |
| COUNTRY X | | | |
| | Non-agreement | 4, 1 | 2, 2 |

*Source*:   Adapted from Blackhurst and Subramanian in K. Anderson and R. Blackhurst (eds) *The Greening of World Issues*, Harvester-Wheatsheaf, London, 1993, p. 251.

**FIGURE 8.5   Prisoners' dilemma**

than 3 if choosing the strategy of agreement), selecting the low abatement strategy because it must share the gains with Country Y. Country Y also selects the non-agreement strategy for the same motives. The implication is that of an under-investment in abatement by both countries. However, the outcome is that each country actually achieves a pay-off of 2 (bottom right-hand quadrant). But if both had chosen a strategy of agreement, they would both have received a pay-off of 3. Hence both would be better of if they had negotiated an agreement.

However, it is also true to suggest that even if they had come to an agreement, an incentive to cheat on the agreement still exists because if one country sticks to the agreement, the pay-off for the other is higher if it cheats on the agreement. In the absence of a global authority to enforce an agreement, both countries would remain with the pay-off of 2, 2.

Relaxing some of the assumptions of this simple model may lead to a conclusion where the prospects for a lasting agreement are much better. In particular, if the game is repeated, each country is more likely to stick to an agreement if the other had demonstrated a will to co-operate by sticking to the agreement in the previous period, or through the threat of retaliation if the agreement is broken. In addition, increasing the number of participating countries in an agreement may reduce the prospects of a lasting agreement because of the greater incentive for an individual country to be a free-rider. Finally, the numbers in the matrix may not reflect all the costs involved in pollution reduction as there may be substantial economic costs that will vary between different countries.

## Conclusion

Policy recommendations concerning the problems of environmental degredation, whether local, national or global, must take into account the fact that individual rationality and collective rationality are not often coincident. If they are not, then intervention is required for the good of the community as a whole. At a national level, this requires the state to intervene using a combination of 'carrot and stick' policies designed to achieve the desired outcome: some measures of taxation and subsidy, some of the regulation of economic activity. This is also true if the community that is affected is the global community, but here we have the problems of co-ordination, monitoring and policing, *if* agreements between nations can be brokered. There exists no world body with the necessary power or authority to supervise such an operation. The Rio Conference was full of good and laudable ideas, but vested interests of the northern industrial nations fail to deliver the will necessary to have an impact.

Who are we to decide whether a rare Amazonian butterfly is of greater value than a Bengal tiger? Who is to know the effect on the ecosystem of the extinction of a rare but seemingly non-essential moth on a remote Pacific island? Should species diversity be a major goal of economists, politicians and policy advisers, given the resources that would be required to achieve this aim? Answers to these and many other questions concerning the environment remain, and always will remain, highly subjective and subject to vested interest and political will.

# CHAPTER 9

# Health and Education

## The importance of the health and education industries

These industries are clearly of crucial importance to the individual. The efficiency of the health service may literally be a matter of life and death; educational success or failure has a crucial effect on an individual's future career and income.

These industries also have an important economic significance. Future output may be determined in large part by the quality of the working population, and this quality results from the effects of these industries. Moreover these industries consume huge quantities of resources as Figures 9.1 and 9.2 show.

In both these industries the major component of spending is on staffing. In the health service, three-quarters of the revenue budget goes on staff because the National Health Service is a major employer. Over a million people are directly employed in the provision of health care in the UK (*Annual Abstract of Statistics*, 1995). Only 60 000 of these are general medical practioners, whilst there are 460 000 nurses and midwives. The rest include a wide range of occupations including non-health-specific jobs such as secretaries and electricians, as well as health professionals such as physiotherapists.

A similar picture emerges in the education industry. In 1995 there were 393 000 full-time equivalent teachers employed in maintained nursery, primary and secondary schools (DFE, 1995). In addition there were 100 000 educational support and administrative/clerical staff in schools. In addition to this there were an unknown number of caretakers, cleaners and canteen staff. Moreover, these figures only apply to maintained schools; in addition, 54 000 teachers work in independent schools and many more in colleges and universities.

The position in the UK is not exceptional. Figure 9.3 shows the importance of health as a share of GDP in a range of countries. Although comparisons can not be precise, for example, because the definition of 'health' may vary, it is clear that in all developed countries, spending on health takes up a significant proportion of the nation's resources.

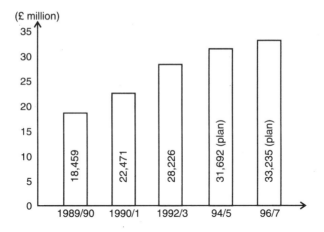

*Source*: Based on data from *The Government Expenditure Plan 1994/5–1996/7*, HMSO, 1994, Cm 2512.

**FIGURE 9.1    Department of health spending (£ billion)**

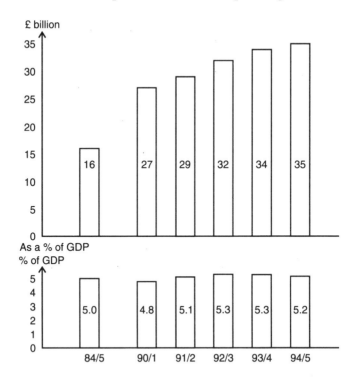

*Source*: Based on data from DFE, *Statistical Bulletin* 5.95, April 95.

**FIGURE 9.2    Education expenditure in the United Kingdom**

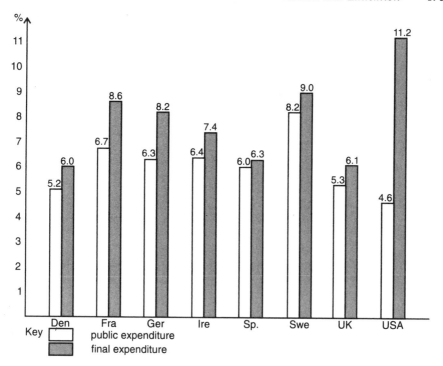

*Source*:    Based on data from *Health Care Systems in Transition*, OECD, Paris, 1990.

**FIGURE 9.3    Total and public health expenditure as a percentage of GDP**

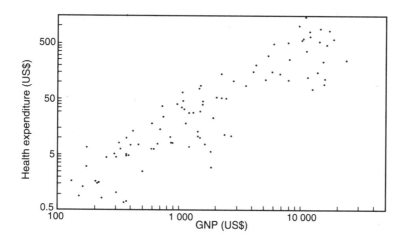

*Source*:    *World Health Statistics*, World Health Organisation, Geneva.

**FIGURE 9.4    Health expenditure and GNP per capita, 1987**

Although the education and health industries are not identical, they both consume a large amount of resources, and it is therefore important to ensure that these are allocated in an optimal way. One way in which this could be done would be to leave decision-making to the market.

### Market failure in health and education

There is a substantial consensus among economists that market forces are the best way to allocate resources to goods as diverse as alarm clocks, hairdressers or decorators. There is little or no government intervention in these industries, and the allocation of resources seems to be satisfactory. What makes education and health different?

The answer is that there is a widespread belief that unregulated markets would not give a satisfactory allocation of resources, for several reasons.

The first is a merit good argument. Although some economists would disagree, there is a strong case for suggesting that education and health have characteristics which are special, and that left to individual choice too few of these goods would be demanded. For example, some people would not buy private health insurance and would not have the money to pay for treatment if they were ill. In many poor countries, there is no universal provision of health services because the country cannot afford it, but even in a rich country, such as the USA, the market-based private insurance system means that millions of people cannot afford insurance and so are denied appropriate medical treatment. Moreover, some people with chronic conditions would not be able to afford private insurance or treatment so in a market system would go untreated. This line of argument is illustrated by the constitution of the World Health Organisation (1958, p. 459) which claims 'The enjoyment of the highest attainable standard of health is one of the fundamental rights of every human being without distinction of race, religion, political belief, economic or social condition'. Hence a fundamental difference between health care and consumer goods is that health care is seen as a moral right.

Similar arguments are applied to education. Children are not thought competent to choose how much education they ought to have and some parents might not be willing to buy education for their children. Hence the need to restrict consumer choice, and for state intervention to enable children to have a suitable education.

There is also an argument for intervention because of the existence of externalities. Smallpox is an example. This terrible disease, which once killed huge numbers of people, has been wiped out by government intervention to provide free vaccination. This argument applies to all other infectious diseases where one person's illness affects others. This market failure gives a strong case for government intervention.

The same argument applies to education. An educated person may benefit from higher earnings, but others also benefit: for example, if children learn acceptable values in school, then society benefits. As Durkheim (1956, p. 123) argues, education is 'above all, the means by which society perpetually recreates the conditions of its very existence'. In economic terms, this implies enormous externalities since if people are not socialised into accepting the values and rules of everyday life, then society as a whole may collapse.

Moreover, it is possible to argue that educated people contribute to higher living standards because they are innovative and that other people will benefit from these innovations. Left to the market, intelligent people may not choose, or may not able to afford, higher education. Hence the need for state intervention.

There is also a case for the government to intervene on the grounds that individuals lack the information necessary to make informed choices – the basic assumption on which the market forces argument rests. Few young people possess the knowledge to choose subjects which will lead to a suitable career; and most adults lack knowledge about health that would enable them to choose suitable treatment. Consequently there is asymmetric information – medical information is held by doctors and other medical staff and, since these are also providers of medical services, consumers may be persuaded to choose medical treatment which is in the interest of the provider rather than in their own interest. A variation of this argument is that 'the role for users of health care is that of patient. The patient role is characterised by trust, passivity, compliance and dependence . . . A consumer in contrast to a patient is a questioning, active and informed decision maker' (Hibbard and Weeks, 1989). Hence there are strong reasons to believe that an uncontrolled market approach is inappropriate for health, and consequently there is a strong case for governments to intervene in this market to correct resource misallocation arising from information failure.

There is a further argument, linked to that put forward by Durkheim. Governments are interested in *control*; above all they want public order. Educated people often threaten the established system because they have ideas which challenge those in authority. This makes governments keen to control the diffusion of knowledge, for example, by introducing a national curriculum.

These arguments are compelling. Every government in the world intervenes in the markets for health and education; but the question remains: exactly *how* should the government intervene?

## The postwar system

Governments can intervene in these markets in a number of ways: for example they could provide finance; alternatively they could actually provide services themselves. Although there are exceptions, the approach adopted in the UK after the Second World War was for the state to provide education and health, though in some cases it paid others to provide the service. In education, most children went to schools owned by local authorities. Many did go to schools owned by religious bodies, but the teachers were paid out of public funds and most of the consumables also came from the public purse. In the health service the hospitals – the most expensive sector – were state owned, and although general practitioners (GPs) were not formally employees of the state, the money to pay them was provided by the taxpayer. The private sector in both industries was relatively small, and most economic decision-making in these industries was essentially undertaken by elected politicians in conjunction with appointed officials.

In the 1970s criticisms were made of this system, usually stemming from the right of the political spectrum. One argument was that the system was 'producer orientated'. Instead of the market responding to the wishes of consumers, as was supposed to happen in market systems, it was argued that in education and health decisions were made in the interests of producers. For example, in education parents were not really consulted about the curriculum since this was felt to be a decision best left to the experts – the teachers. Similarly, it was argued that patients had little say in the health care that they received.

Another argument has been developed by a number of economists led by James Buchanan (1965). 'Public choice economics' suggests that people in government are motivated by self-interest. Thus bureaucrats want promotion and status, and this comes from managing big departments. Hence they favour increases in spending. Similarly, politicians want power, and this is often obtained by giving pressure groups what they want: better services, even though these cost more and put financial burdens on the rest of the country. Consequently economists such as Buchanan argue that the system of government leads to more spending than is desirable.

Moreover, health care is provided at zero cost to the individual (if we ignore costs such as time spent waiting for treatment). Consequently individuals have an incentive to extend demand so long as the benefit received exceeds zero. On the supply side, taxpayers have to pay for the service whilst having to share the service with others. The result is that taxpayers are not willing to pay for the quantity of service which consumers want, so that queues develop. Hence it is argued by some people that the system is inefficient. Another criticism made by right-wing reformers is that in the private sector inefficient firms go bust because the discipline of the market means that they cannot compete; in the public sector government departments can continue to provide goods and services inefficiently since there are few penalties attached to economic inefficiency. There is thus a strong case for introducing the power of market forces whenever possible.

In the 1980s these arguments caused governments in many countries to review the way in which they provided a wide range of goods. In some cases this led to privatisation of nationalised industries. In others it caused governments to contract out services such as refuse collection. In the education and health industries it led governments to introduce internal markets. For example, these arguments, together with rising levels of public spending, caused the Dutch Government to reform the health care system. Part of the change was the introduction of regulated competition (Van de Ven, 1990). Although the context and details are different, the changes proposed by the Dutch Government were consistent with those suggested in the British White Paper.

## Health

### *The internal market in health*

There were a number of intellectual influences behind the introduction of the internal market. One was the work of Buchanan and other public choice theorists. Another influence was also American, for it rested on the ideas of Alan Enthoven (1985) and the experience of health maintenance organisations in the USA. These receive money from public and private sources and then negotiate to purchase treatments from clinics, hospitals and pharmacies (Whynes, 1993, p. 142).

This structure was influential in the ideas put forward in the White Paper *Working For Patients* (Department of Health, 1989), the basic document underlying the changes in health service provision.

This argued that there was a clear need for reform. For example, the cost of treating in-patients varied by as much as 50 per cent between different health authorities, even after allowing for differences in the complexity and mix of cases treated, Similarly, waiting lists for treatment varied enormously in different areas. Most startlingly, there was a twenty-fold variation in the rate at which GPs refer patients to hospital (p. 3).

The aim of the White Paper was to secure two objectives:

- to give patients, wherever they live in the UK, better health care and greater choice of the services available; and
- greater satisfaction and rewards for those working in the NHS who successfully respond to local needs and preferences (pp. 3–4).

In the new system the National Health Service (NHS) will continue to be funded by the government, largely from tax revenues, but the flow of funds will be different. The White Paper distinguished between purchasers of health care and the providers of such care. This is an attempt to replicate the market for consumer goods and services. However, in this case the purchasers will be general practitioners or District Health Authorities who buy services for their patients from hospitals. Instead of invoicing the Department of Health, as happened in the old system, each purchaser was to be allocated a budget from which all operating expenses were to be met. This included treatment by the GP as well as the purchase of hospital care. On the supply side this hospital care could be provided by private as well as public bodies. Most of the provision is by NHS Trusts. These are independent organisations accountable to the Secretary of State. By 1994, as much as 95 per cent of hospital and community services were provided by NHS Trusts (Robinson and Le Grand, 1994, p. 3). The intention was that GPs could choose the most suitable provider. One criterion for this was cost: expensive providers would be forced by competition to become more efficient, just as the market forced inefficient firms in the private sector to cut costs. The flow of funds in this system is illustrated in Figure 9.5.

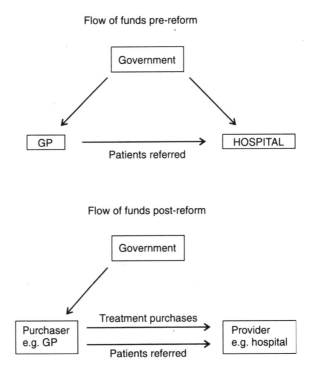

*Source*:  David K. Whynes, 'Economic aspects of healthcare in the UK', in G. B. J. Atkinson (ed.) *Developments in Economics*, vol. 9, Causeway, Ormskirk, 1993.

**FIGURE 9.5    Flow of funds in the NHS**

GPs were not forced to become budget-holders, but there were incentives for them to do so, because the system gave them greater control and they could use 'surpluses' to improve their practice facilities. Consequently the number of budget-holders has risen quickly: by 1993 fund holding practices covered more than a quarter of the United Kingdom population and by 1994 it had risen to two-fifths (Robinson and Le Grand, 1994, p. 3). In fact one theme of the changes is the attempt to create incentives, just as a 'normal' market has incentives. Thus purchasers have an incentive to shop around for the 'best buy'; providers have an incentive to cut the prices they charge and to provide better services, because that way they will continue to attract purchasers. Another incentive is that entrepreneurs will have an incentive to enter the market – for example, privately owned hospitals – because GPs may choose to send their patents to them if the cost and level of services are suitable.

The reforms rest on the assumption that the health care market has sufficiently similar characteristics to other markets that the results of unleashing market forces will also be similar – output will be produced at least cost (assuming no externalities) and that in the long run output will be at the optimum level.

However, there are manifest hazards in transferring these results to the hospital market, as Culyer and Posnett (1990, p. 13) point out:

(a) In competitive markets firms aim to produce profits, but it is possible for non-profit organisations to pursue very different objectives. Indeed these other objectives may conflict with the profit motive.
(b) The benefits from markets rest on the assumption of competition but the conditions required for contestable markets are often absent from the market for health services. For example, there may be only a few suppliers and hence only limited competition in some geographical areas. Too few alternative suppliers means that there are no incentives to force producers to improve their cost effectiveness.
(c) Those demanding services need sufficient information to make optimum choices. This may not be the case in the market for health care.

Another difference is that the health market will continue to be regulated much more than other markets. Health care is characterised by rules and regulations, some of which are restrictive practices, but others are necessary to protect patients. For example, entry is easy in markets such as hairdressing, but there are considerable barriers – particularly legal barriers – which limit the provision of health care.

In addition, in competitive markets the optimum level of output is determined by consumer demand – the consumer is king. In the case of the NHS the overall level of output will be constrained because the main determinant will be the amount of finance that the government is willing to make available. It is thus a political decision made in the light of available funding and political priorities. Consequently, the amount of health care provision may or may not be at an optimum level.

How will providers react to the changing circumstances?

This is difficult to predict, but prior to the reforms the typical hospital provided a very wide range of services. The costings which were introduced as a result of the reforms show that some of these services are much more profitable than others. It therefore seems likely that hospitals will tend to specialise in those activities in which their costs are relatively low. This may seem a desirable result since it will improve efficiency, but in the longer run it will mean less choice for patients since local hospitals may not provide the type of treatment that they need. Moreover, self-governing hospitals may find that their best strategy is to collude, for example by forming a consortium. This would allow them to direct patients to those hospitals with spare capacity. However, it might also encourage them to collude in pushing up prices – not in the public interest. Monopolies and mergers legislation might then have to be invoked.

A further possibility is that competition may not lead to lower costs. In the USA, up to a decade or so ago, hospitals charged on a cost plus basis. Robinson and Luft (1985) found that costs were higher in areas where there were more hospitals competing, even after allowing for such factors as different cases. The reason may have been that the hospitals competed in other ways such as giving more tests or in providing more lavish accommodation. This is what economic theory would predict – non-price competition is a strong characteristic of oligopoly.

### Criteria for judging the reforms

In competitive markets, the usual criterion for measuring success is the level of profits. That criterion is not appropriate for non-profit organisations, particularly those working in markets where competition is limited. So what are the objectives of a successful health service?

The Royal Commission on the NHS (1979, p. 9) suggested that *efficiency* was paramount: the NHS should seek to provide 'a broad range of services to a high standard'. A second criterion which can be applied to judge the reforms is *equity*.

### Efficiency

A simplistic approach to efficiency would be to suggest that it is efficient to meet demand; that since the purpose of the health service is to produce good health then spending should be increased until good health is produced. However, no system can produce 'good health'; in an ideal world it might be possible to expand services until the marginal benefits just equalled the marginal costs, but in the case of health it is not possible to quantify benefits in this way.

Neither would it be appropriate to conclude that efficiency exists when costs are low. For example, one way to cut costs is to have greater selectivity in admitting patents so that only low-cost patients in each category are admitted (Culyer, 1993, p. 171). Another way to reduce costs is to discharge patients early, and there is evidence to suggest that this happens in the USA. This may enable hospitals to treat more patients and so to increase their income, but it may be to the disadvantage of the patient.

It is possible to distinguish three different dimensions to the concept of efficiency (Le Grand *et al.*, 1990). First there is 'output efficiency'. This involves varying the outputs of the health service so that the net social benefit is maximised. This involves cutting services in those areas where they will do least good and concentrating resources where they will have most benefit. The difficulty with this approach is that it is not easy to decide what constitutes most benefit. Consequently, in practice benefit is determined by social priority: for example, a decision to give priority to mental health would be the result of lobbying rather than a comparison of the benefits to be obtained from spending on this rather than some other service such as geriatrics.

One simple measure of output is the number of patients treated. If hospital A and hospital B both cost £10 million to run but hospital A treats twice as many patients as hospital B, then A is more efficient. But here again difficulties arise. For example, if hospitals discharge patients quickly so that they relapse and have to be admitted again the statistics will show two patients treated, whereas the reality is that only one person has been treated, but that the patient has had to suffer the trauma of two admissions.

A second approach to efficiency can be called 'input efficiency'. This involves changing the mixture of resources used as their price changes. For example if some types of medicines became relatively more expensive, alternatives would be used. Similarly community care for the mentally ill could be substituted for residential care if this rose in price. The difficulty with this approach is that outputs are also affected, so that although the change may cut costs, benefits may be cut by more. In addition, in many cases it may not be possible to adjust the mix of resources used in treatment.

A third approach to efficiency is 'technical efficiency'. This means producing the maximum possible outputs from a given amount of inputs. Again, there are problems in using this approach because it is difficult to measure outputs.

One solution to this problem is to use performance indicators. These may permit efficiency judgements to be made about non-profit-making organisations. Again, there are difficulties. Thus one performance indicator might be the number of 'cures'. However, hospitals that produce most 'cures' may do so because the patients they treat are not so ill as those in comparable hospitals. The figures can be adjusted to compensate for this, but such adjustments are never accurate.

The simplest performance indicator is mortality. This has two advantages: firstly, the fact of death is relatively easy to determine – it is much more precise than the answer to a question such as 'How do you feel?'. Second, the facts are easily available, since all deaths have to be recorded. Mortality rates can be used in many ways, for example to compare regional differences. Even here there are difficulties: the death rate in an area with many old people such as Hove will be higher than that in an area with fewer old people. Hence actual deaths need to be compared with those which could be expected, given the age and sex distribution of the population. Once this is done, comparisons can be made. These show that in the Northern Regional Health Authority the number of deaths was 12 per cent more than expected in 1987, in the North West region the figure was 11 per cent. At the other extreme, in Wessex and in South-West Thames the number of deaths was 11 per cent less than expected (Fitzpatrick and Dunnell, 1992, p. 65).

Mortality rates are a useful way of comparing regions, but on their own they do not say much about efficiency. This can be achieved by comparing mortality rates in areas where death is potentially avoidable, for example in pregnancy and childbirth. A hospital which has high death rates in these areas may be regarded as inefficient, though this assumes that the patients it treats are similar to those in other hospitals. Moreover, a simple comparison of mortality takes no account of costs – hospitals with low mortality rates might have many more staff and better facilities.

An alternative approach is to look at the quality of life which results from medical attention. This approach is usually called 'QALYs', an abbreviation of 'quality adjusted life years'. The basic idea of QALYs is that a treatment which makes little difference to the quality of life, or which has only a short-term effect is worth less than a treatment which has substantial and prolonged results. The difficulty here is how to compare, say, the benefits resulting from back pain treatment with a heart bypass. In a QALYs approach this is done by asking panels of people – doctors, nurses as well as patients – to give values to various conditions, and then to adjust this rating to allow for the length of time that the condition lasts. In principle this makes it possible to compare very different kinds of health treatment in relation to their costs. This is done in Table 9.1.

It is not claimed that QALYs enable definitive conclusions to be reached, but they do allow indicative estimates. The results, as in the table, generally favour a greater emphasis on preventative intervention.

The introduction of the internal market will force those involved in buying or providing medical care to have greater regard to costs in particular and to efficiency in general. But it is far from certain that the results will necessarily be an improvement on the previous system. In any case, as this section has shown, we do not really have the analytical tools or the data to make definitive conclusions.

TABLE 9.1 **League table of costs and QALYS for selected health care interventions**

| Intervention | *Present value of extra cost per QALY gained (£)* |
|---|---|
| GP advice to stop smoking | 170 |
| Pacemaker implanted for heart block | 700 |
| Hip replacement | 750 |
| Breast cancer screening | 3 000 |
| Heart transplant | 5 000 |
| Hospital haemodialysis | 14 000 |

*Source*: M. Drummond 'Output measurement for resource allocation in health care' *Oxford Review of Economics and Politics*, 5 (1989) pp. 59–74, quoted in R. Fitzpatrick and K. Dunnell. 'Measuring outcomes in healthcare' in E. Beck *et al.*, *In the Best of Health?*, Chapman & Hall, London, 1992.

*Equity*

If efficiency is one criterion which can be used to judge health systems, its companion must be equity. If efficiency is difficult to define and measure, the problem is significantly greater in the case of equity.

One approach is to say that health care should be provided according to need. But, as Culyer and Wagstaff (1992) point out, it is difficult to see why someone who is sick can be said to need health care regardless of the treatment's ability to improve the person's health. So before 'need' can be regarded as a determinant of provision, there must be some capacity to benefit from the consumption of resources.

In turn, the individual's ability to benefit from the treatment depends on the cost of the proposed treatment. It would be a waste of resources to spend a million pounds on a treatment for some minor condition, even if the patient would benefit. Use of this criterion sometimes gives rise to difficulties. Since resources are limited, is it justifiable to spend a large sum of money on treating an elderly patient who may not live to benefit much from it?

Equality of access is sometimes suggested as a criterion for equity. When this condition is satisfied, all individuals will face the same money and time costs in obtaining treatment. Again, difficulties arise – how do you measure equality of access?

After summarising various alternatives, Culyer and Wagstaff (1992) conclude that none of these criteria is egalitarian in the sense of necessarily promoting a greater equality of health in the community. According to them, if the objective is greater equality of health in the community, then what is required is *unequal* distribution of medical care. This is needed to ensure that those who lack equal care actually receive it.

One way to explore this conclusion is to examine two aspects of equity: vertical and horizontal. Vertical equity requires that people who are unequal should be treated unequally. Thus vertical considerations would require that more resources should be given to those with greater need and greater capacity to benefit, for example, by spending more in disadvantaged areas. Horizontal considerations require that individuals who are equal in relevant aspects should be treated equally.

An important aspect of equity in this context is the distribution of the burden of financing the health service. There are several approaches to this. It is possible that equity occurs when those who make the most use of the service pay most of the cost. Others would argue that this penalises the sick – who are often the least well-off in society – and that a better approach is that contribution to the system should be based on the individual's ability to pay. This removes an additional burden from the sick individual. In the UK the health service is largely financed out of general taxation so that in general those with the highest incomes pay most. In some cases, the principle of 'user pays' applies: for example in some kinds of dental care, for prescription charges (where applicable) and for unorthodox medical treatments such as acupuncture as well as treatment in private hospitals.

Two specific aspects of equity can be discussed. One is regional. There are considerable regional differences in the distribution of illness. In general, poorer areas are characterised by higher mortality rates, and also by higher rates for non-life-threatening diseases. In 1975 a Resource Allocation Working Party (RAPL) was set up to secure a pattern of distribution which would 'reduce progressively, and as far as is feasible, the disparities between the different parts of the country in terms of opportunity for access to health care of people at equal risk' (DHSS, 1976, p. 1). The resulting report suggested that resources to the regions should be determined by a formula – which took account not only of population and age, but also of regional mortality rates. The 1989 White Paper *Working for Patients* claimed that when the formula was introduced regions were on average over 8 per cent away from their targets. By the time of the White Paper 11 of the 14 regions were within 3 per cent, so that there was no need to continue with the system. Instead, the Regional Health Authorities will be funded on a capitation basis 'weighted to reflect the health and age distribution of the population'. It seems likely that this change will be a move away from equity, in the sense of remedying unequal needs.

A second aspect is that of class. People obtain access to health services through their GP; hence we can measure social class access to health services by using statistics of GP visits. Le Grand *et al.* (1990, p. 121) use General Household Survey data to calculate that in 1985 semi- and unskilled manual workers were more likely to visit their doctor than the population as a whole. Similarly, people from low income groups were more likely to visit the doctor than those from high income groups. At first sight this suggests that the health service is promoting equality. One problem with this conclusion is that it takes no account of need: some groups may need more care than others. However, even after this is done the authors find that 'there is something close to equal access for equal need'.

*Evaluating the reforms*

A full analysis of the reforms introduced in the White Paper will take many years, and even then may be subject to controversy, not least because they will be evaluated by special interest groups. Moreover, the changes do not take place in an economic vacuum. The reforms were accompanied by a significant increase in the resources going to the NHS. In 1991–2 these rose by 6.1 per cent in real terms and in 1992–3 the increase was 5.5 per cent (Department of Health, 1993, p. 94). This means that any improvements – for example, in shorter waiting lists – may be the result of more resources rather than from the reforms.

However, it is possible to come to tentative conclusions. On the positive side there is no doubt that, pre-reform, most people in the system had little knowledge of the real costs of their operations. The internal market has changed that. However, it does not need the creation of an internal market to achieve this; appropriate accounting and management procedures could provide the information.

Supporters of the reforms say that District Health Authorities or GP budget-holders will have an incentive to purchase services from least-cost providers. They claim that this will create incentives for providers to increase efficiency. However, outside large urban areas, competition is limited by geographical factors. Research by Appleby *et al.* (1994, p. 45) suggests that even in a relatively urban region such as the West Midlands only 60 per cent of general surgery patients were treated in hospitals subject to effective competition. For more specialised treatment, and in rural areas, the percentage would be much lower.

Moreover, discovering information about costs is not free; and it is not certain that the costs of providing information will be less than the value of the information. What is certain is that transactions costs will rise. Budget-holders and providers will have to obtain information, negotiate the terms on which they will purchase treatment and keep accounts. This will mean more employees in administration, and, since total spending is finite, probably less will be spent on nurses and other medical staff. Thus the number of managers in England rose from 6091 in 1989–90 before the changes, to 20 478 in 1992–3 and 23 350 in 1994–5. In the NHS Trusts, management costs were £817 million in 1995, some 3.9 per cent of income. Whilst the number of managers was rising, the number of nurses fell by 27 235 in the period 1989–90 to 1992–3. (*Guardian*, 1994, 1995). Moreover, collecting money imposes costs. For example, the St George's Hospital in London sends out 2000 bills a month to GP fundholders and health authorities, with a handling cost of each invoice of up to £25. Most of these are for outpatients where the medical costs are not much higher. Before the reforms, there were no bills such as this because the health authorities ran the hospital (*Independent on Sunday*, 1995).

Freedom of choice is a prime benefit claimed for market systems. In the health service, the reforms will make it easier for patients to choose – and change – their doctor, but the choice of hospital may be reduced for several reasons. First, hospitals may choose to concentrate on fewer services, so giving less choice. Second, the patients' freedom to choose a hospital may be limited by the existence of contracts between their GP or District and a particular hospital. This means that patients will have to go to the hospital where his/her GP has a contract rather than the one they would have chosen. Moreover, there is some fear that GPs, perhaps running close to their budget limits, will tend to buy the cheapest treatment rather than the best. On the other hand, Abel-Smith and Glennerster (1995) point out that GP power can be used to benefit patients since they can bully specialists about waiting times and can insist that test results come back quickly.

Another limit to freedom of choice is that there is some evidence of a two-tier system developing. Equity requires that people should be treated on the basis of their medical condition, but there is no doubt that patients on fundholders lists have priority over those on non-fundholder lists.

Competition may have advantages in many markets, but government-appointed advisers (HMSO, 1993) suggested that in specialist services such as childhood leukaemia and heart bypass surgery, co-operation between hospitals was needed rather than competition, because 'Many specialist services are not suited to case insensitive block contracts'.

Hence it is possible to conclude that the changes *may* result in the benefits of the market being transferred to the health service, but this is not certain. What is sure is that demand for health services which are free at the point of delivery will continue to exceed the supply. This raises questions of ethics. Since not everyone can receive the medical treatment they would like, what criteria should be used to decide who benefits?

## Education

*How much education does a country need?*

In the United Kingdom, spending on education rose in real terms during the 1980s as it had in every postwar decade, but the share of education in GDP was 5. 1 per cent in 1979–80 and exactly the same in 1991–2. This suggests that although spending on education may rise, its share of the national cake may have reached a plateau. But is the plateau at the right level? Should we spend more on education, or are higher levels of spending a waste of resources?

In a market economy, quantity would be determined by the interaction of demand and supply, but in an industry such as education, market forces will play only a minor part. They will determine the extent of the private sector, but most education is paid for out of public funds and so is determined by political decision-making.

Those who argue that we need to continue to spend more on education make several points. Research by Denison (1969) suggested that economic growth in the USA had been due to a number of factors: for example a growth in investment, better resource allocation, and the growth of the labour force. In addition, educational factors played a substantial part. Denison calculated that advances in knowledge were responsible for a third of the rise in GDP, whilst education also contributed to 14 per cent of the growth through a rise in increased skills and versatility. Denison's research was followed by others, almost all showing that education made a significant contribution to economic growth.

However, such studies do not take us very far in deciding how much to spend on education. Even if Denison's analysis was correct – and there have been methodological criticisms of his work – there is no guarantee that what happened in the past would apply in the future. And even if education does contribute significantly to growth, the basic question – how much education? – is not answered.

An alternative contribution to this debate can be made by cost-benefit analysis. A private-sector company deciding whether or not to invest in a project can calculate the rate of return it expects to receive on its investment, and then decide whether or not to proceed. The same technique can be applied to education. Psacharopoulos (1985) summarised many of these studies and obtained the results shown in Table 9.2.

TABLE 9.2   Social returns to education, various countries

|              | *Primary* | *Secondary* | *Higher* |
|--------------|-----------|-------------|----------|
| Africa       | 26        | 17          | 13       |
| Asia         | 27        | 15          | 13       |
| Intermediate | 21        | 10          | 8        |
| Advanced     |           |             |          |
| France       | —         | 10          | 11       |
| Japan        | —         | 9           | 7        |
| Netherlands  | —         | 5           | 6        |
| UK           | —         | 9           | 7        |
| USA          | —         | 11          | 11       |

*Source*: G. Psacharopoulos, 'Returns to education', *Journal of Human Resources*, 20 (1985), pp. 583–604.

Psacharopoulos's analysis suggests that investment in education pays off, particularly investment in younger children's education (largely because the costs are less), but again, the basic problem remains because positive returns in the past do not necessarily mean that these will be repeated in the future. Moreover, increases in the supply of educated people in the future may reduce the returns received. An additional criticism of these studies is that the returns may not be the result of higher productivity, but occur because education is used as a screening device in employment so that the high returns may not be due to higher productivity, but may be merely the result of better educated people getting the best jobs.

The argument that the UK needs more investment in education is supported by international comparisons. As early as 1870 the first British Minister of Education was concerned that Britain would 'become outmatched in the competition in the world' (Maclure, 1965, p. 104). Similar fears have been expressed at regular intervals ever since. Thus Finegold and Soskice (1988) take the UK's failure 'to train its workforce to the same level as its competitors as . . . a cause of the nation's poor relative economic performance'.

These concerns have led to international comparisons. Thus Micklewright *et al.* (1989) point out that over half of children leave full-time education at the age of 16. In countries such as the USA and Japan some 85–90 per cent of 16-year-olds are still in education; only Greece among EC countries had a lower proportion.

Table 9.3 gives another international comparison, this time of full-time participation rates by young people; the conclusion is that the UK is lagging behind similar countries in the quantity of education it provides.

Another comparison was undertaken by Steedman *et al.* (1991) This analysed intermediate skills in the workplace: that is, supervisory and technician skills. This concluded that:

> Britain produces only a quarter as many skilled craft employees . . . as either France or Germany. At higher technical level, both British and French flows are substantially higher than in Germany. However, neither Britain or France engages in systematic training of foreman to the equivalent of the *Meister* qualification in Germany.

### TABLE 9.3    Full-time participation rates (%), 1992/3

| Age | USA | Denmark | France | Germany | Sweden | UK |
|-----|------|---------|--------|---------|--------|------|
| 16+ | 91.4 | 92.4 | 92.2 | 95.3 | 89.2 | 69.9 |
| 18+ | 54.0 | 68.5 | 77.9 | 82.8 | 60.8 | 33.0 |

*Source*:   Based on data from DFE *Statistical Bulletin*, 168/95 (1995).

Such comparisons have been criticised. A fundamental weakness of such studies is that they rest on the assumption that other countries have got the 'correct' level of skilled labour. There is little evidence to support this assertion – it is quite possible to spend too much on education as it is to spend too much on any other good or service. Moreover, data can be found to suggest that the UK spends too much on higher education. Murphy (1993) quotes evidence on the percentage of the adult population with a higher educational qualification to show that West Germany with only 6 per cent of its population so qualified would find itself the second poorest country in Europe; Britain with 10 per cent of its population so qualified would be the richest nation in Europe after Belgium.

Even in engineering, where Britain is supposed to lag behind its competitors, the National Economic Development Council (1984) found that the UK was producing more engineers than Germany, since it was producing 15 000 such graduates a year compared to Germany's 7000. Another study by Prais (1988) came to rather different conclusions. His analysis suggested that at master's degree level the numbers of engineering graduates appeared to be under a half of those produced in the other four countries analysed (France, West Germany and Japan). At first degree level Prais concluded that Britain trains as many as France, a third fewer than Germany and the USA and only half the Japanese total. However, the biggest shortfall was at craftsman level where France and Japan train between two and three times as many as Britain in mechanical, electrical and construction occupations.

The difficulties of reaching a definite conclusion about the under- or over supply of skilled personnel are also illustrated by Smithers and Robinson (1989). They analyze the output of graduates in several countries and conclude that the UK is roughly on a par with Germany, but produces considerably fewer graduates than France, Japan and the USA. The shortage may not lie in the graduate market, but in the supply of technicians.

One problem about all these international comparisons is that definitions vary across countries. Terms such as 'graduate' or 'craftsman' do not necessarily mean the same thing in every country, so that international comparisons of the output of graduates may owe more to definitional differences than to real variations. It is quite possible for a country to produce more 'graduates' than another, but for this quantitative comparison to be misleading because the graduates are less well educated than non-graduates in other countries. In the best of all possible worlds, comparisons would use measures of quality not quantity, but since such comparison are very difficult and often impossible, we often have to make do with simple numerical measures.

If, instead of cross-national studies we look at the labour market in the UK, a similar conclusion can be reached: the UK is producing too many graduates because 'the UK has not for a long time been able to absorb the graduates it currently produces' (Murphy, 1993, p. 16). Thus a government enquiry (HMSO, 1990) found that 'a degree was considered essential for only a third of the jobs' which newly qualified graduates were performing. In other words, graduates were taking jobs which did not need graduate skills.

Murphy's analysis is criticised by Johnes (1993a). He argues that investigations at a time of high unemployment will inevitably find that there are unemployed graduates and graduates taking jobs that did not need graduate skills. Moreover, 'the best judge is the relative productivity of qualified and unqualified workers' and 'graduates are significantly more productive than less well educated workers in similar positions . . . it is the unqualified workers who are under-educated, not the other way around'.

Data does not prove the case for or against the argument that the UK spends too much – or not enough – on education. For example, Dolton (1992, p. 113) analyses graduate and national unemployment over thirty years and concludes that there is a close similarity between the two; not surprisingly unemployment among graduates rises when the general level of unemployment rises. This could be used to argue that there is no shortage of graduates, since if employers were wanting more graduates they could easily obtain them when unemployment is high. However, the counter-argument is that few employers would take on more workers when sales are falling. Moreover, as Dolton (p. 126) points out, over the period 1960–90, the number of graduates coming out of the UK education system rose over 500 per cent from 22 000 to over 125 000 whilst the general workforce rose by only 10 per cent. This large increase in graduates was accommodated by the labour market, implying that there was no over-supply.

This section has shown that there is considerable disagreement about the supply of skilled personnel in the UK. It therefore follows that there is disagreement about the extent of educational provision. The only certain conclusion to the question 'How much education is required in the UK?' is agnostic: there is no correct answer, and actual provision will be determined by incremental additions, modified by political factors and the state of the economy.

## How should education be provided?

The traditional pattern of provision of education in the UK – and in many other European countries – has been for the state to provide most education. Most children went to schools owned and run by local education authorities, or by religious organisations where the state provided most of the money to run the schools. A minority of children attended private schools, though these were helped indirectly by the state, for example be giving them charitable status which reduced their tax liability.

But this pattern of provision is not inevitable: it is the result of historical accident, the enthusiasm of local authorities and the successes of religious pressure groups. It is quite possible to argue that the objectives of education would be better served by the introduction of market principles, even if the state continued to provide most of the finance.

One way in which market forces could be introduced into education would be through the use of education vouchers.

The basic idea of a voucher is very simple. The government would issue a voucher equal to the cost of a year's education. Parents would then take this voucher to the school of their choice, and the school would then receive a cheque from the government equal to the value of the voucher.

One argument put forward in favour of vouchers is that they would increase consumer choice. Voucher supporters argue that education is dominated by producers: in particular, teachers decide what is taught and how it is taught. Vouchers would force schools to respond to market forces; if schools were providing an education which was not that desired by parents they would take their children elsewhere. Unpopular schools would lose money and would be forced to change. Popular schools would be rewarded by more money and would therefore be able to educate more children, and the people who worked in successful schools would be rewarded by greater job security and higher financial rewards, just as workers in successful firms benefit. On the other hand, 'Schools that cannot attract applicants will be faced with financial difficulties, possible closure, or take over by more efficient management prepared to cater for the preferences of parents' (Maynard, 1975, p. 26).

The argument that vouchers increase choice was used by the government in 1995 when it announced that all parents of four-year-olds would receive a voucher for £1100 to cover part of the cost of nursery education. It claimed that this would enable parents to send their children to the nursery school of their choice, be it in the public sector or private.

Critics of the scheme claimed that this would be regressive since it would only really benefit well-off parents who already sent their children to fee-paying schools; these would now be subsidised. Parents who sent their children to free council nursery schools would not benefit, and there would be increased bureaucracy since such parents would have to receive a voucher from the local authority, and then take it back to the local authority to enable it to recoup some of the costs of providing nursery education.

The reforms announced in the White Paper *Choice and Diversity* (1992) claimed to enhance parental choice by simplifying the creation of grant maintained schools (i.e. schools which have opted out of local authority control) and proposed a new funding body to finance such schools. This White Paper was building on the foundations laid down in the Education Reform Act (1988). The aim of these reforms was to create a

> consumer-driven market in which schools compete for pupils by trying to offer the best goods and a greater variety of choice. Under this market mechanism, schools which fail will go to the wall. But for those schools which remain, the new system will increase their power and enhance their status (*The Times Educational Supplement*, 1991).

The principal way in which the market was to be introduced was through a scheme called the Local Management of Schools (LMS).

*Local Management of Schools*

The 1988 Education Reform Act marked a revolutionary change in the way in which schools were funded in the UK. Previously, maintained schools were funded directly by the local education authority who paid the teachers and almost all other costs. Schools had little say in the way money was spent; in practice they had discretion only over 'capitation' – a relatively tiny sum of money to be spent on educational materials such as books. They could also decide how to spend any money they raised themselves through fundraising activities.

The 1988 Act gave schools much more control over finance; at the same time it introduced competition between schools, since money followed pupils. Schools gaining pupils would receive more money; those losing pupils would lose it, just as a firm gaining or losing customers would find its income changing. Under the new system, every local education authority (LEA) has a 'general schools budget'. Some of this money, such as capital spending on buildings, is not devolved to schools. In addition, LEAs can keep some money to provide central services to schools such as medical and welfare services. However, the law ensures that almost all the money spent on education is devolved from the local authority to the schools.

The question therefore arises: How should this money be distributed?

The system that has been adopted is called 'formula funding'. In essence, the LEA decides to give a fixed sum of money for each child attending school. This is adjusted for age, older children bringing more money than young ones. Thus, in 1994, the average over England and Wales was £1125 for pupils aged 5 to 10 years, £1645 for those aged 11–16 and £2312 for those aged over 16 (CIPFA, 1994). Adjustments are also made so that schools with particular problems such as split sites or children with special needs receive additional finance.

One concern with this scheme is that it is 'based on an assessment of a school's objective needs, rather than the historic patterns of expenditure' (DES, 1988, para. 104). This has both short- and long-term implications. In the short term, schools with 'expensive' teachers – those at the top of the salary scales because they are experienced – received much less finance than if historic costs had been used. This difficulty was overcome to some extent by bringing in the scheme over several years. In the longer term, however, there is some concern in the teaching profession that the system will mean that schools will tend to appoint younger, less experienced teachers since they are cheaper. The result may be that older teachers find it difficult to obtain teaching jobs.

Each LEA devises its own formula within limits prescribed by the Act. For example, they can choose the pattern of age weighting and the special needs additions. Levačić (1993) investigated the effects of formula funding in one authority. She concluded that the system promoted efficiency because schools with low unit costs benefit. This was because it reduced the number of schools which had large positive discrepancies between their unit costs and the average for their sector. Her results also suggested that changes in pupil numbers and hence in budgets are inversely related to poor examination results, but good examination results had little effect on numbers. This suggests that parents avoid schools with poor results (in terms of GCSE results), but do not, or cannot, move their children to schools with good results. Whether this is entirely desirable is debatable. It may lead to 'sink schools' as suggested below, or it may force some poor schools to improve or to close, just as falling sales would force a firm to adapt or go under.

LMS might promote efficiency in another way. Under the previous system schools had little say in how money was spent. Now, within limits, they can determine their own priorities; choosing, for example, to delay decorating the school and instead employing a foreign language assistant. They can use local knowledge and contacts to ensure that repairs are done quickly and at low cost.

However, the system imposes costs. Headteachers may have considerable knowledge of education but be innocent of accounting procedures: hence the need to appoint staff with specialised financial knowledge. Moreover, the marginal cost of an additional pupil in an existing class is much smaller than the additional revenue brought by the grant for that pupil. Schools therefore have a strong financial incentive to compete for pupils. But competition is not costless. Resources spent on publicity and marketing could have been spent on education.

Moreover, headteachers and governors may be over-cautious. They may fear that the whole future of their school would be threatened if they exceeded their budget. Consequently, they may build up excessive contingency reserves. The result is that money designated for educational use is lying unused in bank accounts whilst children are educated in a school with too few teachers and too few resources.

Nevertheless, LMS has shown that the traditional way of financing education, with control resting with local authorities, may not be the best way; decentralising decision-making to schools may have many beneficial effects. In practice 'The devil is in the detail' (Thomas, 1994, p. 52). In financial matters relatively small changes can have large effects. For example, a local authority which was committed to greater equity could use the formula to direct resources to those schools which catered for disadvantaged children; another could give greater weights to A level, so benefiting middle-class children who tend to have relatively large numbers in such classes.

*Limits to markets*

Despite the undoubted benefits of some aspects of LMS, there are good reasons to argue that education differs from other consumer goods and services.

If there is a shortage of consumer goods, manufacturers can usually increase production in a relatively short period of time. If market forces are operating efficiently, a shortage will lead to a price rise which will encourage existing firms to produce more (for example by putting workers on overtime). If the shortage is thought to be long term, new firms will move into the market to benefit from the high prices.

If this sequence were to apply to education, then a shortage of engineers (for example) would lead to a rise in engineers' salaries. This would encourage more young people to become engineers, institutions training engineers would expand and new training institutions would appear. The result would be the elimination of the shortage.

It is possible that this sequence of events would be followed in practice, but there are considerable limitations. The labour market is imperfect, so that shortages of particular skills can persist for some time without prices rising. Moreover, there are huge information failures in the education market. Young people and their parents may be ignorant of the salaries which can be earned in various occupations. Most people have knowledge of only a few occupations. Hence, even if salaries do rise this may not be followed by a flow of young people into training.

Then there are lags. Production of consumer goods can be increased quickly; people are different. It may be years before more young people choose to enter a shortage occupation; even then it will take several years to train a skilled engineer. Hence, left to market forces, the supply of skilled people will lag behind the changes in demand. Moreover, there is considerable danger of overshoot; an increase in supply that eventually exceeds the demand so that a surplus persists until the message eventually percolates down to those choosing careers. Support for this argument is provided by Guerney (1987). He analysed the relationship between subject-specific unemployment rates and university applications and found that a 1 per cent increase in the subject-specific unemployment rate for agriculture, engineering and science led to a fall in applications of 0.28 per cent – more than double the rate for arts and social sciences. If engineering and science are sensitive to changes in the unemployment rates for graduates of these disciplines, then this, combined with the long lags involved in training, would be expected to lead to an exploding cobweb – where equilibrium is never reached.

Consequently markets fail to provide a satisfactory solution to the problem of producing the correct quantity of skilled people, and there is a need for government intervention to ensure a more satisfactory supply of skilled labour.

Education is concerned with the transmission of knowledge. It is therefore paradoxical that information failures are considerable in the industry. In the UK young people hoping to go to university may read several prospectuses and talk to older friends who are students. They may even visit several universities. But the problem remains: students are choosing courses and institutions on the basis of very little knowledge. The same applies when parents are choosing schools for their children. The government is attempting to rectify this information failure by requiring schools to publish examination results and the results of national curriculum tests, but such information is very partial. Schools with a high ability intake will normally produce good results and schools with many disadvantaged pupils poor ones (though there is strong evidence that schools do make a difference, as Cohn and Geske (1990, p. 185) show: some schools with pupils of similar background achieve much more than others). What parents need is information about which school would be best for their child, and a school with good examination results may not in practice be providing the best education.

The dissemination of examination results may have undesirable side effects. If a school gets a reputation as one which produces good examination results, it will recruit the children of ambitious parents. Since parental interest and ambition is a strong indicator of children's academic achievement, such schools will then produce good results. Schools with poor examination results will then tend to take in children whose parents are not concerned with examination success: a recipe for producing poor results in the future. Hence 'sink schools' develop.

Moreover, examination results are not a very satisfactory measure of a school's performance. Education has goals other than success in examinations. For example, schools run by Christian bodies may have as their first objective to produce good Christians, and non-religious schools may also give priority to goals such as 'encouraging young people to fulfil their potential' or to 'producing moral and civilised adults'. How can a parent judge a school's success in achieving such goals? Parents want their children to be happy at school. They can easily judge their children's preferences for icecream or biscuits, but it is not so easy to decide if children will be happy in a particular school. And the consequences of a wrong choice can be serious. A poor choice of clothing can be discarded, but there are substantial social and psychological costs involved in changing schools and a child leaving part-way through a year may find that the new programme of study does not fit with the one half completed.

Choice is one of the undoubted benefits of the market. But choice in education is limited. Those wanting education in a particular institution may not be able to obtain entry. That is unlikely to be the case in the market for consumer goods. Even at school level, parents may be unable to obtain their first choice since their preferred choice may be full. Geographical factors also limit choice. Young children may be limited to a school in the neighbourhood, and, except in large towns, even secondary school children may be limited to a choice of very few schools. Hence one of the proclaimed benefits of markets may only have limited application in education.

Choice may be limited in another way. In most markets, producers are supposed to respond to consumer choice, though this is disputed by writers such as Galbraith (1975, p. 150f) who argue that in the modern economy consumers are managed by large producers so that they respond to producer decisions. In education there is considerable evidence that producers may also determine what is produced and that consumers accept this offering. A voucher experiment was conducted over several years in Alum Rock in the USA. Existing schools were split into mini schools so that 45 programme options were available to parents, and children were given travel grants so that a wide range of curriculum choice was on offer. The result (Cohen and Farrar, 1977) was that parental choice was increased but 'most parents failed to become more autonomous, powerful or involved'. Consequently producers (i.e. teachers) continued to determine to a large extent what happened in the schools. If this result is transferable to other education systems, it implies that parents will have little say in deciding what is produced (the curriculum) or in how this is delivered.

Competition in education may be limited by producer action. Whilst some schools have embarked on radical marketing schemes in order to attract more customers, many other have been reluctant to embrace this competitive philosophy (Keep, 1992, p. 106), and there have been a number of attempts by schools to avoid competition by establishing co-operative arrangements. In addition, the National Association of Head Teachers has designed a code of conduct to limit competitive behaviour between schools.

There are profound differences between schools and firms. The most obvious is that schools do not aim to make a profit; instead they have to provide education to all those who are entitled to it. This means that they will probably be much less responsive to changes in the market than firms.

Schools also find it difficult to identify their 'customers'. For most schools, the pupils are likely to be seen as 'the customer', but the government seems to view parents as the main customer, and in some cases potential employers are seen as the customer – schools provide an education which can be regarded as a product which will be bought by firms. This leads to confusion because the interests of the three groups may differ. For example, children may wish to pursue an interest at school which their parents do not appreciate and which may not appeal to potential employers. Should schools respond to such 'customer demand'?

Another difference between education and most private-sector markets is that the education market is highly regulated. For example, the government specifies the information that must be given to customers, and also the product range that must be offered (ibid, p. 115). Moreover, for public services such as education and health, the impact of political factors is huge, so that choices such as levels of service and product mix do not result from consumer choices but from political intervention. Thus the National Curriculum did not result from market research into the wishes of customers but was imposed by the Secretary of State. This limits schools' ability to offer a different product to competitors. Nor can state schools sell their capital assets, buy other 'firms' or operate deficit budgets.

Some writers would argue that there is a fundamental contradiction between the principles underlying state education and the free-market principles of consumer choice. Cole (1992) argues that in the last decade or so there has been a shift in the direction of support for free-market economics and a decline in state intervention in the economy. However, in contrast to this, there has been an increase in state intervention in education, which reduces consumer choice. Cole argues that the National Curriculum imposes a uniform and ethno-centric curriculum on state schools, though interestingly it has not been imposed on public (i.e. private) schools. Indeed, 'on the formal curriculum . . . the 1988 changes were in the opposite direction to the "market". Indeed, what can better illustrate more hierarchic control than a circumstance where it is the Secretary of State who now decided where History ends?' (Thomas, 1994, p. 41). Moreover, the government has encouraged schools to opt out of local control and become grant maintained, that is, to be financed by central Government. Some of these schools have expressed a desire to select their pupils, something that the newly created City Technology Colleges also do. Hence this newly privatised sector will result in a wealth of choice for able children and no choice for others. 'In effect, they will have created a situation where, far from parents choosing schools, schools would be choosing parents' (p. 339). This suggests that the free market can provide a basis for the education of the wealthy elite, but it cannot provide a basis for organising education in its entirety.

It is possible to examine the effect of market forces on education. Ball *et al.* (1994, p. 15f) examined the effect of the reforms on 15 schools in three adjacent local authorities over a 39 month period. They found that:

- Education markets are essentially localised, and differ by virtue of their history and their spacial organisation and transport infrastructure.
- There is no simple relationship between enrolment and quality – some good schools are difficult to get into whilst others suffer declining populations.
- There is evidence of a shift of resources away from students with special needs and learning difficulties. Well-established systems of special educational needs teaching are being dismantled or reduced in size and some of the money saved is spent on marketing.

This movement of resources away from less able children within schools is reinforced by the funding system used by LEAs. Smith and Noble (1995, p. 49) found that under LMS:

there is very little variation in the overall budget of schools on the basis of disadvantage – figures for individual schools suggest that overall schools in the most disadvantaged areas receive perhaps 5 per cent more funding per pupil than the bulk of schools in similar types of LEA.

This is a tiny amount compared to the very large differences that exist between schools in the character of their intake.

Another market limitation is that there may be a conflict between efficiency and equity. An education policy requires that the government should allocate resources equitably among individuals of different abilities. Left to the market, those children from better-off backgrounds – both educationally and financially – will consume more education. This may be efficient since if initially if all individuals received the same education the gain in productivity achieved by a marginal increase in the education of an able individual would be relatively high. However, 'Just as the concept of equity – along with progressivity and regressivity – applies to the allocation of inputs, so it must apply to the outputs of the education system' (Johnes, 1993b, p. 70). This means that 'in order to achieve an output allocation that is not regressive we *must* have input progressivity; more resources should be devoted to the education of those with less ability than to that of more able pupils'. There is therefore a role for government to intervene to secure an optimum position in the equity–efficiency trade-off. Smith and Noble (1995, p. 139) suggest that this could be done if the government provided a comprehensive programme of high quality pre-school provision, reductions in class size, special help for poor readers and greater parental involvement. They argue that such a programme, combined with measures such as an increase in child benefit to reduce poverty in the community, could enhance the educational chances of children from poor families.

A final difference between education and conventional markets is that 'You do not have to buy particular good or services in the free market, but you are compelled to "buy" schooling for your children' (ibid, p. 341). Again, in the free market consumers can ensure success in terms of value for money; but in an education system that insists on evaluating children competitively, no parent can ensure a successful purchase.

Hence there are major differences between education and the market for most goods and services, and market-led reforms may not be appropriate. Thomas and Bullock (1994, p. 51) suggest that there is no simple choice to be made between markets and hierarchies as a basis for deciding how educational goods and services should be produced, but that different systems should co-exist. They argue that formula-funding rules should be rewritten so that schools with high levels of pupils with special educational needs should be guaranteed adequate resources. In addition, schools must not be able to decide their own admissions criteria because this would lead to continued vicious and virtuous circles. Instead, regulations must be determined at the level of the school system.

## Conclusion

Market forces will continue to play a crucial role in the provision of heath and education. That is partly because both have considerable privately funded sectors, but the main reason is that the Government, largely for ideological reasons, has introduced market forces into these industries. These do not solve the problems of resource allocation because these services differ fundamentally from conventional product markets. Hence there is a continuing need for government intervention to ensure that equity and efficiency are not reduced by market failures.

# CHAPTER 10

# The Distribution of Income

When investigating the distribution of income there are several important questions that must be addressed: indeed, fundamental questions such as 'To what degree are we interested in equality?' 'To what degree are we interested in re-distribution?' and 'To what extent can government intervention serve to achieve our objectives and aims regarding levels of equity through policies of redistribution?' The answer we give to each of these basic questions will determine our approach to the discussion of the distribution of income. Therefore, as we are concentrating upon micro-economic policy, we will be very interested in the concept of equality, we will have an opinion on the redistribution of income, and government policy and its effectiveness will be high on our agenda. Figure 10.1 illustrates the area of our investigation in terms of the way in which income is determined and thus, the way in which government policy can have a direct effect upon the final distribution of income. Taking the top line of Figure 10.1, 'Earnings from employment' may depend upon incomes policies, 'Occupational pensions' and 'Investment income' may depend upon interest rate policy, and 'Other income' may depend upon other government policies (e.g. Child Support Agency). Therefore 'original income', before government intervention, will itself be dependent upon a variety of decisions made by central government. This is before we approach the four stages of government intervention that interpose upon income distribution before we arrive at the bottom line of 'Final income'.

## Ideology

The investigation of income equality requires first that we find a definition of equality with which to measure the extent of inequality. However, this is not an easy task and is inexorably tied up with ideological beliefs and value judgements. The notion of equality is not a concept that is confined to socialism, utopianism or communism, nor is it necessarily evident in those countries where it is espoused as a virtue of society. One could point to economies as diverse as Cuba and the United States of America where equality is frequently aspired to, but obviously not achieved: in the latter case it can be summed up in the idea that any individual has the opportunity

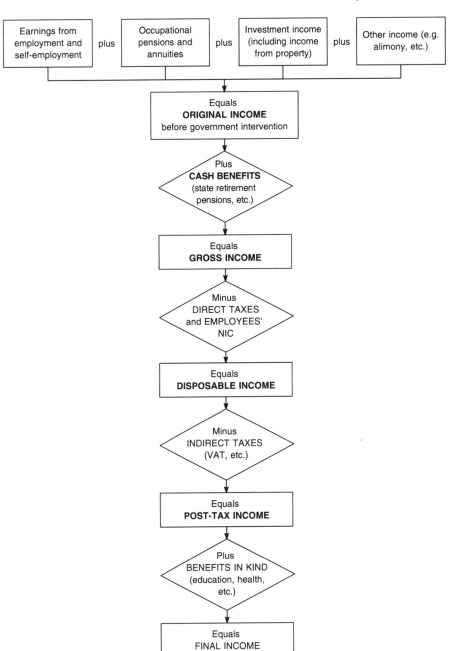

*Source:   Economic Trends,* May 1993.

**FIGURE 10.1   Stages of redistribution**

to be the President of the United States. However, in practice, you must first ensure that you command a great fortune to fund the campaign.

However, equity itself would appear to be inherently bound up with the concept of justice and is sought in a number of areas: for example, equality before the law or equality in citizenship. For our purpose, however, such definitions are far too broad, and instead we will concentrate on the concept of social equity that relates to the distribution of income (and wealth) and then to differences of class, opportunity and the amenity associated with them.

The norm of equity may be expressed in at least three ways:

1.  *Fairness or justice*
    Here we hold it to be wrong to treat two people differently when they are in a like situation. Therefore, justice demands that those found guilty of offences of the same, or similar, gravitas shall receive the exact same penalty. It follows that we should hold with the same conviction the tenet that equal achievements should be equally rewarded. Hence, if two workers are paid differently, that can only be because of a corresponding difference between them in their output, product or performance. It follows therefore that if women are employed alongside men, doing the same work with the same efficiency, the notion of equity holds that they must not be paid less because they are women. We may call this the principle of equal treatment.

2.  *Egalitarianism*
    Egalitarians will argue that the principle of equal treatment does not go far enough in its definition. They would suggest that it would be unfair that some people should be able to earn so much more than others. They would also express their disapproval at the fact that some are able to acquire vast wealth despite a lack of commensurate effort in its formulation. This would be especially true in the case of inherited wealth. For example, if an economist and a labourer were to be paid in accordance with the principle of equal treatment, it may be argued that equality has not been achieved because life has not treated them equally. The economist may be in a position to earn much more than the labourer due to the good fortune of being born to parents well able to provide excellent schooling through the private system, whereas the labourer was required to leave education at the earliest opportunity to seek employment to boost the family income to a reasonable level. In addition, the school that the labourer attended was an underfunded, overcrowded, inner-city school. The question is then raised as to what the outcome would have been had they started at the same level.

    The answer has to be one of conjecture only, but it is a level start that egalitarians are seeking to ensure. Therefore, they aspire to a principle of equality of opportunity. The argument is that however fairly the mechanism of the market operates, the distribution of income that emerges from it will be unfair until life chances have been equalised. Thus, if only equality of opportunity could be secured, the inequalities of income and wealth that arose would be acceptable. The analogy could be used of a national lottery: winning an enormous sum of money on a national lottery is simply a matter of good fortune, as all have the same opportunity to enter, but the inheritance of a large sum, although remaining a matter of good fortune, is confined only to a privileged few.

3.  *Thoroughgoing egalitarians*

    Not all egalitarians would agree with the principle of equality of opportunity. In the case of thoroughgoing egalitarians, equality of opportunity is seen as resulting in inequality of *achievement*, plus the fact that this inequality is an inequality between the more and the less able. That is, it is no longer solely between the more and the less privileged. Hence, in this view, the element that remains omitted from the earlier analysis is a sense of the basic equality between one human being and another. This dissatisfaction with the principle of equality of opportunity is heightened when the possibility of actually achieving it is examined. The major obstacle is that whereas the principle of equal treatment can be attained with relatively minor changes to the existing arrangements, those required for a movement towards equality of opportunity are much more deep-rooted in the economic environment. This raises the question of how far ought we to go? What we require is the use of 'handicaps' or weights – these are seen as fair and just if, and only if, they serve to offset the differences in ability and capability that arise from those factors that are outside an individual's own control. But which factors are, and hence which are not, beyond an individual's own control? This is the question that essentially divides thoroughgoing egalitarians from others, and egalitarians as a whole from their opponents. There will normally be a general agreement that children cannot be held responsible for the amount of resources (in terms of both time and money) that their guardians devote to their own use, keen or careless, of whatever education is provided for them. What is termed 'laziness' in this view is a defect in the same way as lameness, which may be present from birth, or inflicted by mishandling in the early years of life. In exactly the same way, wrongdoers are viewed as not being in some way evil, but as suffering from an illness or debilitated in some way.

    Thus, if all an individual's capabilities, physical, mental and emotional, are regarded as being the product of heredity and environment, then the individual remains as a centre of consciousness without distinguishing characteristics that could be the source of unequal treatment. Thus envisaged, each human being must enjoy equal esteem with each other human being due to the simple fact that all share a common humanity. All that differentiates one individual from another (and would therefore justify treating them differently) is extrinsic to the self at the core between which no distinction of stronger or weaker, or better or worse, can be made. That one person is less clever than another is no more reason for assigning them incomes than that one was involved in an incapacitating accident that another escaped. Therefore, the condition of everyone should be the same, for lack of any reason why they should differ. (For a full discussion of these positions, see Phelps-Brown, 1988.)

Public policy in Britain throughout much of the twentieth century has promoted all three of these norms of equality in a variety of forms and during different epochs. However, the change in government in 1979 brought with it a greater reorientation than had previously accompanied such a change. The values of self-help and 'enterprise' were increasingly raised over those of social welfare and community.

**Philosophical approaches**

There are several philosophical approaches that we can isolate and examine which can be combined with economic analysis to comment upon policies designed to influence the distribution and redistribution of income and wealth. We will examine three of these approaches:

1.  Natural Rights Libertarians – Robert Nozick
2.  Empirical Libertarians – F. A. Hayek and M. Friedman
3.  Liberals – John Rawls.

*1.  Natural Rights Libertarians – Robert Nozick*

For Nozick the subject of justice consists of three main types. The basic position of Justice in Holdings (or ownership) is made up of:

(a)  *The original acquisition of holding* – the appropriation of unheld things. This includes the issue of how unheld things may come to be held; the things that come to be held by these processes, the extent of what comes to be held by a particular process; and so on. This is known as the Principle of Justice in Acquisition.

(b)  *The transfer of holdings from one person to another.*
     (i)   by what process may a person transfer holdings to another?
     (ii)  how may a person acquire a holding from another who holds it?
     Under this heading come general descriptions of voluntary exchange such as gifts, and on the other hand fraud, as well as reference to particular conventional details fixed upon in a given society. This is known as the Principle of Justice in Transfer.

Therefore, if the world were wholly just, what follows would exhaustively cover the subject of Justice in Holdings:

-   A person who acquires a holding in accordance with the Principle of Justice in Transfer, from someone else entitled to the holding, is entitled to the holding.
-   No one is entitled to a holding except by the application of the two above.

Hence, the complete principle of distributive justice would say simply that a distribution is just if everyone is entitled to the holdings that they possess under the distribution. The legitimate means of moving from one distribution to another are specified by the Principle of Justice in Transfer. 'Whatever arises from a just situation by just steps is itself just' (Nozick, 1974, p. 151).

Justice in Holding is obviously historical and it depends upon what actually happened. Therefore, not all situations are generated in accordance with the two principles of Justice in Holdings. Some may steal from others, seizing their product and prevent them from living as they choose, or forcibly exclude others from competing in exchange. None of these are permissible modes of transition from one situation to another. Some persons acquire the holdings by means not sanctioned by the Principle of Justice in Acquisition and therefore the existence of past injustices raises the third major topic under Justice in Holdings:

(c)   *The rectification of injustice in holdings: the Principle of Rectification.* If past injustice has shaped present holdings in various ways, some identifiable and some not, then what now (if anything) ought to be done to rectify these injustices? What obligations do the performers of injustice have towards those whose position is worse off than it would have been had the injustice not been perpetrated? How does this work if these are the decedents of those made worse off? How far back must one go in wiping clean the historical state of injustice? What may the victims of injustice permissibly do in order to rectify injustice done to them? (For example, the victims of apartheid.) These questions tend to go unanswered.

Therefore we are back to the position whereby if each person's holdings are just, then the total distribution of holdings is just. Hence, if the current distribution of income and wealth is arrived at through present injustice or past injustice, it may be changed. However, if the distribution is arrived at through just means, now and in the past, it may not be changed. It follows that taxation, for Nozick, is on a par with forced labour. Taking the earnings of *n* hours labour in taxation is like taking *n* hours from the person. It is like forcing the person to work *n* hours for another person's purpose. The person who chooses to work longer to gain an income more than sufficient for their basic needs prefers some extra goods or services to the leisure that could be taken during these possible non-working hours; whereas the person who chooses not to work the extra time prefers the leisure activity to the extra goods and services that could be acquired. Therefore, if it is illegitimate for a tax system to seize some of a person's leisure (forced labour) for the purpose of serving the needy, how can it be legitimate for a tax system to seize some of a person's goods for that purpose? Hence, according to Nozick, applying these ideas to redistribution is extremely straightforward. Any redistribution other than that sanctioned by the Principle of Rectification is morally unacceptable and should not be undertaken. Obviously this means that policies of redistribution of income and the operation of the welfare state have no place in a 'free' society, nor is there scope for progressive taxation. As regards the welfare state, this will be rejected as immoral, since the pursuit of equality will be a violation of individual liberty.

### 2.   Empirical Libertarians – F. A. Hayek and Milton Friedman

The basic proposition here is that liberty requires the absence of coercion. In *The Road to Serfdom* (1944), Hayek argues that collective tendencies create dangers for personal freedom. For freedom and liberty there must be an absence of coercion. Particular forms of democracy will produce a progressive expansion of government control of economic life, even if the majority of the population wish to preserve a market economy. The reason for this, according to Hayek, is that in a democracy the powers of the majority must be unlimited, and a government with unlimited power will be forced to secure the continued support of the majority, to use its unlimited powers in the service of special interests (particular trades, particular regions, etc.). If a community has a mass of people in favour of a market, Hayek argues that in a market economy in which no single individual or group of individuals determines who gets what, and the shares of individuals always depend upon many circumstances which nobody could have foreseen, the whole conception of social justice becomes meaningless and empty. 'Nothing has done so much to destroy the juridical safeguards of individual freedom as the striving after this mirage of social justice' (Hayek, 1948).

Although the coercive action of the state must be limited to the enforcement of general rules of just conduct, this does not preclude government from rendering services for which it need not rely on coercion (except for raising the necessary finance). Such government services are seen as being entirely compatible with liberal principles so long as the government does not claim a monopoly, and new methods of rendering services through the market are not prevented. In addition, the means must be raised by taxation on uniform principles, and taxation must not be used for redistributive purposes. The wants that are satisfied must be the collective wants of the community as a whole and note merely the collective wants of a particular group, or groups. Hayek argues that we cannot know enough about each person's situation to distribute to each according to their moral merit. His objection is against the attempts to impose on society a pattern of distribution that has been deliberately chosen on behalf of that society. Rather, in a free society Hayek asserts that there will be a distribution in accordance with *value* rather than moral merit: that is, in accordance with the perceived value of a person's actions and services to others. Friedman argues that there is no inconsistency between a free-market system and the pursuit of broad social and cultural goals, or between a free-market system and compassion for the less fortunate – whether that compassion takes the form of nineteenth-century charitable activity or through the assistance of government. However, he argues that there is all the difference in the world between two kinds of government assistance that may seem superficially similar:

(i)   90 per cent agree to impose taxes upon themselves to help the bottom 10 per cent.
(ii)  80 per cent vote to impose a tax on the top 10 per cent to help the bottom 10 per cent.

Therefore, for Friedman, a society that puts equality of outcome ahead of freedom will end up with neither equality nor freedom. The use of force to achieve equality will destroy freedom, and the force introduced for good purposes will end up in the hands of people who use it to promote their own interests. On the other hand, he suggest that a society that puts freedom first will, as a by-product, end up with both greater freedom and greater equality. For Friedman this is very important because a free society releases the energies and abilities of individuals to pursue their own objectives and prevent some people from suppressing others. He recognises that it cannot prevent some people from achieving positions of privilege, but suggests that as long as freedom is maintained it prevents those positions from becoming institutionalised. Thus, freedom means diversity, but also mobility, and it preserves the opportunity for today's disadvantaged to become tomorrow's privileged, enabling everyone to enjoy a fuller and richer life.

Thus, both Hayek and Friedman argue for the primacy of the individual and stress the allocative and efficiency roles of the market mechanism. They stress the non-existence of social justice, it being attached to the individual. Since the market mechanism is an impersonal force, there can be no role for a concept of justice, only for a concept of efficiency. They reject all programmes of redistribution, but temper this by advocacy of government intervention to eradicate absolute poverty. This is called for not on moral grounds, but only on grounds of efficiency and stability in the economic system. The welfare state is similarly criticised, and government intervention is limited to the provision of certain public goods such as defence and the preservation of law and order. These views of the Empirical Libertarians are very different to those of Nozick and the Natural Rights Libertarians because the former base their analysis on pragmatic grounds whereas Nozick bases his analysis on moral considerations.

## 3.    Liberals – John Rawls

The approach begins with a society in an 'original state', in which individuals reach a social contract. This contract, Rawls believes, will lead, via rational negotiation, to the acceptance of a 'Maximin rule'. Such a rule maximises the position of the least well-off member of society and this process leads to three principles:

(i)    *The Liberty Principle*
   • Equality of rights compatible with similar equality for others.
(ii)   *The Difference Principle*
   • Social and economic inequalities are to be arranged so that they are:
     (a)   attached to the greater benefit of the least advantaged.
     (b)   attached to positions open to all under conditions of fair equality of opportunity.
(iii)  *The Priority Principle*
   • Between the first and the second principles, the first has absolute priority.
   • Within the second principle, the second part has priority over the first part.

Rawls assumes a society is a self-sufficient association of individuals who, in their relations with one another, recognise certain rules of conduct as binding and who act in accordance with them. He also assumes that these rules specify a system of co-operation designed to advance the good of those taking part in it. It follows that although society is a co-operative venture, it is typically marked by a conflict, as well as an identity, of interest. As such, there is an *identity of interest* since social co-operation makes possible a better life for all than would be possible if all were to live solely by their own efforts. There is also a *conflict of interests* since individuals are not indifferent as to how the greatest benefits produced by their collective actions are distributed; for in order to pursue their ends, they each prefer a larger to a lesser share. Therefore a set of principles is required for choosing among the various arrangements which determine this division of advantage and determine the proper distribution of shares. These principles are the Principles of Justice.

The problem of distributive justice for Rawls is how the benefits of co-operation are to be distributed or allocated.

$$t + s = T$$

where

$t = $ the product due to the individual
$s = $ the increment due to social co-operation
$T = $ the total product

This can be viewed in two ways: How is the total to be allocated? or, How is the incremental amount due to social co-operation to be allocated? Social co-operation means that one cannot disentangle the contributions of distinct individuals who co-operate. Thus, everything is everyone's joint product, and on this joint product each individual will make claims of equal strength, as no person has a distinctly better claim than any other. Hence it must be decided, by some means, how this total product of joint production is to be divided up. This is the problem of Distributive Justice. Do individual entitlements apply to parts of the co-operatively produced product? Rawls argues that inequalities are justified *only* if they serve to raise the position of the worst-off group in society. If, without the inequalities, the worst-off group would be in an even worse position, then the inequality is justified. These inequalities arise from the necessity to provide incentives to certain people to perform certain activities or fill certain roles that not everyone can do equally well. But to whom are the incentives paid? Rawls assumes that we can disentangle individual contributions to joint social production. He suggests that people can choose principles of justice as a result of a fair agreement or bargain, because in what he calls the 'original position', no one knows their place in society, their class position, or social status, or their natural assets and abilities, strength, intelligence, and so on. What would people in the 'original position' agree to? Rawls suggests that they would agree to two principles:

(*i*)  Equality in the assignment of basic rights and duties.

(*ii*)  Social and economic inequalities are only just if they result in compensating benefits for everyone, and in particular, for the least advantaged members of society.

Clearly such an approach is well suited to the promotion of policies of redistribution, so long as they improve the position of the least well-off, but does not imply horizontal equity. In a similar manner the provision of state-sponsored welfare and state intervention can be acceptable modes of policy, so long as they are successful in assisting the least well-off. Hence, progressive taxation is supported by this approach.

### Inequality in a capitalist economy

Economic inequality arises from the operation of the free market and from unequal wealth holdings which are largely due to the accumulation of vast fortunes that are transmitted from one generation to another. Capitalism refers to a mode of production that distributes and allocates resources in a particular way, given the relations of production that exist. Under capitalism a society's capital equipment, its means of production, are owned by a minority of individuals who use this property for private gain. The distribution of economic rewards that emerges is therefore inevitably unequal. Capitalism is the dominant form of economic organisation, and its supporters see the unequal distribution that emerges as acceptable and justifiable because it is the 'natural' outcome of the impersonal market mechanism. Capitalism, it is argued, is still the dominant system because of the economic growth and full employment that it offered in the 1950s and 1960s which transformed the living standards of the vast majority of people in the affluent industrial nations. For example, between 1950 and 1970, GDP in Britain increased by over 74 per cent in real terms (*Social Trends*, 1993) and, during the same period, unemployment in Britain averaged only 1.8 per cent per annum (Stewart, 1986). Marx, whilst denouncing the human consequences of capitalism, admired its immense productivity. In the *Communist Manifesto* he wrote, 'The bourgeoisie, during its rule of scarce 100 years, has created more massive and colossal productive forces than have all preceding generations together' (Marx and Engels, 1988). Whilst Marx argued that this created the material preconditions for the transition to socialism, liberal political economists have argued that the immense productivity of the capitalist system leads to a greater benefit for all, even if inequality persists, because of the 'trickle-down' of the benefits which improves the absolute, if not the relative, position of the poor.

Adam Smith's *Wealth of Nations* is the most often quoted (and often misquoted) authority in support of the free market and capitalism. Paradoxically, the object of Smith's admiration was not the emerging class of industrial capitalists, but hard working artisans and small businessmen. However, the *Wealth of Nations* served the convenience of the capitalists because of the way in which it asserts that the unrestrained pursuit of self-interest improves the general welfare, and because, implicit in this, is the notion that the principle of *laissez-faire* should apply. Friedman argues that an economy based on the free market and voluntary exchange (a capitalist economy), has the potential to promote efficiency, prosperity and human freedom. In addition, the free-market price mechanism will co-ordinate the activity of millions of individuals each seeking their own self-interest, in such a way as to make everyone better off. The price mechanism, therefore, performs three vital functions in this scheme: First, it transmits information. Second, it serves to provide the incentive to react to information and adopt the lowest-cost method of production. Third, it serves to determine the distribution of income. Friedman has argued that these three functions are intimately connected, and, if we do not allow the price mechanism to determine the distribution of income, then it will be unable to fulfil its other roles. The price mechanism determines the distribution of income on the basis of the value of the product of different individuals. 'If what people get is determined by "fairness" and not by what they produce, what incentive is there to work and produce?' (Friedman and Friedman, 1985). Underlying this argument is the importance of incentives. Human beings are assumed to have aspirations and, as such, an hierarchical distribution of income acts as an incentive to move up the income hierarchy to fulfil these aspirations. Therefore, if inequality of income is removed, then the incentive for individuals to work harder, or to make investments in their human capital, would disappear. The aggregate effect would be a fall in output, employment and, therefore, living standards. Implicit in the analysis of Friedman is the idea that any attempt by the state to achieve its notions of a fairer distribution of income and wealth will inevitably result in a loss of individual liberty and a reduction in economic efficiency.

Further, inequality in wealth holding can also be justified because the owners of accumulated capital should receive the greatest rewards in order to maintain the incentive to abstain from consumption in the current period. The justification for the unequal share of income that goes to the capitalists is that it represents a reward for their willingness to invest and also, as a reward for the factor that they bring to the productive process, namely their 'enterprise'. As such, 'enterprise' is found to be a recurring theme in liberal political economy.

Inequality has an important intertemporal aspect. Each epoch of human history, and therefore each economic system, has had a different economic environment. As such, the political exploitation of the serf in a feudal economy is viewed as an unacceptable level of inequality from the position of a contemporary capitalist environment. However, such inequality was seen as being entirely appropriate, at least by the landlords, in a feudal environment, and rationalised as being necessary to maintain the order of society. In the same manner, neo-classical economists and liberal politicians who fully support the role of the free market in a capitalist system do not deny that inequality exists within the system, but argue that economic inequality is necessary and justifiable because capitalism maintains stability in modern industrial economies.

In addition, the productivity engendered by the capitalist system is said to lead to greater benefits for all in society, but that, because society values the product of different individuals differently, some individuals deserve greater rewards. It also follows that in the absence of inequality there would be no incentive for the individual to increased effort or to invest in education and training. Therefore, this analysis suggests that the inequality that emerges from the capitalist system is a 'natural' process and is a justifiable outcome.

However, we could suggest that the level of economic inequality that is fostered by capitalism is excessive and unjustifiable. Capitalism is an economic system based on a class relationship which in itself is not a force for social stability, but rather is the reverse. It is inherently unstable, dividing society between capitalists and workers amongst whom there is an incompatibility of interests, whereby the capitalists own the means of production and the workers have only their labour power to sell as a commodity. The outcome is exploitation, as with feudalism, but the exploitation is manifested within the economic relationship and not the political system. The capitalists exploit labour by appropriating surplus value to form capitalist profit. Thus, under capitalism, production is organised in a socially divisive way. It is controlled by a small minority of non-producers who own and control the means of production, living off the productivity of the majority. Hence the concept of inequality is fundamental to the system.

## Measurement

The simplest graphical representation of the distribution of income is by means of a frequency distribution which takes the raw data and records the number of incomes found at each income level. Thus we divide the income of either individuals or households into income classes in a block diagram. Thus, Figure 10.2 shows that over 7000 income units had incomes of less than £1500 per year in 1984.

There is also another type of frequency distribution which illustrates the *relative* proportions of total income earned by individuals or households within these income classes. Figure 10.3 shows two types of frequency distribution. The two curves must intersect at the average income of the population as the proportion of units *must* be equal to the proportion of income they receive where, $z = x$. Above the average the $z$ curve will be above the $x$ curve and the area $\varepsilon$ indicates the extent to which these units earn in

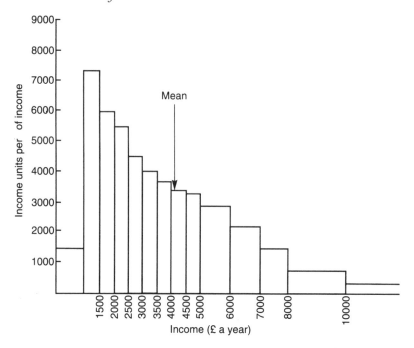

*Source*:    A. B. Atkinson, *The Economics of Inequality*, 2nd edn, Oxford: Clarendon Press, 1983.

**FIGURE 10.2    Frequency distribution – income classes**

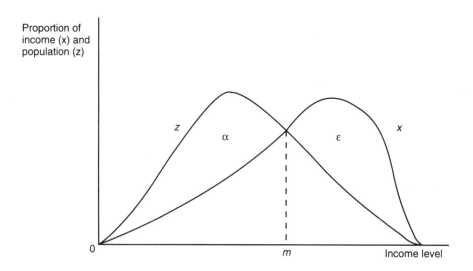

**FIGURE 10.3    Frequency distribution – relative proportions**

excess of the average income. Similarly, below the average income, the relative proportion of earners will be greater than the relative proportion of incomes. The area α thus indicates the extent to which these units receive less that the average income. This gives a graphical indication of the extent of the inequality of income.

However, there are several serious limitations with this type of display when we attempt to compare the distribution of income in two time periods. We could argue that if one of the distributions is less peaked, it indicates that it represents a more equal distribution, but it is highly likely that some of the change will be due to a general inflation of the figures in the intervening years. Mean income may have risen, which would effectively flatten the peak. In addition, it is not obvious as to how incomes at various levels may have been affected differently. Thus, such a display does not address questions as to intertemporal changes in equality, nor does it tell us how certain classes of incomes have altered in relation to the other classes of income.

A better representation is the Lorenz Curve, Figure 10.4. This is formed by cumulating the data. The incomes are arranged in ascending order, from lowest to highest. As we move along the array and cover successively 5 per cent, 10 per cent, 15 per cent, and so on, of all income recipients, we ask the question 'What percentage of total income has been covered so far?' These pairs of percentages of the cumulated total of income are then plotted in the co-ordinates to form the Lorenz Curve. If everyone had exactly the same

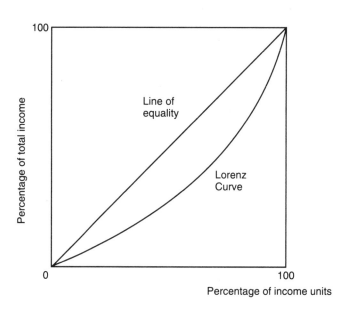

**FIGURE 10.4   Lorenz Curve**

income, the first 10 per cent of recipients would have 10 per cent of the income, the first 20 per cent would have 20 per cent of the income, the first 80 per cent would have 80 per cent of income. Thus, complete equality of income is where all these points would lie. At the other extreme, if no income at all was received by all except one income recipient (and this one had it all), then all the points would lie on the base line until we reach 100 per cent, when the profile would shoot up the vertical axis. Thus, this represents complete inequality. Actual distributions lie between these two extremes. The nearer the curve is to the rectangular boundary, the more unequal is the distribution. Similarly, the closer the curve to the 45° line, the more equal is the distribution. The advantage of this representation of the data is that we can make a direct comparison of two, or more, periods and examine where in the distribution the changes have taken place.

The Gini coefficient reduces the position of the Lorenz Curve to a single figure by measuring the area enclosed between the curve and the diagonal as a percentage of the whole area below the 45° line. Therefore, it varies between zero and unity. At zero, this indicates complete equality, whereas the extreme of inequality is given by unity. This figure can then give us a standard by which to compare distributions between time periods, groups of recipients and even countries.

The definition of income and the choice of unit represent a complex issue. For example, do we include the imputed value of owner-occuplier dwellings? This would raise middle-class incomes in greater proportions than others. In fact there is no indisputable conclusion as to what basic principles should be used. We may however regard income as a *flow* of revenue to the recipient, irrespective of changes in that person's assets over the period studied. Such a definition differs from the concept of income generally adopted by economists, which is the amount that is available for consumption whilst keeping assets intact. There are difficulties. For example, should we include transfer payments? Social benefits make up a large proportion of lower incomes, but they may be seen as paid for by the taxpayer out of his/her income. If a parent gives a child an allowance, we would not expect it to be added to the sum of incomes, and the transfer from the taxpayer to the recipient of social benefit is of the same kind (even though it is compulsory). But when we are recording personal income we are concerned with something more than the composition of the national income. The fact remains that many incomes do contain large elements of benefit, and therefore we must take account of this when we define income.

Should we include elements of income that are not received or recorded in money terms, for example, the provision of a company car? They should be included conceptually, but the difficulty is how to evaluate and record them. In addition there is the problem of where to draw the line between remuneration and amenity. Conditions of work may be provided at some cost to the employer, which may make the job more attractive, but be paid at a lower rate in money terms. The more we add, the less likely it is that we will be able to make international or intertemporal comparisons.

The major sources of information are much the same in kind, (if not in detail) in most contemporary economies. A major source is always found in the returns of direct taxation, although some income that should be assessed for taxation avoids it, and many incomes lie below the exemptions level. There are also surveys of family or household income that are collected through sampling, in a number of countries. In Britain, the Family Expenditure Survey – set up to find the correct weights for the Retail Price index – covered 7418 households in 1992, and they are asked to state their income.

The many definitions of both income itself and of the income unit, bedevil attempts to compare distributions compiled from different sources; indeed since 1979 the basis upon which the figures are collected and presented has changed in subtle ways to make intertemporal comparisons extremely difficult. For example, Social Security statistics do not provide a complete description of the income distribution. Also, the Central Statistical Office (CSO) figures are inconsistent over time in their definition of income. From 1984 onwards all rent/rates/poll tax/community charge rebates and allowances and housing benefit are excluded from gross income. In 1990 the New Earnings Survey changed the basis of employment figures from the list of Key Occupations for Statistical Purposes (KOS) to the Standard Occupational Classification (SOC). The New Earnings Survey also changed in 1983 from Men aged 21 and over and women aged 18 and over, to males and females on adult rates.

If our aim is to answer the question as to whether one distribution of income is more unequal than another, and to answer it by reference to a single index, such as the Gini, then much adjustment in detail is required before such an answer can be given, or the answer must be subject to a great deal of qualification.

## Taxation

Taxation can be viewed as a powerful redistributive tool, one which may have a large impact on the distribution of income and wealth. Taxation falls into two groups, direct and indirect, and therefore the incidence of the tax may be different for different taxes. The formal incidence of taxation falls on those who have the legal liability to pay the tax, whereas the effective incidence refers to those individuals who are finally out of pocket as a result of the imposition of a particular tax. Traders are legally liable to pay value added tax, but are able to pass the burden of payment to someone else, the consumer. Therefore, we should note that the person who is liable to pay the tax is not necessarily the person who is out of pocket because of the tax. Tax collections depend upon the tax base and the tax rate taken together. Hence the amount raised in revenue can vary because of a change in the rate or a change in the base, or a change in both the rate and the base. The tax base is what the tax is imposed upon, for example, income, the value of property, sales, and so on. The tax rate refers to the percentage at which the tax base is taxed, for example, a rate of 20 per cent on a sales tax base of £1000 leads to collections of £200.

In respect to income, taxes are classified as progressive, regressive or proportional. Where the rate of taxation rises as income rises, this is progressive. Where the rate of taxation remains constant as income rises, this is proportional. A regressive tax is where the rate of taxation falls as income rises (Figure 10.5). If the tax is not levied on income, it cannot easily be determined whether the tax is progressive, proportional or regressive by examining the tax rate in isolation. Thus, a proportional tax rate levied on general sales may appear to be equitable, as all pay the same tax rate. However, it may actually be regressive if the ratio of sales to income falls as income rises. This is because, if people on low incomes spend proportionally more of their income on the commodities that are taxed than those on higher incomes, then the ratio of sales taxes paid to the income of the low-income group will be higher than the ratio of sales taxes paid to the income of the higher-income groups. To understand fully the progressivity of the tax system, we must examine the difference between the average and the marginal rates of taxation. The average tax rate is the proportion of income that is taken in tax. The marginal

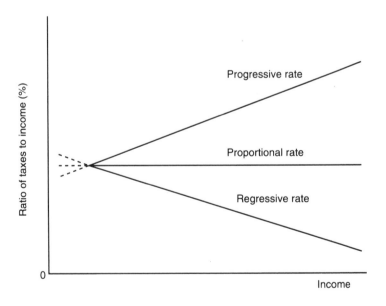

**FIGURE 10.5   Proportional, progressive and regressive taxation**

rate of tax is the fraction of additional earning that is taxed. Hence a progressive tax schedule is one in which the average rate of tax increases with income. A tax rate is progressive only if the marginal rate is higher than the average rate: that is, if one pays a higher rate on any additional earnings than one pays on current earnings.

Figure 10.6 overleaf shows three possible relationships between average and marginal tax rates: Figure 10.6(a) shows the situation where the tax schedule is progressive over most of the income range. On income less than *OA*, both marginal and average rates are rising. At incomes above *OA*, the marginal rate begins to fall, but because it is at such a high level, the average rate continues to increase. Only when we get to incomes higher than *OB* does the average rate begin to fall as the marginal rate falls below the average rate. However this is not a likely schedule, not least because of the Laffer Curve relationship (see below). Figure 10.6(b) illustrates a tax schedule that is linear, and as such is progressive. The amount of income *OX* is exempt from taxation, and the earnings above *OX* are taxed at a rate of *OY*. As income rises, the fraction of total income that is taxed becomes larger, until those on the highest incomes have an average tax rate very nearly equal to *OY*. The progressivity of the schedule is given by the fact that the average tax rate rises steadily with income. The degree of progressivity can be found from the slope of the average tax rate. In Figure 10.6(c), the slope of the average tax rate is steeper and, therefore, the degree of progressivity of the schedule is greater. Thus, it is progressivity that we are looking for if we wish to use taxation as a redistributive tool.

However, because progressivity requires high marginal rates of taxation, a conflict appears in that high marginal rates of taxation generate disincentive effects, causing a conflict in terms of equity and efficiency. This is often illustrated by the supposed relationship of the Laffer Curve (Figure 10.7, p. 221). Beyond *t**, higher tax rates reduce revenue because of the disincentive effect which greatly reduces the quantity being taxed. At 100 per cent tax rate, supply and revenue will be zero again. This is often invoked to support the idea that high tax rates of 70, 80, 90 per cent on the highest income groups would actually raise less revenue. This is because some of the highest income recipients would leave the country and pay nothing to the British Inland Revenue. However, it could be argued that if high rates of taxation lead to Phil Collins, Rod Stewart and Michael Caine leaving the country, then this alone could be justification enough for the imposition of high rates.

### Distribution

The changes in the distribution of income between 1688 and 1978/9 are shown in Figure 10.8. In the period covered there has been a move to greater equality, as the 1978/9 curve is everywhere closer to absolute equality. However, it

220

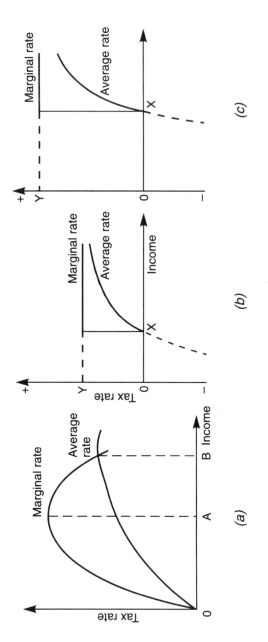

*Source:* J. A. Kay and M. A. King, *The British Tax System*, 5th edn, Oxford University Press, Oxford, 1991.

**FIGURE 10.6 Marginal and average rates of taxation**

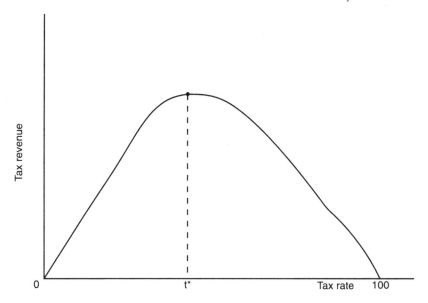

**FIGURE 10.7   Laffer Curve**

would appear that the changes were very much different in the lower 70 per cent of incomes than in the top 30 per cent. That is, in the lower section, incomes had become much more unequal, whereas in the upper section, incomes had become much more equal. Whereas the income at the 70th percentile was nearly four times that at the 10th percentile in 1978/9, the ratio had been only 2:1 in 1867. The average income of the top 10 per cent was 5.3 times the mean of all incomes in 1867. In 1978/9 the ratio was just half of that. The component of income in the top 5 per cent had been reduced even more, to a third of the 45 per cent of all income at which it had stood in 1867. What is the explanation for this striking change in income distribution? It would appear that much of the relative fall in the higher incomes came about through the Second World War.

Although the evidence is far from perfect, there are a number of estimates of national income before and after the war, but there is none that gives us a comparable series to compare the distribution of income until after the war. Using the Survey of Personal Incomes, compiled by the Inland Revenue, is one way of attempting to compare pre- and postwar distributions. However, Table 10.1 does illustrate unmistakable changes in the distribution at the higher income level, in terms of the relative reduction. The component of the top 10 per cent which had been 45.5 in 1867, still stood at 40.5 per cent in 1938/9, but had fallen dramatically to 28.3 per cent in 1954/5. In addition, the rise in the other components was not spread evenly. It was concentrated in the two

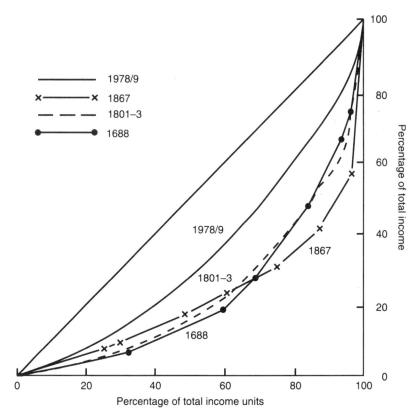

*Note*: The data relate to England and Wales for 1688 and 1801–3, to Great Britain and Ireland for 1867, and to the United Kingdom for 1978/9.
*Source*:   A. B. Atkinson, *The Economics of Inequality* 2nd edn, Oxford: Clarendon Press, 1983, p. 22.

**FIGURE 10.8    Distribution of income in Britain, 1688–1978/9**

middle quintiles, leaving out the poorest: hence the relative rise in middle incomes between 1867 and 1978/9 (Figure 10.8). It can be argued, therefore, that over this period the middle incomes rose faster than those above them and those below them. Rubinstein agrees that there appears to be little doubt that the Second World War marked a turning point in British income distribution. He argues that the 'single most important chronological and causal locus of this clear cut trend to income equality was the Second World War and the immediate post-war period of socialism and Austerity' (Rubinstein, 1986).

There are several arguments that have been put forward to explain this trend. Rubinstein observes that rates of personal taxation reached levels that

**TABLE 10.1  Distribution of personal income in Britain before and after the Second World War**

|  | 1938/9 (%) | 1954/5 (%) | 1974/5 (%) |
|---|---|---|---|
| Quantiles as percentages of the median |  |  |  |
| Highest percentile | 1137 | 558 | 417 |
| Highest decile | 244 | 188 | 191 |
| Upper quartile | 143 | 140 | 142 |
| Lower quartile | 81 | 67 | 66 |
| Average income of top 10 per cent as relative to mean income | 4.0 | 2.8 | 3.2 |
| Quantile components as percentages of total income |  |  |  |
| Top 10% | 40.5 | 28.3 | 24.8 |
| Top 20% | 52.4 | 42.1 | 39.4 |
| 61–80% | 16.1 | 21.4 | 22.9 |
| 41–60% | 12.3 | 16.6 | 17.5 |
| 21–40% |  |  | 12.6 |
| 0–20% | 19.1 | 19.9 | 7.6 |

*Source*:  Royal Commission on the Distribution of Income and Wealth (1977), *Report No. 5*, Cmnd 6999, London.

were without precedent in history: 'A bachelor earning £10,000 had retained £6,222 after income tax and surtax in 1937, but only £3,501 in 1948, despite the fact that inflation had nearly halved the value of the pound' (Rubinstein, 1994). Peden points to the introduction of the welfare state and the policy of full employment as a powerful redistributive measure which much reduced absolute poverty in its extent, although many continued to suffer from relative poverty (Peden, 1991). There is also the rise in average earnings during this period which, allied to the level of employment, must have contributed to the reduction in inequality. Atkinson has shown that the average income in Britain before tax 'rose ninefold, from £344 in 1949 to £3,159 by 1977' (A. B. Atkinson, 1980).

The available statistics show that the change at the top of the income distribution that was so marked after the Second World War continued on a smaller scale afterwards. However, the trend slows after 1973, at the end of the long postwar boom, and, as we shall see, the trend has been reversed since 1979. As we approach the 1980s we begin to suffer from the many changes that have taken place in terms of the availability of statistics and the comparability of these data sources. The table in the National Income Blue Book was dropped in 1970 and only reintroduced in 1975 as a result of the recommendation of the Royal Commission on the Distribution of Income and Wealth (The Diamond Commission). However, the Diamond Commission was itself abolished in 1979 by the incoming Conservative Government on the grounds that enough information on this subject was available from government sources. In 1981, the Rayner Review of the Government Statistical Service recommended a large reduction in the statistics on income and wealth. Hence 1986 is the latest data set available on a comparable basis, shown in Table 10.2. Here we see that middle incomes fall slightly, lower incomes fall, whilst higher incomes rise. Even with redistribution (final incomes) the change is still apparent. But problems arise due to the inconsistency of the statistics themselves from 1979 onwards.

Using the data that we have, it becomes clear that Margaret Thatcher's policies had an effect upon the distribution of both pre-tax and post-tax income in such a way as to end the move towards greater equality in income distribution and move back to the prewar situation. Whereas the richest 1 per

**TABLE 10.2    Income distribution, 1976–86**

| Original income | 0–20% (Group 1) | 21–40% (Group 2) | 41–60% (Group 3) | 61–80% (Group 4) | 81–100% (Group 5) |
|---|---|---|---|---|---|
| 1976 | 44.4 | 26.6 | 18.8 | 9.4 | 0.8 |
| 1978 | 44.8 | 26.7 | 18.7 | 9.2 | 0.6 |
| 1980 | 45.5 | 26.9 | 18.6 | 8.5 | 0.5 |
| 1981 | 46.1 | 26.9 | 18.0 | 8.1 | 0.6 |
| 1982 | 47.1 | 27.2 | 18.2 | 7.1 | 0.4 |
| 1983 | 48.0 | 27.2 | 17.7 | 6.7 | 0.3 |
| 1984 | 48.6 | 27.5 | 17.5 | 6.1 | 0.3 |
| 1985 | 49.2 | 27.3 | 17.2 | 6.0 | 0.3 |
| 1986 | 50.7 | 26.9 | 16.4 | 5.7 | 0.3 |
| *Final income* | | | | | |
| 1976 | 37.5 | 24.0 | 18.1 | 12.8 | 7.6 |
| 1978 | 38.4 | 24.0 | 17.9 | 12.5 | 7.2 |
| 1980 | 38.8 | 24.1 | 18.0 | 12.3 | 6.8 |
| 1981 | 38.6 | 24.0 | 17.9 | 12.4 | 7.1 |
| 1982 | 39.4 | 24.1 | 17.6 | 12.0 | 6.9 |
| 1983 | 39.3 | 24.0 | 17.6 | 12.2 | 6.9 |
| 1984 | 39.0 | 24.3 | 17.5 | 11.7 | 7.1 |
| 1985 | 40.2 | 24.0 | 17.4 | 11.8 | 6.7 |
| 1986 | 41.7 | 23.9 | 17.0 | 11.4 | 5.9 |

*Source*:    Based on data from *Social Trends*, various issues.

cent's share of income halved between 1949 and 1978/9 to 5.3 per cent, by 1981 the figure had risen to 6 per cent and by 1984/5 to 6.4 per cent. The picture was the same for the top 10 per cent, whose share rose from 26.1 per cent in 1979 to 29.5 per cent by 1984/5. With regard to the poorest 10 per cent, they experienced a period of greater shares in pre-tax incomes from 2.5 per cent in 1971 to 2.7 per cent in 1974. However, by 1979 their share of income had fallen to 2.4 per cent and in 1981 to 2.0 per cent. In reality this meant that the richest 10 per cent received £1557 p.a. per head, whilst the poorest lost £82 p.a. per head during the period 1979–82. Various sources suggest that the change in trend set in motion by the Thatcher Government has indeed been sharp, and a continuing process, although none can claim to give a definitive result. For example, the Department of Social Security statistics in *Households Below Average Income 1988–89* show an increase in the number of individuals with a household income below 50 per cent of the national mean. Department of Social Security statistics also show that the bottom 10 per cent of households saw their real disposable income fall by 6 per cent between 1979 and 1989. This compares with a 30 per cent increase in the average income of all households over the same period.

*Social Trends* 1992 confirms that the share going to Britain's poorest people fell throughout the 1980s. The poorest fifth of the population's share of household income fell from 9.9 per cent in 1979 to 7.9 per cent in 1988/9. Only the top fifth of the population finished the 1980s with a bigger share of total income than they had in 1979, this rose from 34.8 per cent in 1979 to 40 per cent in 1988/9. Again, *Social Trends* (1993) shows that, after housing costs are taken into consideration, the real income of the poorest 20 per cent fell by approximately 3 per cent from 1979 to 1990/1, while the incomes of all other groups increased, with the wealthiest fifth of the population achieving a 49 per cent rise. The same study shows that the poorest 20 per cent derived 69 per cent of their income from state benefit in 1990/1, with only 20 per cent coming from employment. Using the Inland Revenue statistics, we can confirm that the latest data set available shows that the Lorenz Curve for 1977/8 lies inside that of 1990/1 for both pre-tax and post-tax income.

Johnson and Webb extrapolate Gini coefficients to show the increasing inequality of income distribution (Johnson and Webb, 1993). They use the annual UK Family Expenditure Survey, with modelled benefit receipts and tax payments to test the sensitivity of income inequality to changes in the tax and benefit system.

They confirm that relative inequality increased between 1979 and 1988, such that the Lorenz Curve for 1979 lies inside that for 1988 at every point. They also confirm that the increase in inequality could be ascribed to changes in personal tax and the benefit system, with changes in pre-tax earnings distribution and the changes in economic activity, taken together, accounting for much of the overall change. Within this, they suggest that tax and benefit changes have had the largest impact.

### TABLE 10.3    UK Gini coefficients

|        | *Gini coefficient* |
|--------|--------------------|
| 1979   | 0.2381             |
| 1982   | 0.2495             |
| 1985   | 0.2611             |
| 1988   | 0.3104             |

*Source*:  P. Johnson and S. Webb, 'Explaining the growth in UK income inequality 1979–88', *Economic Journal*, 103, March 1993.

## Policy

Although the redistribution of income in Britain has its origins in the 1563 Poor Law, policy in the twentieth-century has transformed and extended the scope of redistribution beyond recognition. In particular, since the Second World War the scale of the redistribution and the types of methods employed have steadily risen in real terms. The benefits of redistributive policy have been in both cash and kind. Those benefits that accrue in kind are primarily in the form of merit goods that are assumed to be made freely available to everyone in equal amounts (however, it could be argued that the better-off receive more education goods because they are more likely to enter higher education). Such goods can be consumed in equal amounts by the richest as well as the poorest in society, but the provision of merit goods remains redistributive as the costs of their provision are not spread evenly throughout the population. They bear much more heavily on the upper-income groups. Health care and education are the most obvious examples. The benefits paid in cash include old age pensions, income support, child benefit, unemployment benefit and sickness benefit.

The basis for economic policy immediately after the Second World War was the maintenance of full employment. This had enormous implications for all departments of the economy, not least in terms of the redistribution of income. Full employment meant high levels of consumption and therefore high levels of demand. Full employment also made it much easier to leave one job and to find another, as well as giving greater power to the trade union movement to negotiate on behalf of its members to secure higher remuneration: 'The moral fervour which has gathered round the idea of full employment has been due as much as anything to the hope that, with labour acquiring scarcity value, workers would be able to insist on reasonable assurances about their own treatment and the general policies of their industries' (*The Economist*, 13 July 1946, quoted in Youngson, 1960). The maintenance of full employment meant that workers had little difficulty in finding and then keeping a job in which they could earn a 'living' wage. However, this increase in the ability to keep and maintain a household at a 'reasonable' standard of living did not result in a contraction of social services. Indeed, they expanded at a considerable rate. Expenditure on education rose at both secondary and university level. The Education Act of 1944 raised to fifteen the school-leaving age which, in time, required the construction of new schools and the upgrading of the existing school buildings. The need for a highly skilled and technically trained work-force led to an increase in university student members, and thus an expansion of existing universities and the construction of many new universities.

The National Health Service was proposed in a White Paper of 1944 and came into operation in 1948. The basic underlying principle was that medical attention should be available to all who required it. The Act proposed that no one should pay directly for any medical services. However, some charges were introduced in 1951 to reduce the cost to the Exchequer. The other major social measures of the immediate post war period was the so-called Beveridge Plan. Assuming full employment (defined as 3 per cent unemployment) the plan proposed a comprehensive scheme of social insurance using a system of tripartite contributions from the insured person, the state and the employer, which would provide retirement pension, grants covering maternity, marriage and death, benefits covering sickness, unemployment, childhood and widow-hood. All of the population between the ages of 16 and 65 were to be the contributors. These proposals were accepted by the state in a series of Acts between 1945 and 1948.

The introduction of what was to be the welfare state goes a long way to explain the change in trend in terms of inequality that was discussed above, a trend that appeared to continue until the late 1970s.

As already noted Atkinson has shown that the average income in Britain before tax 'rose nine fold from £344 in 1949 to £3,159 by 1977' (A. B. Atkinson, 1980). However, with the Thatcher Government's fiscal policy coming into force after 1980, income distribution has been radically altered. According to Field, Thatcher's policy regarding distribution has halted 'the gentle trend towards greater equality in income that marked the post-war years and actually put the whole process in reverse' (Field, 1989). Although figures vary, it is estimated that in the early 1960s there were nearly 4 million people receiving means-tested benefits compared to over 7 million in 1983. Similarly, there is thought to have been at least 1.3 million people living on the poverty line in 1960, with the number rising to 2.7 million by 1981. This pattern has continued throughout the 1980s and the early 1990s.

Peden notes that poverty had been greatly reduced by 1951, mainly due to full employment and the introduction of the welfare state. Indeed, the level of national assistance benefits in 1963 was worth half as much again as in 1948. By 1973 the rate of long-term supplementary benefit was worth double the level thought to be sufficient in 1948 (Peden, 1991). Hence, until Thatcher came into office in 1979, there were movements towards greater equality of income. In addition, Stark has argued that between 1925 and 1980 wealth distribution showed a 'strong underlying trend to less inequality' (Stark, 1987).

Thatchers's policy reforms had an effect upon the distribution of both pre-tax and post-tax income in such a way as to end the move towards greater equality in distribution, and to actually reverse the trend of the previous 34 years. Whereas the richest percentiles' share was halved between 1949 and 1978/9 to 5.3 per cent, by 1981 the figure had risen to 6.0 per cent, and 6.4 per cent by 1984/5. The picture was the same for the top 10 per cent whose share rose from 26.1 per cent in 1979, to 29.5 per cent by 1984. As regards the poorest 10 per cent, they experienced a period of greater shares in pre-tax income from 2.5 per cent in 1971 to 2.7 per cent in 1974. By 1981 their share of income had fallen to 2.0 per cent. This meant that the richest 10 per cent received £1557 per annum, per person, whilst the poorest lost £82 per annum per person during the period 1979–82.

Obviously, a major factor influencing the distribution of income is the changes to the tax system. Amongst the top 10 per cent income group, the post-tax share fell from 27.1 per cent in 1949 to 23.1 per cent in 1975/6. This figure rose slightly in 1978, but the greatest changes came about during the period of the Thatcher Government, with a rise to 25.6 per cent in 1981–2. The situation for the poorest 10 per cent as regards post-tax income was very different, with their share declining each year from 3.2 per cent in 1975, to 2.4 per cent by 1982. Atkinson has shown that of the £4.17 billion in tax cuts in 1979, 44 per cent went to the richest percentile, whilst the lowest 25 per cent income group only receives 3 per cent in cuts (Townsend, 1984). Indeed, Townsend suggested that 'the present government has declared its priorities by relieving the very rich of high rates of income taxation and doubling the threshold of capital transfer tax' (Townsend, 1984). According to Townsend, those who had higher incomes were seeking overseas investment at the rate of £4.6 billion per year. The abolition of exchange controls made it harder to tax the rich effectively, and to encourage overseas investment led to falls in wage and employment levels, which ultimately altered the distribution of income.

In 1977 direct taxation represented 38 per cent of total taxation, with indirect taxes representing 38 per cent. By 1987 direct tax stood at 28 per cent and indirect at 43 per cent, showing how the combination of taxes has altered since the late 1970s. The amount a person expects to contribute through taxation can affect many areas of the individual's life, as well as the general income distribution. For example, increases in taxation will affect the desire to work, as it will reduce the amount of income retained from doing overtime. Thus, a worker may prefer to work fewer hours to avoid paying higher taxes. On the other hand, if a workers earns less money as a result of the imposition of higher taxes they may wish to work longer hours to regain the earnings level otherwise lost in taxation. If people are earning less in post-tax income, they will spend less on goods and services and in some instances will become dependent upon the state. In this way, income distribution can be altered as the number of people in certain income groups has changed dramatically.

The other very important factor is the level of employment. As we have seen, the immediate post-war period saw high levels of employment which contributed to the move towards greater equality in the distribution of income and living standards. By 1979 unemployment had begun to increase and many more people were claiming social security benefits to ease the pressure of being unemployed. Poverty and debt increased, and the number of claimants of benefit by 1983 was over 7 million. Since 1981, long-term unemployment has risen, which has meant that income distribution has altered due to the high numbers claiming benefits. Hence the number of poor people in Britain is much larger now than during the 1970s. Figures relating to the number of social security benefit recipients have also risen due to the change in the age profile of the population in terms of the large numbers of elderly population that are on or below the poverty line. It has been argued that, over the 1980s, the total percentage living on low income rose from 60 per cent to 68 per cent (Townsend, 1984).

Social security benefits came under attack after 1979, both in terms of their real value, and individual entitlement. There were 38 major changes to the entitlement of the unemployed to social security benefits during the period 1979–88, reducing social security payments to the unemployed by £510 million per year (Rowthorn, 1992). In addition, the State Earnings Related Pension Scheme also became subject to pressures from the government through the reduction in the benefits of the scheme in 1986. There has followed a sustained attempt to persuade people to opt out of the state-sponsored scheme by offering financial inducements to move to pension arrangements organised by the private sector.

In the immediate postwar period both Labour and Tory governments employed a policy of raising most social security benefits in line with real earnings, reflecting economic growth – to distribute the benefits of economic growth throughout the income groups of the economy. Indeed, the Labour Government of the 1970s increased child benefit and old age pensions significantly faster than the contemporary increase in average earnings. The Thatcher administration reversed this policy and broke the link between economic growth and the level of benefits. The policy became one of increasing the majority of benefits in line with inflation, which rises more slowly that incomes. As such, in real terms, most benefits remained roughly constant throughout the period 1979–91. The real value of child benefit in 1991 was virtually the same as it had been in 1978 for a recipient with two children. During this period, the relative value of all the major social security benefits fell substantially in comparison to average earnings. The vast majority of benefits fell in relative value by approximately 20 per cent (Rowthorn, 1992). Thus there has been a complete reversal of the so-called postwar consensus surrounding the policy towards social benefits.

**TABLE 10.4  Tax revenue as percentage of GDP: international comparisons, 1970–89**

|       | USA  | Japan | Germany | France | UK   | EEC  |
|-------|------|-------|---------|--------|------|------|
| 1970  | 29.2 | 19.7  | 32.9    | 35.1   | 37.0 | 30.8 |
| 1971  | 27.8 | 20.0  | 33.4    | 34.5   | 34.8 | 31.5 |
| 1972  | 28.7 | 20.7  | 34.7    | 34.9   | 33.3 | 31.5 |
| 1973  | 28.7 | 22.5  | 36.3    | 35.0   | 31.4 | 31.4 |
| 1974  | 29.2 | 23.0  | 36.5    | 35.5   | 35.0 | 32.3 |
| 1975  | 29.0 | 20.9  | 35.7    | 36.9   | 35.7 | 33.4 |
| 1976  | 28.3 | 21.8  | 36.8    | 38.7   | 35.5 | 34.4 |
| 1977  | 29.1 | 22.3  | 38.1    | 38.7   | 34.8 | 35.0 |
| 1978  | 29.0 | 24.0  | 37.9    | 38.6   | 33.1 | 35.1 |
| 1979  | 29.0 | 24.4  | 37.7    | 40.2   | 32.7 | 35.2 |
| 1980  | 29.5 | 25.5  | 38.0    | 41.7   | 35.4 | 36.4 |
| 1981  | 30.0 | 26.2  | 37.6    | 41.9   | 36.7 | 37.0 |
| 1982  | 29.9 | 26.7  | 37.4    | 42.8   | 39.2 | 38.0 |
| 1983  | 28.4 | 27.2  | 37.3    | 43.6   | 37.5 | 39.2 |
| 1984  | 28.4 | 27.4  | 37.5    | 44.6   | 38.0 | 39.4 |
| 1985  | 29.2 | 28.0  | 38.0    | 44.5   | 38.0 | 39.4 |
| 1986  | 28.9 | 28.9  | 37.6    | 44.1   | 37.8 | 40.1 |
| 1987  | 30.1 | 30.1  | 37.7    | 44.8   | 37.2 | 40.6 |
| 1988  | 29.8 | 31.3  | 37.4    | 44.4   | 37.3 | 40.8 |
| 1989  |      |       | 38.1    | 43.9   | 36.5 |      |
| 1970–9 | 28.8 | 21.9 | 36.0    | 36.8   | 34.3 | 33.1 |
| 1980–9 | 29.4 | 27.9 | 37.7    | 43.6   | 37.4 | 39.0 |

*Source*:  OECD *Revenue Statistics*, 1965–1989, quoted in C. Johnson, *The Economy under Mrs Thatcher 1979–1990*, Penguin, Harmondsworth, 1991.

Table 10.4 shows that the average tax burden in Britain during the 1970s was 34.3 per cent. However, this increased during the 1980s to 37.4 per cent. Johnson also shows how the total tax burden was higher at the end of the decade than it had been at the beginning when Thatcher became Prime Minister (Johnson, 1991). The basic rate of income tax was cut from 30 per cent to 29 per cent in 1986, and again reduced to 27 per cent in 1987 and to 25 per cent in 1988. Johnson comments that: 'The cuts in personal taxes went mainly to middle and even to high income groups and it is doubtful how much effect they had on work incentives' (Johnson, 1991). The last of the income tax rate reductions came in 1992 with the introduction of a new 20 per cent band on the first £2,000 of taxable income. In terms of indirect taxation, the Budget of 1991 increased the standard rate of VAT from 15 per cent to 17.5 per cent. In addition, the Budget of March 1993 introduced a widening of the

VAT base since the introduction of VAT in 1973. Despite the announcement in the Second Budget of 1993 of compensatory measures to offset the effects of this widening of the VAT base, many householders will remain worse off due to the changes. Although many pensioners will find the compensation sufficient to offset the imposition of VAT on domestic fuel, households on means-tested benefits will not receive equivalent compensation and, as a result, will be worse off. The worse affected will be low-income households with children.

Giles and Johnson suggest that the overall effect of the tax changes since 1985 has been to increase household disposable income by an average of £4 per week. However, this figure relates to the *average* gain, and in fact, the gains were very unevenly distributed: they show that 47 per cent of households gained, whereas 37 per cent lost. Moreover, within this, it has been high-income households that have gained substantially with the negative impact of increases in indirect taxes being more than offset by the reduction in direct taxes. The overall effect for poorer households, however, has been a reduction in their post-tax incomes as they gained little from the reduction in direct taxes (Giles and Johnson, 1994). Table 10.5 illustrates that the higher the decile, the greater is the average gain; whereas the lowest deciles lose on average as a result of the changes in taxation.

The study by Giles and Johnson also shows that the direct tax changes were regressive, reducing the proportion of income that the higher deciles paid in tax by a greater degree than is the case for the lower decile.

TABLE 10.5    **Impact of tax changes, 1985–95, by decile group**

| Decile | % losing | % gaining | Average gain/loss (£ per week) | Average gain/loss (% of net income) |
|--------|----------|-----------|-------------------------------|--------------------------------------|
| 1 | 66 | 7 | −3.0 | −2.9 |
| 2 | 44 | 13 | −1.4 | −1.4 |
| 3 | 47 | 23 | −1.8 | −1.5 |
| 4 | 43 | 40 | −1.1 | −0.8 |
| 5 | 37 | 50 | 0.7 | 0.4 |
| 6 | 33 | 57 | 1.6 | 0.7 |
| 7 | 29 | 64 | 3.1 | 1.2 |
| 8 | 25 | 69 | 4.4 | 1.5 |
| 9 | 23 | 72 | 6.3 | 1.8 |
| 10 | 20 | 76 | 31.3 | 5.8 |
| All | 37 | 47 | 4.10 | 1.70 |

*Source*:   C. Giles and G. Johnson, *Taxes Down, Taxes Up: The Effects of a Decade of Tax Changes*, Institute of Fiscal Studies, commentary no. 41, London.

the largest tax reduction was enjoyed by the top decile whose direct tax burden fell from about 34.25 per cent to about 30.5 per cent [1985-1995]. The numbers for the top decile are in fact heavily affected by the very rich households in that decile – the top 1 per cent of the income distribution. The top percentile's direct tax burden fell from 46.2 per cent to 36.2 per cent over the period – a drop of 10 percentage points (Giles and Johnson, 1994).

Increased regressivity is also in evidence in terms of the changes to indirect taxation. In relation to the highest decile whose share of gross income taken in indirect taxes will be 8 per cent in 1995, the share for the lowest decile will be 20 per cent. Giles and Johnson conclude that the changes toward greater indirect taxation has reduced the progressivity of the tax system and therefore has benefited the higher-income recipients at the expense of the lower-income recipients.

Finally, the Rowntree Report of 1995 confirms that income inequality in Britain grew rapidly between 1977 and 1990, reaching a higher level than at any time since the Second World War. Inequality increased faster in Britain during this period than in any other industrialised nation, with the exception of New Zealand. Between 1979 and 1992 the poorest 20–30 per cent of the population failed to benefit from economic growth, which is in contrast to the general trend since the war.

The report cites multiple causes for this change in the trend, and highlights greater dependence on state benefits caused by increases in unemployment, with a rising gap between income from employment and income from state benefit. Incomes of those on benefit have fallen behind, as benefit levels have generally been linked to prices since the early 1980s. Income from employment had an effect also, as hourly wages for the lowest-paid men were lower in real terms in 1992 than in 1975, with median wages rising by 35 per cent over the same period.

The report confirms that the long-term trend towards greater equality of incomes ended in the late 1970s with inequality rising rapidly throughout the 1980s. Since 1979 there has been a rapid rise in the share of the top 10 per cent and a fall in the share of the poorest fifth, with the real incomes of those in the poorest 20–30 per cent failing to increase significantly during the 1980s.

# CHAPTER 11

# Unemployment

The chequered history of British unemployment is matched by the variety of policies that have been employed to combat the problem. From the great depression of the late Victorian economy, through the record levels of the early 1930s and the reintroduction of mass unemployment since the late 1970s, policies and policy proposals dealing with unemployment have formed a major focus for both politicians and economists. The orthodoxy may have changed over the century, but each was concerned, at its core, with unemployment: how to reduce it, how to explain it, or perhaps even how to justify its existence. The 'Treasury View' of the 1920s and 1930s, with its emphasis on balanced budgets, the Keynesian revolution and the use of state intervention to reflate the economy, and back to the deflationary monetary policy, beginning with the Callaghan Labour Government of the mid to late 1970s, and continued with much vigour by the Thatcher Governments of the 1980s: all, implicitly or explicitly, were concerned with policy involving the role of the unemployment in a mature capitalist economy. Whilst economists may argue over causes and cures, it is the role of the politicians to either justify the existence of unemployment of attempt to eradicate it from the economy.

## Definition

General discussion of unemployment may well treat the phenomenon as being synonymous with being out of work and claiming unemployment benefit. However, particularly in lesser developed countries where benefit systems (if they exist at all) tend to be far from comprehensive or adequate, *under*employment is the major problem. With a lack of a benefit safety net, people cannot be unemployed and survive. Hence, when discussing unemployment, one should remember that the definition may be crucial in terms of the policy proposals that follow. Indeed, even in economies with relatively sophisticated welfare systems, unemployment benefits may be paid only to a proportion of those of working age who are without work. This is particularly true of the British economy. There are more than 20 million people in the OECD who are in receipt of benefits other than unemployment benefit (e.g. early retirement on a state pension, invalidity benefit) (Blondal and Pearson, 1995, p. 136). Blondal and Pearson show that in approximately 50 per cent of OECD countries there are more people receiving invalidity benefits than there are people registered as being unemployed (Blondal and Pearson, 1995).

It may be argued that unemployment is simply the state of being out of paid employment, interested in paid employment at a realistic rate of pay, and available for work. However, Layard argues that different people will have different intensity with which they seek paid employment. Some people, for example, may not be actively seeking work on a daily or weekly basis, but would be prepared to work if the opportunity presented itself. On the other hand, many people may be actively seeking work following a long absence from the labour market and would not be classed as in a state of unemployment, being ineligible for unemployment benefit: many women may find themselves in this situation (Layard, 1988).

For the economist, the definition tends to depend upon ideological and philosophical perspectives. To greatly oversimplify, for the 'right' wing, unemployment is not an outcome of market failure and is referred to as a voluntary activity. For the 'left' wing, it is involuntary inactivity and is therefore the result of market failure. The approach that is adopted will obviously produce very different policy proposals, and so the definition of the problem has a fundamental bearing on the economic policies that are adopted.

## Measurement

The measurement of unemployment in Britain is somewhat idiosyncratic in that those classed by government statistics as being unemployed have to be in receipt of unemployment benefit or income support. This 'claimant count' tends to reduce the official figures, making inter-country comparisons very difficult. In addition, changes to the way in which the statistics are compiled (about 32 changes since 1979) mean that intertemporal comparisons are also difficult, if not impossible, to calculate.

The International Labour Organisation (ILO) definition includes people without a paid job in the reference week who were available to start work in the next fortnight, and who had either looked for work at some time in the past four weeks, or were waiting to start a job already obtained.

The Royal Statistical Society has argued that the claimant count should be replaced because people believe that the government has been activity fiddling the figures (*Financial Times*, 5 April 1995). The 'headline' measure counts the number of people who are without work and who successfully

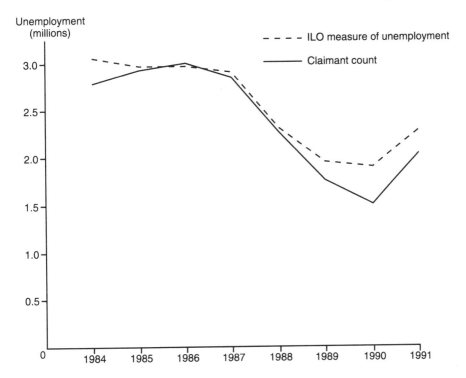

*Source:* Based on data from *Employment Gazette*, July 1992.

**FIGURE 11.1** **Comparison of alternative measures of unemployment 1984–1991**

claim unemployment benefit or income support. The Society report states that the claimant count is not based on any agreed concept of unemployment, is not consistent over time, due to the changes in the claimant system, and cannot be used for international comparisons.

Several groups are omitted from the official statistics in Britain. For example, the disabled, married women who have either been out of the labour market for a period of time, or have never been previously employed, redundant workers, school-leavers who do not take up the offer of training programmes, those of independent means who do not register as being unemployed, and those who are on government-sponsored training schemes are not included. In addition, changes in unemployment are driven by the supply of labour as changes occur in the workforce. We may see a reduction over a twelve-month period in unemployment, but Department of Employment figures in January 1994 show that the number of people in part-time work increased over the year to September 1993, whilst those in full-time employment fell. Although the trend over 1993 was that new jobs being created were mostly part-time and for women, the Department's figures published in March 1994 appear to show that the trend in unemployment of the previous decade has been reversed. The figures for employees in employment showed full-time employment rising by 19 000 between September 1993 and December 1993, while part-time employment fell by 5000. However, the Labour Force Survey (6000 households) appeared to show the opposite: between the summer and autumn of 1993 part-time employment rose by 90 000, while full-time employment fell by 17 000.

The *Employment Gazette* (August 1995) shows the trend towards more employment for females and greater emphasis on part-time work. Table 11.1 illustrates this point. Total full-time employment rose by 3.3 per cent in the ten years 1984–94; but, within this, male full-time employment fell by 1.9 per cent, while female full-time employment rose by 16.1 per cent. Over the same period, total part-time employment rose by 26.6 per cent, female employment in this category increasing by virtually the same percentage as with full employment, but male part-time employment rose by 97.1 per cent during the decade.

We can illustrate how the measurement of unemployment can be used to reinforce a particular view. In the extreme we can quite plausibly suggest a figure for unemployment in Britain that is over four times the official figure. We do this as follows:

In winter 1994/5 there were 44.352 million people in Britain over the age of 16; around 10 million of these were pensioners. A total of 25.221 million were classified as being in employment, with 2.417 million officially unemployed as defined by the claimant count. Thus, taking the 16+ population of 44,352 million and subtracting the 25.221 million in employment, we arrive at a figure of 19.131 whom we may classify as being 'economically inactive'. Then, subtracting the 10 million pensioners leaves us with 9.131 million who are 'economically inactive of working age'. Next we assume that of the 25.221 million who are classified as being in employment, 0.820 million are working part-time but would prefer full-time work, 0.283 million are on training schemes and 0.240 are temporary workers, all of whom would prefer permanent full-time employment (*Social Trends*, 1995). We now arrive at a figure of 10.474 million who we can classify as interested in full-time employment.

Hence:    $\dfrac{10.474}{44.352} = 23.62$ per cent

However, we need to take account of 10 million pensioners

Therefore:    $\dfrac{10.474}{34.352} = 30.49$ per cent

**TABLE 11.1**   Full-time and part-time workers in Great Britain, (seasonally adjusted) (000s)

*FULL-TIME*

| Spring | Total | Men | Women |
|--------|-------|-----|-------|
| 1984 | 18 395 | 13 050 | 5 346 |
| 1985 | 18 525 | 13 107 | 5 417 |
| 1986 | 18 513 | 13 035 | 5 479 |
| 1987 | 18 642 | 13 055 | 5 587 |
| 1988 | 19 264 | 13 429 | 5 837 |
| 1989 | 20 037 | 13 807 | 6 230 |
| 1990 | 20 213 | 13 852 | 6 361 |
| 1991 | 19 667 | 13 438 | 6 230 |
| 1992 | 19 343 | 13 051 | 6 292 |
| 1993 | 19 973 | 12 737 | 6 236 |
| 1994 | 19 009 | 12 800 | 6 209 |
| 1995 | 19 256 | 12 955 | 6 301 |

*PART-TIME*

| Spring | Total | Men | Women |
|--------|-------|-----|-------|
| 1984 | 4 851 | 558 | 4 292 |
| 1985 | 4 952 | 564 | 4 388 |
| 1986 | 5 041 | 567 | 4 475 |
| 1987 | 5 231 | 643 | 4 587 |
| 1988 | 5 399 | 710 | 4 689 |
| 1989 | 5 541 | 719 | 4 823 |
| 1990 | 5 606 | 772 | 4 834 |
| 1991 | 5 627 | 784 | 4 842 |
| 1992 | 5 898 | 978 | 4 920 |
| 1993 | 5 971 | 1 004 | 4 967 |
| 1994 | 6 118 | 1 100 | 5 017 |
| 1995 | 6 146 | 1 126 | 5 020 |

*Source*:   *Employment Gazette*, August 1995.

We now have an unemployment rate that represents those of working age who are not employed on a permanent, full-time basis but wish to be if the opportunity arises. The official unemployment figure at this time was 7.04 per cent.

## Types of unemployment

Some theories take as their premise the idea that unemployment is an efficient outcome of market activity and thus advocate *laissez-faire* policies to reduce the level of unemployment. Other theories pinpoint market failure as the cause. In the latter case, different types of market failure can be identified as causing unemployment and, as such, require different economic policies to tackle the problem.

### 1. Frictional unemployment

Frictional unemployment results from the length of time that it takes workers to move between jobs. It is the consequence of short-run changes in the market for labour, as workers search for jobs that they consider as being better than the one that they already have. The time spent between jobs is considered to be worthwhile as workers search for better opportunities, through an investment which will bear fruit in the form of higher earnings and/or greater job satisfaction. In addition, the economy as a whole may benefit from this frictional unemployment as workers search for better opportunities, through higher productivity, as workers match their skills to the appropriate jobs. The reduction of frictional unemployment is therefore possible through measures designed to reduce the search time involved in changing jobs. This may be achieved with an efficient system of employment centres, giving accurate and up-to-date information on the availability of employment opportunities. Joan Robinson commented that 'completely full-employment can never be seen. Nor is completely full-employment desirable. The attainment of full employment in this absolute sense would require strict controls, including direction of labour' (Robinson, 1979, p. 21). There must be an amount of unemployment in an economy because of frictional unemployment. If not, it would mean that the state is in a position to dictate who works where, and there can be no movement between jobs.

### 2. Structural unemployment

This results from longer-term changes in the structure of the economy which leads to changes in the demand for, and supply of, labour in particular industries, regions and occupations. This can be further reduced into different types of structural unemployment:

(a) *Regional unemployment*: We can clearly see in Table 11.2 the disparity between regions which has been a feature of the British economy for many years.

The traditional explanation for this regional disparity has been the over-reliance of certain regions on 'staple' industries that have gone into decline, for example, coal, textiles and shipbuilding. Consequently policy recommendations tend to focus on the need for geographical mobility of both firms and the labour force, as well as the need for retraining.

TABLE 11.2   **Regional unemployment (%)**

|  | 1986 | 1989 | Feb 1994 | Feb 1995 |
|---|---|---|---|---|
| UK | 11.8 | 6.3 | 9.8 | 8.4 |
| North | 16.4 | 10.0 | 11.8 | 10.6 |
| Northern Ireland | 18.1 | 15.1 | 13.2 | 12.1 |
| South-East | 8.7 | 3.9 | 9.6 | 8.1 |
| East Anglia | 9.0 | 3.6 | 7.8 | 6.4 |

*Source*:   Based on data from the Department of Employment.

*(b)   Occupational unemployment*: Here, certain industries tend to suffer disproportionately as far as unemployment is concerned. The construction industry is a good example in this area, with over 25 per cent unemployment in 1982 and 1991/2. Also, the unskilled are much more likely to be unemployed than non-manual workers. Policies may centre on state help for individual industries, particularly during a recession, and concentrating on employment subsidies where demand has fallen.

*(c)   Technological unemployment*: Technological progress may allow more output to be produced in a given industry with less labour, also making certain skills no longer required, for example, the changes in the print industry in the 1980s. Policy would tend to concentrate on the need for retraining and the transfer of workers to new industries and occupations.

*(d)   Seasonal unemployment*: Where workers are only required at certain times of the year, where the demand for labour varies considerably over the year. Examples are found in the tourism industry, where demand may be much higher in the summer months, the demand for Father Christmases, which will be particularly low in July, and even county cricketers who will be unemployed from October to March. There is a limit to the effectiveness of policy in this area, but attempts to match skills to out-of-season employment may have some impact.

Hence structural unemployment is a problem of skills and locations not matching those required for unfilled vacancies. Therefore high levels of structural unemployment are likely when there is a rapid decline in an economy's traditional products, and the labour market is unable to adjust quickly enough to the changes. The ultimate answer is tied up with the retraining and relocation of workers, incentives for firms to relocate, or new firms to locate in these areas of high unemployment, and for the introduction of new products and methods of production.

Whether the problem of unemployment is caused by frictional or structural matters is very important to the policy-maker, as this makes a very important difference to the whole matter of unemployment. For example, does 13 per cent unemployment represent 13 per cent of the population unemployed for a year, or every one of the population unemployed for 13 per cent of the year? The first case would represent a structural problem and could be addressed by one set of policies, whereas the latter case suggests a frictional problem and would require a totally different set of policy proposals.

Consider Table 11.3 in terms of the structural change in the British labour market:

### TABLE 11.3   Changes in employment

*Sectors which have lost jobs in the past five years*

Overall manufacturing
Car industry
Chemical/manmade fibres
Electrical/electronic engineering
Banking/finance
Local government services
Sectors which have added jobs in the past five years
Medical/health services
Education
Charities
Sport/other recreational
Business services
Sanitary/other cleaning

This suggests a structural shift in the British economy away from manufacturing industry and towards the service sector. Some economists have argued that this is a good thing for the British economy. In particular, Patrick Minford has suggested that '[The] service sector is the key to our employment prospects – that is where the UK's comparative advantages lie' (*Financial Times*, 13 September 1995). However, others would argue that such a structural change cannot be a driving force for increasing employment opportunities, and indeed will lead to the reverse. To suggest that we have a comparative advantage in services neglects the whole point of Ricardo's theory of comparative advantage. Except for the category 'Business services' in Table 11.4, none of the other sectors represent export potential. Whereas the sectors that have lost jobs all have a high export potential, with the exception of local government services. Hence, serious balance of payments problems are likely to arise with implications for aggregate demand which are compounded by the fact that jobs in the service sector are more likely to be low paid and part-time than those in the manufacturing sector, and as aggregate demand falls, unemployment will rise, giving the opposite outcome to that suggested by Professor Minford.

## Theories of unemployment

*1. The classical view*

Unemployment in this view is due to the wage being too high. More workers would like to be employed, but, at the present level of wages, employers cannot afford to take them on. In Figure 11.2, the present wage is set at $w'$, giving a level of employment of L. The point $L^*$ represents the level of full employment and, given the conditions of supply and demand in the labour market, this could only be achieved if the wage level were to be reduced to $w^*$. In other words, the level of unemployment engendered by the wage level $w'$ is equal to $OL^* - OL'$. The answer, therefore, is to reduce the wage level and thus increase the level of employment that firms are willing to offer. Hence the trade unions are the villains here, in that they represent a monopoly of labour, keeping wages above the rate required for full employment. A policy of reducing the power of trade unions to negotiate wage levels would be advocated, to be replaced by the introduction of individual, rather than collective, wage bargaining.

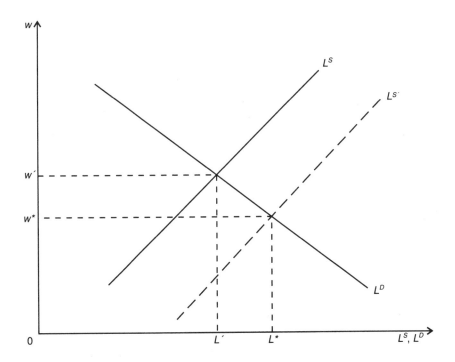

**FIGURE 11.2 Classical view of unemployment**

## 2. Demand deficient unemployment

The classical view held the orthodoxy until the late 1930s when Keynes severely criticised the logic of this argument. Keynes argued that the policy recommendations of the Classical view would in fact have the opposite effect. That is, they would create more unemployment. If wages are reduced this would reduce aggregate demand reducing the demand for goods and services, causing firms to adjust their output downwards and thus reducing their demand for labour. Hence unemployment, in this view, is associated with too little aggregate demand for goods and services in the economy as a whole. Any of the elements that make up aggregate demand could be the cause of demand deficiency: consumer spending may fall, investment spending may fall, government expenditure may be reduced, or net exports may decline. In each case, it is within the power of the government to act to reverse the trend, as only the state has an overview of the needs of the economy. Figure 11.3 illustrates the way in which state intervention could be used to reduce the level of unemployment in the economy. At the equilibrium level of activity, shown by $C + I + G + (x - m)$, the level of employment is at $Y'$, below the

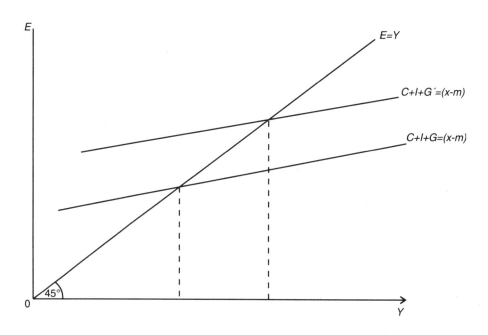

**FIGURE 11.3   Keynesian view of unemployment**

level of full employment ($Y^*$). By acting to increase the level of aggregate demand to $C + I + G' + (x - m)$, the government can take the economy to the new equilibrium level of activity which will produce full employment, $Y^*$.

### 3. *The monetarist/supply-side approach*

This view tends not to be concerned with the separation of unemployment into its constituent parts as already described, and in this respect is totally opposed to the Keynesian view. They argue that, for any economy, at any given point in time, there is a Natural Rate of Unemployment (NRU), given by the state of the labour market. The NRU is therefore the amount of the labour force that will remain unemployed even when the supply of labour is in equilibrium with the demand for labour, brought about by changes in the real wage rate. Figure 11.4 shows the equilibrium level of unemployment ($L_N^*$), and, hence, the difference between this level of employment and the available amount of labour in the economy will be the NRU.

In addition, the NRU is seen as being the only level of unemployment consistent with a stable rate of inflation. Therefore, according to this theory, if

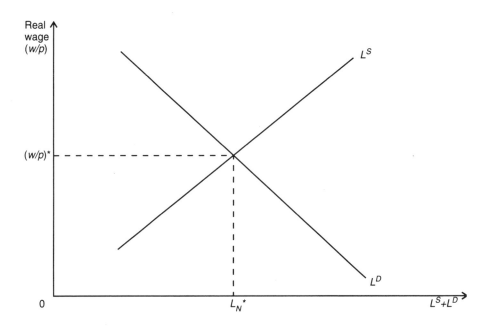

**FIGURE 11.4   Monetarist/supply-side view of unemployment**

the government wishes to increase the level of employment (that is, reduce the level of unemployment below the NRU), it can only achieve this by continuously stimulating the economy, causing accelerating inflation. Thus there can be no long-term trade-off (à la Phillips). It follows that macro-economic policy will be ineffective in the long run as far as unemployment is concerned. It is considered to be a micro-economic problem, and efforts should be concentrated on the improvement in the responsiveness of the labour market to reduce the NRU. The policy recommendations that follow include the need to improve occupational and geographical mobility, reduction of trade union restrictive practices and the provision of suitable wage differentials within the labour market and between the employed and the unemployed.

*4.  New classical school*

Unemployment according to this theory is driven from the supply side using a model of labour-market-clearing equilibrium. The 'rational' worker is interested in planning for the supply of labour across all periods. That is, the individual seeks to take leisure in periods where the opportunity cost is best, and thus withdraws from the labour market when the wage level is low, re-entering the market when the wage level rises. Leisure is therefore taken when it is least costly in terms of forgone earnings. In this model the labour market always clears, and any unemployment that remains must be the result of voluntary decisions taken by workers to withdraw their labour from the market, although still being classed as unemployed. Therefore, if unemployment exists, it is entirely voluntary.

*5.  Marx's reserve army of labour*

The reserve army of labour is, for Marx, essential to the workings of capitalism, to counteract the tendency for the rate of profit to fall. Wages do not fall, but the reserve army are there to keep the growth of wages to that which the economy can afford. Much of the unemployment for Marx is technological in character because, as the economy reaches the top of the cycle, firms substitute 'expensive' labour for capital machinery, creating a reserve army of labour as a counter-weight to the power of labour. For Marx, accumulation and innovation are bedfellows, and capital accumulation is linked inseparably to technical change. It follow that accumulation not only brings in new types of machinery, but it also ushers in new methods of production, and an increasing division of labour. All of the technology is described as being of the embodied variety, that is, new capital goods embody the latest technology, and therefore the accumulation of fixed capital and innovation are synonymous. An individual capitalist will attempt to increase productivity through the substitution of constant capital (plant and machinery) in place of labour power. Hence production of the commodity will be possible using smaller amounts of labour embodied than will their competitors. This suggests a tendency inherent in the capitalist system for technical change to be biased towards labour-saving innovations. One important implication of this is that the economy will not proceed on a balanced equilibrium growth path. The capital goods sector will be producing an increasing proportion of total output. If technological change is predominantly labour saving, the employment of labour power will grow less rapidly than does constant capital. It follows therefore that the demand for labour power is a function of the accumulation of capital, and since accumulation increases the proportion of constant capital in output, the growth in the demand for labour must be slower than the growth of constant capital. Competition forces other capitalists to introduce the same methods of production ensuring an increase in constant capital throughout the economy and producing a rising reserve army of labour. The rising unemployment is therefore not due to deficiencies in aggregate demand because it exists when all existing capital is fully staffed. The rate of technological change is conditioned, for Marx, by the relative scarcities of the appropriate inputs. Thus, if in any period there is an excess demand for labour, such that wages increase and the rate of profit falls, the application of labour-saving technology will be accelerated, thus reducing the demand for labour power.

The reserve army of labour allows the total domination of capital over labour. It is the key economic force which keeps the real wage down to subsistence level, ensuring that the techniques of increasing the productivity of labour increase the rate of exploitation, and thus the relative share of the capitalist class in net output.

## 6. The non-accelerating inflation rate of unemployment (NAIRU)

Layard has argued that, whether they will admit it or not, the Government has been using unemployment to contain, or reduce, inflation. He therefore examined the relationship between unemployment and inflation. He concluded that if unemployment is low, inflation will tend to rise, and as employers find it more difficult to fill vacancies they will attempt to attract workers by paying more than the going rate. In addition, trade unions will feel in a much stronger position to push for wage increases. Therefore it follows that if unemployment is high enough, inflation will fall (as was the case in the early 1980s). Thus there exists a critical level of unemployment at which inflation will neither be rising, nor falling, and this is NAIRU. In Figure 11.5, if unemployment is pushed below NAIRU, inflation will increase.

Conversely, if unemployment is pushed above NAIRU, inflation can be reduced. The model works through expectations as inflation feeds on itself. If inflation is stable this process is halted. NAIRU itself is determined in the labour market, as shown in Figure 11.6. At any particular point in time there is a limit to the living standards which the economy can provide. Thus, there

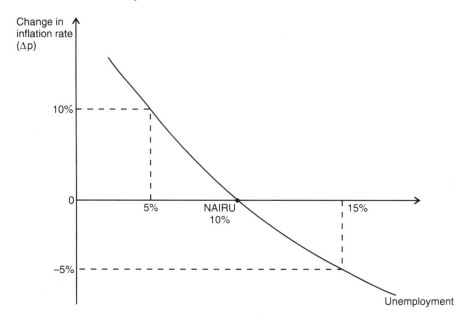

**FIGURE 11.5    Non-accelerating inflation rate of unemployment**

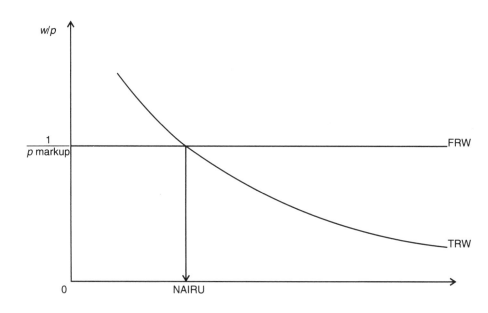

**FIGURE 11.6    Determination of NAIRU**

exists a Feasible Real Wage (FRW). If workers attempt to get more than this, inflation will rise, with wages accelerating and prices following them upwards. Hence, stable inflation has to be set at the wage bargaining table. This can be assured by having just enough unemployment in the economy. The correct level of unemployment will ensure that the target real wage (TRW) equals the feasible real wage. If there is too little unemployment, wages will be pushed too high and wage inflation will increase. If there is too much unemployment, wage and price inflation will fall. This theory represents a synthesis of the Keynesian demand-deficiency argument, the supply-side market equilibrium theory and the Marxian reserve army of labour. The power relations of the two sides of the capitalist economy underlie the conditions in the macro-economy, and the higher the level of unemployment, the greater the power of capital to reduce the wage level, and hence reduce inflationary pressure.

It is clear that economists vehemently disagree about the causes of unemployment, and therefore the policies that would best be suited to alleviate, or eradicate, the problem of unemployment. Broadly, the Keynesians talk in terms of demand deficiency and the ability of the government to address the problem through intervention to overcome market failure. The supply-siders consider present levels of unemployment in terms of the NRU having risen to purge inflation from the system. The classical school blamed supply-side factors and Marxists generally believe that unemployment is necessary in a capitalist economy to keep a check on the wage level, and thus maintain profits.

### The history of unemployment policy

Due to the unreliability of the few statistics that are available, we do not have a clear picture of the extent of unemployment before the First World War. However, Beveridge, using data from the trade unions, estimated that between 1881 and 1913 an unemployment rate of 4.8 per cent was the average amongst skilled and semi-skilled workers. Within this there were fluctuations, with a maximum of approximately 10 per cent in 1886 (Beveridge, 1944). The extent of unemployment in late Victorian Britain was not that different in recessionary periods in comparison with the twentieth century. However, Floud argues that employment was much more insecure in the latter half of the nineteenth century, with employers able to change employment at will. Given that employment protection was non-existent, eligibility for assistance from the Poor Law was not available to the able-bodied, and trade union funds only covered a small number of the labour force, unemployment caused enormous hardship for individuals and families. Indeed, Floud has suggested that, 'it was no wonder that unemployment was regarded as the best recruiting agent that the army and navy could ever have' (Floud, 1994).

There were chronological and cyclical variations with estimates that vary due to the data problems. There is no reliable measure of the incidence of disguised unemployment through underemployment and casual employment. Underemployment occurred in agriculture and casual employment was most prominent in the docks and the building trade. In general, underemployment and casual unemployment were most prevalent in the older traditional sectors of the economy and this declined only gradually as more people became employed in the newer industries and occupations.

The welfare reforms of the Liberal governments of 1906–1914 included the provision of unemployment insurance. Although the Poor Law remained, new forms of state assistance supplemented the existing system, extending the scope of government intervention, but not the level of expenditure. Unemployment insurance benefits were first paid in 1913, but the majority of workers who contributed to the fund were skilled and male. The payments were on a small scale and contributions were made on a flat scale which made them regressive taxes (MacKinnon, 1994).

After the First World War, the speculative boom of 1919–20 gave way to depression. Average unemployment 1921–39 was 14 per cent of the insured workforce (Constantine, 1994). Two peaks are evident, and in 1921 unemployment stood at 16.9 per cent, and at 22.1 per cent in 1932. The unemployment figure never fell below one million between 1921 and 1939. Constantine estimates that in the worst months of the depression in the early 1930s, 6 or 7 million people in the UK were living on the dole. Long-term unemployment increased in the 1930s, with over 400,000 unemployed for 12 months or more by August 1932, representing 16.4 per cent of the unemployment total (Constantine, 1994). There was also a regional dimension, with much lower rates of unemployment in the south-east than in the industrial areas. Staple industries had higher levels of unemployment, while non-tradable industry faired relatively better.

In the classical view, rigidities in the labour market are to blame, and to reduce unemployment the wage level must fall. The Harrodian view is that the proportion of the population of working age rose: from 1924 to 1937 population growth was 0.4 per cent, but working population growth was 1.5 per cent per annum (Aldcroft, 1987). In addition, we see an increase in the participation of women, which may have been a contributory factor.

In the classical tradition, Benjamin and Kochin have pointed to the National Insurance scheme as being a significant contributory factor through the replacement ratio (benefit level: real wage of the economy) (Benjamin and Kochin, 1982, 1979): the result being an increase in the level of search unemployment and voluntary unemployment. They examine actual labour supply ($S^A$) and effective labour supply ($S^E$). They conclude that the effective labour supply is reduced, due to a high replacement ratio and, as the benefits to wage ratio rises, this causes $S^E$ to shift further to the left (Figure 11.7), causing an increase in unemployment. While it is true that National Insurance was extended in 1920 to cover approximately 11 million workers, Benjamin and Kochin's conclusion that the unemployment rate would have been a third lower without National Insurance is not generally supported. In particular, Crafts found that, on a sectoral basis, only three of the 12 sectors that he examined were significant in terms of the benefits to wage ratio. In addition, unemployment in the 1920s tended to be short term, whereas in the 1930s long-term unemployment was much more prevalent, and this does not suggest a strong relationship.

In reality there are no mono-causal explanations for the high levels of unemployment in the interwar period. There was a cyclical element with the booms and slumps in the economy and population-related factors. Booth and Glynn have argued that about 80 per cent of the problem can be ascribed to structural problems in the British economy (Booth and Glynn, 1975), although this figure may be an exaggeration. Another factor may be that of hysterisis. The argument here is that a persistent change in an economy can be caused by a transitory disturbance. Thus short-term unemployment leads to long-term unemployment, which then becomes inbuilt into the system as it becomes self-generating (Isaac, 1994). There will also exist interrelationships between these

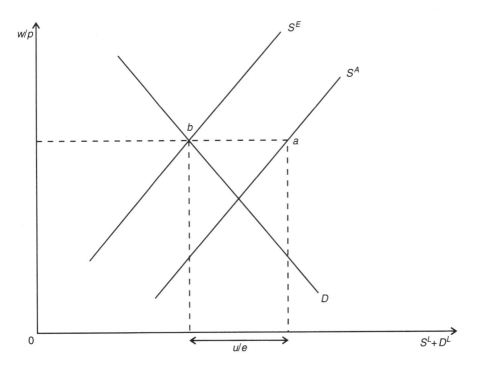

FIGURE 11.7   Effect on labour supply of high replacement ratio

separate factors. For example, structural problems will feed through into technological change, and hence affect the rate of investment, leading to a fall in the output of capital goods, causing unemployment in the capital goods sector. This may result in a reduction in aggregate demand, causing a fall in output in the consumption goods sector, leading to an increase in unemployment in that sector, giving the familiar multiplier effect.

This was the basis of Keynes' critique of the classical view of unemployment. Whilst successive governments had believed that the best policy to combat unemployment was to revive the free market at home and facilitate this by minimising its own role and allowing private enterprise to be the main agent of recovery, Keynes argued that only intervention in aggregate could address the problem. He asserted, in essence, that the orthodoxy maintaining that in the long run demand always equals supply was misguided. Orthodoxy was turned on its head in the Keynesian revolution that followed. Demand deficiency and the need for government intervention came to the fore, and for almost three decades the problem of unemployment appeared to have been solved.

The immediate postwar years of full employment gave way to a return to the mass unemployment of the interwar period, and the abandoning of the Keynesian 'solution'. In its place came a rejuvenation of the orthodoxy of the 1920s and 1930s, and its policy prescriptions.

The unemployment of the 1980s was attributed to several familiar factors. It was seen to be cyclical, caused by the world recession of 1980–2. The trade unions were blamed for their insistence on real wage increases rather than limiting their demands to preserve jobs, and the lack of pressure on the unemployed to take employment at low wages due to the high replacement ratio. In the face of a doubling of unemployment between 1979 and 1981 and a continuous rise of another 50 per cent over the next five years to more than 3 million, the Thatcher Government refused to use macro-economic policy, believing that a stimulation of the economy would be inflationary without creating employment in the long term. The best way to reduce unemployment, they argued, was to allow market forces their head to adjust conditions in the labour market. Thus policy was designed to facilitate market forces, and the villains of the piece were the trade unions, acting as a monopoly on labour, and – for some economists – the Government itself for offering too generous benefits. On this latter point, Minford wrote:

> wage flexibility is substantially reduced by the fixed (flat rate) benefit level. This is because benefits do not vary with wage levels. Hence as wages fall, benefits do not fall in proportion and act as a floor below wages reducing their flexibility. Our first proposal is therefore to introduce a maximum statutory ratio ('benefit capping') of 70 per cent for total unemployment benefits to net income in work . . . It would, according to our estimates, bring about a sizeable reduction in unemployment – about $\frac{3}{4}$ million in 4 years (Minford, 1985).

## Policy

As already discussed, much of the history of unemployment has involved policy prescriptions that adhere to the market-oriented analysis. One could argue that the interventionist decades of the immediate postwar era represent little more than a 'blip' in the orthodoxy. The supply-side package that was introduced in the 1980s thus had its emphasis on the freeing-up of markets. Trade union reform, reductions in earnings-related benefits and the introduction of numerous retraining schemes were all intended to create the environment within which the free market could be allowed to reach an equilibrium and maintain a 'natural rate of unemployment' consistent with stability of prices. Table 11.4 lists the main initiatives of the Department of Employment from 1980 to 1990.

TABLE 11.4   Department of Employment activities, 1980–90

| | |
|---|---|
| 1980 – | Employment Act (secondary action, closed shop, postal ballots) |
| 1982 – | Employment Act (union damages, closed shop, trade disputes) |
| – | Community Programme, Young Workers' Scheme, Enterprise Allowance |
| 1983 – | Youth Training Scheme (16–18) |
| – | Job Splitting Scheme |
| 1984 – | Trade Union Act (secret ballots) |
| – | Technical and Vocational Education Initiative (14–18) |
| 1985 – | Job Clubs |
| – | National Council for Vocational Qualifications |
| 1986 – | Wages Act (councils) |
| – | Sex Discrimination Act (hours of work) |
| – | Restart |
| – | Job Training Scheme |
| – | Jobstart Allowance |
| 1987 – | Compacts |
| – | New Workers' Scheme |
| 1988 – | Employment Act (closed shop, members' rights) |
| – | Employment Training (18–34) |
| – | Career Development Loans |
| 1989 – | Employment Act (deregulation, training) |
| – | Business Growth |
| – | Training |
| – | Claimant Advisers |
| 1990 – | Employment Act (job protection, unofficial action) |
| – | Training and Enterprise Councils |
| – | Youth Training |

*Source*:  Adapted from C. Johnson, *The Economy under Mrs Thatcher, 1979–1990*, Penguin, Harmondsworth, 1991, p. 223.

The consequences of high and persistent levels of unemployment are not confined to the waste of human resources in the economy: Shapiro and Ahlburg have argued that as unemployment rises the number of suicides also rises (Shapiro and Ahlburg, 1983). In addition, they suggest that each 1.0 per cent increase in unemployment has been associated with an increase in deaths from heart disease of 1.9 per cent, a 3.4 per cent rise in the incidence of mental illness, a 4.0 per cent increase in committals to prison and a 5.7 per cent rise in murders. Long periods of unemployment lead to demoralisation and demotivation which is recognised by potential employers who actively discriminate against the long-term unemployed, adding to the problem. Hence the policy initiatives have served only to reorganise the labour market in terms of increasing the supply of labour and in attempting to increase the flexibility of the existing supply. The effect of this is to reduce wage levels in the way that was advocated in the 1920s and 1930s.

Perhaps in the light of historical evidence the theory of hysterisis is as plausible as any explanation for the persistently high level of unemployment in the British economy in the 1980s and 1990s. If so, a new set of policies are required to tackle the problem. Even so, supply-side economists could still argue a case for their policies based on an interpretation of hysterisis as the cause, suggesting that policies should be concentrated on a reduction in the 'natural rate'. Marx would clearly understand the process at work and also agree with the hysteresis line of argument, but in terms of a totally expected outcome of the capitalist system. The policy recommendation would be for a fundamental change to the relations of production to reverse the trend.

What is clear is that the current set of policies are not reducing significantly the level of unemployment, or, even more significantly, the incidence of long-term unemployment. Indeed, Layard and Nickell have attributed approximately 75 per cent of the rise in unemployment in the 1980s to the policies adopted by the Thatcher Governments. One could be cynical about the whole episode and suggest that the only truly successful policy to reduce unemployment over the past 21 years has been the manipulation of the unemployment figures.

# CHAPTER 12

# *Inflation*

The economic significance of the rate of inflation and the need to specifically target economic policy towards the reduction of inflation has come to the fore in the latter part of the twentieth century in all Western capitalist economies, supplanting unemployment as the 'great evil' of our time. Perhaps this is not quite so surprising given that prices have risen faster over the past fifty years than in any similar period since 1694, with the index of prices rising threefold between 1694 and 1948, but rising twenty-fold since (MacFarlane and Mortimer-Lee, 1994). This is illustrated in Figure 12.1. Apart from the inflationary period of the First World War, low rates were recorded throughout the twentieth century until the 1970s.

**TABLE 12.1 Average inflation rates in the UK (geometric averages) %**

| | |
|---|---|
| 1900–1913 | 1.3 |
| 1914–1918 | 15.3 |
| 1919–1939 | −1.2 |
| 1940–1945 | 4.3 |
| 1946–1949 | 2.6 |
| 1950–1959 | 4.3 |
| 1960–1969 | 3.5 |
| 1970–1979 | 12.5 |
| 1980–1989 | 7.4 |
| 1990–1993 | 5.1 |

*Source*: H. MacFarlane and P. Mortimer-Lee, 'Inflation over 300 years', *Bank of England Quarterly Bulletin*, 34, 2, May 1994.

Therefore, for the past twenty years governments have tended to be preoccupied with formulating policies to combat inflationary pressure which has necessitated a greater emphasis on cause, theory and cure. Policy priorities have dictated that low and stable inflation has replaced low

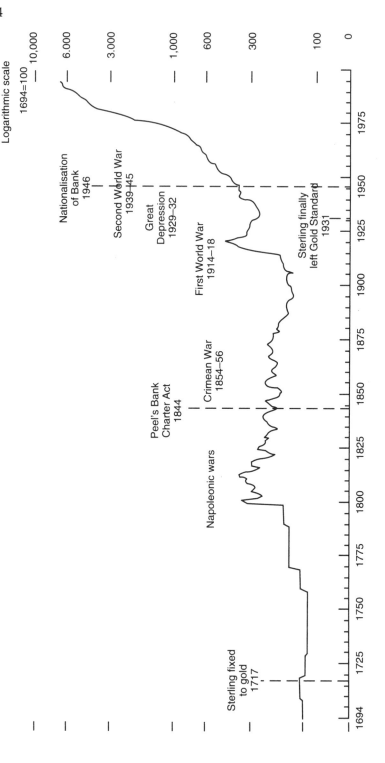

FIGURE 12.1   UK rate of inflation 1694–1994

*Source:*   H. MacFarlane and P. Mortimer-Lee, 'Inflation over 300 years', *Bank of England Quarterly Bulletin*, 34, 2, May 1994, p. 157.

unemployment as the target for governments, and in many ways the evolution of economic theory in this area is a reflection of this change in priority.

## Measurement

The measure that is normally used is the Retail Price Index (RPI). This represents a basket of goods and services that is purchased by the 'average' household given by the annual household survey. Each item is given a weighting according to its importance relative to other expenditures and can be presented in the form of an index (Figure 12.2).

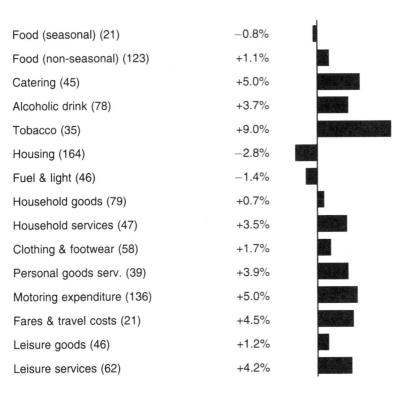

| | |
|---|---|
| Food (seasonal) (21) | −0.8% |
| Food (non-seasonal) (123) | +1.1% |
| Catering (45) | +5.0% |
| Alcoholic drink (78) | +3.7% |
| Tobacco (35) | +9.0% |
| Housing (164) | −2.8% |
| Fuel & light (46) | −1.4% |
| Household goods (79) | +0.7% |
| Household services (47) | +3.5% |
| Clothing & footwear (58) | +1.7% |
| Personal goods serv. (39) | +3.9% |
| Motoring expenditure (136) | +5.0% |
| Fares & travel costs (21) | +4.5% |
| Leisure goods (46) | +1.2% |
| Leisure services (62) | +4.2% |

Figures in brackets are weights in retail prices index in parts of 1.000
Percentages represent annual % change to December 1993.

*Source:* *Financial Times,* 20 January 1994.

**FIGURE 12.2  Weighting of expenditures**
**(UK inflation rate: +1.9%; RPI: 141.9 in December 1993)**

The rate of inflation is then usually represented as the twelve-monthly change in the RPI. However, other measures of inflation can be employed and the Tax and Price Index (TPI) was introduced for a short period in 1979 to measure changes in real spending power. This takes account not only of changes in prices, but also those in take-home pay. Thus the TPI is a composite of the change in prices and the change in direct taxes and National Insurance contributions.

As Figure 12.3 illustrates, this meant that the rate of inflation measured by the TPI was lower in 1979 and 1980, but when it rose above RPI in 1981 and 1982, it fell out of use as the 'correct' measure of inflation.

The Government has consistently argued that the RPI as a measure of inflation is biased upward in comparison to other European economies because of the inclusion of mortgage repayments and other 'incidental' items, such as the council tax. Hence they often quote the *underlying* rate of inflation which excludes rent, council tax and mortgage repayments and has come to be known as ROSSI. For example, the headline rate of inflation in September 1994 was 3.9 per cent, but the underlying rate (ROSSI) was 3.1 per cent. Thus, large differences can be recorded depending upon the definition of what should, and should not, constitute the basis for inflation.

**Problems of inflation**

High inflation can cause several problems. Living standards will be eroded if rising prices mean that we are able to buy fewer goods and services than before. If inflation becomes cumulatively worse, then the expectations of inflation held by workers and by firms will be built into wage claims and price-setting calculations. The result will be a self-justifying outcome leading, possibly, to hyper-inflation which occurs when prices rise at a faster and faster rate until the economy reaches a position where confidence in the value of the monetary unit is totally destroyed. This occurred, for example, in Germany in 1923 when the value of the mark reached the situation where 1 gold mark was equal in value to one billion paper marks and a similar position was reached by the Brazilian economy in the 1980s. There will also be effects on the distribution of national income. Here the effects are arbitrary as they do not affect us all equally, and this fact leads some to describe inflation as an arbitrary tax. The incomes of firms and of shareholders are closely tied to the price level, management may be in a position to fix their own salaries to keep up with current price rises, and highly organised workers may have the bargaining strength to prevent their real wages from being eroded by inflation. However, the burden of inflation will fall on those whose incomes are relatively fixed. These include the low paid, some pensioners, students and some public-sector employees. Their position is made even worse if the price of basic essentials, such as food, housing and fuel are among the fastest rising,

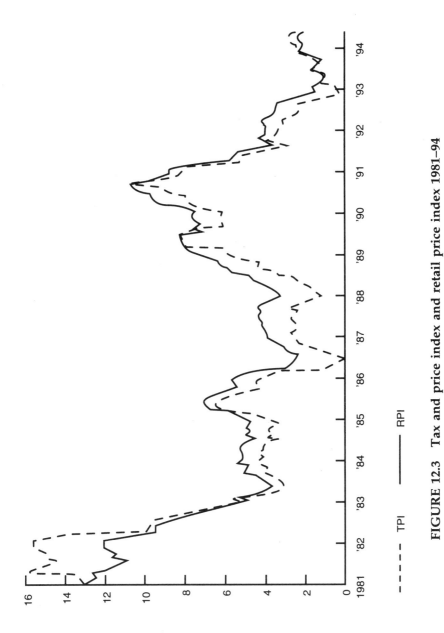

% change on one year earlier

----- TPI    ——— RPI

FIGURE 12.3    Tax and price index and retail price index 1981–94

because low income groups spend a greater proportion of their incomes on these items than those in the higher income brackets. Inflation also has an impact on savings, as rising prices reduce the real value of savings. This may be offset by the rate of interest earned, but at many times during the 1970s and 1980s the rate of inflation has far exceeded the rate of interest. Where this is the case, the incentive to save may be totally destroyed.

Such problems may be overcome through government intervention, using policies such as the indexation of pensions and benefits to maintain real standards of living and by ensuring a rate of interest at least on a par with the rate of inflation. However, for any economy involved in international trade, this will not be sufficient. In order to maintain international competitiveness, prices must not be rising substantially faster than those of economies in competition in world markets. For example, if Britain's prices are rising at a faster rate than those of its competitors then it makes it more difficult to sell its exports and easier for other countries to penetrate Britain's markets, causing balance of payments difficulties. This was the case in the mid-1970s when, although all Western capitalist economies suffered large increases in their rates of inflation, Britain was less successful in containing the initial increases in the price level, and subsequently was less successful in reducing inflation to 'acceptable' levels.

## Causes

Inflation was seen as a reflection of a national crisis preceding a fall in the value of the currency. Traditionally this has been the result of expensive wars and their aftermath being a potent source of inflationary pressure. In more recent times this could be said to apply to the Korean and Vietnam wars. The mechanism at work is that governments are attempting to squeeze more and more out of a hard-pressed wartime economy, putting excessive strain on the productive capacity of the economy in the use of resources to produce arms and equipment and in the payment of the armed service personnel.

Wartime inflation and the methods of minimising, or avoiding, it was the main theme of Keynes' pamphlet, 'How to Pay for the War'. In an economy fully stretched in producing the necessary output to conduct a successful war, extra government expenditure serves only to bid up the prices of output in the economy. Hence a *sustained* rise in expenditures by the state in these circumstances will lead to a *persistent* tendency for prices to increase. It was generally assumed that once the economy returned to the 'normal' state of affairs, the price level would remain more or less stable if government refrained from putting undue strain on the productive capacity of the economy. In the prewar period inflation had continued, but on the whole prices tended to move in sympathy with the general level of economic activity. In other words, the economic cycle of regular expansions and contractions in

the scale of output and the level of employment was a continuing phenomenon which affected the movement of prices. Hence, in the upswing, prices
would rise, and in the downswing they would, in general, fall. This cyclical
inflation was never considered to be a particularly serious problem for the
economy or of such a magnitude as to require state intervention. After the
Second World War inflation continued up to 1953, at which time inflationary
pressure appeared to have disappeared throughout the West. It continued to
exist, but by contemporary standards this could be considered to be modest.
Annual rates of 2–4 per cent were regarded as the price worth paying for full
employment, which was the overriding objective of the immediate postwar
governments. They were committed to a Keynesian programme of continually
stimulating expenditure whenever unemployment appeared likely to increase. However, the somewhat transient nature of inflation observed before
the Second World War now became regarded as an integral part of the
economics of a mixed economy. This therefore required a wages policy
because, with full employment, the nature of the wage bargain is changed
in favour of workers and generally against employers. The apparent prosperity of the 1950s and 1960s appeared to justify the acceptance of creeping
inflation to achieve the objective of full employment and the respectable
growth rates that were recorded. This applies not only to Britain, but to the
other mature capitalist economies (Figure 12.4).

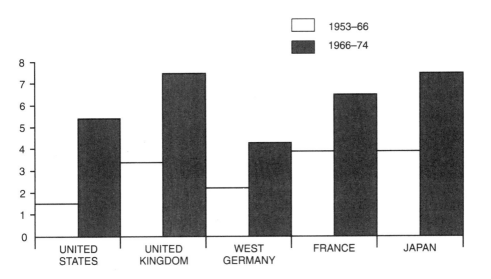

*Source*:   Based on data from *OECD Economic Indicators*, various issues.

**FIGURE 12.4   Average rates of inflation**

After 1967 things altered, as shown in Table 12.2. For the first time in the postwar era, inflation showed a persistent tendency to accelerate throughout the West. Indeed, the rates of inflation reached 23 per cent in Japan in 1974 and 26.9 per cent in Britain in 1975.

## Theories of inflation

### (i)   Demand-pull inflation

The various plans of households, firms and the government add up to a total in excess of the value of full-employment output, measured in current prices. Hence, in Figure 12.4, the total demand in the economy is exceeding the total supply (aggregate demand > aggregate supply).

Thus, at full employment, any excess demand in the economy can only show itself in the form of higher prices. Prices are 'pulled up' by increased

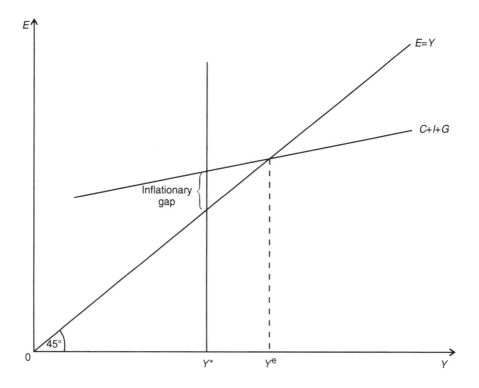

FIGURE 12.5   Demand-pull inflation

expenditure as various groups of spenders in the economy are, in effect, forced into bidding resources away from each other. For example, there is no reason why a firm should not set up a business in an area where there is already full employment. However, it can only do so by attracting land and labour away from their present uses, through offering a higher price. If we generalise this throughout the economy, then we will have demand-pull inflation. This was seen to be a very likely condition in mixed economies where the state accepted a wide range of social responsibilities and was practising Keynesian stabilisation techniques. Partly it is an outcome of attempting to do too much. That is, the government wants resources for welfare programmes, health, education, defence spending and for public-sector firms. In addition, it is stimulating the private sector to undertake more investment and to expand production. Consumers are also constantly bidding to increase their material standards of living as expectations rise. Thus competing demands may easily exceed the output that is possible from the available resources.

If the state is committed to maintaining full employment, it is difficult to know how to combat demand-pull inflation without a reduction in social expenditure and a consequent increase in unemployment, because the solution is to dampen down demand, reducing consumer spending by raising taxes, reducing private-sector investment by raising interest rates and cutting government expenditure through public spending cuts. Obviously this would not be a politically attractive package of measures and in fact even if the policy is successfully introduced, one could not be certain that the basic cause of inflation had been identified.

### (ii)  Cost-push inflation

Cost-push theorists tend not to deny the possibility that excess demand can lead to inflationary pressure. However, even when demand is quite evidently not excessive, inflation can still appear in the economy through pressures that are operating on the supply side. When the prices that are set by firms are generally composed of costs, plus a mark-up for profits, rising costs will be reflected in rising prices, regardless of the state of overall demand, as businesses struggle to maintain their profit margins.

Hence:

Prices = Cost + mark-up for profit

$$P = C + r$$

Then, if costs rise, the firm is faced with a choice

either  (a)    $P = \uparrow C + \downarrow r$

or       (b)    $\uparrow P = \uparrow C + r$

Given choice (a) prices remain at the same level as before the cost increase and the mark-up for profit is reduced. Given choice (b), the mark-up for profit remains at its previous level and the increase in cost is passed on in the form of an increase in the price. Obviously there is a third option, to share the increase in costs between lower profits and higher prices. However, given the pressure from shareholders and the objective of profit maximisation, it is considered more likely that the firm will choose to pass on the rise in costs in the form of price rises. Therefore it is the upward pressure of various costs that go to make up price increases and hence inflation. The most obvious of these costs is wages. One result of the success in maintaining full employment is the increased bargaining power of the trade unions. They can demand wage increases above those that are justified by increased output per worker, and the employers concede because the consumer will pay through higher prices. However, consumers are also workers who, seeing the increase in prices will demand further wage increases to maintain their real wage. Thus is set in train a wage-price spiral that would appear to have no solution.

The higher cost of raw materials may also at times play an important role in pushing up prices. The oil crises of OPEC I (1973–4) and OPEC II (1978) are pointed to by cost-push theorists as the trigger for the high rates of inflation experienced in the mid-1970s and early 1980s. Firms may also increase prices to cover the expense of new investment or to increase their profit margins. In addition, the government may contribute to inflation by increasing taxes (corporation tax, business rate) which firms then attempt to pass on to consumers.

Ultimately the solution was seen to be the devising of an acceptable prices and incomes policy to break the inflationary spiral. Direct government intervention was seen as necessary, both in terms of the wage bargain and the pricing policy of firms. Again this is a deeply unpopular policy which will tend to antagonise both sides of the economy, the capitalists and the workers, and proves to be politically damaging to the government that introduces the prices and incomes policy.

*(iii)   Phillips Curve trade-off*

In 1958 Professor A. W. Phillips wrote his celebrated paper 'The relationship between unemployment and money wage rates in the United Kingdom 1861–1957.' Phillips had reason to believe that there existed an inverse relationship between the level of prices and aggregate demand. Inflation could obviously be measured, but there appeared no way of measuring aggregate demand. Phillips asked the question 'Is there any economic variable that will move systematically with aggregate demand?' He used unemployment because he found that an inverse relationship existed between the level of employment and the level of aggregate demand. Using the rate of money wage change $(w = f(U))$ he appeared to have unearthed a relationship between unemployment and the rate of money wage change that had remained for 96 years (Figure 12.6). Coupled with the theory of mark-up pricing, this had enormous policy implications as there appeared to be a trade-off relationship (Figure 12.7).

It was not long before the full implications of a stable price curve were seen by the macro-economic policy-makers. That is, the dangers of an increase in public spending to reduce unemployment, could lead to price inflation. The Phillips Curve was seen as a constraint on policy: a point on the curve had to be chosen. In Figure 12.7, Point A is where the government will be reducing inflation, and Point B is where they are attempting to reduce unemployment. Hence there exists a 'menu of choice'. At any point chosen there is a combination of unemployment and inflation that can be maintained into the foreseeable future, making policy a matter of preference between inflation and unemployment. Both demand-pull inflation and cost-push inflation now called for the same solution, if price stability was to be the main priority, it could be achieved only by codifying the objective of full employment. It was argued that deliberately created unemployment, of relatively minor proportions, would kill both birds with one stone. It would strike at the roots of any excess demand and reduce the strength of the trade unions to bring cost-push under control.

However, it can be argued that a given Phillips Curve is only a temporary one, and it is impossible to maintain through time as there are an infinite number of Phillips Curves (Figure 12.8). Here it is the underlying position of the labour market that will cause the short-run Phillips Curve to shift. Figure 12.8 shows how, according to Friedman, the trade-off position $P_1^e U_1$ cannot be maintained indefinitely because an individual who expected zero inflation would soon realise that inflation is occurring and take action to ensure that the money wage bargain protects against inflation. As a result inflation quickens, pushing the Phillips Curve to a higher position at $U_1$, and inflation expectation increases ($P_2^e$). Friedman suggests that only at $U^*$ will inflation be stable and this equates to the Natural Rate of Unemployment (NRU). At all points to the left of $U^*$ inflation will accelerate, and at all points to the right inflation will fall. Only at $U^*$ will actual inflation equal expected inflation. Hence, this is the expectations-augmented Phillips Curve. If Friedman's proposition is true, then there is no point in the government pursuing ambitious employment policies. In the late 1960s and early 1970s the Phillips Curve relationship appeared to break down as stagflation occurred. Unemployment was rising but money wage rates were also rising, something that could not occur according to the Phillips relationship. Trade union militancy in bargaining for money wage increases increased rather than diminished in the face of rising unemployment. The result was that rising unemployment was accompanied by still faster rising inflation. By 1975 Britain had an unemployment rate of 4 per cent and inflation above 26 per cent. However, according to Friedman, the answer was to reduce aggregate demand, raise unemployment,

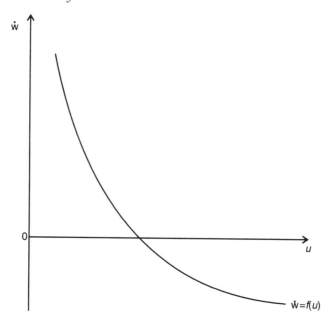

**FIGURE 12.6   Phillips Curve**

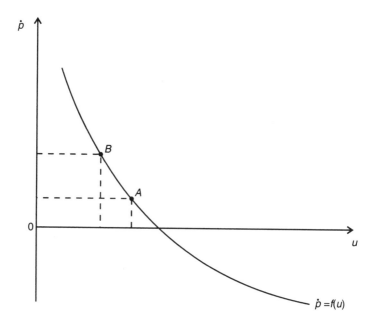

**FIGURE 12.7   Phillips Curve trade-off**

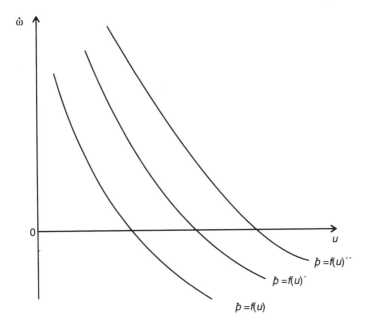

**FIGURE 12.8    Short-run Phillips Curves**

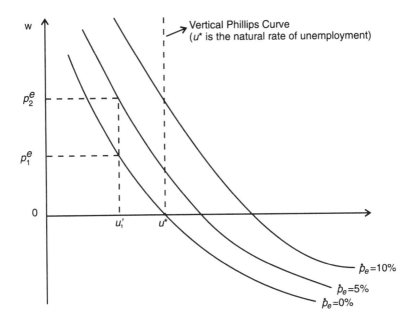

**FIGURE 12.9    Natural rate of unemployment (NRU)**

and thereby bring about a revision of inflationary expectations. Hence, the main thrust of monetarist policy was to use deflationary demand-management policies.

*(iv)    Monetarism*

Monetarists argue that all inflations of moderate duration are caused by increases in the size of the money stock. Thus, price increases are only produced by the excess issue of money by the central bank. Therefore inflation can only be brought under control by the action of the government to restrict the money supply. The mechanism by which this was shown to be the case was the 200-year-old Quantity Theory of Money which Keynes had ravaged fifty years earlier. The Quantity Theory of Money is associated with David Hume, David Ricardo, John Stuart Mill and Alfred Marshall. Thus, the Quantity Theorists of the late eighteenth and early nineteenth centuries became the monetarists of the late twentieth century. The modified version of the Fisher equation of exchange is:

$$MV = PY$$

Where:   $M$ = the money supply
$V$ = the transactions velocity of circulation of money
$P$ = the price level
$Y$ = real income/output

Thus, by definition, $MV$ is national spending and $PY$ is national expenditure. The total amount spent on the output of the economy is equal to the total value of that output. Hence the equation is a mere tautology. However, Friedman and Schwartz (1963) compiled a massive study to show that, over a long period of time, the correlation between the money supply and the level of economic activity had, for industrial economies, been an extremely close one. In effect, they argued that $Y$ can change in the short run, but in the long run its rate is fixed by real forces in the economy such as the growth of productivity or the supply of factors of production. In addition, $V$ was regarded as only fluctuating to a very negligible extent. Therefore they were able to rewrite the original equation as:

$$M\bar{V} = P\bar{Y}$$

It follows that if $V$ and $Y$ are constants, then:

$$M = P$$

If this is true then   $\dot{M} = \dot{P}$

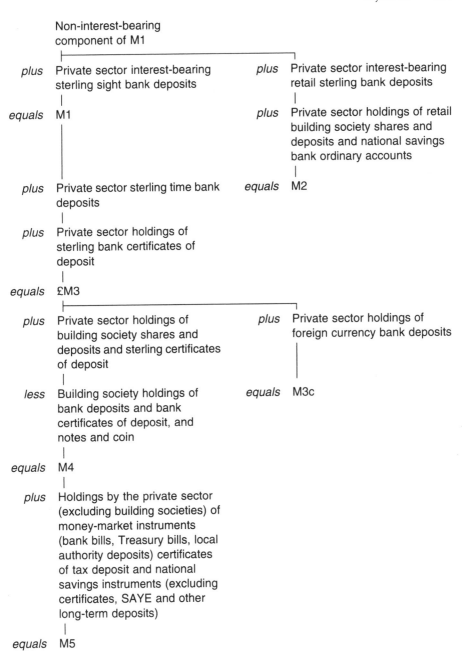

Source:  *Bank of England Quarterly Bulletin,* p. 214, May 1987.

**FIGURE 12.10    Relationships among monetary aggregates and their components**

That is, the rate of growth of the money supply is equal to the rate of growth of the price level (the rate of inflation).

For example, if

$$
\begin{array}{ccccccc}
M & \times & V & = & P & \times & Y \\
5 & \times & 4 & = & 1 & \times & 20 \\
\text{If } M^s \ 10 \quad 10 & \times & 4 & = & 2 & \times & 20 \\
\text{If } M^s \ 20 \quad 20 & \times & 4 & = & 4 & x & 20
\end{array}
$$

Thus they argue that $\uparrow \dot{M} \rightarrow \uparrow \dot{P}$.

Hence, for the monetarist, if the quantity of money is increased, then prices increase (for Keynes increasing the quantity of money leads to a reduction in the rate of interest which in turn leads to an increase in investment). Hence the policy proposals that follow are that the government should take action to control the rate of growth of the money supply, the objective being to allow the supply of money to grow at a rate equal to the rate of growth of real income. Inflation can only be cured, according to this view, by reversing the policies that caused the inflation in the first place. Hence a regime of strict monetary restraint will be accompanied by unemployment rates in excess of the NRU to erode inflationary expectations Monetary control is, for monetarists, the only way to conquer inflation. Prices and incomes policies will be harmful because of the government interference that they involve in the process of wage and price determination. They accept that their policy solution involves a considerable period of under-utilisation of capacity and high unemployment, but this is regarded as a penance that the economy must pay for the inflationary binge undertaken by the government in a previous period.

However, there are several important criticisms of the theory and the implementation of the policy prescriptions that need to be addressed. First of all the theory rests to a large extent on the assumption that the variables $V$ and $Y$ can be regarded as constants. Hendry and Ericsson (1983) undertook to reassess the work of Friedman and Schwartz. In their conclusions they pointed to the unjustified manipulations of the data that enabled Friedman and Schwartz to obtain the answers that they were looking for. They cast serious doubt on the validity of the proposition that the two variables in question could be treated in this manner. Even if this were not the case, there is still the problem of cause and effect: in the original scheme, the rate of growth of the money supply equals the rate of growth of the price level. It is then assumed that an increase in the rate of growth of the money supply *leads to* an increase in the rate of growth of the price level. It may be just as plausible to suggest that the relationship is the other way round, such that an increase in the rate of growth of the price level leads to an increase in the rate of growth of the money supply. Again even if the theory is correct, there still remains the problem of how to implement the policy recommendations that follow. In reducing the rate of monetary expansion the government is supposed to set strict targets for the rate of increase of the money supply, but the salient question to ask is, 'What is money?' Figure 12.10 illustrates the difficulty for the government. Which of the definitions of money is the correct one for policy purposes? Indeed, even if a 'correct' definition could be agreed, Goodhart's Law suggests that control of the monetary variable is not possible: Goodhart's Law states that any variable that has been stable and predictable over long periods of time will become unstable and unpredictable if targets are set for its rate of growth. This appeared to be the case in the 1980s when the Government failed to achieve target rates of growth for several definitions of the money supply and after only a few years abandoned money supply targets as policy instruments, preferring to use $M_0$ as an 'indicative' variable.

*(v)   The rational expectations school*

Partly in response to the criticisms of the monetarist model, the new classical wing of the monetarists (sometimes called the 'Young Fogeys') attempted to salvage the policy recommendation. They argue that all that is necessary is that the economy works 'as if' the monetarist model is correct. They suggest that since the private sector is a party to the 'correct' model of the economy (the monetarist model), all that the government need to do is to announce money supply targets for years to come and reach those targets, thus quickly eroding inflationary expectations with minimal extra unemployment and forgone output. The mechanism at work would be as follows: the government set a target for monetary expansion of 5 per cent. Assuming that inflation stands at 7 per cent, wage bargainers will expect inflation in the coming year to fall to 5 per cent because they believe the monetarist model. The outcome will be an inflation rate of 5 per cent, not because of a 5 per cent expansion in the money supply, but because of the 5 per cent increase in money wages based upon the expectations around the bargaining table. It is therefore a self-fulfilling outcome. All that is required is for the government to consistently hit its targets for monetary expansion and to steadily reduce its targets. On this point Graham has written that, 'while strict versions of adaptive expectations require mankind to be totally stupid, rational expectations require mankind to be too clever by half' (Graham, 1985, p. 231).

*(vi)   Conflict theories of inflation*

Rowthorn (1984) proposes that in a capitalist economy there exist no redistributional effects from fully anticipated inflation because people will take action to allow for future inflation. The redistributive effects of inflation only occur as a result of unanticipated inflation. In the model it is assumed that, in the private sector, an amount of income is available to be distributed between capitalists and workers, after taxes and import costs have been accounted for. The actual distribution is decided upon by negotiation between the capitalists and the workers. The workers attempt to achieve wage increases that increase their standard of living, and the capitalists set their prices to achieve a target rate of profit after the wage settlement has been agreed. The prices that are set may be in conflict with the wage settlement however, because these claims together may exceed the amount available. In addition, the real income of the working class as a whole will depend upon the increase in prices. Therefore, the shares that are received depend on whether the level of prices that was anticipated at the time of the negotiation turns out to be the actual level after the capitalists have made their pricing decisions. If capitalists achieve their target rate of profit based on what was agreed in the negotiation, then there is no conflict. However, if the pricing policy is different to that agreed in the wage bargain, then there will exist a conflict. Rowthorn calls this the Aspiration Gap, and shows the extent to which the claims of the capitalists are inconsistent with other claims on total private-sector income. If the wage bargain results in the capitalists share being lower than their target rate of profit, then they will increase their prices to compensate. Such price rises will constitute unanticipated inflation, in the sense that they were not anticipated at the time of the wage negotiation. The outcome of this unanticipated inflation is a redistribution of income from the workers to the capitalists, as real wages are less than what was expected at the settlement but the capitalists have been able to maintain their target rate of profit through a change in their pricing policy.

The Aspiration Gap is the crucial factor in determining the level of inflation via the pricing policy of the capitalists. It is itself determined by the relative market power of the capitalists and the workers. Workers use their market power to obtain money wage increases and the capitalists use their market power to set prices. Therefore, one would expect to find a large Aspiration Gap, and hence a rate of unanticipated inflation that is high, unless the market power of the workers is low relative to that of the capitalists. This would suggest that when the level of employment is high in the economy the market power of the workers is also high. Whereas, when unemployment is high the workers are in a weak bargaining position. It follows, therefore, that there exists a relationship between the level of employment and the rate of inflation arising out of the conflict between capitalists and workers given by the Aspiration Gap. At full, or near full, employment, the mechanism is similar to that explained by cost-push inflation and rests on the ability of the capitalists to pass on the increase in costs to the consumers in the form of price rises. However, as with cost-push inflation, the mechanism can be initiated by increases in costs other than wage costs: in particular, an unanticipated increase in import costs or an unanticipated rise in taxes.

## Interest rates

The use of interest rates as an anti-inflationary policy instrument is associated with both Keynesian and monetarist doctrine. For Keynesians, the rate of interest can affect the components of aggregate demand to dampen down economic activity in both the internal and external environment. A policy of high interest rates can reduce consumption, particularly at a point of, or near, full employment, to reduce demand-pull inflation. It will also tend to reduce the level of investment in the economy as the marginal efficiency of investment falls. However, there may exist a conflict between the internal objective of reducing inflation and the external effects of high interest rates – high interest rates will attract capital from abroad and tend to appreciate the currency, causing exports to be uncompetitive and reducing the price of imports. Depending upon the price and income elasticities of exports and imports, it could lead to a deficit on the current account of the balance of payments, which would require low rates of interest to bring the balance of payments back to equilibrium. However, until 1972 and the collapse of the Bretton Woods system of fixed but adjustable exchange rates, the position of sterling had been the major determinant of interest rates. This was in line with the current Keynesian thinking. This suggested that interest rates should not be used for the purpose of macro-economic stability, and relegated monetary policy to a subservient position in relation to fiscal policy.

Although monetarists argue that it is the control of the rate of growth of the money supply that is the appropriate monetary policy to defeat inflation, with the failure of the Medium Term Financial Strategy, the Conservative Government reverted back to interest rates as a means of controlling the exchange rate and, therefore, influencing the real economy. Interest rates were used as a deflationary tool, high interest rates protected sterling and dampened down aggregate demand, thus attacking inflationary pressure in terms of both internal and external mechanisms. The protection of the exchange rate prevented a devaluation which would have caused inflationary pressure from rising import costs, and internally the high rate of interest caused a fall in the level of investment which in turn reduces employment. It can be argued that the Phillips Curve relationship ensures that this dampening down of economic activity leads to an easing of inflationary pressure. It would seem that the use of interest rates to control inflation involves a much more complex mechanism than may at first sight appear to be the case. Not only does a policy of high interest rates affect the exchange rate and investment, but also consumption and the labour market. The reduction in the rate of return to productive investment puts downward pressure on the real wage in an effort to reduce costs, which adds to the reduction in aggregate demand. Add to this the policy of reducing the Public Sector Borrowing Requirement, and we have an extremely deflationary policy package. Therefore, the rate of interest has strong anti-inflationary effects but at the expense of other variables in the real economy.

## Policy

The policy for inflation in the immediate postwar period was in the form of price controls. Approximately 50 per cent of consumer spending was subject to price control, which remained in place until 1950 when some items were removed. Nearly all controls were abandoned by 1953 with only house rents, coal and rail and bus fares remaining subject to control. This policy appears to have been successful in keeping prices in line with costs during this period. Monetary policy was assigned to a subordinate role, having little independent influence on economic activity until the change of government in 1951 (Cairncross, 1994).

From 1951 to 1964 'stop-go' policies were predominant, designed to stop the economy from overheating. This became known as 'Butskellism' as both the main parties accepted the belief in economic management and the need to maintain a high level of employment. The Conservative Government removed all wartime restrictions and revived the use of monetary policy. At the beginning of 1957 strong inflationary pressure resulted in cuts in public investment and the introduction of hire purchase restrictions. This can be equated with a reaction to overheating of the economy at a high level of employment, in accordance with demand-pull theory deflationary action. However, in September 1957 Chancellor Thorneycroft appeared to prioritise the fight against inflation over the objective of full employment by suggesting that unemployment be allowed to increase to 2–3 per cent. He talked in terms of controlling the money supply using money GDP. His proposals were rejected by Cabinet in 1958 and Thorneycroft resigned.

The Radcliffe Committee Report of the summer of 1959 regarded money as the most important of a range of liquid assets and insisted on the existence of variability of the velocity of circulation, warning not to expect too much from the control of money. The main policy employed between 1945 and 1957 was incomes policy, as wage inflation was regarded as the main danger, following the theory of cost-push, given the level of employment. The Government fell back on deflation after 1957 but Selwyn Lloyd's 'pay pause' of 1961 reintroduced incomes policy. This remained the preferred policy to control inflation down to 1970.

When the Heath Government came to power in 1970, they did so promising to reduce state intervention in the economy and rejecting the use of incomes policy. However, as unemployment increased simultaneously with wages and prices, and the Phillips Curve relationship appeared to have broken down, Heath was forced to increase intervention in public-sector pay negotiations in an attempt to counter this stagflation. Following the coal strike of January/ February 1972, which was settled on a pay increase of 17–20 per cent, a statutory 90-day wage and price freeze was introduced on 6 November 1972. This was followed by a link between increases in pay and prices which proved to be disastrous. Retail prices had already risen by 9 per cent 1971–2, and then rose by 48 per cent over the next two years. This led to an acceleration of wage increases that were well above the 7 per cent limit imposed by the incomes policy. In October 1973 the oil crises developed and the mineworkers rejected a 13 per cent wage offer. When a ballot gave support for a strike, Heath called a General Election. Wages were rising at 28 per cent, prices were rising at 20 per cent, unemployment was increasing and the balance of payments current account went into record deficit.

The incoming Labour Government continued the incomes policy after settling the coal dispute, and inflation was checked in 1974–5. Much of this was achieved with the introduction of tight monetary policy and attempts to reduce the growth of public expenditure, designed to check the growth of demand. Unemployment rose from 100,000 in 1974 to 500,000 in 1975. A renewed crisis in 1976 saw the Labour Government asking for a $5.5 billion of standby credit from the European Central Banks, which required recourse to the International Monetary Fund (IMF). This meant an acceptance of terms set by the IMF including cuts in public expenditure in 1977–8 of £1 billion and further cuts of £1 billion in the following year. In fact, both cuts had already been undertaken. Although the IMF had insisted on the introduction of monetary targets for the control of inflation, the Chancellor, Healey, had already announced the conversion to a more 'monetarist' policy, accepting that control of the rate of growth of the money supply is a necessary condition for the control of the rate of inflation (Howson, 1994). By October 1975 the Government had already adopted a £$M_3$ target, public expenditure cuts and a sharp increase in interest rates, before its application for the standby loan.

Healey's combination of policies (incomes policy, public expenditure cuts, tax increases and monetary targets) allowed cost-push Keynesians, demand-pull Keynesians and monetarists to all claim that their theory and policy to be responsible for the fall in the rate of inflation. However, inflation still continued to present a problem, particularly after the second oil shock in the winter of 1978–9. The incomes policy continued with a 5 per cent norm, which led directly to the 'winter of discontent' and by May 1979 inflation was at 13 per cent (Cairncross, 1994).

The incoming Thatcher Government was convinced that no conflict existed between low inflation and high rates of economic growth and that, with the aid of supply-side measures, one would lead to the other. The Conservative Party manifesto of 1979 argued that '[t]o master inflation, proper monetary discipline is essential, with publicly-stated targets for the growth of the money supply – At the same time a reduction in the size of the Public Sector Borrowing Requirement is also vital' (Johnson, 1991). Incomes policy was rejected as being incompatible with Conservative free-market philosophy, but a 'crypto' incomes policy was employed through the holding down of increases in public-sector pay. The 1980 budget introduced the Medium Term Financial Strategy (MTFS) which outlined the Government's anti-inflationary policy of controlling the rate of growth of the money supply, using the rate of interest, outlining public expenditure plans and setting targets for the reduction in the PSBR to avoid over-reliance on interest rates. However, problems arose immediately over the choice of monetary instruments. Initially $£M_3$ was chosen for control purposes, reducing the rate of growth of $£M_3$ through reduction in the PSBR. Howe's first budget announced that the PSBR was to be reduced from 5.5 per cent of GDP to 4.5 per cent 1979–80, and the $£M_3$ target was cut from an increase of 11–12 per cent to one of 7–11 per cent. Table 12.2 shows the descending target ranges for the monetary instruments and illustrates the lack of success in achieving these targets. With interest rates at 17 per cent they were nullified to a large extent as an instrument for tackling the inflationary problems, but did cause rising unemployment and industrial closures as a rising exchange rate made exports unprofitable.

$£M_3$ continually overshot the targets that were set and the banks had the ability to create credit faster than money, due to the lack of credit controls and the use of overseas deposits, and with increases in capital that were not within the monetary aggregates. This is an example of the operation of Goodhart's Law. Milton Friedman, in giving evidence to the Treasury Select Committee in 1980, suggested that 'the key role assigned to targets for the Public Sector Borrowing Requirement . . . seems to me unwise . . . . There is no necessary relation between the PSBR and monetary growth' (Johnson, 1991, p. 41). The toughest budget of the decade was introduced in March 1981, moving from monetarism to fiscalism with an even greater emphasis on the PSBR, and admitting that $£M_3$ was not a good indicator of monetary conditions and, as

TABLE 12.2   The outcome of monetary targeting of $£M_3$

| Year of target | Percentage increases | |
| | Target range | Outcome |
| --- | --- | --- |
| 1979–80 | 7–11 | 16.2 |
| 1980–81 | 7–11 | 18.4 |
| 1981–82 | 6–10 | 12.8 |
| 1982–83 | 8–12 | 11.1 |
| 1983–84 | 7–11 | 9.5 |
| 1984–85 | 6–10 | 11.9 |
| 1985–86 | 5–9 | 16.3 |
| 1986–87 | 11–15 | 18.7 |

*Source*:   Adapted from C. Johnson, *The Economy Under Mrs Thatcher 1979–1990*, table 9, pp. 274–5, 1991, taken from the Financial Statement and Budget Report, *Financial Statistics*, Bank of England.

such, it should not be implied that future inflation would follow the growth in the money supply. The budget was attacked in a letter to *The Times* by 364 economists who argued that there was no basis in economic theory for the belief that deflating demand would bring inflation permanently under control, and monetarism therefore should be rejected. However, the rate of inflation fell from a peak of 22 per cent in May 1980 to 4 per cent in April 1983. This appeared to vindicate the MTFS and Lawson continued the policy of reducing the PSBR, giving targets for both PSBR and monetary aggregates for the next five years in his first budget. Money GDP was introduced as a monetary variable to be targeted, giving three variables in all, $M_0$, $£M_3$ and now money GDP. But in October 1985 $£M_3$ was suspended as a target in Lawson's Mansion House speech. Finally, in October 1987, monetary targets were scrapped in favour of a free market in money, and the rate of interest became the instrument to control inflationary pressure. Lawson also began to shadow the D-mark as a prelude to entry into the Exchange Rate Mechanism (ERM). As Chancellor, Major abandoned the monetarist doctrine in his Autumn Statement of 1989, ending the MTFS and adopted a fixed exchange rate as the discipline the economy required to hold down inflation, and the rate of interest was now given a subordinate role.

Throughout this episode what has been clear is that the British governments from the mid-1970s have gradually returned to the Treasury orthodoxy of the 1920s and 1930s of balanced budgets and sound money. The outcome has been a reduction in the rate of inflation on average and over the period. However, the deflationary measures that were employed, whether under the short period of monetarist doctrine or the more substantial period of supply-side orthodoxy, have served to weaken the position of the labour force and strengthen the hand of capital. This has occurred, not through the imposition of an explicit income policy, but through the massive increase in unemployment that the policies caused. This has re-established the Phillips Curve relationship that appeared to have broken down in the period of stagflation, through the mechanism described by Rowthorn in his conflict theory of inflation. Capitalism is a continuous conflict over the allocation of the surplus between capital and labour, but even when labour appears to have the upper hand and can negotiate higher real increases in its share, the capitalist class as a whole maintains its own share by increasing the price of its output. Thus, either way the working class are in a no-win situation. If they gain increases in money wages, they will be eroded by inflation and if inflation is eradicated from the system, this has been achieved by reducing the power of labour through large injections of unemployment which mean that money wage rises are greatly curtailed.

# CHAPTER 13

# *International Trade*

## Introduction

The British economy has for many years been a particularly open economy, evidenced by the high level of exports and imports as a percentage of GDP. Exports as a percentage of GDP in 1993 were 25.3 and imports were 26.6 per cent of GDP in the same year (OECD, 1995).

The ratio of total manufactured imports to GDP was only 12 per cent in 1963, but had increased to almost 25 per cent by the end of the 1970s as imports penetrated the domestic market. A high level of dependence on international trade will therefore have enormous implications in terms of British economic policy. There may often exist conflicts between the use of policy instruments for internal and external objectives which involve the policy-maker in value judgements as to the relative importance of the internal and external objectives.

For example, the use of the interest rate to 'cure' an external imbalance may well affect the level of investment in the domestic economy. In addition, the lower level of investment resulting from an increase in the rate of interest to protect the exchange rate may reduce output in export-oriented industry and cause the balance of payments position to deteriorate on the current account. So these actions and interactions of instruments and objectives add complications in the case of an open economy , and the greater is the 'openness', the greater will be the conflict. Also, because the British economy is such an open economy, and its trade has been dependent upon manufacturing industry, the decline in the competitiveness of Britain's manufactured output in world markets presents serious problems for the British economy.

## Trade theory

### (i) Mercantilism

Mercantilism prevailed in sixteen- and seventeenth-century Europe: this theory basically suggested that as wealth is a necessary condition for the enhancement of national power, a country should encourage export discourage imports, in order to increase the wealth of the nation. The policy that mercantilism encouraged were: the promotion of manufacturing through subsidy, seizure of colonies, the introduction of tariffs and trade limitations, and the support of domestic agriculture, keeping overseas competitors out of the domestic market by taxing food imports. However, mercantilism required that one nation's gain was another's loss, and the result would ultimately be that no international trade could be undertaken due to the lack of purchasing power in the world economy when one nation, or group of nations, had procured all the wealth.

### (ii) Absolute advantage

Adam Smith developed the *Theory of Absolute Advantage* through his recognition of the importance of specialisation and the division of labour. This led Smith to advocate free trade, as two countries will benefit from trade if they can provide each other with a product, or products, more cheaply than they could be produced domestically.

Therefore, each country should specialise in those products in which it has a greater level of efficiency. Both economies will then gain from trade through the concept of opportunity cost. The higher is the level of specialisation, the greater will be the potential gain from trade and, in contrast to the mercantilist theory, both parties will gain from trade.

### (iii) Comparative advantage

David Ricardo highlighted the problem involved in the theory of absolute advantage. That is, if a country has an absolute advantage in the production of all, or most, goods, then we are back at the mercantilist position. So Ricardo showed that both nations can benefit from trade even in the situation where one of the countries has an absolute advantage in the production of all goods, by specialising in, and exporting, the commodities in which it is comparatively more efficient. It should then import those commodities in which it is relatively less efficient.

For Ricardo, the source of trade between countries lies in the differences in technologies, or labour productivities. The basic model of comparative advantage reasons in terms of a single factor of production, labour, and the way in which labour, and therefore labour productivity, differs between countries. An alternative to this simple model was offered by the Heckscher-Ohlin model of comparative advantage, which has since become the orthodox theory of international trade. Here, countries differ in their relative stocks of all of the factors of production which, in turn, will influence the relative costs of production of different goods. For example, a country which has plentiful supplies of labour, but is scarce: in capital, will concentrate production in

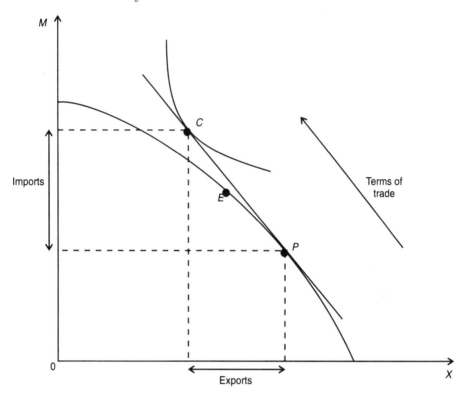

**FIGURE 13.1    Free trade equilibrium**

labour-intensive goods. Figure 13.1 illustrates the position of equilibrium with free-trade in the Heckscher-Ohlin model, given balanced trade between two neo-classical economies. If one country has a comparative advantage in the production of a labour-intensive good (good *X*), the internationally traded price of this good is higher than the autarky price, giving an incentive to increase production of good *X*, at the expense of the production of another good (good *M*) which is capital-intensive good, and as such is relatively expensive to produce. Autarky equilibrium is represented by the point *E*, but, with trade specialisation, consumers are able to choose point *C* because real income has increased and consumers are able to attain a higher social indifference curve. The Heckscher-Ohlin theorem thus products that the pattern of international trade will follow the proposition that a country will export the good that is intensive in its abundant factor and import the good that is intensive in its scarce factor. However, there are several important assumptions that are required to achieve this outcome: There are no transport costs in the model and perfect competition is assumed in all markets. It assumes that the production processes exhibit constant returns to scale and the economy is always in equilibrium, due to instantaneous adjustment mechanisms. Finally, the model assumes full employment of the factors of production and that the preferences of consumers can be represented by a set of social indifference curves. It may be suggested that not all of these assumptions are realistic in the real world and therefore the conclusions regarding the benefits of free trade must come into serious question. However, the Heckscher-Ohlin model remains as the 'orthodox' model and the one on which the major international institutions, to which Britain subscribes, rely for policy purposes.

## International trade policy

During the depression of the 1930s international trade became much restricted as countries imposed tariffs and other barriers to trade in an effort to mitigate the effects of unemployment by protecting their domestic markets for domestic producers. The outcome of these protectionist measures was a sharp decline in the level of world trade, due to increasing incidence of retaliatory protective policy. The General Agreement on Tariffs and Trade (GATT) was formulated in 1947 with the objective of avoiding further tariff wars and the consequent diminution in world trade volumes. The key principle of GATT is non-discrimination in trade relations, and the move towards completely free trade on a global scale. GATT negotiations have made slow progress since its inception, but progress has been made over the course of the various 'rounds': the Kennedy Round of the 1960s, the Tokyo Round of the 1970s and the Uruguay Round of the 1990s. Agreements have been reached in each round, with negotiations tending to centre on the disagreements between the principal participants of the US, Japan and the EU. Much of the disagreement between the main participants has been in the area of agricultural subsidy, and, in particular, on the role of the Common Agricultural Policy of the EU. In all these negotiations the position of the developing countries has tended to be of secondary importance and, in reality, GATT represents attempts to safeguard the trading positions of the advanced industrialised economies. Thus Britain, as a signatory to the Uruguay Round of GATT, is committed to a regime of free trade amongst the leading industrial nations, as well as fulfilling its obligations in terms of the EU as a free-trade association encompassing the Single European Market.

## The exchange rate regime

Because the international economic transactions take place, for the most part, in different currencies, the relative price of one currency against another becomes very important in such transactions. Thus the exchange rate regime that is employed is a crucial policy instrument for any government. At one extreme, the exchange rate may be allowed to float freely, and in this case market forces of supply and demand in the financial markets will determine the exchange rate. At the other extreme, the monetary authorities intervene to fix the exchange rate at a given level, through their ability to maintain a par value, using international reserves – gold, foreign currency and other assets that may act as international mediums of exchange. Therefore the central bank has to be willing to trade currencies with the private sector at the per value in the foreign exchange market. To successfully maintain a fixed exchange rate, the central bank must ensure that asset markets remain in equilibrium.

Figure 13.2 illustrates the short-run equilibrium of the economy, where the central bank sets a par value for the exchange rate, at *e*. The output level of the economy is at *Y*, and it is assumed that the rate of interest in the domestic economy is equal to the foreign rate, clearing the market. We now assume that the monetary authorities decide to increase output by increasing the money supply, through the purchase of domestic assets.

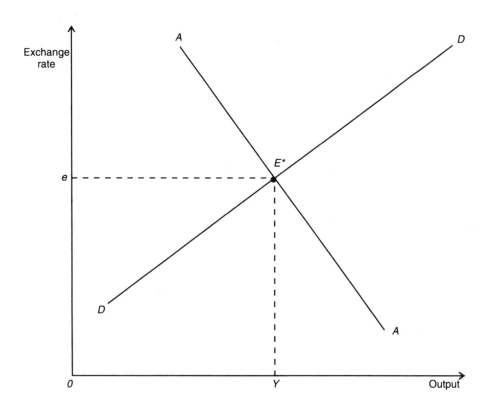

**FIGURE 13.2   Short-run equilibrium**

The effect of this is shown in Figure 13.3. If a floating exchange rate regime were in operation, the market equilibrium curve (*AA*) would shift to the right, to *A″A″*, giving a new equilibrium at *E*** and a currency depreciation. However, under a fixed exchange rate regime, the central bank must sell foreign assets for domestic currency, and the money received by the bank goes out of circulation, shifting the market equilibrium policy instruments are unable to affect the domestic economy's output or its money supply. The effect of monetary policy is on international reserves, as an increase in the central bank's domestic assets will be exactly offset by a decrease in the bank's international reserves. By the same token, the sale of domestic assets, designed to produce an increase in the reserves, will prevent the money supply as a whole from changing. However, although monetary policy cannot be used for domestic stabilisation under the fixed rate regime, fiscal policy may play this role. Figure 13.4 shows the effect of expansionary fiscal policy. The fiscal expansion shifts the output–market equilibrium curve (*DD*) to the right, to *D′D′*. If no intervention were to take place, then this would cause a currency

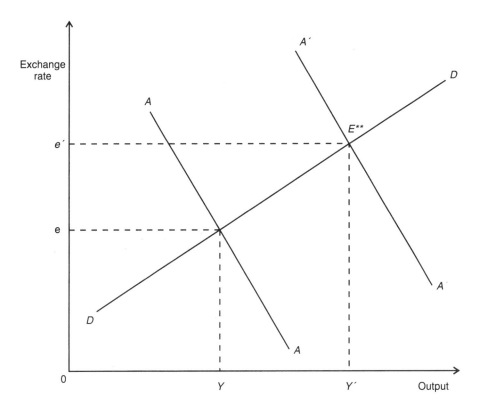

FIGURE 13.3   Effect of a shift in equilibrium

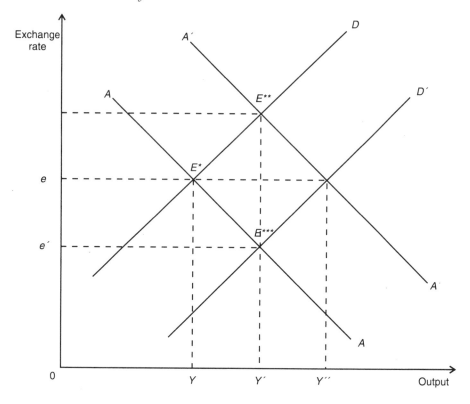

**FIGURE 13.4    Effect of explaining fiscal policy**

appreciation, as the exchange rate falls to $e'$, due to a rise in the domestic rate of interest, and output would rise to $Y'$. To stop this appreciation, the central bank must buy foreign assets, causing an increase in the money supply, shifting the asset–market equilibrium curve ($AA$) to the right, $A'A'$. At the new equilibrium ($E^{***}$) the exchange rate is unchanged and output is at the higher level of $Y'$. This would not tend to be the case under a floating exchange rate regime, as the fiscal expansion would be accompanied by a domestic currency appreciation which would make domestic goods and services more expensive in foreign markets and counteract the positive effects on aggregate demand.

## Balance of payments adjustment

Adjustment of the balance of payments when it is in deficit depends very much on the view one takes of the adjustment mechanism. One school of thought suggests that automatic forces will reverse surpluses or deficits, and hence government intervention may be harmful. This automatic adjustment occurs through the 'price-species flow mechanism'. It assumes that there is a positive relation between each country's reserves and its money stock, and between its price level and its money stock. For example, in a two-country model, if country 1 is in surplus on its current account, it must gain reserves from country 2. The money supply, and thus prices, in country 1 will tend to rise relative to prices in country 2. However, such a model does not consider the possibility that real income in country 1 may be growing faster than in country 2, and in such a situation the demand for money, and hence reserves, would be rising faster in the former than in the latter. With a fixed exchange rate, this would result in a persistent tendency to surplus in country 1. Under a floating exchange rate regime, if country 1 is in surplus, residents in country 2 must pay more to the residents of country 1 for their imports than they are earning from their exports. A result of this is that there is a higher demand for the currency of country 1 than there is supply of it. The outcome under the automatic adjustment theory is that the currency of country 1 will rise in value against the currency of country 2, reducing the surplus.

Interventionists, however, argue that changes in prices, labour, goods and assets can be ignored in the analysis because of their inflexibility. National income can change via the multiplier in respect to changes in the components of aggregate demand. One of these components is exports. Given our two-country model, there is no reason to expect that their current accounts will be in balance, as these depend upon income levels. Since income levels in the two countries are interdependent, in the sense that a boom in one country will raise export prices in the other, there is reason to believe that the deficit in one country, due to an increase in income, will produce an increase in income in the other country through the surplus generated. This would then move both countries back into balance. A current account deficit may produce a drain on reserves which the government may counter with a deflation of domestic demand or through a devaluation of the currency. However, the interventionist school argues that devaluation is not a reliable method of restoring the balance. In fact, if the domestic demand for imports and the foreign demand for exports are particularly inelastic, the outcome will be the reverse of that desired. In addition, the higher cost of imports may push up costs of production, producing rising prices of domestically produced goods and services and therefore weakening further the economy's competitive position in international markets. For these reasons, the interventionist school tends to oppose the policy of a floating exchange rate regime.

In general it has been suggested that floating exchange rates contain an inflationary bias, whereas fixed rates contain a deflationary bias. For these reasons alternative systems for determining exchange rates have been sought and implemented in attempts to reduce the volatility of international trading conditions. The adjustable peg system was introduced after the Bretton

Woods conference in 1944. This fixed, but adjustable, exchange rate regime was introduced to eliminate the competitive devaluations employed during the 1930s, which were held to be responsible in part for the world depression. Currencies under the Bretton Woods arrangement were fixed at agree parities, and the participating governments committed themselves to supporting these parities. However, it was recognised that adjustments in exchange rates would be necessary from time to time in cases of fundamental disequilibrium. Although this phrase was never explicitly defined, in practice it referred to a situation where a country was running a persistent deficit or surplus. The Bretton Woods system therefore represented a compromise between a fixed exchange rate regime and a free floating regime.

A further variant is the managed or 'dirty floating' system. Here, exchange rates are allowed to adjust on a day-to-day basis, but the government may intervene when it deems necessary to aid adjustment. The authorities will have in mind a parity level that may change, given an alteration in external or internal conditions, and will attempt to maintain this parity. This was the system that most governments adopted after the collapse of the Bretton Woods System.

## Balance of payments experience in Britain

The statistics compiled by Mitchell and Deane show that between 1854 and 1939 Britain's trade balance was always in deficit (Mitchell and Deane, 1962). However, invisible trade, particularly from overseas investments, meant that the current account was in surplus up to the Second World War. This was mainly due to the tremendous acceleration of overseas investment from 1870 to 1914. Annual outflow of capital from Britain averaged around 4 per cent of national income, but actually reached 7 per cent by 1913 (Kenwood and Lougheed, 1992). In the interwar years the average trade deficit was £340 million, and invisible trade was not sufficient to offset this deficit (Mitchell and Deane, 1962). The Second World War caused the balance of payments to fall into serious disequilibrium, but a fairly dramatic recovery took place immediately after the war, and by 1948 the balance of payments on current account was in surplus. It remained in surplus until 1950. This was short-lived, however, as Britain's share of world exports continued to decline, as it had before the war. This trend decline was also true in terms of Britain's share of world output and imports (Thirlwall, 1986).

In 1956 and 1958 Britain recorded surpluses on the trade balance, a situation that had only occurred on three previous occasions since 1800, in 1816, 1821 and 1822. From 1959 onwards, the balance of payments moved into disequilibrium and a conflict emerged between the policy of maintaining full employment and the balance of payments. The trade deficit worsened considerably from £119 million in 1963 to £543 million in 1964, caused by a rapid expansion of demand, reflected in an increase in the value of imports from £4450 million to £5111 million, giving the largest peace-time deficit on the balance of payments up to that point of £749 million (Thirlwall, 1986). Devaluation was widely advised to be the correct response to this crisis, but the Labour Government responded to the deficit with a demand deflation and the introduction of a surcharge on all imports (with the exception of food and raw materials) of 15 per cent. The surcharge remained in operation until November 1966. Devaluation was finally adopted in 1967 as a result of a speculative attack on sterling in the foreign exchange markets. Sterling was devalued from $2.80 to $2.40, leading to a competitive advantage, although the conflict between internal and external equilibrium remained.

After the breakdown of Bretton Woods in 1972, exchange rate volatility became very high, and rather than freeing monetary policy for internal stabilisation, interest rates have tended to be employed in consideration of the balance of payments. Sterling depreciated against the dollar by 10 per cent after floating in 1972, and the balance of payments position worsened as a result of the increase in import prices, producing a merchandise trade deficit of over £2000 million in 1973, and on the current account the deficit in 1973 stood at £1000 million. The oil crisis of 1974 led to a trade deficit of £5000 million and a current account deficit of £3000 million (Thirlwall, 1986). Sterling fell below $2 on 5 March 1976 and by May had fallen below $1.80, a depreciation of 12.5 per cent from January to May. This was reversed in 1977 and by the following year the current account had moved into surplus.

The election of the Conservative Party to Government in 1979 and the introduction of tight monetary policy, coupled with the weakness of the dollar, saw a rise in the exchange rate. The Thatcher Government removed all exchange controls which gave rise to an increase in capital outflows. In addition, 1979 was the year of the second oil crisis, and the visible trade deficit rose to over £3000 million. Between 1979 and 1990 the current account was in balance only twice, in 1979 and 1986. It was a hope of the time that, due to North Sea oil, the oil balance would come to the rescue of the current account. However, this was not the case, as oil prices fell in 1986. It was also suggested that the relaxation of exchange controls would reap rewards in the form of a large surplus on the invisible side of the account. But, the invisible surplus was unable to prevent the increasing deficit over the 1980s. The position in July 1995 was a trade deficit of £1100 million, with the import volumes rising faster than export volumes. It would appear that the recessions of the 1980s were induced by the restrictive monetary policy of the British Government, and the reduction in manufacturing industry that this cased has had long-term implications for the balance of payments: first of all, through the rise in manufactured imports and a failure to make up the gap with invisible earnings, and secondly due to the appreciation of the exchange rate that made British industry uncompetitive in overseas markets.

TABLE 13.1    UK balance of payments on current account

|      | Current balance (£m) | Visible balance (£m) | Invisible balance (£m) |
|------|---------------------|----------------------|------------------------|
| 1985 | 2 238               | −3 345               | 5 583                  |
| 1986 | −864                | −9 559               | 8 695                  |
| 1987 | −4 813              | −11 582              | 6 769                  |
| 1988 | −16 475             | −21 480              | 5 005                  |
| 1989 | −22 398             | −24 683              | 2 285                  |
| 1990 | −19 293             | −18 809              | −484                   |
| 1991 | −8 533              | −10 284              | 1 751                  |
| 1992 | −9 468              | −13 104              | 3 636                  |
| 1993 | −11 042             | −13 379              | 2 336                  |
| 1994 | −1 648              | −10 594              | 8 910                  |

Source: *Economic Trends*, October 1995, table 2.13.

## Exchange rate policy

The dominating force in economic policy in the 1920s was the currency question. That is, the attempts to stabilise exchange rates and to return to the gold standard after its suspension during the First World War. Many countries held the belief that the gold standard would resolve the economic problems caused by the war. These beliefs were quite quickly shattered as, far from correcting the underlying maladjustments, the resurrected gold standard was itself subject to serious problems from the beginning and it quickly disintegrated. This raises the question as to how mechanism that had apparently worked so well before 1914 failed to function to the benefit of the international economy after the war. The gold standard was created in the latter half of the nineteenth century and quickly replaced silver as the currency of international acceptability. With the large-scale discovery of new supplies of gold in the 1890s, there came a worldwide transition to gold. Gold encompasses two important features: it commanded universal acceptance as a means of clearing international payments, and most currencies were readily convertible into gold. These were seen as being sufficient reasons to regard the gold standard as the guarantor of international economic stability. The classical view of the automatic adjustment mechanism under the gold standard depended upon the emphasis that was placed on adjustment via the trade balance. Given a disequilibrium between countries, the money flows that occur, arising out of such an imbalance, would tend to bring about downward price adjustments in countries running a deficit and upward price adjustments in countries running a surplus. These adjustments would then restore former price and cost relations. This 'automatic' adjustment mechanism was facilitated by the so-called 'rules of the game', which the central banks were supposed to adhere to: discount rates were raised and credit tightened in countries losing gold, with opposite policies in surplus countries. The effects were that interest rate changes stimulated short-term capital movements from surplus to deficit countries and the variations in interest rates and credit policy reinforced price and cost adjustments that were necessary to restore equilibrium. However, such an interpretation was too simplistic for practical purposes. The classical view emphasises price relationships, but ignores the effects of income adjustments. There is also an over-emphasis on the retification of the current account balance, and this view overlooks the compensatory mechanism that operates within the capital account of the balance of payments. The system appeared to work well in the era before the First World War, mainly because of an absence of conflict between internal and external needs of the major international economies. It was only after the war that domestic and external needs came into conflict, a situation which finally led to the demise of the gold standard. The gold standard had worked for the major industrial powers, mainly due to the fact that it was never subjected to serious strain. It can be argued that any regime of fixed exchange rates will only work in a smooth fashion if the countries that adhere to it are already in fundamental equilibrium. The strength of the gold standard system came from the pre-eminence of London as the single financial centre. Sterling and gold were virtually interchangeable, and this gave the Bank of England the role of regulator of the gold standard and the international payments system. The war totally disrupted the international monetary system, but most governments had a strong resolve to return to the gold standard as quickly as possible, and at prewar parity for their currencies. Although few were able to attain prewar parity, by 1928 the process was virtually complete. But within three to four years the whole regime had collapsed. It collapsed mainly because there was a failure on the part of the authorities to recognise that the economic environment that had prevailed before 1914 no longer existed and, indeed, had been replaced with a completely different international economic order.

The system contained several fundamental weaknesses, not least of which was the position of London. In the postwar system, London and New York were required to hold larger stocks of gold than for normal trading purposes, as foreign claims could be withdrawn at short notice. New York held large stocks of gold and relatively small liabilities, but London had large claims against it and low stocks of gold, and thus was the weak link in the system. As a result, sterling was continually under pressure in the 1920s. Exchange rate parities tended to be chosen in an uncoordinated and haphazard manner, which inevitably meant that countries ended up with the wrong parity. Many were overvalued, others were undervalued, but those countries that restored their currencies to prewar parity were generally overvalued, and this was particularly the case with sterling. So the system began from a position of disequilibrium, with very little prospect of adjustments taking place to restore equilibrium. Those countries with overvalued currencies faced an extremely difficult situation. They could not devalue their currency so quickly after restoration as this would have involved a tremendous loss of confidence and prestige, and as the currency that was the most out of line was sterling, this would have undermined the whole process of the restoration of the gold standard regime. The alternative to devaluation was to deflate the domestic economy to come in line with the exchange rate at the existing parity. However, the British authorities were reluctant to deflate by the amount necessary, given the high level of unemployment that existed in the economy. As a result internal and external objectives were in conflict in a manner in which they had never previously been.

No sooner had the gold standard been restored than pressures developed which were to undermine the whole system. Countries on the gold standard introduced deflationary policies as a reaction to balance of payments deficits and internal disequilibrium, which aggravated a downswing in economic activity which was already well under way. Gold became vulnerable as the situation raised the ratio of claims on gold to the amount of gold that was available to match those claims. There was a steady contraction of international credits from mid-1930 as confidence was eroded. This led to an increase in bankruptcies, exchange depreciation and bank failures. The major crisis in banking occurred in the US and France in 1930–1, which intensified the pressure on London as France liquidated its sterling holdings. Debtor countries were losing gold at an accelerating rate and deflation proved to be no solution. In the summer of 1931 the German banking system collapsed and a panic ensued. London was at the forefront as it remained one of the few places still prepared to grant accommodation. Between July and September 1931 the financial crisis in Europe caused a rapid withdrawal of sterling balances, and the loss of reserves was made worse by the loss of confidence in Britain's ability to maintain solvency as its balance of payments position deteriorated. As much as £43 million was withdrawn from the London money market in three days after 15 September, which made a total of nearly £200 million withdrawn in two months. This proved to be too much for the British authorities and Britain officially left the gold standard on 21 September 1931. Devaluation of the currency became preferable to the British authorities than the internal deflation that would have been necessary under the gold standard. Many other countries followed the British example and this marked the end of the gold standard system.

There were several immediate benefits for the British economy. The devaluation gave a competitive advantage over those economies that had remained on the fixed exchange rate regime, and monetary policy was removed from the constraints imposed by the 'rules of the game', which had resulted in a high rate of interest in an attempt to stem the outflow of reserves. A policy of cheap money was followed from 1932 to 1939, which may have had benefits through consumption and investment, making monetary policy permissive of the recovery. However, the collapse of the gold standard was reflected in a period of international economic instability, world depression and a lack of international liquidity. Countries were unable to finance balance of payments disequilibrium, and the international trading environment became one of competitive devaluation and protectionism as tariffs were introduced throughout the world economy in the 1930s.

It was with the problems of the 1930s in mind that the major industrial powers came to the conference at Bretton Woods in 1944. Bretton Woods re-established fixed, but adjustable, exchange rates, with countries obliged to maintain the exchange rate within 1 per cent either side of its par value, by means of intervention in the market. The International Monetary Fund (IMF) was established to oversee the operation of the system and to agree adjustments of over 10 per cent in the par value of a currency if it could be convinced that the balance of payments of the economy involved was in 'fundamental disequilibrium'. Under the regime agreed at Bretton Woods, national currencies were convertible into gold and, from that time, the dollar became the reserve asset of the international monetary system. Built into the agreement was the recognition that the balance of payments adjustment under a fixed regime requires interest rates to rise and prices to fall, and therefore, because of a lack of price flexibility, income and employment would be the variables to suffer under the adjustment process. Hence, given the postwar priority of full employment, the IMF provided countries in temporary disequilibrium with the facility to borrow funds sufficient to overcome their problems without recourse to employment-threatening adjustment policies. In addition to the IMF, the agreement at Bretton Woods created the International Bank for Reconstruction and Development (the World Bank) charged with the role of international allocator of last resort to 'assist and supplement private international investment, not to supplant it' (Panić, 1995).

Panic suggests that the Bretton Woods system did not operate in the manner that was envisaged by those who created it. Rather than the system being managed by the institutions set up for the purpose, it became dominated by the United States, and therefore dependent upon the economic policies and performance of the US (Panić, 1995). This dominance of one economy eventually led to the collapse of the system in 1971–2. The position of the dollar as the key currency in the system proved to be its weakness. A general lack of liquidity in international markets meant that the US could be allowed to run balance of payments deficits to add to international reserves. However, dollar liabilities began to increase, and the ability of the dollar to be convertible into gold came into serious doubt. Confidence in the dollar eventually fell to such a level that convertibility into gold was suspended in August 1971. Par values were restored by the Smithsonian Agreement in December 1971, which devalued the dollar by approximately 8 per cent and widened the bands of fluctuation to 2.5 per cent from the original 1.0 per cent. However, sterling came under intensive speculative pressure and it was floated in 1972. This began a period of floating exchange rates as the major currencies were quickly allowed to float (Thirlwall, 1986).

Many saw the return to a floating exchange rate regime as an opportunity to release monetary policy into the service of internal stabilisation. In particular, Milton Friedman argued in favour of a policy of benign neglect in exchange markets, with no intervention and the use of monetary policy to achieve a steady rate of growth of the money supply. Another option existed in terms of intervention to 'lean against the wind', and to resist a change in the exchange rate dictated by the market, through the use of official transactions in the money market and interest rate policy. Essentially these were the policy options available to the British Government after the decision to allow sterling to float in 1972. Lack of intervention was the preferred policy until the pound weakened in mid-1973. For the next three years the Bank of England supported sterling in the market. The weakness of sterling continued, however, and reached a crisis in 1976, forcing Chancellor Healey to introduce a deflationary package to restore confidence in the currency as part of the IMF conditionality attached to a standby loan. With the strengthening of the pound, aided by market confidence from North Sea oil, the authorities attempted to hold back currency appreciation by selling sterling on a large scale and allowing a fall in interest rates.

A 'U' turn took place in 1977 as sterling was allowed to rise and interest rates moved steadily upwards. The 'U' turn coincided with the 'conversion' of the Labour Government to the monetarist doctrine, and hence the requirement to employ monetary policy to attend to the rate of growth of the money supply. The election of the Thatcher Government in 1979 saw the continuation of the benign neglect policy and a consensus with the Labour Government's assessment that it was not in the best interests of the economy to participate in the Exchange Rate Mechanism (ERM) of the European Monetary System (EMS). The ERM was introduced in March 1979 as an anti-inflationary policy with members fixing their exchange rates to that of the D-mark and using monetary policy to keep their currencies within bands of fluctuation of 2.25 per cent. The British Government preferred to employ interest rates directly as the anti-inflationary instrument, with exchange rates being set by the market. However, by 1985, Chancellor Lawson was shadowing the D-mark, despite still not having joined the ERM. In October 1985 Lawson proposed to Cabinet, with the support of the Bank of England and other Cabinet Ministers, that the time was right to enter the mechanism, but his proposal was vetoed by Thatcher, advised by Alan Walters (Johnson, 1991). Lawson continued to press for Britain's membership of the ERM and finally resigned in October 1989 over Thatcher's refusal to dispense with the services of Walters, who was the chief opponent of British entry. Thatcher relented later and Major took Britain into the ERM on 8 October 1990. Britain joined at a relatively high exchange rate, suggesting that this would encourage industry to bear down on unit labour costs (Johnson, 1991). It has been argued that entry into the system at the appreciated rate of 2.95 DM was a signal of the anti-inflationary intentions of the Government, and produces 'slack' in labour and output markets, tending to put downward pressure on inflation (Masson, 1995). Sterling entered at the wider fluctuation band of + 6 per cent of the central parity, but both the Chancellor, Lamont, and the Prime Minister gave a commitment to remain in the fixed exchange rate regime and to enter the narrower band of + 2.25 per cent in 1992. This declaration coincided with a speculation crisis in September 1992, as the financial markets began to test the resolve of the government to remain within the fixed exchange rate regime and not to devalue. These speculative pressures finally forced the Government to abandon its commitment and to float the currency.

Kenen has highlighted the similarities between the crises of 1992–3 and those of 1971–3. In particular, he argues that although the systems had been designed to combine short-term stability with long-term flexibility, the interplay between the financial markets and the monetary authorities 'ossified the exchange rate regime' (Kenen, 1995). He also points to the similarities in terms of the reaction of the economy at the centre of each system. In each case, he argues, they failed to arrange an orderly realignment of the exchange rate and caused damage to the system. In the collapse of the Bretton Woods system, the US imposed an import tax and closed the gold window, and in the ERM crisis the German authorities put pressure on those central rates, through market forces, that it had expressed doubts about (Kenen, 1995).

It may also be true to say that the collapse of the gold standard in the 1930s shows the same symptoms. in terms of the failure of the central currency to perform in the way expected of it, a failure of the system to withstand speculative pressure and the internal/external conflict that forces monetary policy out of the area of external equilibrium and into the need for internal stabilisation.

### Conclusion

McCombie and Thirlwall have argued that in Britain the unemployment–balance of payments trade-off has deteriorated, in the sense that, in the 1950s and 1960s, a balance of payments equilibrium was compatible with approximately 500 000 unemployed. By the 1970s the level of unemployment required was 1 million, and in 1992 the figure was approximately 3 million (McCombie and Thirlwall, 1992). Under the Keynesian orthodoxy of the 1950s and 1960s, consumption booms were ended by balance of payments crises, as imports rose in relation to exports, and the exchange rate came under pressure. Therefore the rate of growth of GDP tended to be determined by the level of exports. Interest rates were the policy instrument favoured to restore external equilibrium, but this was in conflict with internal objectives. Central to the problem of external equilibrium is the role of manufacturing industry, as its output is tradeable whereas much of the output of the service sector is not. The so-called 'shake out' of 1979–81 saw a 17 per cent fall in manufacturing production, which the Government saw as cutting out the dead wood, to enable the manufacturing sector to become better able to compete in international markets. However, manufacturing was becoming less important in the economy, and it was argued that services, and particularly financial services, could take over the role of provider of economic growth. Earnings from financial services did indeed increase in the first 6 years of the Thatcher Government, but have stagnated since in terms of foreign exchange earnings. Hence Britain has become a high-unemployment, internationally indebted and slow-growth economy. The problem, paradoxically, lies within the solution. Deflation of the British economy to reduce imports will cause an increase in unemployment, and high interest rates to defend sterling will reduce investment.

With a small manufacturing base, a devaluation may produce a competitive advantage in international markets in the short run, but will also fuel inflation as the domestic price of imports rises, adding to manufacturing costs. The scenario is strikingly similar to that of the 1930s when the answer lay in the restructuring of the British economy. Then, as now, this could only be achieved with extensive state intervention, but the climate of opinion makes this strategy highly unlikely.

# CHAPTER 14

# Economic and Monetary Union

## What is 'economic and monetary union' (EMU)?

'No man is an island' wrote John Donne. 'Ask not for whom the bell tolls, it tolls for thee'.

Donne was pointing out that people are not isolated from the actions of others; and this is also true of countries. The actions of one country – particularly if it is an economic giant – will have a significant effect on its trading partners. In this sense, national sovereignty is something of a myth, since every country is constrained in the actions it can take by the actions of others.

However, EMU is different, because countries formally give up the right to make many economic decisions in the hope that this renunciation will bring benefits. This chapter examines the background and the costs and benefits of economic and monetary union in Europe.

EMU is the highest form of integration short of complete political union. It builds on foundations such as a free trade area where goods can circulate between member states without any barriers. A closer form of integration is a customs union where the countries have a common external tariff – this involves ceding power over tariffs to a co-ordinating body. Even closer union involves the free movement of labour between countries.

Monetary integration goes beyond this and has two essential components, both having significant implications. The two components are *exchange rate union* and *capital market integration*. An exchange rate union exists when member countries have what is essentially one currency. In principle, an exchange rate union can exist with the participating countries continuing to have separate currencies, so long as the exchange rates are permanently and irrevocably fixed. However, if this is the case – if, for example, a pound sterling always equals eight French francs, there is effectively no difference between the two. Capital market integration is largely implied by an exchange rate union. It means that there is complete freedom of movement for capital between member countries.

The implications of EMU are considerable. Because there is a single currency there needs to be some organisation to manage it; hence it implies a single central bank. Since there is one currency, there needs to be central control of the money supply and hence of interest rates. And it also implies a common pool of foreign exchange reserves.

All this means that there is effectively complete integration of the financial end economic sectors of participating countries, and indeed some supporters favour EMU because they see it as a step towards a federal Europe. Whether or not this is the eventual result, there is no doubt that it requires individual countries to cede power to a transnational authority.

### Steps towards EMU

Although EMU is an economic phenomenon, the motivation behind it is largely political. Indeed, this is true of the European Union itself. When the Treaty of Rome was signed in 1957, its advocates were politicians who had experienced the suffering of two great wars and who were determined to prevent another European war. They believed that the way to do this was to integrate the European economies since they thought this would also lead to political closeness; hence the Rome Treaty specifically mentioned 'ever closer union'. Hence EMU can be seen as a logical conclusion to this process. This is recognised by opponents of EMU such as Nigel Lawson who in 1989 was Chancellor of the Exchequer and who asserted 'It is clear that Economic and Monetary Union implies nothing less than European government – albeit a federal one – and political union: the United States of Europe. This is simply not on the agenda now, nor will it be for the foreseeable future' (quoted in Dyson, 1994, p. 1). Whilst a 'United States of Europe' may be an exaggeration, there is no doubt that EMU will lead to less political power for national governments.

The Treaty of Rome did not mention economic and monetary union: that was too far in the future. But it did introduce policies which led to EMU. For example, Article 106 stipulates that exchange controls should be eliminated to the extent necessary to make possible the movement of goods, services, capital and people. In practice, however, at that time the EC was concerned to implement a common market with no internal tariffs and to establish a Common Agriculture Policy; EMU was a distant goal. Indeed, countries were more concerned with domestic priorities than with European obligations. Thus in 1969 France devalued the franc by 11 per cent and Germany revalued the mark by 9 per cent.

Paradoxically these fluctuations led European leaders to realise that changes such as these were destabilising – for example, making German exports to France 20 per cent more expensive. Consequently the Hague summit in 1969 declared that the intention of the Community was to proceed progressively in stages to the goal of economic and monetary union. The result was the Werner Report of 1970.

This report by the Prime Minister of Luxembourg was a considerable achievement; not least because it overcame disagreement between two groups of countries and because in essence it eventually led to the Delors report which was the foundation of the Maastricht Treaty.

The disagreement faced by Werner was between what were called the 'economist' group of countries, led by Germany, and the 'monetarists', led by France. The economists argued that before monetary unification could be achieved it was necessary to reach economic convergence by setting targets (for example, for unemployment and inflation) and by co-ordinating economic policies to achieve these.

The monetarists argued that this was the wrong way round; what was needed was to narrow exchange rate fluctuations. Then economic convergence could follow.

The Werner Report agreed that the first stage should be to narrow exchange rate fluctuations, to co-ordinate monetary policy and to set up a European Exchange Stabilisation Fund to provide credit facilities for countries whose currencies were in danger of depreciating. In this plan, European currencies were supposed to move together against the dollar (hence this system was sometimes called 'the snake').

Despite its forward looking nature, the Werner Plan was doomed to failure because of changes in the world economy. The most significant of these was the quadrupling of world oil prices in 1973. This led to currency speculation, forcing currencies to leave the snake. For example France left in 1974, rejoined in 1975 and left again in 1976. From April 1972 to March 1979 the 'fixed' parities of the system were altered 31 times (Hitiris, 1994, p. 142). These changes made progress towards monetary union impossible.

However, in 1979 the Community introduced a new plan; though far removed from full EMU, it laid the foundations. This was the European Monetary System (EMS). All the member states automatically became members of the EMS which had a number of features. One of these was the introduction of the ecu as a unit of account for EU transactions. At the heart of the EMS was the Exchange Rate Mechanism. This was a system of fixed, though adjustable exchange rates. Currencies were allowed to diverge only slightly from the fixed parity, and there were credit facilities to help countries whose currencies were under pressure.

The next big step forward was the plan devised by Jacques Delors which became the basis of the Maastricht Treaty (Council/Commission of the European Communities, 1992). Delors was building on the relative success of the EMS, since although there had been realignments, the overall picture was one of stability and co-operation between member states. This stability was reinforced by the Single European Act of 1987 which led to the removal of many barriers to the free movement of goods and services, and which also set out the goal of economic and monetary union.

Delors, the President of the Community, was determined to make real progress towards EMU. His committee met in the period 1988–9 and decided that the creation of EMU should be a single process, but that this process should be in stages which would lead to the ultimate goal.

The result was the Maastricht Treaty which was signed in February 1992, though only approved by the member countries after much difficulty – the Danish electorate at first rejected the Treaty, and the UK took the opportunity to opt out of both the social chapter and, like Denmark, is not committed to joining EMU. If the provisions of the Treaty are satisfied, then the European Union will have achieved an economic and monetary union.

The Treaty proposed three stages:

- *Stage one*: This required the freeing of capital flows and the integration of financial markets; all countries were required to participate in the exchange rate mechanism.
- *Stage two*: This was to start in 1994 and involved the creation of a new Community institution, the European Monetary Institute, which will eventually become the European Central Bank. This was to oversee the changes necessary for the implementation of a single currency, including the co-ordination of national monetary policies.
- *Stage three*: This is due to begin in 1999 when exchange rates will be irrevocably fixed for participating countries, and the European Central Bank will be responsible for European monetary policy.

Provision was made for some countries to join EMU in 1997, but subsequent events have made this unlikely.

Countries will only join the single currency if they fulfil the following criteria:

1. *A high degree of price stability*. This is defined as an average rate of inflation that does not exceed by more than 1.5 per cent that of the three best performing countries.
2. *Low interest rates*. Member states have to have long term interest rates that do not exceed by more than 2 per cent that of the three best performing member states.
3. *Low budget deficits*. Budget deficits should not exceed 3 per cent of GDP.
4. *National debt*. The protocol does not define this, but it seems likely to mean that membership requires a ratio of debt to GDP that does not exceed 60 per cent.
5. *Currency stability*. Membership requires that a country should not have devalued its currency against any other member currency in the last two years.

These are very strict provisions, and in the recession which followed Maastricht very few countries would have qualified for membership. However, Article 6 of the Protocol states: 'Council shall acting unanimously on a proposal from the Commission and after consulting the Parliament. . . adopt appropriate provisions to lay down the details of the convergence criteria . . . which shall then replace this Protocol.'

In other words, the strict criteria can in practice be modified if all the members agree.

The most difficult criteria for countries to achieve are those relating to budget deficits and the national debt. In 1995 only Luxembourg and Germany met criteria (3) and (4) above, and some failed by huge margins. Greece, for example, had a public debt to GDP ratio of 120 per cent compared to the 60 per cent required, and its budget deficit was 13 per cent of GDP. Consequently, almost all are taking measures to achieve the criteria. Economic growth will help, but there are two other ways: to cut public spending or increase taxes. *The Economist* claims that most countries are responding by putting up taxes rather than cutting spending and that this is likely to be unsuccessful. 'Between 1964 and 1992, different OECD countries imposed sharp cuts in their budget deficits 52 times (sharp meaning deficit reductions of more than ½ per cent of GDP).' Only 14 were successful in reducing the public debt by five percentage points of GDP and in the successful cases, 80 per cent of the reduction came from spending cuts. *The Economist* (1995, p. 16) also notes that the criterion of low public debt is not really a requirement for EMU since the two countries with the highest and lowest ratios of debt-to-GDP are Belgium and Luxembourg. These countries have shared a common currency for decades.

Overall, the criteria reflect the strong German concern about inflation. If there is a trade off between inflation and unemployment, then these come down very strongly on the side of low inflation.

The Maastricht Treaty had hardly been ratified when it was blown off course, rather to the surprise of even the most distinguished economists. Thus Currie, in March 1992, could write: 'ERM must be judged an appreciable success; much more durable than its critics expected, and much more successful in establishing a credible and stable framework for anti-inflationary policy'.

However, stresses soon arose, caused in part by the economic strains imposed by German reunification which caused higher interest rates in Germany and which then pressured other countries to raise their rates. This was accompanied by widespread recession. The result was that between September 1992 and August 1993 two currencies left the ERM and there were seven realignments before the system was amended in August 1993 to allow currencies to float to plus or minus 15 per cent (Directorate General, 1994, p. 91). In effect this was such a wide band that the old system of fixed exchange rates more or less disappeared, and critics of EMU suggested that the proposal was doomed – at one point only Luxembourg met all the criteria for membership of EMU. This pessimism was misplaced: supporters began putting forward specific recommendations, and at the same time the European Monetary Institute began to make the preparations necessary for EMU.

## Theory of Customs Unions

The underlying theory is that of optimum currency areas. This theory tries to make clear whether a common currency offers more or less advantages than the alternative of separate currencies.

An optimal currency area is defined in terms of internal and external balance. Internal balance implies low inflation and unemployment, and external balance refers to a balance on the current account of the balance of payments.

The early literature in this field started from the Phillips Curve trade-off between inflation and unemployment which suggested that countries could choose between different positions on this trade-off, partly by devaluing their currency to maintain competitiveness. Joining a common currency rules out this possibility, and member countries have to accept the consequences of a fixed exchange rate. This would mean that some countries would end up with more or less inflation and unemployment than they would choose. Hence, in this approach, a common currency is only recommended when countries have long-term monetary stability and common approaches to the unemployment/inflation trade off.

More recently, however, the belief has grown that there is no steady long-term trade-off between inflation and unemployment. If there is no trade-off, then the main benefit for a country of being able to vary its exchange rate is the ability to choose a different inflation rate from other countries. Of course, the 'long term' may be very long; if so, this conclusion would be less firm and countries could benefit from varying their exchange rate for considerable periods of time.

The modern theory of optimum currency areas was developed by Mundell (1961). Assume for simplicity that there are two regions (or countries) and only one good which is produced in region (or country) A and one good produced in region (or country) B. Then assume an asymmetric demand-side shock so that consumers in region A buy less of their product and more of B's product. The result is that region B booms, leading to a rise there in wages and prices and also to a surplus on B's current account of the balance of payments.

Equilibrium will be restored by wages and prices falling in A so that B's products become less competitive, and by labour moving from A to B, so reducing the pressure on wages in B. If wages are not flexible, and if there is little labour mobility, then problems will arise. Equilibrium will eventually be restored by inflation in B, making its products uncompetitive compared to those in A.

Alternatively, equilibrium can be restored by devaluing A's currency. This will cut its prices relative to those in B. However, if A and B are part of a single currency area, this option is no longer possible. A better response to an asymmetric shock is for the exchange rates between the two countries to be adjusted.

The conclusion reached by this analysis is that currency unions will have undesirable effects unless wages are flexible and labour is mobile. Since the evidence suggests that wages in Europe are sticky downwards, and that labour mobility between countries is very limited, the conclusion is that EMU is undesirable.

However, supporters of EMU contest this conclusion. Thus Bofinger (1994) makes several criticisms to show that this argument is not applicable because it depends crucially on the assumptions underlying the model. In the first place, all EU countries are highly diversified, so that the 'one country one sector' assumption made by Mundell is a completely inadequate approximation of reality in the EU. Moreover, Mundell assumes *asymmetric* demand shocks; the reality is that most EU trade is *intra*-industry based – the UK exports cars to France and France exports cars to the UK – so that it is most unlikely that a demand shock in one country would lead to an increase in demand in another. Any factor which affected the demand for cars in one country would almost certainly affect others, so that demand shocks will affect several if not all EU countries. Thus a shock which affected the industrial areas of Europe would not be much ameliorated by changes in the exchange rates of those countries.

Bofinger quotes research by BiniSmaghi and Vori (1993) to the effect that the divergencies in the structure of manufacturing of EU countries amount to only half the size of divergencies that can be observed for the 12 US Federal Reserve Districts. The implication of this research is that if the Mundell optimum currency area approach is accepted, then the USA would be better off abandoning its single currency. A simple review of the costs and benefits of this shows its ridiculous nature; by the same argument, the EU would benefit from a single currency.

Another argument that casts doubt on the optimum currency critique of EMU is that nominal exchange rate changes have only a temporary effect on a country's competitiveness. If a country devalues to maintain its competitiveness, then one result will be an increase in inflation caused by the rise in the price of imports. This will lead to a rise in costs and prices of exports so that the advantage derived from devaluation will only be temporary – Currie (1992, p. 253) estimates two years – unless a policy of continuing devaluations is adopted or unless workers are willing to accept real pay cuts.

Thus the theoretical arguments are inconclusive and Currie's conclusion (1992, p. 253) is probably most appropriate: 'My reading of the optimum currency literature is that it provides a compelling case neither for, nor against, monetary union.'

## The case for EMU

The *political* argument for and against economic and monetary union lies outside the scope of this chapter; at its heart, however, lies disagreement about the benefits or otherwise of nationalism. Opponents of EMU stress national sovereignty, supporters emphasise the wars which result from nationalism and the benefits of international co-operation. John Stewart Mill (1848, p. 176) a century and a half ago, put the central political argument in favour: 'So much of barbarism, however, still remains in the transactions of most civilised nations, that almost all independent countries choose to assert their nationality by having, to their own inconvenience and that of their neighbours, a peculiar currency of their own.'

The 'inconveniences' mentioned by Mill are largely micro-economic, and are summarised by Baldwin (1991):

- The most obvious benefit of a single currency is the reduction in transaction costs. If a single currency replaces the national currencies of the EU, then the resources devoted to money changing can be used to produce goods and services that contribute directly to welfare. In addition, this would reduce the resources which firms currently have to devote to multi-currency accounting.

   The Commission of the EU estimates that these transaction costs are one-half of 1 per cent of EU GDP. However, critics of EMU such as Minford (1995, p. 126) dispute these costs because 'currency risk is diversifiable in a world of many currencies and investment vehicles' and he argues that since money exchanges can now be made electronically, transactions costs should tend towards zero.
- Despite the Single Market, capital markets are not fully integrated. Investors tend to invest in their own country, even though capital could be more efficiently invested in others. A single currency would reduce this misallocation of resources. Moreover, the cost of financial services varies considerably between countries; if the capital market were truly integrated, competition between financial institutions would have equalised the price of financial services.
- The existence of separate currencies affects portfolio choice. With multiple currencies, investors have to consider money demand and supply shocks arising in many countries. This increases risk.
- Financial asset prices do not correctly reflect the true risk and return on underlying physical assets. For example, a German investor faces different transaction costs on a Spanish asset from those on a German asset.
- Flexible exchange rates distort investment decisions and can lead to capital outflows from countries where there is a need for capital. Such decisions may arise from monetary rather than real considerations: for example, because interest rates are higher in one country than another. Profit-maximising firms facing greater uncertainty – which will usually be the case when firms invest in a country with a different currency – will require higher returns, especially where an investment involves sunk costs (i.e. where costs cannot be recovered).

Since there is a high proportion of sunk costs in fixed business investments such as factories, EMU should encourage more long-term cross-border investments.

Moreover, fluctuations in the exchange rate rather than real considerations may determine investment. For example, suppose a German and a British firm are bidding for a factory in the UK. If the mark is strong, the German company's ability to self-finance the investment will be artificially high compared to the British firm's ability, so that the German firm will be able to afford a higher price. Thus spurious changes in exchange rates can have real effects on investments.

Consequently, exchange rate uncertainty prevents the EU capital market from being a truly unified market and reduces the gains which arise from the Single Market.

- There is a medium-term induced capital formation effect. The points mentioned above show that a single currency will lead to improved productivity of labour and capital. This will improve the investment climate and lead to increased investment, which in turn increases EU income.

- In the long term, supporters argue that an efficient economic structure – which would be encouraged by EMU – promotes economic growth. This would be reinforced by behaviourial changes by economic agents (Emerson, 1990, p. 19) who come to recognise that the systemic changes not only affect them directly through the Single Market and single currency, but also change the behaviour of others so that the whole system becomes more competitive. This expectations effect may also lead to greater macro-economic stability.

These micro-economic effects are difficult to quantify, not least because the benefits of the Single Market overlap with the benefits of a single currency. Baldwin (1991) however, makes an attempt.

He suggests that the static effects such as cutting transactions costs and integrating capital markets would boost EU GDP by more than 0.55 per cent. In addition, induced capital formation would add to this but is difficult to calculate because it depends on such factors as differing discount rates and multipliers. To this should be added the long-term growth effects which Baldwin estimates to be 1.8 per cent of GDP. Even if these figures are exaggerated, this analysis suggests that the benefits will be substantial.

*Macro benefits*

Supporters of EMU suggest that there will also be considerable macro-economic benefits. One is that member countries will pool their foreign exchange reserves. This will economise on the use of foreign exchange reserves since it is unlikely that all member countries will go into deficit at the same time. Moreover, intra EU trade will no longer be financed by foreign exchange so that this trade can be expected to flourish. The pooling of reserves also means that the ecu foreign exchange market will be 'thicker' than the market for individual currencies and so should be less volatile than the market for individual currencies. This stability should encourage international trade.

Another advantage is that the integration of the capital market means that if a member country is in deficit it will be helped automatically by the European Central Bank.

The size and importance of the EU means that the ecu would become a major international currency and so be able to enjoy the benefits of seigniorage. In other words, the EU would be able to finance balance of trade deficits because foreign countries would hold the ecu as part of their foreign exchange reserves. This is difficult to quantify. Alogoskoufis and Portes (1991, p. 241) quote research to the effect that when sterling was still a major currency, seigniorage was almost zero. On the other hand, because so many dollars are held outside the USA, seigniorage benefits for the USA may amount to 0.2 per cent of American GDP. It is unlikely that EU benefits would approach this level.

Ashdown (1995, p. 26) also claims that joining a monetary union would mean lower inflation.That is because the European Central Bank would be greatly influenced by European – particularly German – attitudes towards low inflation and would adopt policies which would ensure low inflation for the EU as a whole.

Again, this line of argument is criticised by Minford (1995, pp. 125f) on the grounds that price stability can be pursued effectively by domestic means. All that is required is the political will to set some form of domestic nominal target such as the money supply or nominal income and to ensure that these targets are met.

Ashdown goes on to claim that joining an EMU would mean lower interest rates. That is because the currency markets expect sterling to depreciate relative to the German mark. Hence the UK government needs higher interest rates to prevent falls in sterling. A single currency would enable the UK to benefit from low German interest rates.

Finally, the case for EMU, so far as the UK is concerned, is that there would be costs in staying out. There would perhaps be less direct foreign investment into the UK since foreign firms would want to be at the core of Europe and not the periphery. Moreover, if the UK was outside the EMU the decisions of the European Central Bank would have a significant effect on the UK economy, but the UK would have no say in its decisions; the UK would be effectively marginalised.

### The case against EMU

Not surprisingly, there is disagreement about the costs of monetary union.

One theoretical argument against union argues that there will be losses which arise because there is an enforced departure from internal balance.

Assume three countries, 'Domestic', 'Neighbour' and 'Foreign', and that Domestic needs to devalue to maintain internal and external balance whilst

Neighbour needs to revalue. If Domestic and Foreign were partners in a monetary union they could either devalue or revalue, but not both. In these circumstances, an alteration in the exchange rate could either leave Domestic with an external deficit, forcing it to deflate its economy and so causing recession and unemployment, or it would lead to a surplus forcing it to accumulate foreign reserves or allowing prices and wages to rise.

The argument can be put another way. Tinbergen (1952) showed that countries need to have at least as many instruments of economic policy (e.g. financial) as they have objectives (e.g. low inflation). In this case we can assume two objectives – internal and external balance, and two instruments – financial (which includes both fiscal and monetary policy) and the exchange rate. Monetary union would mean the loss of one instrument, and make it impossible for a country to achieve internal and external balance simultaneously.

The consequence of this loss of instruments may be higher unemployment. That is because if a country has external imbalance (a deficit on international trade) the policy to adopt is to devalue the currency and cut domestic spending. Monetary union makes devaluation impossible, so the country is forced to have greater reliance on cutting the domestic expenditure. The result is recession and higher unemployment.

However, this conclusion has been criticised because it assumes that there is a simple Phillips Curve type trade-off between inflation and unemployment. If this is not so – if unemployment is at its natural rate – then the result will not be higher unemployment (since this is determined by such factors as the flexibility of the labour market).

The deflationary bias of a fixed exchange rate system can be argued another way. Under fixed exchange rates and where capital is free to move outside national boundaries, countries allow the money stock to adjust to the exchange rate and the interest rate. Hence, when exchange rates are fixed, countries lose the ability to control inflation by varying the money supply, since this is determined by the demand for money at the interest rate across the monetary union. This means that countries have to accept the inflation rate which exists across the union.

If a country does not accept this rate, its prices will rise, so its exports become uncompetitive, and the result is higher unemployment which may eventually damp down the inflation. Until this happens, however, the country will export its inflation since the other members of the monetary union will receive more demand for their lower-priced exports. This increase in demand will cause their prices to rise.

Overall, it is argued that the system causes deficit countries to adapt policies which will deflate their economies, and the effects of this will spread to other countries which do not need to deflate.

Even this might not cure inflationary pressures, as a group of German economists have argued (Steinherr, 1994, pp. 72–3). They argue that monetary union is a desirable goal, but suggest that the arrangements made at Maastricht are not satisfactory. One reason is that 'A consensus to regard price stability as priority, as has traditionally prevailed in Germany, has not been evident throughout Europe'. Without this consensus, it will not be possible to pursue price stability since this requires that public opinion supports the state's policies on wages and public finances.

These economists also suggest that the weaker countries in an economic and monetary union will be exposed to greater competitive pressures and that this will lead to rising unemployment. They suggest that what is needed is not union at an agreed date in 1999, but a gradual move so that union is achieved after a substantial period of convergence, so that the economies which join are very similar economically. In practice, this means that some countries might never be able to join the union, since it will clearly be very many years before countries such as Greece and Portugal achieve economic convergence with Germany.

Minford and Rastogi (1990) use the Liverpool computer model of the economy to estimate the effects of EMU. This is essentially a rational expectations model with an emphasis on nominal contracts and monetary surprises. They conclude that the world as a whole would be better off under a system of floating exchange rates. So far as the UK is concerned, 'Tying the currency to a foreign vehicle exposes the economy to greater instability and supply side shocks that floating largely protects against' (p. 65), and they conclude that for the UK 'the consequences would be severe'. Of course, different underlying assumptions would lead to a different conclusion: computer simulations can never be conclusive.

*Regional difficulties*

One of the most difficult problems associated with economic and monetary union is the widely differing economic circumstances of the countries in the EU. This is a regional problem writ large. Although there are substantial regional differences *within* every EU country, these pale into insignificance when compared with those within the EU as a whole. Armstrong (1994, p. 355) points out that the most affluent ten regions within the EU have GDP per capita values more than three times higher than those in the bottom ten. Moreover, at the beginning of the 1990s, the worst 25 regions had unemployment rates more than five times higher then those in the best-performing regions. This has consequences for economic and monetary union, since there is a definite core–periphery pattern to these differences: the poorest regions are those in the periphery such as Greece, Portugal and Ireland as well as the north of Scotland and Northern Ireland. Critics of EMU argue that a single currency will create considerable cohesion problems because firms will tend to move to the core, so exacerbating the regional problem.

The argument is that economic development is a process of cumulative causation: rich regions attract new industry because of the markets they offer; this then makes them more attractive to other new industries, and so the process continues. For poor regions, the position is reversed, as firms in poor regions have smaller markets, local authorities have lower tax bases, so the area becomes unattractive and firms move out, creating a downward multiplier process.

It is argued the EMU will exacerbate these tendencies; Armstrong lists the reasons:

1. *Economies of scale*: Firms seeking to exploit economies of scale are more likely to be attracted to the core of the EU since they have the strongest markets and access to the whole EU market is easiest from central locations.
2. *Location economies*: These arise when firms in the same industry locate close to each other because they can then benefit from the proximity of trained labour, and can easily sub-contract work. When firms from many different industries locate closely together, they give rise to agglomeration economies such as better transport and financial facilities. This is more likely to occur in core rather than peripheral regions.
3. *Lack of competitiveness in peripheral regions*: Armstrong quotes research (IFO 1990) to show that peripheral regions face severe problems in meeting the competitive challenge posed by the core. The reasons include poor location, weak infrastructure and low skilled labour forces. One reason for this low skill is that highly qualified workers tend to migrate to more prosperous areas.

If this line of argument is accepted, then a single currency will exacerbate the EU's regional problem because it will strengthen the forces leading to a single market whilst at the same time weaken the ability of individual governments to take measures such as devaluation which might help these areas.

This line of argument has its critics. Market forces, they argue, will solve the problem so long as governments do not interfere. If market forces are prevalent, then in areas of high unemployment there will be less demand for labour, so wages will fall. This will attract new industry. At the same time workers will emigrate, so reducing the unemployment problem. In more prosperous areas, the influx of workers will tend to push down wages, but so long as wages remain relatively high firms will tend to move out. The overall effect will be a movement towards equilibrium, with wages and employment levels tending towards equality. Supporting evidence for this line of argument comes from trade unions in rich countries which fear competition from low cost producers in the periphery.

In this view of the world, there is no real regional problem; just problems caused by government interference in the operation of market forces. Hence there is no need for an EU regional policy; this will just tend to introduce inefficiencies.

So which theory is true? Not surprisingly, it is impossible to give a definitive answer as evidence is mixed. In the United Kingdom, for example, regional differences have persisted for many years; a map of unemployment in the 1930s would show many similarities to a map drawn today. For example, in both cases unemployment would be highest in Northern Ireland (though this is not conclusive because there are special factors operating there).This rigidity suggests that market forces will not solve the problem.

In any case, the operation of cumulative causation or market forces is very long term: for example, the consequences of the 1992 Single European Act will take many years to work themselves out. Nevertheless, Armstrong (1994, p. 364), reviewing the evidence suggests that 'cumulative causation has not occurred, nor is likely to occur in the EC'. Regional disparities narrowed over a long period until the mid 1970s when they widened for a few years. These now seem to have stabilised. Further evidence comes from the USA where regional differences have diminished over the years. Hence the evidence suggests that 'convergence forces at work eventually come to predominate over the divergent forces'.

If this is true, then the regional argument against EMU is weakened in the long run; but the problem is that in this case the long run is probably very long, so that to achieve cohesion within the EU substantial funds will be needed to reduce regional differences, and it is open to question whether or not the richer countries will be willing to pay the price.

*Political arguments*

The strongest arguments against EMU are put by those who emphasise the loss of sovereignty. Some of their arguments have already been mentioned. A country which controls its own money supply has more instruments than one in an economic union. Thus, assuming that there is a trade-off between inflation and unemployment – at least in the short run – a country may choose to have higher or lower rates of inflation or unemployment than those chosen by the supra-national authority. In addition, control over some aspects of fiscal policy might have to be abandoned under EMU since there will be strong pressures towards fiscal harmonisation.

However, the political arguments usually focus on the idea of the nation state. The United Kingdom, it is argued, is an independent country with the power to make its own decisions. Why should we cede this power to Brussels bureaucrats who may be acting in their own interest or in the interests of other countries? Decisions made outside this country are unlikely to be made in the interests of this country.

Critics of this line of argument suggest that 'sovereignty' is largely a myth. In practice, the powers of government are limited in a number of ways. If a multinational company decided to put up its prices, or transfer its factories elsewhere, there is little that the government can do to stop it. Similarly, if (say) the Bundesbank puts up its interest rates, money will flow from other countries to Germany, and this can only be stopped if interest rates in other countries are also increased. Hence national governments cannot really determine the interest rate. They add that by giving up power, countries may actually gain it, since at present they have no power over the decisions of the Bundesbank whilst in the decisions of a European Central Bank, all countries would have a say.

The arguments for and against EMU are nicely summarised by Crockett (1994, p. 183):

> Nobody can dispute that EMU will involve a combination of benefits and costs for participating countries. The benefits arise from the greater market integration and lower transaction costs that a single currency will permit. The costs arise from the loss of the exchange rate instrument as a means of maintaining external competitiveness, as well as from the inability to use an independent monetary policy as a means of responding to cyclical or other disturbances.

There is no final answer as to whether the costs will outweigh the benefits; as elsewhere in economic policy making, the values of the person making the judgement – in this case the extent of nationalistic feelings – will greatly affect the calculation.

## An independent central bank

One complication which arises in discussing EMU is that it is possible to be in favour of the idea, yet to dislike the actual arrangements made at Maastricht. The arguments of the German economists summarised above are an example.

The 1992 Treaty on European Union (Maastricht) made provision for an independent central bank. Its primary objective 'shall be to maintain price stability. Without prejudice to the objective of price stability, it shall support the general economic policies in the Community with a view to contributing to the achievement of the objectives of the Community' (Art.2 of the Protocol). Article 3 sets out its main tasks:

- to define and implement the monetary policy of the Community
- to conduct foreign exchange operations . . .
- to hold and manage the official foreign reserves of the Member states
- to promote the smooth operation of payment systems.

The Bank will have a small executive of six people who are responsible for the current business of the European Central Bank (ECB) and act in accordance with the instructions of the Governing Council, which is made up of the Executive, plus the Governors of the national central banks. The Governors will meet at least ten times a year, and voting will normally be on a qualified majority basis – i.e. there does not need to be unanimous agreement.

The case for central bank independence can be put quite simply. Proponents argue that inflation is the supreme economic evil; that it is caused by excessive increases in the money supply, and that governments do not have the willpower to control money supply. Instead they are liable to increase it when economic difficulties arise – or, for example, to stimulate the economy when elections are expected. An independent central bank can take a longer-term view, without having to worry about political considerations. Moreover, central bank independence will affect expectations about inflation, so that its very existence will modify behaviour, causing inflationary pressures to be reduced.

There is some evidence to support this argument. Neumann (1991) for example, analyses the performance of five European central banks, and the results, reproduced in Table 14.1 show that there is indeed evidence to suggest that independence is linked to low inflation.

However, the case for central bank independence is not universally accepted. In the first place, 'independence' is a matter of degree, and has several components. For example, central banks can differ in the extent to which they are required to make credit available to the government. At one extreme, this is done automatically, at low interest rates. At the other extreme, such loans are for short periods at market rates of interest. Similarly, in some countries the bank sets the discount rate; in others it does not. Perhaps more important, there is a political dimension to independence. In cases where the bank is largely independent, the governors are not subject to political direction, and they are appointed for long periods so that government's power to lean on them is limited.

TABLE 14.1   Average inflation record

| Central bank | 1960–88 | 1979–88 |
|---|---|---|
| Deutsche Bundesbank | 3.5 | 2.6 |
| Schweizerische Nationalbank | 3.9 | 2.6 |
| Banque de France | 6.9 | 7.1 |
| Bank of England | 7.9 | 7.4 |
| Banca d'Italia | 9.3 | 10.8 |

Source:  M. J. M. Neumann, 'Central bank independence as a prerequisite of price stability', *European Economy*, special edn no.1, Commission of the European Communities, pp. 77–106.

Using these dimensions, the proposed ESB will be on the 'very independent' end of the spectrum. That is not surprising, since its constitution is based largely on that of the German Bundesbank. It is therefore possible to argue that the ESB will be as successful in keeping down inflation as the German prototype has been.

However, the evidence between independence and low inflation is largely correlational. It may be true that countries with low inflation have central banks which are largely independent of government control; but this does not prove cause and effect. It is equally plausible that countries have low inflation for another reason – that the national culture is one which is strongly opposed to inflation, so that the country's institutions and practices are geared to this end. Where this is the case, bank independence is just one facet of the picture and not the cause. This is the reason why the German economists quoted above are not confident that the proposed ESB will succeed in keeping down inflation. The argument is developed by Currie (1992) who points out that monetary policy will be set by a committee of the governors of the central banks. This means that it will be possible for the policy preferences of the inflation-prone countries to dominate those of Germany and other low-inflation countries.

Sawyer (1994) puts another argument against central bank independence. He argues that giving the pursuit of low inflation top priority can have substantial adverse effects on other policy objectives; for example it can mean high interest rates which then lead to low growth and higher unemployment. Moreover, it may be that the relationship between money supply and prices is not that assumed by monetarists; possibly changes in the price level influence the money supply rather than the other way round. If this is so, then a central bank which had as its top priority the control of the money supply would be doomed to failure; but the consequences would be higher unemployment than would result from a policy which had different priorities.

## Conclusion

Economic and monetary union – if it comes about – will have a profound effect on the countries that participate, and also a significant effect on those that do not. The economic arguments are controversial, and in any case often subordinated to the political, but there is no doubt that there are powerful forces pushing for EMU by the end of the century. The precise form that this will take is still under discussion, and there are many details still to be determined, from the design of the coins to the date at which everyday transactions will take place in a single currency.

# Bibliography

Abel-Smith B. and Glennerster H. (1995) 'Labour and the Tory health reforms', *Fabian Review*, 107, 3, June, pp. 1–4.

ACAS (1992) *Annual Report*.

Adam Smith Institute (1994) *But Who will Regulate the Regulators*, London.

Akyuz, A. (1995) 'Taming international finance' in J. Michie and J. Grieve Smith (eds) *Managing the Global Economy*, Oxford University Press, Oxford.

Alchian, A. A. and Demsetz, H. (1972) 'Production, information costs, and economic organization', *American Economic Review*, 62, pp. 777–95.

Aldcroft, D. H. (1986) *The British Economy, vol. 1, Years of Turmoil 1920–1951*, Harvester, London.

Aldcroft, D. H. (1987) *From Versailles to Wall Street, 1919–1929*, Pelican, Harmondsworth.

Allen, J. and Massey, D. (1988) *The Economy in Question*, Sage, London.

Alogoskoufis, G. and Portes, R. (1991) 'International costs and benefits from EMU' in *European Economy*, Special edn no. 1.

Amin, A. and Robins, K. (1990) 'The re-emergence of regional economies? The mythical geography of flexible specialisation', *Environment and Planning D*, 8, pp. 7–34.

Amin, A. (1994a) 'The difficult transition from informal economy to Marshallian industrial district', *AREA*, 26, pp. 13–24.

Amin, A. (ed.) (1994) *Post Fordism: A Reader*, Blackwell, Oxford.

Anderson, K. and Blackhurst, R. (eds) (1993) *The Greening of World Issues*, Harvester-Wheatsheaf, London.

*Annual Abstract of Statistics* (1993), London, HMSO.

Appleby, J., Smith, P., Renade, W., Little, V. and Robinson, R. (1994) *Evaluating the NHS Reforms*, 'Monitoring Managed Competition' in R. Robinson and J. Le Grand, King's Fund Institute/Policy Journals, Newbury.

Armstrong H. W. (1994) 'EC Regional policy' in A. M. El-Agraa (ed.) *The Economics of the European Community*, Harvester Wheatsheaf, Hemel Hempstead.

Ashdown, P. (1995) 'The case for a single currency', *Economist*, 4, March, London.

Asheghian, P. (1995) *International Economics*, West Publishing, St Paul MN.

Atkinson, A. B. (1978) 'The Wealthy and the wealth tax', *New Society*, 9 Feb.

Atkinson, A. B. (1980) *Wealth, Income and Inequality*, 23nd edn, Oxford University Press, Oxford.

Atkinson, A. B. (1984) *The Economics of Inequality*, 2nd edn, Clarendon, Oxford.

Atkinson, J. (1984) 'Manpower strategies for flexible organisations', *Personnel Management*, Aug, pp. 28–31.

Atkinson, S. E. (1983) 'Pollution permits and acid rain externalities', *Canadian Journal of Economics*, 16, pp. 704–22.

Authers, J. (1994) 'London is biggest winner of regeneration funds', *Financial Times*, 7 December.

Bachtler, J. and Michie, R. (1993) 'The restructuring of regional policy in the European Community', *Regional Studies*, 27, 8, pp. 719–25.

Bacon R. and Eltis (1976) *Britain's Economic Problem: Too Few Producers*, London, Macmillan.

Baker, P. (1993a) 'The role of the small firm in locality restructuring', *AREA*, 25, pp. 37–44.

Baker, P. (1993b) 'Production restructuring in the textiles and clothing industries', *New Technology, Work and Employment*, 8, pp. 43–55.

Baker, P. (1995) 'Small firms, industrial districts and power asymmetries', *International Journal of Entrepreneurial Behaviour and Research*, 1, pp. 8–25.

Baldwin, R. E. (1991) 'On the microeconomics of the European monetary union', *European Economy*, special edition no. 1, Commission of the European Communities.

Ball, S. J., Bowe, J. and Gewirtz, S. (1994) 'Market forces and parental choice' in S. Tomlinson (ed.) *Educational Reform and Its Consequences*, IPPr/Rivers Crom Press, London.

Balls, E. (1993) 'Immigration route to labour market Flexibility', *Financial Times*, 8 November.

Barrett, S. (1991) 'Global warming: the economics of a carbon tax' in D. Pearce (ed.) *Blueprint 2: Greening the World Economy*, Earthscan, London.

Bassett, P. (1986) *Strike Free*, London, Macmillan.

Batchelor, C. (1995) 'Concerns increase over job security', *Financial Times*, 7 August.

Baumol, W. J. and Oates, W. E. (1988) *The Theory of Environmental Policy*, 2nd edn, Cambridge University Press, Cambridge.

Beatson, M. (1995) 'Progress towards a flexible labour market', *Employment Gazette*, February, pp. 55–66.

Beck, E., Lonsdale, S., Newman, S. and Patterson, D. (1992) *In the Best of Health?* Chapman and Hall, London.

Beesley, M. E. (1993) *Major Issues in Regulation*, Institute of Economic Affairs and London Business School.

Beesley, M. E. and Hamilton, R. T. (1984) 'Small firms' seedbed role and the concept of turbulence', *Journal of Industrial Economics*, 33, pp. 217–31.

Begg, I. Gudgin, G. and Morris, D. (1995) 'The assessment: regional policy in the European Union', *Oxford Review of Economic Policy*, 11, 2, pp. 1–17.

Benjamin, D. K. and Kochin, L. A. (1979) 'Searching for an explanation of unemployment in inter-war Britain', *Journal of Political Economy*, 3.

Benjamin, D. K. and Kochin, L. A. (1982) 'Unemployment and unemployment benefits in twentieth century Britain', *Journal of Political Economy*, 2.

Best, M. (1990) *The New Competition*, Polity, Oxford.

Beveridge, W. H. (1944) *Full Employment in a Free Society*, Allen & Unwin, London.

BiniSmaghi, S. and Vori, S. (9193) 'Rating the EU as an optimum currency area', *Banca d'Italia Temi di Discussione*, No. 187, January.

Binks, M. and Jennings, A. (1986) 'Small firms as a source of economic rejuvenation' in J. Curran, J. Stanworth and D. Watkins (eds) *The Survival of the Small Firm*, Gower, Aldershot.

Birch, D. (1979) *The Job Generation Process*, MIT Programme on Neighbourhood and Regional Change, Cambridge, Mass.

Blondal, S. and Pearson, M. (1995) 'Unemployment and other non-employment benefits', *Oxford Review of Economic Policy*, 11, 1, pp. 136–69.

Blyton, P. and Turnbull, P. (1994) *The Dynamics of Employee Relations*, London, Macmillan.

Bofinger, P. (1994) 'Is Europe an optimum currency area?' in A. Steinherr (ed.) *30 Years of European Monetary Integration: From the Werner Plan to EMU*, Longman, Harlow.

Bolton Report (1971) *Report of the Committee of Enquiry on Small Firms*, Cmnd. 4811, HMSO, London.

Booth, A. E. and Glynn, S. (1975) 'Unemployment in the inter-war period: a multiple problem', *Journal of Contemporary History*, vol. 10, pp. 611–36.

Borrie, G. (1993) 'How can UK competition policy be improved?' in M. E. Beesley, *Major Issues in Regulation*, Institute of Economic Affairs and London Business School.

Bosanquet, N. (1983) *After the New Right*, Heinemann, London.

Boyer, R. (1988) 'Defensive or offensive flexibility?' in R. Boyer (ed.) *The Search for Labour Market Flexibility*, Clarendon, Oxford.

Brown, A. J. (1972) *The Framework of Regional Economics in the United Kingdom*, Cambridge University Press, London.

Brunskill, I. (1992) *Making It*, Institute for Public Policy Research, London.

Buchanan, J. M. (1965) *The Inconsistencies of the National Health Service*, Institute of Economic Affairs, London.

Buckley, N. (1993) 'Burton cuts 2,000 full time jobs in move to part-time working', *Financial Times*, 8 January.

Budd, A. (1994) 'Economic policy – too important to be left to economists?', The Second Hilton Memorial Lecture, Southampton University, 8 February.

Button, K. J. (1994) *Transport Economics*, 2nd edn, Edward Elgar, Aldershot.

C.S.O. (1995) *Economic Trends*, no. 504, HMSO, October.

Cairncross, A. (1990) 'The United Kingdom' in A. Graham with A. Seldon (eds) *Government and Economies in the Postwar World*, London, Routledge.

Cairncross, A. (1994) 'Economic policy and performance 1964–1990' in R. Floud and D. N. McClosky (eds) *The Economic History of Britain Since 1700*, 2nd edn, vol. 3, Cambridge University Press, Cambridge.

Cameron, G. C. (1990) 'First steps in urban policy evaluation in the United Kingdom', *Urban Studies*, 27, 4, pp. 475–95.

Campbell, M., Daly, M., Gallagher, C. and Robson, G. (1991) 'Job creation 1987–1989: the contributions of small and large firms', *Employment Gazette*, November, pp. 589–94.

Capecchi, V. (1990) 'A history of flexible specialisation and industrial districts in Emilia-Romagna' in F. Pyke, G. Becattini and W. Sengenberger (eds) *Industrial Districts and Inter-Firm Co-operation in Italy*, ILO, Geneva.

Caporaso, J. A. and Levine, D. P. (1992) *Theories of Political Economy*, Cambridge University Press, Cambridge.

CBI Manufacturing Council (1992) *Making it in Britain*, London Confederation of British Industry.

Childs, D. (1979) *Britain Since 1945*, London, Methuen.

CIPFA (Chartered Institute of Public Finance and Accounts) (1994) *Education Statistics Estimates*, London.

Coase, R.H. (1960) 'The problem of social cost', *Journal of Law and Economics*, 3, pp. 1–44.

Coates, D. (1991) *UK Economic Decline: A Review of the Literature*, University of Leeds Centre for Industrial Policy and Performance.

Coates, D. (1995) 'UK Economic Underperformance: Causes and Cures' in G. B. J. Atkinson (ed.) *Developments in Economics*, vol. 11, Causeway, Ormskirk.

Cochrane, A. (1993) *Whatever Happened to Local Government?* Open University Press, Buckingham.

Cohen, D. K. and Farrar, E. 'Power to the Parents?' *The Public Interest*, 48, Summer, pp. 72–97.

Cohn, E. and Geske, T. G. (1990) *The Economics of Education*, Pergamon Oxford.

Cole, M. (1992) 'Education in the market place: a case of contradiction', *Educational Review*, 44, 3, pp. 325–43.

Constantine, S. (1944) *Unemployment in Britain between the Wars*, Longman, London.

Cooke, P. and Morgan, K. (1994) 'Growth Regions under Duress: Renewal Strategies in Baden Wurttemberg and Emilia-Romagna' in A. Amin and N. Thrift (eds) *Globalization, Institutions, and Regional Development in Europe*, Oxford University Press, Oxford.

Council/Commission of the European Communities (1992) *Treaty on European Union*, Brussels.

Coutts, K. and Godley, W. (1992) 'Does Britain's balance of payments matter any more' in J. Michie (ed.) *The Economic Legacy 1979–1992*, Academic, London.

Cowling, K. and Mueller, D. C. (1978) 'The Social Costs of Monopoly Power', *Economic Journal*, 88, December, pp. 727–48.

Cowling, K. and Sugden, R. (eds) (1990) *A New Economic Policy for Britain*, Manchester University Press, Manchester.

Crafts, N. F. R. (1988) 'British economic growth over the long run', *Oxford Review of Economic Policy*, 4, 1, Spring, i–xx1.

Crafts, N. F. R. and Woodward, N. (1991) (eds) *The British Economy since the War*, Oxford University Press, Oxford.

Crang, P. and Martin, R. (1991) 'Mrs Thatcher's vision of the "new Britain" and other sides of the Cambridge phenomenon', *Environment and Planning D*, 9, pp. 91–116.

Crick, M. (1985) *Scargill and the Miners*, Penguin, Harmondsworth.

Crockett, A. (1994) 'The role of convergence in the process of EMU' in A. Steinherr (ed.) *30 Years of European Monetary Integration*, Longman, London.

Cropper, M. L. and Oates, W. E. (1992) 'Environmental economics', *Journal of Economic Literature*, 30, pp. 675–740.

Culyer, A. J. (1993) 'Health care insurance and provision' in N. Barr and D. Whynes (eds), *Current Issues in the Economics of Welfare*, Macmillan, Basingstoke.

Culyer, A. J. and Posnett, J. 'Hospital Behaviour and Competition' in A. J. Culyer, A. K. Maynard and J. W. Posnett (1990) *Competition in Health Care*, Macmillan, Houndmills.

Culyer, A. J. and Wagstaff, A. (1992) *Need, Equity and Equality in Health and Health Care*, University of York Centre for Health Economics.

Curran, J. and Blackburn, R. (1994) *Small Firms and Local Economic Networks: The Death of the Local Economy?* PCP, London.

Currie, D. (1992) 'European monetary union: institutional structure and economic performance', *Economic Journal*, March, pp. 248–64.

D.E.S. (1989) *The Education Reform Act: Local Management of Schools*, 7/88, D.E.S. London.

Daly, M. and McCann, A. (1992) 'How many small firms?' *Employment Gazette*, February, pp. 47–51.

Daly, M., Campbell, M., Gallagher, C. and Robson, G. (1991) 'Job creation 1987–1989: the contributions of large and small firms', *Employment Gazette*, November, pp. 589–94.

Dasgupta, A. K. (1985) *Epochs of Economic Theory*, Blackwell, Oxford.

Dasgupta, P. S. (1990) 'The environment as a commodity', *Oxford Review of Economic Policy*, 6, pp. 80–108.

Davoudi, S. and Healey, P. (1995) 'City challenge: sustainable process or empty gesture?' *Environment and Planning C: Government and Policy*, 13, 1, pp. 79–95.

Deakin, S. and Wilkinson, F. (1991) 'Labour law, social security and economic inequality' *Cambridge Journal of Economics*, 15, pp. 125–48.

Denison, E. F. (1969) *Accounting for United States Economic Growth 1929–1969*, Brookings Institute.

Department of Health *(1989) Working for Patients*, London, HMSO.

Department of Health (1993) *The Government's Expenditure Plans 1993/1994 to 1995/96*, Department Report, Cm 2212, HMSO, London.

Department of Trade and Industry (1988) *Review of Restrictive Trade Practices Policy*, Green Paper, Cmnd 331, HMSO, London.

Devine, P. J., Lee, N., Jones, R. M., Tysons, W. J. (1985) *An Introduction to Industrial Economics*, 4th edn, George Allen & Unwin, London.

DFE (Department for Education) (1993) 'International statistical comparisons of the participation in education and training of 16 to 18 year olds', *Statistical Bulletin*, 19/93.

DFE (1995) *Department for Education and Employment News*, 161/95.
DHSS (Department of Health and Social Security) (1976) *Sharing Resources for Health in England*, HMSO, London.
DHSS (1983) *Health Care and its Costs: the Development of the NHS in Britain*, HMSO, London.
Dietrich, M. (1992) 'The foundations of industrial policy' in K. Cowling and R. Sugden (eds) *Current Issues in Industrial Economic Strategy*, Manchester, Manchester University Press.
Dietrich, M. (1994) *Transaction Cost Economics and Beyond*, Routledge, London.
Directorate General for Economic and Financial Affairs (1994) 'ERM tensions and monetary policies in 1993', *European Economy*, 56, Brussels.
Doeringer, P. and Piore, M. (1971) *Internal Labour Markets and Manpower Adjustment*, D.C. Heath, Lexington, MA.
Dolton, P. (1992) 'The market for qualified manpower in the UK', *Oxford Review of Economic Policy*, 8, 2, pp. 103–29.
DTI (1989) *Opening New Markets: New Policy on Restrictive Trade Practices*, White Paper, Cmnd 727, HMSO, London.
DTI press notice, 20 October 1993 (p/93/615).
DTI (1995) *Small Firms in Britain: Report 1995*. HMSO, London.
Durkheim, E. (1956) *Education and Sociology*, trans. S.O.Fox, Free Press, Free Press.
Dyson, K. (1994) *The Process of Economic and Monetary Union in Europe*, Longman, London.
Eatwell, J. (1982) *Whatever Happened to Britain?* London, BBC.
Eatwell, J. (1994) 'Institutions, efficiency, and the theory of economic policy,' *Social Research*, 61, pp. 35–54.
*Economist, The* (1995a) 'Labour market trends', 29 July, p. 92.
*Economist, The* (1995b) *Economist Intelligence Unit Yearbook, 1994–95*, London.
Eichengreen, B. and Mclean, I. W. (1994) 'The supply of gold under the pre-1914 gold standard', *Economic History Review*, 47, 2, pp. 288–309.
Eichner, A. S. (1983) *Why Economics is Not Yet a Science*, Macmillan, London.
El-Agraa A. M. (ed.) (1994) *The Economics of the European Community*, 4th edn, Harvester Wheatsheaf, Hemel Hempstead.
Eldridge, J., Cressey, P. and MacInnes, J. (1991) *Industrial Sociology and Economic Crisis*, Harvester Wheatsheaf, Hertfordshire.
Emerson, M. (1990) 'One market, one money' in K. O. Pohl (ed.) *Britain and EMU*, Centre for Economic Performance, London School of Economics.
Enthoven, A. C. (1985) *Reflections on the Management of the National Health Service*, Nuffield Provincial Hospitals Trust, London.
EOC (Equal Opportunities Commission) (1995) *Targeting Potential Discrimination*, Manchester, EOC.
European Communities (1991) *European Industrial Policy for the 1990s*, Brussels, Bulletin of the European Communities Supplement, 3/91.
Feinstein, C. (1988) 'Economic growth since 1870: Britain's performance in international perspective', *Oxford Review of Economic Policy*, 4, 1.
Feinstein, C. (1990) 'Benefits of backwardness and costs of continuity' in A. Graham with A. Seldon (eds) *Government and Economies in the Postwar World*, London, Routledge.
Ferguson, P. R. and Ferguson, G. J. (1994) *Industrial Economics: Issues and Perspectives*, 2nd edn, Macmillan, London.
Field, F. (1989) *Losing Out*, Blackwell, Oxford.
*Financial Times, The* (1994) 'OECD criticises record of Tecs', 6 July.
Fine, B. and Harris, L. (1985) *The Peculiarities of the British Economy*, Lawrence & Wishart.

Finegold, D. and Soskice, D .(1988) 'The failure of training in Britain', *Oxford Review of Economic Policy*, 4, 3, pp. 21–2.

Fisher, A. and Peterson, F. M. (1976) 'The environment in economics: a survey', *Journal of Economic Literature*, 14, pp. 1–33.

Fitzpatrick, R. and Dunnell, K. (1992) 'Measuring outcomes in health care' in E. Beck *et al*, *In the Best of Health?* Chapman & Hall, London.

Floud, R. (1944) 'Britain 1860–1914: a survey' in R. Floud and D. N. McCloskey (eds) *The Economic History of Britain since 1700*, 2nd edn, vol. II, Cambridge University Press, Cambridge.

Fothergill, S. and Gudgin, G. (1982) *Unequal Growth*, Heinemann, London.

Freeman, C. (1982) *The Economics of Industrial Innovation*, London, Francis Pinter.

Friedman, M. and Friedman R. (1980) *Free to Choose*, Penguin, Harmondsworth.

Friedman, M. and Schwartz, A. (1963) *A Monetary History of the United States*, Princeton University Press, Princton, NJ.

Galbraith, J. K. (1975) *Economics and the Public Purpose* Penguin, Harmondsworth.

Galbraith, J. K. (1977) *The Affluent Society*, 3rd edn, Deutch, New York.

Galbraith, J. K. (1985) *The Anatomy of Power*, Corgi, Uxbridge.

Garnsey, E. and Cannon-Brookes, A. (1993) 'Small, high technology firms in an era of rapid change: evidence from Cambridge', *Local Economy*, 7, pp. 318–33.

George, K. (1989) 'Do we need a merger policy?' in J. A. Fairburn and J. Kay (eds) *Mergers and Merger Policy*, Oxford, Oxford University Press.

Geroski, P. A. (1990) 'Encouraging investment in science and technology' in K. Cowling and R. Sugden (eds) *Economic Policy for Britain*, Manchester University Press.

Giddens. A. (1981) *The Class Structure of the Advanced Societies*, 2nd edn, Hutchinson, London.

Giles, C. and Johnson, P. (1994) *Taxes Down, Taxes Up: The effects of a Decade of Tax Changes*, Institute of Fiscal Studies, Commentary no. 41, London.

Gilmour, I. (1983) *Britain can Work*, Martin Robertson, Oxford.

Glyn, A. (1995) 'The assessment: unemployment and inequality', *Oxford Review of Economic Policy*, 11, 1, pp. 1–25.

Goodhart, D. (1994) 'Sock shop becomes a follower of fashion', *Financial Times*, 26 January.

Graham, A. W. M. (1985) 'Inflation and unemployment' in D. Morris (ed.) *The Economic System in the UK*, 3rd edn, Oxford University Press, Oxford.

Granovetter, M. (1985) 'Economic action and social structure: the problem of embeddedness', *American Journal of Sociology*, 91, pp. 481–510.

Grant, W. (1993) *The Politics of Economic Policy*, Harvester Wheatsheaf, Hemel Hempstead.

Grant, W. and Nath, S. (1984) *The Politics of Economic Policymaking*, Blackwell, Oxford.

Gravelle, H. and Rees, R. (1992) *Microeconomics*, 2nd edn, Longman, Harlow.

Gray, J. (1990) 'Hayek on the market economy and the limits of state action', in D. Helm (ed.) *The Economic Borders of the State*, Oxford University Press, Oxford, pp. 127–43.

Griffiths. A. and Wall, S. (1993) *Applied Economics*, 5th edn, Longman, London.

*Guardian* (11 October 1995) 'Boom in NHS top staff'.

*Guardian* (9 March 1994) 'Grey suits face cuts in NHS purge'.

Gudgin, G. (1995) 'Regional problems and policy in the UK', *Oxford Review of Economic Policy*, 11, 2, pp. 18–63.

Guerney, A. (1987) 'Labour market signals and graduate output: a case study of the university sector' in H. Thomas and T. Simkins (eds) *Economics and the Management of Education*, Falmer Press, Lewes..

Hahn, F. (1993) 'James Meade and benevolence' in A. B. Atkinson (ed.) *Alternatives to Capitalism: The Economics of Partnership*, Macmillan, London.

Hakim, C. (1989) 'New recruits to self-employment in the 1980's', *Employment Gazette*, June, pp. 286–97.

Harberger, A. C. (1954) 'Monopoly and Resource Allocation', *American Economic Review*, vol. 45, May, pp. 77–87.

Hare, P. and Simpson, L. (1993) *British Economic Policy: A Modern Introduction*, Harvester Wheatsheaf, Hemel Hempstead.

Harrison, S., Hunter, D. J. and Pollitt, C. (1990) *The Dynamics of British Health Policy*, Unwin Hyman, London.

Hay, D. (1993) 'The assessment of competition policy', *Oxford Review of Economic Policy*, 9, 2, pp. 1–26.

Hayek, F. A. (1944; reprinted 1976) *The Road to Serfdom*, Routledge & Kegan Paul, London.

Hayek, F. A. (1980) *Unemployment and the Unions*, London, Institute of Economic Affairs.

Hayes, P. and Smith, K. (eds) (1993) *The Global Greenhouse Regime: Who Pays?* Earthscan, London.

Healey, N. M. (ed.) (1995) *The Economics of the New Europe*, Routledge, London.

Heath, A., Jowell, R. and Curtice, J. (1991) *Understanding Political Change*, Pergamon Press, Oxford.

Helm, D. (ed.) (1990) *The Economic Borders of the State*, Oxford University Press, Oxford.

Hendry, D. F. and Ericsson, N. R. (1983) 'Assertion without empirical basis; an econometric appraisal of Friedman and Schwartz' monetary trends in the United Kingdom', *Bank of England Panel Paper no.22.*

Henry, N. (1992) 'The new industrial spaces: locational logic of a new industrial era?' *International Journal of Urban and Regional Research*, 16, 375–96.

Hibbard, J. H. and Weeks, E. C. (1989) 'Does the dissemination of comparative data on physician fees affect consumer use of services?', *Medical Care*, 27, 12, pp. 1167–74.

Hirst, P. and Zeitlin, J. (1992) 'Flexible specialisation versus post-Fordism' in M. Storper and A. J. Scott (eds) *Pathways to Industrialization and Regional Development*, Routledge, London.

Hitiris, T. (1994) *European Community Economics*, 3rd edn, Harvester Wheatsheaf, London.

HMSO (1965) *The National Plan*, London.

HMSO (1977) *A Policy for the Inner Cities*, Cm 6845, London.

HMSO (1989) *Employment for the 1990s*, HMSO, London.

HMSO (1989) *Working for Patients*, HMSO, London.

HMSO (1990) *Highly Qualified People: supply and demand*, HMSO, London HMSO.

HMSO (1992) *Choice and Diversity: A New Framework for Schools*, Cm 2021.

HMSO (1993) *Access to and Availability of Specialist Services*, Clinical Standards Advisory Group.

HMSO (1994a) *Assessing the Impact of Urban Policy*, HMSO, London.

HMSO (1994b) *Competitiveness: Helping Business to Win*, Cm 2563, London, May.

HMSO (1994c) *Social Trends*, no. 24, HMSO, London.

HMSO (1995) *Forging Ahead*, Cm 2867, May, London.

HMSO *Social Trends*, various issues, London.

Hobsbawm, E. (1968) *Industry and Empire*, Pantheon, New York.

Hodgson, G. (1984) *The Democratic Economy: A New Look at Planning, Markets and Power*, Penguin, Harmondsworth.

Hodgson, G. (1988) *Economics and Institutions: A Manifesto for a Modern Institutional Economics*, Polity, Cambridge.

House of Commons (1994) *Competitiveness of UK Manufacturing Industry*, Trade and Industry Committee, Second Report, HMSO, London.

Howson, S. (1994) 'Money and monetary policy in Britain 1945–1990' in R. Floud and D. N. McCloskey (eds) *The Economic History of Britain since 1700*, 2nd edn, 3, Cambridge University Press.

Hutton, W. (1994) 'Gentlemanly capitalism and the loss of British industrial vitality', *University of Leeds Centre for Industrial Policy and Performance Bulletin no. 6.*

Hutton, W. (1995) *The State We're In,* Jonathan Cape, London.

IFO (1990) 'An empirical assessment of the factors shaping regional competitiveness in problem regions. A study carried out for the EC Commission'.

Imrie, R. and Thomas, H. (eds) (1993) *British Urban Policy and the Development Corporations,* Paul Chapman, London.

*Independent on Sunday,* 17 September 1995, 'Cost of red tape strangling NHS'.

IOD (Institute of Directors) (1992) *Small Firms in the UK Economy: A Business Leader's View,* IOD, London.

Isaac, A. G. (1994) 'Hysterisis' in P. Arestis and M. Sawyer (eds) *The Elgar Companion to Radical Political Economy,* Edward Elgar, Aldershot.

Jacobs, M. (1991) *The Green Economy, Environment, Sustainable development and the Politics of the Future,* Pluto, London.

Jacquemin, A. P. (1990) 'Mergers and competition policy' in P. H. Admiraal (ed.) *The European Community,* Basil Blackwell, Oxford.

Jessop, B. (1992) *Changing forms and function of the state in an era of globalization and regionalization,* Paper presented to EAPE Conference, Paris, 4–7.

Johnes, G. (1993a) 'A degree of waste: a dissenting view', *Oxford Review of Education,* 19, 4, pp. 459–64.

Johnes, G. (1993b) *The Economics of Education,* Macmillan, Basingstoke.

Johnson, C. (1991) *The Economy under Mrs Thatcher 1979–1990,* Penguin, Harmondsworth.

Johnson, P. and Webb, S. (1993) 'Explaining the growth in the UK income inequality 1979–1988', *Economic Journal,* 103, March.

Johnston, R. J. (1989) *Environmental Problems: Nature, Economy and State,* Belhaven, London.

Joseph Rowntree Foundation (1995) *Inquiry into Income and Wealth, vol. 1,* Joseph Rowntree Foundation, York.

Kaldor, N. (1970) 'The case for regional policies', *Scottish Journal of Political Economy,* Nov, pp. 337–48.

Kamerschen D. R. (1966) 'An estimation of the welfare losses from monopoly in the American economy', *Western Economic Journal,* 4, Summer.

Kay, J. A. and King, M. A. (1991) *The British Tax System,* 5th edn, Oxford University Press, Oxford.

Keasey, K. and Watson, R. (1993) *Small Firm Management: Ownership, Finance and Performance,* Blackwell, Oxford.

Keep, E. (1992) 'Schools in the market place' in G Wallace (ed.) *Local Management of Schools,* Bera Dialogue no. 6, Multilingual Matters Ltd, Cleveland.

Kenen, P. B. (1995) 'Capital controls, the EMS and EMU' *Economic Journal* Vol 105, No. 428, January.

Kenwood, A. G. and Lougheed, A. L. (1992) *The Growth of the International Economy 1820–1990,* 3rd edn, Routledge, London.

Keynes, J. M. (1936) *The General Theory of Employment, Interest and Money,* London, Macmillan.

Keynes, J. M. (1944) *How to Pay for the War,* Macmillan, London.

Klamer, A. (1984) *The New Classical Macroeconomics,* Wheatsheaf, Brighton.

Koutsoyiannis, A. (1979) *Modern Microeconomics,* 2nd edn, Macmillan, London.

Labour Party (1989) *Meet the Challenge, Make the change,* London.

Labour Party (1994a) *Winning for Britain,* London.

Labour Party (1994b) *Rebuilding the Economy,* London.

Laidler, D. and Estrin, S. (1989) *Introduction to Microeconomics,* 3rd edn, Philip Allan, London.

Lancaster, K. (1983) *Introduction to Modern Microeconomics*, 2nd edn, Costello, Tunbridge Wells.

Lawless, P. (1991) 'Urban policy in the Thatcher decade: English inner city policy, 1979–1990', *Environment and Planning C: Government and Policy*, 9, pp. 15–30.

Layard, R. (1988) *How to Beat Unemployment*, Oxford University Press, Oxford.

Layard, R. (1995) 'A skilful step to the future', *Financial Times*, 5 September.

Layard, R. and Nickell, S. (1985) 'The causes of British unemployment', *National Institute Economic Review*, April.

Layard, R., Nickell, S. and Jackman, R. (1994) *The Unemployment Crisis*, Oxford University Press, Oxford.

Lazerson, M. (1993) 'Factory or putting-out? Knitting networks in Modena', in G. Grabher (ed.) *The Embedded Firm: On the Socioeconomics of Industrial Networks*, Routledge London.

Lazonick, W. (1993) *Business Organization and the Myth of the Market Economy*, Cambridge University Press, Cambridge.

Le Grand, J., Winter, D. and Woolley, F. 'The National Health Service: safe in whose hands' in J. Hills (ed.) *The State of Welfare*, Clarendon, Oxford.

Letwin, O. (1988) *Privatising the World*, Cassell, London.

Levačić, R. (1993) 'Assessing the impact of formula funding on schools', unpublished ms.

Littlechild S. C. (1981) 'Misleading calculations of the social costs of monopoly power', *Economic Journal*, 91, June, pp. 348–63.

Loveman, G. and Sengenberger, W. (1990) 'Economic and social reorganisation in the small and medium-sized enterprise sector' in W. Sengenberger, G. W. Loveman and M. J. Piore (eds) *The Re-Emergence of Small Enterprises*, ILO, Geneva.

Machin, S. and Wadhwani, S. (1991) 'The effects of unions on organisational change and employment', *Economic Journal*, 101.

MacKinnon, M. (1994) 'Living standards 1870–1914' in R. Floud and D. N. McClosky (eds) *The Economic History of Britain since 1700*, 2nd edn, vol. II, Cambridge University Press, Cambridge.

Maclure, S. *(1965) Educational Documents*, Methuen, London.

Magatti, M. (1993) 'The market and social forces: a comparative analysis of industrial change', *International Journal of Urban and Regional Research*, 17, pp. 213–31.

Mahon, A., Wilkin, D. and Whitehouse, C. (1994) 'Choice of hospital for elective surgery: GPs' and patients' views' in R. Robinson and J. Le Grand (eds) *Evaluating the NHS Reforms*, King's Fund Institute/Policy Journals, Newbury.

Malecki, E. J. (1991) *Technology and Economic Development: The Dynamics of Local, Regional and National Change*, Longman, Harlow.

Maler, K-G, (1990) 'International economic problems', *Oxford Review of Economic Policy*, 6, pp. 80–108.

Marginson, P. (1993) 'Power and efficiency in the firm: understanding the employment relationship', in C. Pitelis (ed.) *Transaction Costs, Markets and Hierarchies*, Blackwell, Oxford.

Marglin, S. (1974) 'What do bosses do? The origins and functions of hierarchy in capitalist production', *The Review of Radical Political Economy*, 6, pp. 33–60.

Markandya, A. (1991) 'Global warming: the economics of tradeable permits' in D. Pearce (ed.) *Blueprint 2: Greening of the World Economy*, Earthscan, London.

Marsh, D. (1992) *The New Politics of British Trade Unionism*, London, Macmillan.

Marshall, A. (1892) *Elements of Economics of Industry*, Macmillan, London.

Martin, R. (1988) 'Industrial capitalism in transition: the contemporary reorganization of the British space economy', in D. Massey and J. Allen (eds) *Uneven Re-Development: Cities and Regions in Transition*, Hodder & Stoughton, London.

Marx, K. and Engels F. (1988) [1848] *The Communist Manifesto*, Pathfinder, New York.

Mason, B. and Bain, P. (1993) 'The determinants of trade union membership in Britain: a survey of the literature', *Industrial and Labour Relations Review*, 46, 2, pp. 332–51.

Mason, C. (1988) *Explaining Recent Trends in UK New Firm Formation Rates: Evidence From Two Surveys in South Hampshire*, Urban Policy Research Unit Working Papers, Department of Geography, University of Southampton.

Masson, P. R. (1995) 'Gaining and losing ERM credibility: the case of the United Kingdom', *Economic Journal*, 105, May.

Matsumoto, G. (1992) 'The work of the Ministry of Trade and Industry' in K. Cowling and R. Sugden (eds) *A New Economic Policy for Britain*, Manchester University Press.

Maynard, A. (1975) *Experiment with Choice in Education*, Institute of Economic Affairs, London.

McCombie, J. and Thirlwall, T. (1992) 'Comment: the re-emergence of the balance of payments constraint' in J. Michie (ed.) *The Economic Legacy 1979–1992*, Academic Press, London.

McFarlane, H. and Mortimer-Lee, P. (1994) 'Inflation over 300 years', *Bank of England Quarterly Bulletin*, 34, 2 May.

McGregor, A. and Sproull, A. (1992) 'Employers and the flexible workforce', *Employment Gazette*, May, pp. 225–34.

McIlroy, J. (1991) *The Permanent Revolution: Conservative Law and the Trade Unions*, Spokesman, Nottingham.

Metcalf D. (1989) 'Trade unions and economic performance: the British evidence', *LSE Quarterly*, 3, pp. 21–42.

Metcalf, D. (1990) 'Movement in motion', *Marxism Today*, September, 32–5.

Michie, J. and Grieve Smith J. eds (1994) *Unemployment in Europe*, Academic Press, London.

Michie, J. and Grieve Smith, J. (eds) (1995) *Managing the Global Economy*, Oxford University Press, Oxford.

Michie, J. and Wilkinson, F. (1992) 'Inflation policy and the restructuring of labour markets' in J. Michie (ed.) *The Economic Legacy 1979–1992*, Academic Press, London.

Micklewright, J., Pearson, M. and Smith, S. (1989) 'Has Britain an early school leaving problem?', *Fiscal Studies*, 10, 8, Feb, pp. 1–16.

Miliband, R. (1982) *Capitalist Democracy in Britain*, Oxford University Press, Oxford.

Mill, J. S. (1848) *Principles of Political Economy*, vol. 2, Parker, London.

Miller, D. (1990) 'The future of local economic policy: a public and private sector function' in M. Campbell (ed.) *Local Economic Policy*, Cassell, London.

Minford, P. (1985) *Unemployment: Cause and Cure*, 2nd edn, Blackwell, Oxford.

Minford, P. (1991) *The Supply Side Revolution in Britain*, Edward Elgar, Aldershot.

Minford, P. (1995) 'What price European Monetary Union' in N. M. Healey (ed.) *The Economics of the New Europe*, Routledge, London.

Minford, P. and Rastogi, A. (1990) 'The price of EMU' in K. O. Pohl (ed.) *Britain and EMU*, London Centre for Economic Performance, London Select Economics, pp. 47–67.

Mitchell, B. R. and Deane, P. (1962) *Abstract of British Historical Statistics*, Cambridge, Cambridge University Press.

Morgan, E. J. (1995) 'EU competition policy and the single market', *Economics and Business Education*, III, 1, Spring.

Morris, D. (ed.) (1985) *The Economic System in the UK*, Oxford University Press, Oxford.

Mueller, D. (1980) *The Determinants and Effects of Mergers: An International Comparison*, Cambridge, Oelgeschlager, Gum and Marin.

Mundell, R. (1961) 'A theory of optimum currency areas', *American Economic Review*, 51, pp. 657–65.

Murphy, J. (1993) 'A degree of waste: the economic benefits of educational expansion', *Oxford Review of Education*, 19, 1, pp. 9–31.

Murray, F. (1987) 'Flexible specialisation in the "Third Italy"', *Capital and Class*, 33, pp. 84–95.

Murray, R. (1991) *Local Space: Europe and the New Regionalism*, CLES, Manchester.

National Economic Development Council (1984) *Competence and Competition*, London.

Neumann, M. J. M. (1991) 'Central bank independence as a prerequisite of price stability', *European Economy*, special edn no. 1, Commission of the European Communities, pp. 77–106.

Nickell, S. *et al.* (1989) 'Unions and productivity growth: evidence from UK company accounts data 1972–86', *London School of Economics Quarterly*, June.

Normand, C. E. M. (1990) 'Reflections on the reform of the National Health Service', *European Economic Review*, 34, 2/3, pp. 625–31.

Nozick, R. (1974) *Anarchy, State and Utopia*, Blackwell, Oxford.

Oates, W. (ed.) (1992) *The Economics of the Environment*, Edward Elgar, Aldershot.

OECD (1995) *Main Economic Indicators*, October, OECD, Paris.

Office of Fair Trading (1973) *Mergers*, HMSO.

Ormerod, P. (1994) *The Death of Economics*, Faber & Faber, London.

Panić, M. (1995) 'The Bretton Woods system: concept and practice' in J. Michie and J. Grieve Smith (eds) *Managing the Global Economy*.

Parker, D. (1995) 'Has privatisation improved performance?' in G. B. J. Atkinson (ed.) *Developments in Economics*, vol. 11, Causeway, Ormskirk.

Parkinson, M. and Evans, R. (1990) 'Urban development corporations' in M. Campbell (ed.) *Local Economic Policy*, Cassell, London.

Pearce, D. (ed.) (1991) *Blueprint 2: Greening of the World Economy*, Earthscan, London.

Pearce, D. and Turner, R. K. (1990) *Economics of Natural Resources and the Environment*, Harvester Wheatsheaf, Hemel Hempstead.

Peck, J. and Emmerich, M. (1993) 'Training and enterprise councils: time for change', *Local Economy*, 8, 1, 4–20.

Peden, G. C. (1991) *British Economic and Social Policy: Lloyd George to Margaret Thatcher*, 2nd edn, Philip Allen, Oxford.

Phelps-Brown, H. (1988) *Egalitarianism and the Generation of Inequality*, Oxford, Oxford University Press.

Phillips, A. W. (1958) 'The relation between unemployment and the rate of change of money wages in the UK 1861–1957', *Economica*, 25.

Pigou, A. C. (1932) *The Economics of Welfare*, 4th edn, Macmillan, London.

Piore, M. J. and Sabel, C. (1984) *The Second Industrial Divide: Posibilities for Prosperity*, Basic Books, New York.

Pollert, A. (1988) 'Dismantling flexibility', *Capital and Class*, 34, pp. 42–75.

Prais, S. J. (1988) 'Qualified manpower in engineering' *National Institute Economic Review*, 127, Feb, pp. 76–83.

Price, C. (1994) 'Economic regulation of privatised monopolies' in P. M. Jackson and C. M. Price (eds) *Privatisation and Regulation*, Longman, London.

Price, Victoria Curzon (1981) *Industrial Policies in the European Community*, London, Macmillan for the Trade Policy Research Centre.

Psacharopoulos, G. (1985) 'Returns to education: a further international update and implications', *Journal of Human Resources*, 20, Fall, 583–604.

Rainnie, A. (1991) 'Just-in-time sub-contracting and the small firm', *Work, Employment and Society*, 5, pp. 353–75.

Rainnie, A. (1993) 'The reorganisation of large firm subcontracting: myth and reality', *Capital and Class*, 49, pp. 53–75.

Rawls, J. (1973) *A Theory of Justice*, Oxford University Press, Oxford.

Riddell, P. (1983) *The Thatcher Government*, Martin Robertson, Oxford.

Robinson, F. and Shaw, K. (1994) 'Urban policy under the Conservatives: in search of the big idea?' *Local Economy*, 9, 3, pp. 224–35.

Robinson, J. (1979) *Contributions to Modern Economics*, Basil Blackwell, Oxford.

Robinson, J. and Luft, H. 'Competition and the cost of hospital care', *Journal of Health Economics*, 4, pp. 333–56.

Robinson, R. and Le Grand, J. (1994) *Evaluating the NHS Reforms*, King's Fund Institute/ Policy Journals, Newbury.

Rowntree Foundation (1995) *Inquiry into Income and Wealth*, Joseph Rowntree Foundation, York.

Rowthorn, Bob (1984) *Capitalism, Conflict and Inflation*, Lawrence & Wishart, London.

Rowthorn, Bob (1992) 'Government spending and taxation in the Thatcher era' in J. Mitchie (ed.) *The Economic Legacy 1979–1992*, Academic, London.

Rowthorn, R. (1995) 'Capital formation and unemployment', *Oxford Review of Economic Policy*, Oxford.

Royal Commission on the Distribution of Income and Wealth (1977) Report No.5, Cmnd 6999, London.

*Royal Commission on the NHS* (1979) HMSO, London.

Rubenstein, W. D. (1986) *Wealth and Inequality in Britain*, Faber & Faber, London.

Rubenstein, W. D. (1994) *Capitalism, Culture and Decline in Britain 1750–1990*, Routledge, London.

Rubinstein W. D. (1988) 'Social class, social attitudes and British business life', *Oxford Review of Economic Policy*, 4, 1.

Samuels, W. J. (ed.) (1979) *The Economy as a System of Power*, Transaction, New Brunswick.

Sanderson, M. (1988) 'Education and economic decline 1890–1980s', *Oxford Review of Economic Policy*, 4, 1, pp. 38–58.

Sapir, A., Buigues, P. and Jacqueman, A. (1993) 'European competition policy in manufacturing and services: a two speed approach?', *Oxford Review of Economic Policy*, 9, 2, pp. 113–32.

Saul S. B. (1965) 'The export economy, 1870–1914', *Yorkshire Bulletin of Economic and Social Research*, 17, pp. 5–18.

Sawyer, M. (1992) 'On the theory of industrial policy' in K. Cowling and R. Sugden (eds) *Current Issues in Industrial Economic Strategy*, Manchester University Press.

Sawyer, M. (1994) 'The case against an independent central bank', *University of Leeds Centre for Industrial Policy and Performance Bulletin no. 4*, Spring.

Sawyer, M. C. (1989) *The Challenge of Radical Political Economy: An Introduction to the Alternatives to Neo-Classical Economics*, Harvester Wheatsheaf, Hemel Hempstead.

Scambler, G. (1992) 'Recruitment and remuneration in health care' in E. Beck *et al*, (eds) *In the Best of Health*, Chapman & Hall, London.

Schotter, A. (1990) *Free Market Economics*, 2nd edn, Blackwell, Oxford.

Schumpeter, J. (1942) *Capitalism, Socialism and Democracy*, Harper & Row, New York.

Scitovsky, T. (1951) 'The State of welfare economics', *American Economic Review*, 41, 303–15.

Sen, A. (1970) *Collective Choice and Social Welfare*, Holden-Day, San Francisco.

Sen, A. (1987) *On Ethics and Economics*, Blackwell, Oxford.

Shand, A. H. (1990) *Free Market Morality: The Political Economy of the Austrian School*, Routledge, London.

Shapiro, M. and Ahlburg, D. (1983) 'Suicide: the ultimate cost of unemployment' *Journal of Post Keynesian Economics*, pp. 276–80.

Sheldrake, J. and Vickerstaff, S. (1987) *The History of Industrial Training in Britain*, Avebury, Aldershot.

Shone, R. (1989) *Open Economy Macroeconomics: Theory, Policy and Evidence*, Harvester Wheatsheaf, Hemel Hempstead.

Sked, A. and Cook, C. (1984) *Post-War Britain*, 2nd edn, Penguin, Harmondsworth.

Smith, A. (1776) Reprinted 1970. *The Wealth of Nations*, ed. A.S. Skinner, Penguin, London.

Smith, P. and Morton, G. (1994) 'Union exclusion: the next steps', *Industrial Relations Journal*, 25, 1, pp. 3–14.

Smith,T. and Noble, M. (1995) *Education Divides*, Child Poverty Action Group, London.

Smithers, A. and Robinson, P. (1989) *Increasing Participation in Higher Education*, School of Education, University of Manchester.

Snower, D. (1995) 'Evaluating unemployment policies: what do the underlying theories tell us?', *Oxford Review of Economic Policy*, 11, 1, pp. 110–35.

Stark, T. (1987) *Income and Wealth in the 1980s*, Fabian Society, London.

Steedman, H., Mason, G. and Wagner, K. (1991) 'Intermediate skills in the workplace: deployment, standards and supply in Britain, France and Germany', *National Institute Economic Review*, 136, May, pp. 60–76.

Steinherr, A. (ed.) (1994) *30 Years of European Monetary Integration*, Longman, London.

Stewart, M. (1977) *The Jekyll and Hyde Years: Politics and Economic Policy Since 1964*, J.M. Dent, London.

Stewart, M. (1986) *Keynes and After*, 2nd edn, Harmondsworth, Penguin.

Stewart, M. (1992) 'Local management – the Kent scheme' in G. Wallace (ed.) *Local Management of Schools*, Bera Dialogue no. 6, Multilingual Matters, Cleveland.

Stille, F. (1990) 'Industrial policy in the 1980s' in K. Cowling and H. Tomann (eds) *Industrial Policy after 1992*, Anglo-German Foundation for the Study of industrial Society, London.

Stoneman, P. (1990) 'Technology policy in Europe' in K. Cowling and H. Tomann (eds) *Indistrial Policy after 1992*, Anglo-German Foundation for the Study of Industrial Society, London.

Storey, D. and Strange A. (1993) 'Entrepreneurship in Cleveland 1979–1989: a study of the effects of the enterprise culture', *Employment Department Research Series 3*.

Storey, D.J. (1982) *Entrepreneurship and the New Firm*, Croom Helm, London.

Storey, D.J. (1994) *Understanding the Small Business Sector*, Routledge, London.

Storey, D.J. and Johnson, S. (1987) *Job Generation and Labour Market Change*, Macmillan, London.

Sugden, R. (ed.) (1993) *Industrial Economic Regulation*, Routledge, London.

Sundrum, R.M. (1992) *Income Distribution in Less Developed Countries*, Routledge, London.

Talbot, J. (1988) 'Have enterprise zones encouraged enterprise? Some empirical evidence from Tyneside', *Regional Studies 22*.

Taylor, R. (1995) 'Tecs struggle to pull their weight', *Financial Times*, 26 April, 6, 507–14.

Thirlwall, A.P. (1986) *Balance of Payments Theory and the United Kingdom Experience*, Macmillan, London.

Thomas, A. (1994) *Third World Atlas*, 2nd edn, Open University Press, Buckingham.

Thomas, H. (1994) 'Markets, collectivities and management', *Oxford Review of Education*, 20, 1, pp. 41–55.

Thomas, H. and Bullock A. (1994) 'The political economy of Local Management of Schools' in S. Tomlinson (ed.) *Educational Reform and its Consequences*, IPPR/Rivers Cram Press, London.

Thomas, H. and Simkins, T. (eds) (1987) *Economics and the Management of Education: Emerging Themes*, Falmer Press, Lewes.

Thomas, I.C. (1994) 'The relationship between local authorities and TECs in metropolitan areas', *Local Government Studies*, 20, 2, pp. 257–305.

Thomas, M. (1988) 'Slowdown in the pre-World War One economy', *Oxford Review of Economic Policy*, 4, 1, pp. 14–24.

*Times Educational Supplement* (1991) 'Everyday is market day', 25 October, p. 11.

Tinbergen, J. (1952) *On the Theory of Economic Policy*, North-Holland, Amsterdam.

Tomann, H. (1992) 'Germany' in K. Cowling and R. Sugden (eds) *A New Economic Policy for Britain*, Manchester University Press.

Tomlinson, S. (ed.) (1994) *Educational Reform and its Consequences*, IPPR/Rivers Cram Press, London.

Totterdill, P. (1992) 'The textiles and clothing industry: a laboratory of industrial policy' in M. Geddes and J. Benington (eds) *Restructuring the Local Economy*, Longman, Harlow.

Townsend, A. R. and Champion, A. G. (1992) 'The urban/rural shift' in P. Townroe and R. Martin (eds) *Regional Development in the 1990s: the British Isles in Transition*, Regional Studies Association, London.

Townsend, P. (1984) *Why are the Many Poor?* Fabian Society, London.

Trevithick. J. A. (1980) *Inflation: A Guide to the Crisis in Economics*, 2nd edn, Penguin, Harmondsworth.

Trevithick, J. A. (1992) *Involuntary Unemployment: Macroeconomics from a Keynesian Perspective*, Harvester Wheatsheaf, Hemel Hempstead.

TUC (Trades Union Congress) (1995) *Black and Betrayed*, London, TUC.

Turk, J. (1983) 'Power, efficiency and institutions: some implications of the debate for the scope of economics' in A. Francis, J. Turk and P. Wiliman (eds) *Power, Efficiency and Institutions*, Heinemann, London.

Turvey, R. (1963) 'On divergences between social cost and private cost', *Economica*, n.s., 30, pp. 309–13.

Van de Ven W. P. M. M. (1990) 'From regulated cartel to regulated competition in the Dutch health care system', *European Economic Review*, 34, 2/3, pp. 632–45.

Vickerman, R. W. (1984) *Urban Economies*, Philip Allan, Oxford.

Wadhwani, S. (1990) 'The effect of unions on productivity growth, investment and employment: a report on some recent work', *British Journal of Industrial Relations*, 28, 3, pp. 371–84.

Wallace, G. (ed.) (1992) *Local Management of Schools*, Bera Dialogue no. 6, Multilingual Matters, Clevedon.

Warwick, P. (1985) 'Did Britain change? An enquiry into the causes of national decline', *Journal of Contemporary History*, 20, pp. 99–133.

Weale, M. *et al.* (1990) *Macroeconomic Policy: Inflation, Wealth and the Exchange Rate*, Unwin Hyman, London.

Weir, C. (1993) 'Merger policy and competition: an analysis of the MMC's decisions', *Applied Economics*, 25, pp. 57–66.

Wells, J. (1995) *Crime and Unemployment*, Employment Policy Institute Economic Report, 9, 1, February.

Whynes, David K. (ed.) (1993) 'Economic aspects of health care in the UK' in G. B. J Atkinson (ed.) *Developments in Economics*, vol. 9, Causeway, Ormskirk.

Wiener, M. J. (1981) *English Culture and the Decline of the Industrial Spirit*, Cambridge University Press.

Williamson, J. and Milner, C. (1991) *The World Economy*, Harvester Wheatsheaf, Hemel Hempstead.

Williamson, O. E. (1975) *Markets and Hierarchies: Analysis and Anti-Trust Implications: A Study in the Economics of Internal Organization*, Free Press, New York.

Williamson, O. E. (1985) *The Economic Institutions of Capitalism: Firms, Markets, Relational Contracting*, Macmillan, London.

Wood, L. (1995) 'Wages council loss hits pay', *Financial Times*, 30 August.

World Bank (1992) *World Development Report 1992: Development and the Environment*, Oxford University Press, Oxford.

World Economic Forum (1995) *The World Competitiveness Report*, Geneva, World Economic Forum.

World Health Organisation (1958) *The First Ten Years of the WHO*, Geneva.

Yarrow, G. (1996) 'Competition policies and industrial policies' in M. Mackintosh *et al.* *Economics and Changing Economies*, Open University and London International Thomson Business Press.

Youngson, A. J. (1960) *The British Economy 1920–1957*, Allen & Unwin, London.

# Index

absolute advantage, 277
Adam Smith Institute, 54
Advisory, Conciliation and Arbitration
    Service, ACAS, 115, 124
Ahlburg, D., 252
Akyuz, A., 17
Alchian, A. A. & Demsetz, H., 33
Aldcroft, D. H., 248
Alogoskoufis, G. & Portes, R., 302
Amin, A., 9, 95
Amin, A. & Robins, K., 95
Anderson, K., 171
*Annual Abstract of Statistics*, 173
Appleby, J. *et al.*, 187
Armstrong, H., 301–2, 306
Ashdown, P., 299
Ashegian, P., 4–5
assignment rule, 5
Atkinson, A. B., 223, 227, 228
Atkinson, J., 105, 108
Austrian approach, 40
Austrian School, 29
autarky, 275
Authers, J., 146

Bachtler, J. & Mitchie, R., 136
Baker, P., 93, 94, 95, 96
balance of payments, 3–4, 240, 258, 273,
    282–6
Baldwin, R. E., 300, 301
Ball, S. J. *et al.*, 199
Balls, E., 127
Bank of England, 2
Barrett, S., 168
Bassett, P., 122
Batchelor, C., 19, 120
Beatson, M., 128
Beecham, Sir J., 146

Beesley, M. E. & Hamilton, R. T., 87
Begg, I. Gudgin, G. & Morris, D., 150
Benjamin, D. K., 248–9
Berlin Conference (1995), 165
Beveridge plan, 227
Beveridge, W. H., 247
BiniSmaghi, L. & Vori, S., 299
Binks, M. & Jennings, A., 89
Birch, D., 81, 83, 136
birth of firms, 86–7
Blackhurst, R., 171
Blondal, S., 234
Bofinger, P., 296
Bolton Committee, 81
Booth, A. E., 249
Borrie, G., 51, 56
Bosanquet, N., 29
Boyer, R., 9
Bretton Woods, 6, 8, 268, 284–5, 289, 291
Bridlington Principles, 123
British Coal, 111
British Disease, 118–19
Brown, A. J., 140
Buchanan, J., 178
Buckley, N., 108
Budd, A., 10
Bullock Commission/Report, 7, 124
Business Expansion Scheme, 90
Business Links, 90
Butskellism, 7, 272
Button, K. J., 156, 158

Cairncross, A., 272, 273
Callaghan, J., 10, 233
Cameron, G. C., 136
Capecchi, V., 94
capitalism, 211–13
Caporaso, J. & Levine, D. P., 32

325